THE POLITICS OF BELGIUM

JOHN FITZMAURICE

The Politics
of Belgium

A Unique Federalism

WITH A FOREWORD BY
GUY SPITAELS

HURST & COMPANY, LONDON

First published in the United Kingdom by
C. Hurst & Co. (Publishers) Ltd.,
38 King Street, London WC2E 8JZ
© John Fitzmaurice, 1996
All rights reserved.
Printed in England

ISBNs
1-85065-209-0 (cased)
1-85065-215-5 (paperback)

FOREWORD

I warmly welcome this second and wholly rewritten edition of a book that has become something of a standard work on Belgium in the English language. Much has indeed changed since the first edition was published in 1983. New and significant phases of the Reform of the State in 1988 and in 1992/3 have reaffirmed the federal nature of Belgium that was only incipient then. The communities and regions have been translated into an irreversible and living reality.

It seems to me of significance and of symbolic value in that regard that the author should have asked a political personality who has deliberately chosen the regional level, rather than a national political figure, to preface this new edition.

John Fitzmaurice, an Englishman living in Brussels for twenty years, who has been closely concerned with Belgian political life even to the point of joining a Belgian political party, is well placed to show Belgian political developments in an accurate and positive light, as he is a sympathetic though not uncritical observer.

At a time of growing ethnic conflict in central Europe, with tragic human consequences, it is worth looking at the Belgian experience of peaceful and democratic transition to a federal structure. Surely that is a positive achievement that many can only envy. The author shows how the processes of Belgian federalism contribute to that goal.

To the credit of Belgian federalism, it should be said that it respects the specificities and sensibilities of the different entities that make up the state and rests on the firm principle of federal loyalty and cooperation.

However, our federal system is complex and I can well understand that it is hard to grasp for the foreign observer, even one who is well informed. I would consequently invite that observer to read John Fitzmaurice's excellent book for its sensible and relevant analysis.

I hope that this second edition, giving as it were new life to an old standard, will have the same success as the first.

GUY SPITAELS

Guy Spitaels is President of the Walloon Regional Council (Walloon Parliament) and former Minister-President of Wallonia.

v

CONTENTS

AUTHOR'S PREFACE AND ACKNOWLEDGEMENTS

Every author's and publisher's nightmare has just happened: a general election has been called in Belgium for 21 May 1995, right in the middle of the production process of this book. By the time you read this, the election will have been held and perhaps the political contours of the new fully federal Belgium will have become clearer. We have chosen to move ahead with publication, but to add this update.

The election due at the very latest on 24 December 1995 was called early by Prime Minister Jean-Luc Dehaene on 20 February 1995. His plan was for Parliament to adopt a number of essential budgetary measures, some politically popular reforms relating to the political system, and a more or less technical Declaration of Revision of the Constitution, covering those articles revisable, but not revised, in the last legislature. Under the Prime Minister's game-plan, this would then automatically lead to the dissolution of Parliament on 10 April and the subsequent election on 21 May.

The ostensible reason for this early election was to enable a new government to prepare the 1996 budget that will be vital to Belgium's capacity to meet the Maastricht convergence targets for the third phase of economic and monetary union. However, political calculation was clearly not absent from the decision, and this was indeed evident in the immediate support given to the Premier by all four of the centre-left coalition partners and by the less than total enthusiasm of the opposition parties. Avoiding conflict over difficult budgetary issues, taking advantage of the present fairly good economic indicators, avoiding any possible implosion of the coalition nearer to the election (as happened in 1991), with all the electoral consequences that could flow from it, and, perhaps more speculatively, concern over new revelations such as those now merging about the Flemish Socialists – all these factors may well have entered the calculations of the coalition partners. In short, an early election may well have seemed the best way to ensure a new mandate for the present coalition.

In any event, the elections represent an important watershed in Belgian history, as they trigger the full implementation of the new federal structure established in the *Accord de la St Michel* and enacted in a constitutional reform package in 1993. This would bring in the smaller 150-member House of Representatives, the new-style Senate and the autonomous regional assemblies. Thus, on 21 May voters were to elect the new federal House, the directly-elected part of the new Senate (forty senators) and the directly-elected regional and community parliaments. It was now possible that in time different, asymmetrical coalitions would be formed at the

federal level and in the various regions and communities, though observers did not expect that this would happen in 1995.

The European elections and local and provincial elections of 1994 and
subsequent opinion polls all reflected a certain stabilisation of the electoral
position of the coalition parties. The CVP and PSC expected a reasonable
election, with small gains being possible for the CVP, coming back from
its low point. The PS seemed to have partly recovered from the scandals
and internal divisions of 1994. The biggest question-mark hung over the
Flemish SP, which was affected by a new wave of corruption scandals just
before the election campaign. The Liberal opposition and the Greens were
not expecting large gains. The greatest danger lay, therefore, in new gains
by the far right in Flanders, Wallonia and Brussels, in an 'anti-politician'
reaction.

A continuation of the present four-party coalition, with perhaps some
regional variants, especially in Brussels where the Liberals are set to enter
the regional coalition, still seemed the most likely outcome as the campaign opened but became less so as it developed. In any event the complex
interlocking negotiations needed to form the six coalitions needed at
different levels will be long and arduous.

As it was, the election result saw more political stability than had at
first been expected. Dehaene's gamble had paid off. The coalition retained
its majority in the House, as CVP and quite unexpected SP gains out-
weighed the losses of the two Walloon coalition partners. Liberal gains
were real but modest. The Greens fell back for the first time. The gains of
the far right were significant but not massive in Flanders and were more
marginal in Wallonia and Brussels. Jean-Luc Dehaene was thus in a good
position to reform his outgoing centre-left coalition and resist any calls
for a reversal of alliances. In record time for Belgium, governments were
formed at all levels by 23 June 1995, and everywhere except Brussels,
where the French-speaking Liberals were a necessary component with the
PS, the format was that of a centre-left coalition.

Acknowledgements

I owe thanks to a very large number of people, too large to mention them
all individually, for guiding me in the complexities of Belgian politics and
enriching my own knowledge, experience and analysis in ways which
often led me to see various matters in a new light.

I would, however, particularly like to thank Mr Jansens, Director of the
Elections Department of the Ministry of the Interior, and his Deputy Mr
Pieron for giving me their time and expertise to understand the com-
plexities of the electoral system. The Documentation and Committee
Secretariats of the two Houses of Parliament were also most helpful. The

political parties responded unstintingly to my requests for their programmes and statutes, and for details about their history and organisation.

Many Belgian political leaders have over the years given me the benefit of their views and experience, which have greatly enriched this book, I would particularly like to mention Mr Spitaels, Mr Tindemans, Mr Van Miert, Mr Oscar Debunne, Mr Ernest Glinne, Mrs Spaak, Mr Gendebien and Mr Deleuze, who together cover a wide range of both Flemish and Walloon opinion.

Thanks are due to many Belgian friends, who have also contributed to my understanding of their political system, though I do not expect them all to agree with what I have written! I would like to mention in particular my friend and colleague Mr Jean-Louis Salmon, whom I would like to thank for many hours of stimulating discussion about Belgian political life and socialism, to which we are both attached.

Nor must I forget Mrs A. Isaac for once again coping so well with my intractable handwriting and disordered method of work. Finally, all opinions expressed in this book are my own responsibility and in no way engage any other person or institution.

Brussels,   J. F.
January 1996

ABBREVIATIONS

Parties

AGALEV	Anders Gaan Leven (Flemish Ecologists)
CVP	Christelijke Volkspartij
Ecolo	Walloon Ecologists
FDF	Front Démocratique des Francophones
FN	Front National
PCB/KPB	Parti Communiste Belge/Kommunistische Partij van België
PL	Parti Libéral (Brussels)
PLP	Parti de la Liberté et du Progrès (old Liberal Party)
POB	Parti Ouvrier Belge (1885-1945)
PRL	Parti Réformateur Libéral (1978)
PRLW	Parti des Réformes et des Libertés Wallones (1977)
PS	Parti Socialiste (1978-)
PSB/BSP	Parti Socialiste Belge/Belgische Socialistische Partij
PSC	Parti Social Chrétien
PVV	Partij voor Vrijheid en Vortuitgang
RW	Rassemblement Wallon
SP	Socialistische Partij (1978-)
UDRT/RAD	Union Démocrate pour le Respect du Travail/Respekt voor Arbijd en Democratie
VL BLOK	Vlaams Blok (splinter from VU)
VLD	Vlaams Liberalen en Democraten (1992-)
VU	Volksunle

Others

CSC	Confédération des Syndicats Chrétiens
EEC/EC	European Community (the post-Maastricht terminology EU is not used)
FEB	Fédération des Entreprises Belges
FGTB	Fédération du Travail de Belgique
MOC	Mouvement Ouvrier Chrétien
MPW	Mouvement Populalre Wallon
RTBP	Radio-Television Belge Francophone

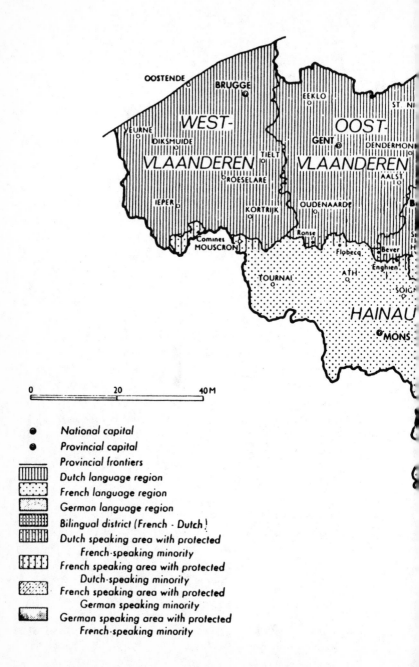

National capital
Provincial capital
Provincial frontiers
Dutch language region
French language region
German language region
Bilingual district (French - Dutch)
Dutch speaking area with protected
    French-speaking minority
French speaking area with protected
    Dutch-speaking minority
French speaking area with protected
    German speaking minority
German speaking area with protected
    French-speaking minority

xvi

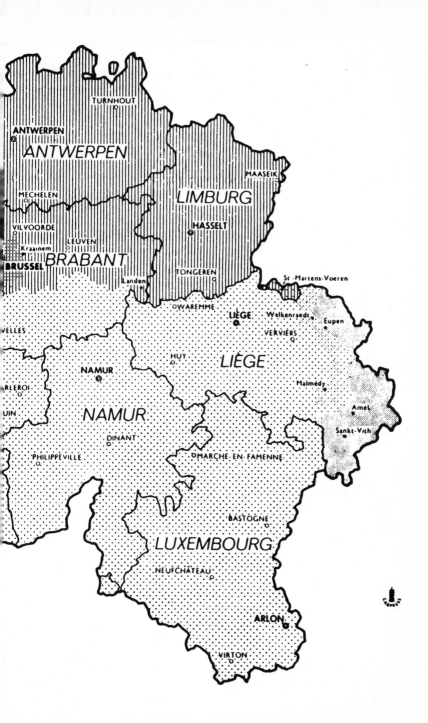

INTRODUCTION

Belgium is a small democracy, comparable with many other small states in Western Europe but also with its own quite special dynamics, deriving from its multilingual character. It is acutely aware of its economic and political interdependence and vulnerability, and has always been significantly influenced by cultural and political trends from its close neighbours, especially France. It was the first continental nation to take up the industrial revolution, and its economy soon became, and still remains, wide open. Trade represents more than 50% of its GDP, and there is heavy dependence on trade with EC partners, which take 72% of exports. The Belgian economy is therefore inevitably highly sensitive to even marginal changes in the economic environment in the neighbouring states; indeed, it is by any indicator one of the most open and interdependent in all Europe. As a consequence, Belgium was an early believer in all forms of European economic and political integration, founding the Benelux and becoming an enthusiastic member of both the Coal and Steel Community and later the European Economic Community (EEC). Within these bodies it has always been a supporter of more rapid economic integration and has tied its currency closely to the German Mark.

Belgians have also been acutely aware, ever since gaining political independence, that this was reliant upon a precarious and shifting balance of power in Europe. Indeed, without great power support, it would never have been won in 1830 and, having been won, would have been short-lived. Between 1839 and 1914, Belgian independence and neutrality were internationally guaranteed by all the major powers. Occupation by an invading army in two world wars showed the limitations of such arrangements, but these experiences gave Belgium a determination to promote both European integration and the Atlantic Alliance, for political as much as for economic reasons. Thus Paul-Henri Spaak early recognised the need, because it was in the Belgian national interest, for some kind of reconciliation with Germany. The country has always supported integration, but with prudence and moderation, seeking to mediate first between France and the others and then between Britain and the others.

European integration has also impacted on the internal constitutional debate in Belgium. Up till the fall of Communism in 1989, it was a force that worked in favour of retaining the existing state structure in western Europe and hence the essential unity of the Belgian state. It was then considered that the only *interlocuteurs* of the European Community could be the existing states themselves, which exercised a degree of centralising

1

pressure. It was also considered that the creation of any new states out of the existing member-states would automatically involve the Community, which would tend to resist such a development. The development of the single market, the push towards economic and monetary union with a single currency, a common foreign policy and the creation of new states in central and eastern Europe out of the dismembered elements of Yugoslavia, Czechoslovakia and the Soviet Union reduced the force of these arguments. The creation of new states was no longer a taboo. The unthinkable was possible, but at the same time the development of the Community opened up another option, as the concept of subsidiarity made it more open to accommodating decentralised or even federalised states within the Union.

The party spectrum in Belgium has also been much influenced from outside, following the classical norm with three dominant political families: Catholics, Liberals and Socialists, to which the Communists had come to be added by the 1920s. In the 1930s Belgium also saw significant rightist and fascist political forces, but – a sign of things to come – these assumed different forms in Flanders and in the south of the country. No unified 'nationalist' movement developed either before or during the wartime occupation.

Following patterns observable in the other Benelux countries, in Austria and to some extent also in the Nordic countries, a political system emerged based on consensualism between three pillars (*zuillen* in the academic literature) or networks, one for each of the three political families and each with its own system of party, trade union, social and cultural organisations. As society becomes more mobile, more atomised and more individualistic, people's collective sense of identity and loyalty to such networks has significantly declined. People in Belgium tend to adopt more of a 'supermarket' approach, shopping around for their parties, unions, health care, cultural and social activities. This is certainly a development that is common to western post-industrial societies, but its structural impact is greatest and potentially most dangerous in countries where such consensualism is the key to the functioning of the political system itself. The possible demise of the consociational model, or at least its serious weakening, may open a void and lead to alienation, filled by extreme populist forces. This development is on the horizon with the success of the Vlaams Blok since the late 1980s.

General trends in society, political organisation and international relations are common throughout western societies, although their intensity may vary. Belgium could be said, as a very open society, to be influenced by them to an above-average degree. However, cutting across these general trends is a specific Belgian trend that came to the surface by the late 1960s in a way that could no longer be ignored. The old unitary, centralised Belgium was becoming ungovernable. The language or community cleavage that overlaid the socio-economic cleavages was becoming the dominant factor in Belgian political life. By the early 1970s, the three traditional political families had split into three pairs, making six community-based parties. These were joined by three specific Flemish, Walloon and Brussels-based parties. The long road to federalism, culminating in 1992 with the *Accord de la St Michel* (St Michael's Agreement, so named because of the day when it was agreed, 28 September), had become inevitable. Belgium is now openly and irrevocably a federal state and, as we shall see, a laboratory of political change.

The Politics of Belgium: Crisis and Compromise in a Plural Society, published by this author in 1983, shortly after the 150th anniversary of the Belgian Revolution, had already noted signs of an increasing lack of national cohesion and national consciousness that underlined the artificiality of the Belgian state. Belgium is artificial in two different ways. First, it was clearly the European great powers that supported the Revolution or at least allowed it to succeed and thereby undid their own equally artificial creation of some fifteen years earlier at the Congress of Vienna, namely the United Netherlands. Secondly, beyond the rhetoric, the Revolution was at best only democratic in the French-speaking areas and if the majority Flemish population were ignored. The Revolution was initiated, led and controlled by the French-speaking bourgeoisie for whom the Orangist régime was linguistically, politically and economically disadvantageous. The victorious revolutionaries created a state in their own image and serving their own interests, first electing a French prince as king until that choice was vetoed by the great powers. They created a liberal constitutional monarchy, based on a limited property-related franchise, with French as the sole language of government, dedicated to promoting the interests of the nascent Belgian industrial revolution.

Much of the story of the intervening 150 years has been of how the Flemish movement emerged in the mid-nineteenth century, grew through the progressive extension of the franchise, and came to formulate cultural and then political demands that ultimately could not be denied. Despite setbacks in the immediate aftermath of both world wars, the movement made steady progress on the ratchet principle, taking up again each time from a more advanced position than where it had left off.

By the early 1980s, Belgium was rapidly moving towards becoming a federal state, though many did not then wish to admit as much. Furthermore, the complexities and institutional creativity of successive compromises, of which the 1992 *Accord de la St Michel* is the latest and most impressive, have created structures that bear little relation to the classic models of federalism found in Anglo-Saxon legal and political science literature. This has hidden the underlying reality and the irreversibility of the process. Since the enactment of the *Accord de la St Michel*, Belgium has been formally a federal state. This is the culmination of a long process by which the regions and communities that make up the country have become real and living political entities. The debate now is more about concern to avoid separatism and ensure a minimum residual solidarity between the regions.

Yet Belgium has always been sensitive to its external environment. The world, and indeed the Europe of the 1990s, are very different from the Europe of the early 1980s. The Yalta syndrome is over. With the collapse of Communism and the division of Europe, the old Yalta-Helsinki taboo on questioning frontiers and the integrity of existing states in Europe has disappeared. The map of Europe is being remade. We are in one of those transitional periods when anything is possible. One state (the GDR) has disappeared and, in addition to the collapse of the former Soviet Union, at least five more have appeared (the three Baltic republics, Slovenia and Croatia). The dismantling of Yugoslavia will require the redrawing of borders between Croatia and Greater Serbia. Czechoslovakia, already a federal state, split quite peacefully. Before 1989 Belgium was as much condemned to continue to exist as was any other European state, but now the unthinkable can be thought. That is not to say that Belgium will break up, but only that if it continues it must be by conscious choice, since there is no longer a geopolitical alibi for inertia.

In the early 1980s Belgium's membership of the European Communiy was seen as another external constraint in favour of a continued state unity. In a weak EC with a confederal tendency, in which the member nation-states were the key building blocks and the main actors, this was in-evitable. The post-Maastricht Community of the 1990s, on its way to becoming a European Union, with a pronounced federal character, no longer represents the same pressure towards a unitary Belgian state. Belgium has the self-confidence to accept and integrate the more pro-nounced regionalism of the 1990s; thus a looser federation or even confederation would pose no real problems for it. In a Community which has become a single economic space with a single currency and with all strategic economic policy-making instruments centralised, the arguments for retaining the Belgian nation-state are weaker. Again there is no longer an external alibi. The choice would be for the Belgians alone.

Belgium may thus be a major institutional laboratory with much to teach us. There is an urgent need in central and eastern Europe for new institutional structures that permit political and hence non-violent solu-tions to ethnic conflicts, and provide governability for areas in which opposed communities lie in close proximity and indeed live with clearly delineated territorial ghettos: this is the tragedy of Yugoslavia and it can arise elsewhere.

The 'Belgian method' has been based precisely on the creation of complex institutional shock-absorbers which subject all problems to lengthy discussion, compromise and rational solution, in the process co-opting new actors into the system and canalising their radicalism into institutional processes and hence away from violence. There is, of course, a down-side to this Belgian method, which imposes heavy costs. This down-side is heavily emphasised by the press and media, both in Belgium and abroad, and the very real benefits are taken for granted or under-rated. That said, what are the main costs of this extreme cosociationalism?

Clearly, the country can only function by co-opting all significant actors into the system and binding them in. This applies to the main political 'families' (Christian Socialists and Liberals), the community parties, the Christian and Socialist trade unions, the employers' organisations, the middle class and professional organisations and the Boerenbond (Flemish farmers' association). The result is very broad coalitions, expensive compromises and duplication of administrations. It means compromises, not only on the substance of issues, but also on the content of the political agenda. Issues can only be dealt with when there is a consensus to deal with them and at least a considerable degree of consensus over how to deal with them.

Conflict is considered dangerous and de-stabilising. Change can only be very slow and very gradual. There are so many shock-absorbers in the system that even a major shock is contained and diverted with only a small impact on the policy output. The Belgian ship of state can be compared to a modern oil-tanker: a massive heave on the tiller will only produce an imperceptible movement some fifty miles on. Elections seem to have but little impact on government formation. The political class seems to feel no compulsion to respect the signals coming from the voters, and indeed it has to be said that in a complex multi-party system, with at least three regional sub-systems, these may be contradictory, enabling politicians to read them as they prefer. The sheer length of government crises (147 days in 1987-8 and more than 100 days in 1991-2) also serves to create distance between the outcome of elections and the formation of government and its policies.

An inevitable danger is a degree of alienation of voters from the political process and a sense that democratic institutions do not function as they should; a sense that the political class does not listen to the voters, and indeed both ignores and fears them. This was illustrated by the cobbling together of the outgoing coalition in 1992 to avoid fresh elections only months after the 1991 elections. This has led to a degree of criticism of the political institutions and an increase in parties that have, from various standpoints, made such criticism central planks in their platforms: for example, the Green parties and the parties of the extreme right, such as the Vlaams Blok and the Front National. In this sense Belgium is also a political laboratory as it tries to balance the very real advantages of consensualism and non-violent change against the political dangers that could come from increasing alienation from the political process.

1

A SHORT HISTORY OF BELGIUM[1]

The Belgian state of today is not only, as we have seen, a very modern creation, but it was also to a considerable extent an artificial one. Paradoxically, it came into existence both as a reaction against its arbitrary fate resulting from historical accident and the machinations of the great powers, and at the same time as the direct result of those very machinations.

Belgium, then, has a long 'pre-history' stretching far back before the Revolution of 1830. The various influences which flowed across this narrow but strategic strip of the North European plain have all chaotically left their mark on the social, political and religious culture of the area. Above all – and this is an important factor in understanding the origins of many of the difficulties of modern Belgium – these various influences created more diversity than unity, more basis for conflict than for a folk memory of common experience, lived together as Belgians.

Between 57 and 52 BC, Julius Caesar conquered Belgium, which was previously inhabited by six different Celtic tribes, related to the Gauls,[2] and established Roman rule, which was to last until the fifth century AD. Initially the administrative division of Gallia Belgica covered what is today Belgium, but this was later split into three provinces. The Romans established order and government as well as good communications and trade. The third century saw the coming of Christianity. However, the Belgian provinces were on the marches of the Empire and as early as 275 came under Frankish attack. In order to defend the outlying areas, the Romans permitted allied peoples, such as the Rhenish Franks, to move north, which quickly adulterated Roman civilisation and led, except in isolated areas, to degeneration and breakdown of any kind of overall control. The Franks settled in the north and west, leaving the Gallo-Roman people in the south, creating already the linguistic boundary which still exists to this day.

The next period is confused and chaotic. The Huns were repulsed in 451 by the energetic leadership of Merovée and Clovis (481-511), creating a large Frankish kingdom stretching from the Danube to the Pyrenees, but after his death there followed a long period of disorder, partly broken by

6

the reigns of Clothaire (613-28), Dagobert (629-39), Charles Martel who won the crucial battle of Poitiers against the Arabs in 732, and Pepin le Bref (741-68). These kings attempted a strong policy of centralisation within defensible frontiers.

Only with Charlemagne (born in 742 near Liège) was this policy fully successful. This vast empire recreated the old Pax Romana and re-established a beginning of law, culture and trade. However, after his death, his heritage was slowly dissipated by his son Louis le Pieux (814-40), whose sons divided the Empire at the fateful Treaty of Verdun (843). This Treaty created three kingdoms: a Frankish kingdom stretching into what is now Flanders (modern France), Francia Orientalis (a German state) and between these strong, compact and rival kingdoms the weak but strategically vital Francia Media, which itself soon split again (855). One kingdom was created in Italy, a second in Provence and Burgundy and a third between the sea, the Rhine and the Meuse covering most of what is today Wallonia (Lotharinga). Thus by 843 and certainly by 855 the die was cast for the history of the next millennium: a secular rivalry between the two large Frankish successor-states, later France and Germany, of which the 'Middle Kingdom' would be the principal victim.

Belgium had already acquired several of its salient characteristics.[3] The cultural and linguistic division was established; it had already acquired its position as 'the cockpit of Europe' and it had become the object rather than the subject of history. All these characteristics acted as a *leitmotif* throughout the ages of Belgian history.

Flanders in the ninth century developed in a more favourable way than the southern part of Belgium which, as we have seen, belonged to Lotharinga. The Counts of Flanders, especially Baudouin I and Baudouin II, were able to maintain considerable independence within the Frankish state. During the tenth century, trade and industry, drainage and the building of polders developed rapidly in Flanders.

In Lotharinga, schism and barbarism were the order of the day. The *Regnum Lotharii*, which resulted from the division of the Middle Kingdom in 855, was again divided in 959 after intensive struggles, into Lower Lotharinga (Wallonia) and Upper Lotharinga. There too, though only in the tenth century, economic conditions constantly improved.

By the tenth century feudalism had become the dominant form of political and social organisation in both Flanders and lower Lotharinga, as elsewhere in Europe. The system provided effective military protection against the Muslims in Spain, and against the Norsemen, Slavs and Hungarians who in turn threatened western Europe, but at the same time it diluted and parcelled out political and economic power to such an extent that it tended to create anarchy, chaos and inefficiency, quite apart from its gradually more and more repressive nature, although in theory it was a system enshrining both rights and obligations. Over the next century

Flanders was to blossom to a much greater degree than Lotharinga. Baudouin V expanded it both to the west (Artois) and into Zeeland in the north and east.

Lotharinga was part of the Holy Roman Empire and in 1012 was given by the Emperor Henry II to Godefroi I, who sought to break the power of local barons. His successor attempted to raise the whole of the Low Countries in an alliance against the Empire, but failed. Nevertheless, after 1100 central authority was much eroded in favour of a number of more local dukedoms: Brabant, the *comtés* of Hainaut, Luxembourg and Limburg, and the independent principality of Liège (its prince being the bishop of that see), which was able to expand into the lower Meuse valley. Godefroi III (1190-1235) attempted to redress the situation by means of a delicate balancing act, the main purpose of which was to weaken Flanders. Jean I was able to gain Luxembourg after his victory over Imperial troops at the battle of Worringen (1288). Hainaut, however, was united with Flanders as early as 1180.

The rise of urban democracy

By 1250 important social changes had occurred, which were to be of vital importance in the next period. The Crusades and considerable inflation had seen the decline of feudalism, with the weakening of the large feudal landowners. Many smaller lords had been reduced to the level of the peasantry and many serfs had been able to purchase their freedom from feudal obligations. This led to the establishment of a more secure and prosperous agriculture.

However, there was a parallel development of even more significance, namely the development of vigorous self-confident urban centres, especially based on the wool trade: Bruges (70,000 inhabitants), Ypres (40,000) and Ghent (45,000). These towns were able to obtain charters which guaranteed them and their citizens important economic rights, such as freedom from feudal obligations, the right to levy taxes, and later virtual self-government under complex systems of guilds and corporations, in which power was in the hands of the richer merchants.

At the same time the state was modernising its institutions, with a consequent gain in central authority. Philippe d'Alsace set up a new non-hereditary body of royal officers (*baillis*), responsible for justice, order and taxation. Law was codified (Code of 1292) and more questions were removed from feudal to royal jurisdiction.

At the opening of the fourteenth century Flanders was once again, as in the early thirteenth century, embroiled in the secular Anglo-French wars. As in 1226 (the Treaty of Melun), it was an Anglo-Flemish Treaty (the Treaty of Lierre of 1294) which provoked the crisis. Above all, the autonomy of the Count of Flanders and his tendency to ally with England was unacceptable to Philippe le Bel, who in 1301 suppressed Flemish autonomy.

Now the towns[4] were to show their new-found power. A revolt led by Pierre de Coninck, leader of the Bruges weavers, led to a massacre of non-Flemish elements. An army of 20,000 men, raised mostly from among the townspeople of Flanders, defeated the French forces at the battle of the Eperons d'Or near Courtrai on 11 July 1302. An attempt to expand Flemish influence into Zeeland failed, but 'French Flanders' was occupied. Peace negotiations were exceedingly long-drawn-out, only being concluded in 1320. Flemish autonomy was reestablished, but Lille and Douai had to be abandoned.

The rest of the century was dominated by serious social conflict and civil war, from which however international rivalries, especially the spill-over of the Hundred Years War, were rarely absent. The heavy fines imposed under the 1320 Treaty led to a tax revolt by the coastal dwellers which spread to Bruges. Only intervention by the sovereign, King Charles IV of France, saved the Count of Flanders who had been captured at Courtrai by the rebels. This French intervention followed a new pattern which was to be repeated on several occasions.

In 1337, another revolt of the proletarian weavers broke out in Ghent as a result of the loyal support of the Count to the anti- English foreign policy of France, which led to the closing of the English market and severe consequential economic distress. In Jan van Artevelde the rebels found an energetic and effective leader. He organised an alliance of the three dominant Flemish towns of Ghent, Bruges and Ypres, and this alliance, called 'the Three Members of Flanders', worked in close alliance with England, especially under Edward III. At the same time, in 1339, defensive and free trade treaties were concluded with Luxembourg, Brabant, Hainaut, Holland and Zeeland. These external alliances were directed against France. However, the dominance and repression exercised by the weavers against other classes provoked a strong reaction, and van Artevelde was seriously challenged and then assassinated in 1345. The policy of consolidation continued, albeit in a more confused manner. Under the Treaty of Ath (1357) Flanders obtained Antwerp and Malines, but in return for a pledge of neutrality Gallican Flanders was returned by the French King.

Severe social unrest was to dominate the next twenty years. This took the form of a struggle between a primitive type of urban proletarian democracy, of which the weavers were the vanguard, and the other social classes led by the Count of Flanders, sometimes supported by the King of France. The weaver Yoens seized power in Ghent in 1379 and the city was subject to three severe sieges. At the battle of Beverhout near Bruges (1382), Philippe van Artevelde (son of Jan van Artevelde) led the forces of Ghent to a crushing victory, but their triumph was short-lived. King

Charles VI intervened in support of the Count and won the decisive battle of West Rozebeke in which van Artevelde was killed. Ackerman continued the struggle with English support, and with general war-weariness on both sides, a compromise peace was concluded at Tournai in 1385 which saw the confirmation of both the sovereignty of the Count and the privileges of the cities.

During the same period there were important constitutional innovations in Brabant, many of which were to last till the end of the *ancien régime* in the 1790s. The democratic split arrived much later there than in Flanders, but its conquest was more serene and durable, finding expression more in constitution-building than in violence and social revolution. Much as in England, it was the perennial indebtedness of the rulers and nobles which led to reform. Creditors took to sequestering the property of merchants to meet the debts of rulers. This situation was intolerable, and thus in return for adequate revenues the rulers were forced to concede a series of charters which guaranteed the rights of citizens and ensured some participation in government. The Charter of Cortenberg (1312) established rights for the citizens and set up a council of four nobles and ten burghers to ensure respect for those rights. After Jean III attempted to break it, two new Charters confirming the previous one and imposing severe limitations on the Duke were adopted in 1314 (the *Chartes Romanes*). In 1356 the '*Joyeuse Entrée*', a codification of earlier customary rights and charters, was adopted and was to remain in force till the 1790s. Citizens were assured of important individual civil rights and equality before the law. The powers of taxation and legislation of the Rules were limited in favour of the three orders (nobles, clergy, burghers). This did not prevent disorders, similar to those in Ghent, breaking out in Louvain in 1360, although they never reached the same proportions. The same struggle for democratic rights was also going on in Liège, leading to the creation of a Legislative Assembly of the three orders (*Paix de Fexhe*), and an arbitral tribunal to consider alleged violations of citizens' rights by the Prince-Bishop (*Paix des XXII*).

The Burgundian period

The early Burgundian period down to the reign of Philippe le Bon (1419-67)[5] was marked by quiet and unspectacular consolidation of the new equality. Marguerite de Male, the Burgundian inheritor of Flanders, Artois, Burgundy and Franche-Comté, married Philip the Bold (1384-1404) who made peace with England and remained neutral in the Anglo-French conflict. His successor Jean Sans Peur (1404-19) continued this work of consolidation.

Philippe le Bon[6] unified under him as many as possible of the diverse states making up the Low Countries, giving them a certain degree of unity and centralisation, to limit their particularism. Many factors, such as increasing trade and the absence of barriers to trade between the various states of the Low Countries, were favourable to these designs, not least because a strong Flanders faced a weakened France and a disparate group of small states to the south which the English had not been able to group together. By a series of dynastic marriages he was able successively to incorporate Zeeland (1432), Holland (1432) and Hainaut (1432) after the Concordat of Delft, having already obtained Namur (1429) and Brabant (1430). He was able to purchase the Duchy of Luxembourg in 1441. Now the whole of the Low Countries was under one ruler, except for Liège over which he was nevertheless able to extend a protectorate. If this work of unification was to be durable, it was necessary to provide the new realm with more solid political institutions. Philippe sought to pursue a certain degree of centralisation without breaking his obligations under earlier charters and customary rights. He established two *Chambres du Conseil* at Lille and in The Hague, which for the times were models of financial organisation. The Estates were reorganised or reactivated in each Province, and a *Grand Conseil* under a chancellor was established which prepared and administered legislation and justice. Despite a high degree of pragmatism and prudence, Philippe inevitably came into conflict with those seeking to defend their rights and privileges, in particular the urban merchants involved in the wool trade who were facing extinction from English competition. There were insurrections in both Bruges (1437) and Ghent (1451) and in both towns radical elements took control. These revolts were put down severely.

The successor to Philippe le Bon, Charles le Téméraire (1467-77), was not a great success. However, despite several internal revolts, conflict with the Estates General (1476) and an unsuccessful foreign policy aimed at securing Lorraine, he was able to continue and complete the centralisation policy of his predecessor. By dividing the *Grand Conseil* he created the *Conseil d'Etat*, responsible for drafting laws and decrees, and the *Parlement* of Malines which acted as an appeal court. Both his attempted imposition of French as the exclusive administrative language and a severe taxation policy, made necessary by his largely unsuccessful military adventures, provoked conflict with the Estates and saw the loss of the territories in Lorraine, called '*par delà*', and the Jura. Charles himself was killed at Nancy in January 1477.

The Habsburg period

Charles was succeeded by his only daughter Marie, who ruled up till her death in 1482. Following a revolt in Ghent, the Estates seized their chance of recovering their privileges and undoing the centralisation of the last century, as did the Flemish towns of the *Membres de Flandres* (Ghent,

Bruges and Ypres) under the *Grand Privilège* (1477). The Estates further-more had to approve declarations of law, taxation etc. A *Grand Conseil* was set up to supervise the sovereign, and if in a certain sense this represented a step backwards, it in no way called into question the territorial unification undertaken by the Burgundians. On the contrary, it provided the whole of the Netherlands with a constitution and political institutions.

Assailed from the south by Louis IX of France, the Low Countries needed the protection of a powerful leader, and so the Estates pressed Marie to marry Maximilian of Austria, which she did in August 1477. The French army was defeated at Lunegatte near St Omer in 1479 and the English Alliance was restored in 1481.

When Marie died, her son Philippe was only four years old and the regency was assumed by Maximilian. There followed more serious disor-ders resulting from conflicts with the Estates and the *Trois Membres*. In a first phase, Maximilian was forced to make serious concessions, but in 1483 he dismissed the Regency Council and in 1485 forced the capitula-tion of Ghent and Bruges. In 1487 civil war broke out again, and Maxi-milian was held prisoner by the city of Bruges. He was forced to accept the reintroduction of the *Grand Privilège*, but once freed led an unsuc-cessful assault with Imperial troops. Under Philippe de Clèves, Marie's son, the Netherlands found both leadership and a clear nationalistic political programme.

However, the civil war was a mere corollary to the wider European struggle between Maximilian and Charles VIII of France. The cities of Flanders were gradually worn down, and with the Peace of Cadzand on 30 June 1494 they lost their privileges for ever. With them Flemish pre-eminence in the Netherlands was to disappear: it was the end of a long era.

In 1493, Maximilian became Holy Roman Emperor and left the government of the Netherlands to his son Philippe, who reigned from 1494 till 1506. In the first period of his reign, he distanced himself from his father's expansionist policy, remaining neutral and concluding an impor-tant trade treaty with England in 1496. When the death of Don Juan, son of Ferdinand and Isabella of Spain, opened to him the succession to the throne of Spain and possibly in time the Imperial crown itself, he moved closer to his father's line, but died before the likely effects of this could be felt in the Low Countries. In domestic policies he had sought to co-operate with the Estates.

His successor Charles of Luxembourg was only six years old. The regency was assumed by Marguerite of Austria whose policy was one of reconciliation in domestic affairs and neutrality in foreign policy. In 1515 Charles (later Charles V) came of age and in 1517 inherited the Spanish Habsburg possessions (Spain, Naples, Sardinia, Sicily and the Empire in the Americas); in 1542 he was elected Holy Roman Emperor. The safe and effective Burgundian foreign policy was now replaced by Imperial considerations, and the rich Low Countries were thrown into the maelstrom of a generalised European conflict between France and the Emperor and of the religious strife which swept Europe after 1517.

In domestic policy – except, as we shall see, in religious matters – Charles V was conciliatory and tolerant. He largely respected the rights and privileges of what was more or less a confederation of states. He undertook some limited reorganisation of the machinery of government by creating three councils with advisory functions: the *Conseil d'Etat* (foreign policy, religious matters etc.), the *Conseil Privé* (drafting and legislation, justice), and the *Conseil des Finances* (taxation and expenditure). However he was severe in repressing the various new religious movements arising from the Reformation – Lutheranism, Calvinism and Anabaptism – which were in any case marginal in the Low Countries.

In economic life there were important changes. The decline of Bruges was irreversible, and Antwerp took its place as the most important trading centre. New industries replaced the old Flanders wool trade, now in mortal decline, and agriculture too was developed considerably in this period.

However, the Low Countries were more and more drawn into the wars resulting from Habsburg dynastic ambitions.[7] They were able to remain almost untouched by the first two wars, of 1524-6 and 1526-9, which ended respectively with the treaties of Madrid and Cambrai, under which France abandoned its sovereignty over Flanders; but they were devastated by the ebb and flow of armies in the third (1536-8), fourth (1542-4) and, especially, the fifth (1551-6) wars. By the end of the period they were freed of French sovereignty, and Gelderland, Utrecht and Friesland had been added; an alliance with Liège had been concluded in 1518. In 1548, the Imperial Diet adopted an Act (the Augsburg Transaction) whereby the Low Countries became independent within the Empire, their sole obligation being to provide troops for common defence against the Turks – this being balanced by a guarantee of Imperial assistance in the event of French invasion. In 1549, the Diet also approved the Pragmatic Sanction, which unified the inheritance of all the Seventeen Provinces (see below) under one prince in an indissoluble 'package'. By the mid 1550s, the Low Countries had reached their full territorial extent and had become independent of arbitrary dynastic changes. From this period the name 'Seventeen Provinces' came into use to designate what today constitutes Belgium, the Netherlands and Luxembourg.

On the abdication of Charles V in 1555, Philip II of Spain became ruler of the Low Countries. He was rarely there, and ruled through a series of governors-general, to whom he unfortunately allowed only very little latitude. He imposed on them two priorities, which were bound to provoke resistance: first, absolutism and 'hispanisation' of the Provinces, and secondly, Counter-Reformation Catholicism with vigorous measures against heresy. Philip II was to follow a much harder line in his dealings with the Netherlands than his predecessor, and his reign is remembered as one of the unhappiest periods in Belgian history. The first of his governors, Margaret of Parma, was 'controlled' by the Secret Council (*Consuela*) of three, dominated by Antoine de Granvelle, who was entirely an instrument of Philip's policy. Without the approval of this body the Governor could take no important decision. The State Council (*Conseil d'Etat*) now had effective power, and several patriotic noblemen who were members of it, e.g. the Counts of Egmont and Horn and William of Nassau, organised opposition to Granvelle's policy in alliance with the clergy, who saw the reform of the diocesan structure of the Netherlands (1559) as an attack on their privileges and influence. This alliance demanded and obtained the withdrawal of Spanish troops (1561) and Granvelle's recall (1563).

However, these concessions in no way involved a more moderate line on the part of Philip II, but were merely a tactical retreat. The ever more open and provocative behaviour of the now numerous Calvinists in such towns as Tournai, Mons and Valenciennes could hardly fail to evoke a reaction. Heavy repression imposed by Philip caused considerable emigration by skilled Calvinist workers. The *Conseil d'Etat* was extremely concerned by this development and sought to moderate Philip's line – but without success. Even Margaret was appalled by his instructions, which would have required the execution of 60,000 people. Emigration inevitably increased.

Faced by this situation, a group of nobles led by Jean Marnix and Louis de Nassau met at Spa in 1565 to found a league, later named the *Compromis des Nobles* based on a text which both Protestants and moderate Catholics could support, calling for recognition of ancient privileges and an end to the work of the Inquisition in the Low Countries. It was decided in April 1566 that a petition with 2,000 signatures should be presented to Margaret, who agreed, while awaiting the King's response, to moderate the application of the religious measures, especially against those who made no public display of their reformist beliefs. This was a considerable victory. However, the more extreme reformers broke the fragile compromise and set in train a movement which, incited by open-air preachers, quickly spread from Armentières all over Flanders, Holland, Zeeland and Friesland. Deceived by Philip's apparent moderation, the nobility themselves organised the suppression of the iconoclasts and dissolved their alliance. Margaret had possibly conceded too much to the Calvinist wing. Under pressure from moderate Catholics she demanded a new oath of allegiance to the King, which split the ranks of the nobility. This led to civil war.

The King then dispatched the Duke of Alba, officially as a military commander although as the King's confidant he held all real power. The Calvinists were holding the Tournai area and Southern Hainaut. The attack by Marnix on Antwerp (January 1567) failed. Alba soon imposed his authority over the country, Margaret becoming increasingly powerless and leaving her post in December 1567. The Council never met, and moderate Catholics were excluded from influence. Alba established a *Conseil des Troubles*, which inflicted a reign of terror claiming some 8,000 victims, among whom the most famous were the Counts of Egmont and Horn.

The Prince of Orange, with some Protestant allies, organised the first campaign of liberation. However, at this stage the alliance was insufficiently strong to break Spanish control. All that was left to the people was passive resistance against the ever-increasing repression and against taxation imposed without respect for ancient rights. In the spring of 1572, preceded by guerrilla activity in the woods and on the coast by *corsaires*, Zeeland and Holland went over to open rebellion. William of Orange invaded Gelderland and Brabant; French Huguenots occupied Valenciennes and Mons. Alba seemed lost but, faced with a divided enemy, recovered; soon only Holland and Zeeland remained in arms against him. The winter campaign of 1572-3 was severe, but Alba was able to take Haarlem and only Alkmaar resisted. However, by early 1573 the war was virtually at a stalemate, and after a short interlude when the moderate Medina was governor (1572-3) Alba left in December 1573. He was replaced by Requessens, who succeeded in defeating the rebels at Mook (near Nijmegen). However, a mutiny of his troops, who had not been paid for twenty-eight months, prevented him from exploiting this victory. At the same time, in line with Philip's new tactics, he issued an amnesty, withdrew some taxes, and limited the powers of the *Conseil des Troubles*. However, these concessions were too small and too late to pacify the Estates General of 1574, and the rebels in Holland and Zeeland merely ignored them and continued the struggle. In 1576 Requessens died and Spain was virtually bankrupt.

The 1576 Estates General was both constructive and hopeful. Faced with the pressing danger of mutiny among the unpaid troops of Spain, the States of Brabant and Hainaut imposed their authority on the *Conseil d'Etat* and sought a rapprochement with Holland and Zeeland. Reviving the Transaction of Augsburg of 1548, they summoned the Estates General, which set up an independent government for the Southern Provinces and opened negotiations with Holland and Zeeland in October 1587 at Ghent. This led to the Pacification of Ghent, an agreement which created a federation of the Seventeen Provinces, decreed a general amnesty, and adopted a compromise on the religious issue whereby Catholicism was to be the main religion in fifteen provinces, with considerable tolerance for Protestants, and two provinces (Holland and Zeeland) were to be Protestant. This compromise was the weakest link in the arrangement and led to its failure, but the mere conclusion of the pact had been significant.

Philip nominated Don Juan of Austria as the new governor. His position seemed impossible, but the unresolved divisions among the signatories of the Pacification of Ghent were an important card in his hands. The moderate Catholics and nobles still sought a reconciliation with Spain, and the Estates entered into negotiations and concluded a 'package deal' with Don Juan. The Estates voted the First Union of Brussels (1577), which imposed Catholicism as the sole religion for all the Seventeen Provinces. Don Juan issued the Edict of Marche-en-Famenne which confirmed ancient privileges and pledged moderation, but not content with this compromise he recalled the Spanish army to the Netherlands and tore up the Edict. This provoked a violent reaction. Rebels took control in Brussels and called in Prince William of Nassau, known as 'William the Silent', who was elected Regent of Brabant; however, his tolerance and moderation made enemies in both the Catholic and Calvinist camps. The noble faction brought in the nineteen-year-old Archduke Mathias, brother of the Emperor, as sovereign of the Low Countries. Real power remained in the hands of William, who imposed a second Union of Brussels, annulling the first. Thus on 18 January 1578 Mathias was inaugurated as King of the Low Countries and William was appointed Lieutenant-General.

Meanwhile, Don Juan had concentrated his forces in Luxembourg, and from there counter-attacked and won the important battle of Gembloux on 31 January 1578, forcing Mathias to withdraw on Antwerp. The constant internal disputes between Catholics and extremist Calvinists, such as those of Ghent who had established a republic in that city, prevented any effective military organisation. William was once more forced to seek outside help. He forged an alliance with the ambitious Duke of Anjou, a younger son of the King of France, who was a moderate Catholic and whom the Estates named 'Defender of the Freedom of the Low Countries'. The military help brought by this new ally created a breathing space. The rebels won the battle of Rymenan on the Dyle near Malines and forced Don Juan to withdraw to Namur, where he died in October 1578.

Once more internal divisions prevented this new respite from lasting for long. Extreme Calvinist elements and discontented soldiers organised the Malcontents' Revolt. Anjou was forced to crush the Calvinists in the Arras, Lille and Valenciennes triangle. The new and moderate governor, Prince Farnese, found that his overtures fell on fertile ground only among the Catholics in terror of Calvinist extremism. This was not enough. Artois, Hainaut and Gallican Flanders reacted by signing the Confederation of Arras and the Peace of Arras, which established the primacy of the

Catholic religion and the powers of the Estates, and banned foreign (i.e. Spanish) troops.

The response was rapid. In January 1579, the Seven Provinces (Holland, Zeeland, Utrecht, Gelderland, Overyssel, Friesland, Groningen) and some Flemish towns signed the Union of Utrecht, which consecrated the separation of the Low Countries into what were to become Belgium and the Netherlands. The Union readopted the religious provisions of the Pacification of Ghent. By the treaty of Plessis-lez-Tars, William, in a gesture of openness and moderation, accorded the title of Hereditary Sovereign of the Union to the Duke of Anjou. However, his attempts to bring about a religious compromise on the ones of the religious Peace of Augsburg (1555), which applied in the Empire, failed almost everywhere. The battle-lines were now tightly drawn. No compromise was possible and the issue would be settled by force of arms. The struggle began in earnest in late 1581.

Apart from the Flemish towns, the Union constituted a compact and defensible mass of territory. In its defensive strategy, the towns in their forward positions were largely abandoned to the siege warfare of Farnese. Anjou had proved a poor choice. He sought first to marry Elizabeth I of England and then, having been repulsed, to establish an absolute monarchy with the aid of French and Swiss mercenaries. He failed and was forced to flee (1583). William was assassinated on 10 July 1584, a fact which made the possibility of any reconciliation still more remote. The Calvinist towns fell one by one – Dunkerque, Ypres, Bruges (1584), Brussels (1585), and finally Antwerp in August 1585. Farnese was the complete master of the southern Low Countries and the division was complete and irrevocable. The war moved to the frontiers of Brabant, Gelderland and Zeeland, without either side gaining any decisive advantage. Spanish priorities were elsewhere – with the Armada (1588) and in France (1590-2) – which drained off forces from the 'side-show' in the Low Countries. In 1595, Henry IV of France invaded the Spanish Low Countries and was only ejected after a heroic struggle which made possible the compromise peace of Verviers (1598) whereby Calais and much of Picardy were ceded to France. This marked the end of a phase. Spanish power was weakening and the situation had reached a *de facto* stalemate.

During this long period of confusion, the principality of Liège was able to remain largely neutral. Its internal constitution, the Peace of St Jacques (1507), held up and the few heretics and Protestants in the principality were treated with toleration. Despite its largely fictive position as an Imperial city, Liège turned less and less to either Spain or Germany, but looked increasingly to France.

Before his death in 1598, having ensured the territorial, military and internal security of the Spanish Netherlands, Philip II created an independent state, which he made over to his daughter Isabella and her husband Albert; if they died childless, the territory would revert to the Spanish Crown and in the meantime Spanish troops remained in the major cities. The new monarchs were moderate and restricted any 'hispanising' tendencies. However, they rejected attempts by the Estates General of 1600 to open peace negotiations. The war intensified and entered a new phase with attacks on the coast and the battle of Nieuwpoort (1600), where the Spaniards suffered a heavy defeat. However, in 1604 they took Ostend after a three-year siege.

The time was ripe for a general truce; this was concluded in 1609 and lasted twelve years (1609-21). The Seven Provinces were thus recognised by Spain as an independent state, whereas the accession of the Spanish Netherlands to semi-independence had proved more and more illusory. The period of the truce, after forty-two years of war, enabled a few minimal economic and social measures to be taken.

By 1621, the Thirty Years War had broken out and there were new hostilities with the Dutch. The 'foreign war' and the loss of Maastricht led to the search for a solution which would enable peace to be restored. Some negotiated with the Dutch for a partitioning of the Spanish Netherlands between France and the Netherlands; others sought to expel the Spaniards with the aid of France to found an independent Belgian state. The Estates General of 1632-4, the last to be called before the Brabançonne Revolution of 1787, was however loyalist and patriotic; it ordered the despatch of a peace delegation to The Hague, but in the event no arrangement proved possible.

In 1633, Isabella died. The Spanish Netherlands, without Antwerp and thus reduced to ten Provinces, was in a difficult position; its fortunes, linked to Spain, were in serious decline, and it had to suffer assaults from other powers, since Spain still refused to abandon her 'world role'. It was now to fall victim to a Franco-Dutch alliance organised by Cardinal Richelieu. In 1634, these powers agreed to offer the Spanish Netherlands a choice between partition or becoming a Catholic federal republic of reduced size. In 1635, they concluded a formal alliance and their forces marched on Brussels. Cardinal Mazarin, after 1642, was even more radical: he sought to give France 'natural frontiers'. However, his Dutch ally, content with its sea power and with secure frontiers, went on the defensive, being more concerned over rising French power rather than with Spain.

The diplomatic settlements of the Thirty Years War which concern us here are the treaty of Munster (1648) whereby Spain recognised the independence of the United Provinces and ceded Breda, the southern portions of Maastricht and Northern Flanders (Hulst and Axel), and the treaty of the Pyrenees (1659) between France and Spain whereby Spain ceded Artois and several fortresses in the Sambre-Meuse valley to France.

With the decline of Spain, hegemony in Europe was within the grasp of Louis XIV of France.[8] In this he was opposed during the period 1667-1713 by a series of *ad hoc* alliances which usually involved Spain and the United Provinces, the former enemies now reunited against rising French power. Five wars were fought across the Spanish Netherlands, and supremacy oscillated between Louis XIV and the allies, whose lack of unity, especially after their series of victories during the War of Spanish Succession, prevented Louis' total defeat, However, the net result was that maritime Flanders (Dunkerque), Gallican Flanders (Valenciennes), Morlenbourg, Philippeville and Thionville were added to earlier losses to France with the Treaty of Utrecht (1713). By a complex series of treaties – Utrecht, Rastadt (1714), Bade (1714) and Antwerp (1715) – the Spanish Netherlands were added to the United Provinces 'in favour of the House of Austria', and a series of 'barrier' fortresses, garrisoned by the Dutch, was set up against the French.

Eighty years of intermittent war and religious persecution had led to much Protestant emigration and a general depopulation of all the towns except Brussels. Agricultural production fell so low that food had even to be purchased from the Netherlands, officially an enemy country. Trade was also considerably affected but some industries, especially lighter textile production, did prosper in the war years.

Austrian rule

Although the fate of what had been the Spanish, and were the now the Austrian, Netherlands was still determined by outside forces, the Austrian period[9] was more tranquil, and favourable to a degree of economic reconstruction. It saw the repopulation of the smaller towns, important development of transport infrastructure, considerable prosperity for the port of Ostend and some industrialisation in the south with coal mining, slate, metallurgy, and textile manufacture. The economic situation of the principality of Liège was even more favourable. The Austrian regime was generally more relaxed and benevolent than its predecessor. However, it was still foreign; even the progressive Joseph II (1780-7) was unpopular precisely because his reforms took no account of the conditions of the country.

The first Emperor, Charles VI, pursued a moderate domestic policy. He respected the form of the Ancient Privileges, but hardly their spirit. He never summoned the Estates General, nominated few Belgians to senior posts in the administration, divided the *Conseil d'Etat* into three separate sections, and established a supreme Council for the Low Countries in Vienna, its four members including only two Belgians. Coupled with additional taxation, these measures provoked a revolt led by Anneessens (1719): this was severely put down, and Anneessens was executed, becoming a martyr. The death of Charles VI in 1740 provoked the War of Austrian Succession, with the position of his heir Maria Theresa being contested by Spain, Poland, Prussia, Saxony and France, which placed the Austrian Netherlands in an exposed position. Only the support of Britain and Hungary enabled the Empress to survive. Ostend was the scene of fighting between France and Britain in 1742-3 and France defeated the Austro-British army at Fontenoy in 1745. Brussels and Liège fell in 1746 and the Netherlands were incorporated into France. The peace of Aix-la-Chapelle (1748) ended the war in an honourable draw. The Netherlands were returned to Austria. When the previous alliances were reversed in the Seven Years War of 1756-63, with Britain and Prussia opposing Austria and France, the Netherlands were spared involvement in the conflict.

Reform and Counter-Revolution

Political life in much of Western Europe entered a new and more hectic phase in the 1770s, and this was to establish the outline of Belgian politics for the next century. As early as 1736 Pierre Rousseau in Brussels had started to issue his *Journal Encyclopédique*, and in 1785 the *Journal Général de l'Europe* appeared. These publications were the sum of the new progressive thought of the Enlightenment, as manifested in Belgium. However, the reform movement[10] came less from below than from the 'enlightened despotism' of the Austrian Emperor, who introduced a series of important religious and secular reforms in 1781-2. Catholicism was no longer to be the official state religion, civil marriage was introduced, and episcopal seminaries were closed; new administrative and judicial bodies were created, and the authority of traditional feudal assemblies was reduced. But, far from being welcomed, these reforms provoked wide-ranging opposition which, though temporarily unified, was composed of two factions. Of these the *Statistes* under Van der Noot and Van der Eupen were dominant; they were mostly an aristocratic and clerical group seeking to defend privilege. The 'Vonckists', led by Vonck, Verlooy and Van der Meersch, were politically more progressive, seeking the introduction of a broader franchise, at least within the Third Estate, but they were mostly not anti-clerical. However, a small part of this group, led by the Liège lawyer Doutrepont, was more radical and anti-clerical: its influence was small, but its very existence created tension between the *Statistes* and the Vonckists which was to prove fatal.

A successful revolt was organised from Breda, led by Van der Meersch. The imperial forces were defeated at Turnhout, and Brussels was captured in December 1789. The Estates General met in Brussels on 10 January

1790 for the first time since 1632 and a United States of Belgium was proclaimed. The power of the Church and the Estates was restored. The *Statiste* faction was at first dominant. Limited power was in the hands of a central government led by Van der Noot and Van der Eupen, with a Sovereign Congress of ninety members. The unity of the rebels, however, was short-lived. Both Verlooy and Vonck published projects for a more progressive constitution, which led to the Vonckists being attacked by the Church as anti-clericals, and banished or imprisoned. This occurred as early as April 1790.

Joseph II's successor Leopold II offered the new rebel state autonomy within the Empire. The offer was not accepted, and alliances were sought with both Prussia and France. A French alliance would have implied a rapprochement with the Vonckists, but this was made impossible by the agitation of the more reactionary *Statistes*. So it was that, undermined from within, the new state was rapidly captured by Austrian forces, with Brussels falling on 3 December 1790. Meanwhile in the same year a progressive rebellion in the independent prince-bishopric of Liège, which covered much of modern Wallonia, had brought down the *ancien régime*.

In this period the lines of force of the liberal-Catholic struggle in the nineteenth century are already to be seen.

The French period

The French Revolution spilled over into Belgium, and the fate of the country depended totally on the ups and downs of the revolutionary and Napoleonic wars[11] until, again without any consideration of Belgian views, the great powers created the United Netherlands as a buffer between France and Prussia as part of the 'reconstruction' of Europe undertaken by the Congress of Vienna. Indeed, it was Austrian hostility to the Revolutionary regime in France that first caused Belgian territory to become involved in the conflagration. After the battle of Jemappes on 6 November 1792, where the French defeated the Austrian army and occupied Belgium, the victorious General Dumouriez proclaimed Belgium a republic and appointed '*représentants provisoires*' until a National Convention could be elected. The French were not welcomed as liberators, except by a small *Comité Révolutionnaire des Belges et Liégeois* led by Dumonceau. Even the *Comité Révolutionnaire* sought to ensure control by Belgian revolutionary elements.

Austrian control was restored in March 1793 and the *ancien régime* re-established; however, this last Austrian restoration was short-lived and ended with the second French occupation in June 1794, when the Austrian armies were defeated at Fleurus. After a period of military government, Liège, the former Austrian Netherlands and the duchy of Bouillon were incorporated within France and as such were given representation in the Revolutionary Assemblies (successively less revolutionary) which followed after Napoleon Bonaparte became First Consul in 1799 and then Emperor in 1804. Belgian voters largely boycotted elections to these Assemblies, and were in any case a small minority among the French. Nevertheless, some political figures who were to play an important role in the struggle for independence (Gendebien, Merode, de Brouckère) began their political and parliamentary careers here. As the Napoleonic '*gloire*' became more and more costly in men and *matériel*, French rule became correspondingly unpopular, except among industrialists in textiles and iron-working to whom it brought considerable prosperity.

The United Netherlands

The future of Belgium after the Napoleonic era was in the hands of the dominant great powers. As early as 1814 it was decided, largely under British pressure, that a greater United Netherlands should be created as a buffer state on the borders of France, incorporating the whole of modern Belgium, Luxembourg with the exception of the Eupen-Malmédy area, and the modern Netherlands. What is today Luxembourg was at the same time to be a member of the German Confederation. The great powers accorded their full approval to this new arrangement in the Second Treaty of Paris (1815), which gave life to the decisions of the Congress of Vienna.[12]

The Dutch constitution of 1814 was to be applied with minor adjustments worked out by a twenty-four member commission (eleven Belgian, eleven Dutch and two Luxembourg members). Under it, royal power was strong and centralised, and the role of the 110-member States-General (fifty-five Belgian members) was limited, especially in budgetary questions. The basic liberal-Catholic division, which came to dominate Belgian political life throughout the century, was well in evidence. The dominant Catholic faction among the fifty-five Belgian members of the States-General was strongly opposed to the royal government, especially its policy of reducing the role of the Catholic Church in public life, and this led to severe conflict over the application of the Dutch constitution to the new territories and over education policy in the years 1814-17 and later in 1825-7.

Liberal opinion, though in substance also opposed to Catholic claims, was sensitive to the issue of religious freedom involved. From 1827, a 'national' coalition of Catholics and Liberals, with the Liberal-Catholic group acting as a bridge, came into being, and made the Revolution of 1830 not only possible but all but inevitable. It was Paul Devaux (Liberal) who in 1827 first argued the case for national reconciliation between Liberals and Catholics. Beginning in progressive Liège, this Unionist movement spread rapidly to Brussels and Ghent. At first only a small disparate group of doctrinaire anti-clericals, and officials and industrialists who profited from the Orange regime, remained to support the United Netherlands.

The concessions of the Dutch King William I on religious and linguistic issues were too little and came too late. The 1830 July Revolution in France was the necessary catalyst that caused the Unionist coalition to move from mere opposition into action. Severe social and economic unrest, above all in Brussels, also fuelled the flames. The 'September Days' saw open revolt in the streets of Brussels. Attempts at mediation and compromise around the idea of an 'administrative separation' failed when William I broke off negotiations. A large volunteer force streamed in from Wallonia to defend Brussels – successfully – against the Dutch army. On 24 September a nine-member provisional government was set up. It considered its task to be limited and transitional, but in its short life it took several political decisions of vital importance.

The new state

The most urgent tasks of the new government were to obtain international recognition by the powers which had underwritten the 1815 settlement, and particularly Britain. Closely linked to that aim, the achievement of which would enhance the new state's credibility, was the enactment of a constitution which would give the new state a basis of popular support.

The provisional government proclaimed Belgium's independence on 4 October 1830,[13] and the decision was confirmed by the newly-elected National Congress on 24 November 1830 while the London conference on the Belgian question, which had opened 4 November 1830, was still sitting. Most of the powers (Russia, Austria, Prussia) were opposed to Belgian independence; only France and, to a limited extent Britain, were sympathetic. It was the simultaneous outbreak of revolution in Poland that prevented a concerted Russian-Austrian-Prussian military intervention in support of 'legitimate' authority represented by William I and against the rebellious Provinces. A change of government in England, with Lord Palmerston replacing the Tory Lord Aberdeen, was also opportune in that the new government supported recognition: a Franco-British coalition imposed exactly such a reversal on the London conference, which approved Belgian independence in January 1831. That decision provided that Luxembourg should go to the Netherlands while remaining in the german Confederation (it did so till 1866) and that the powers would guarantee the permanent neutrality of Belgium and its independence. A second protocol settled the division of the national debt of the old state.

The National Congress,[14] in an understandable but dangerous show of independence, almost wrecked the settlement on Belgium's frontiers, adopting an over-optimistic interpretation of the London protocol over

Limburg. However, it was able to obtain satisfaction on enough of the territorial exchanges proposed, and those were enshrined in the treaty of the 18 Articles (June 1831), which the National Congress ratified on 9 July 1831 by 126 votes to 70. The treaty was not accepted by the Netherlands, and on 2 August Dutch troops invaded the country and, after several easy victories at Hasselt and Louvain, reached the outskirts of Brussels on 12 August. Only the intervention of the French at Wavre, forcing the Dutch army to withdraw, prevented total defeat. This was the 'Ten Day Campaign'. A new treaty was signed in London, the 24 Articles, whereby Maastricht, the mouth of the Scheldt and southern Luxembourg were to go to the Netherlands. For eight years the Netherlands refused to accept the Treaty, and Belgium retained *de facto* control over those areas. Both the original Treaty (ratified by only 59 votes to 38 with two abstentions) and its final execution in 1839 (58 votes to 42) provoked serious opposition in Belgium and in 1832 led to conflict between the King and his Cabinet, which resigned *en bloc* in protest against the moderate royal policy towards the Netherlands which was largely dictated by British pressure.

A much more serious issue, in that it brought Belgium into collision with its most important protector without which it could not have survived, was the choice of a monarch. The constitution had been adopted on 7 February 1831, and the system of hereditary constitutional monarchy had been voted for by an overwhelming majority (174 to 13). On 24 November 1830 the National Congress had formally declared that William of Orange was no longer King of Belgium. After the decision of the London conference to support Belgian independence, the Duke of Nemours, second son of King Louis-Philippe of France, was elected King of Belgium by the Congress – by only 97 votes, as against 74 votes for the Duke of Leuchtenberg (of the Beauharnais family, connected with Napoleon I through the Empress Joséphine) and 21 for Archduke Charles of Austria. However, coming up against British opposition, Louis-Philippe refused this offer, and the President of the Congress, Surlet de Chokier, was elected regent until a king could be elected. After consultation with the powers, the choice fell, with 152 votes in favour, on Leopold of Saxe-Coburg (uncle of Queen Victoria and widower of Princess Charlotte of Great Britain, only child of George IV). Leopold accepted only after the Congress had ratified the Treaty of the 28 Articles, and took the oath on 21 July 1831, ending a five-month regency. The Belgian state was thus established in late August 1831, both internally and internationally.[15]

The 1830 Constitution

Parallel to the workings of great power diplomacy and the Belgians' efforts to influence it in favour of their cause, the internal process of constitution-making was set in train. No doubt in part due to great power sensibilities, but also because the majority of Belgians were ardent traditionalists, the few republicans among the revolutionaries of 1830 had little chance of imposing their view. As we have seen, the choice of monarch fell on Leopold I largely for international reasons, which forced the leaders of the new state to accept the rather more 'monarchical' reading of their constitution desired by Leopold himself.

The 1830 Constitution stood in its time as a model of 'modern' liberal constitutions, despite the fact that it had been drawn up and adopted with great rapidity. Such speed was of course dictated partly by the need to present the great powers with a *fait accompli*. The provisional government which came into being during the 'September days' quickly set about establishing an elected National Congress which was able to meet by November. In the meantime, an *ad hoc* committee had prepared the draft of a constitution on which the Congress would work. This draft was ready by 23 October and was approved without amendment by the provisional government and transmitted to the Congress when it opened on 10 November 1830.

The basis of the franchise for the Congress, though a slight improvement on the Dutch franchise, was in reality extremely strict, being based on age, payment of a minimum amount in taxes, and academic qualifications. There were only 46,099 voters (a mere 0.11% of the population) of whom only some 30,000 (0.075% of the population) actually voted to elect the 200 members of the National Congress. The Congress contained ninety-eight members elected in Flanders, seventy-five in Wallonia and twenty-seven in Brabant. The middle class was overwhelmingly represented, but there were also some fifty nobles and thirteen priests. There were no organised parties in the modern sense, but most belonged to the 'Unionist' tendency with either Liberal or Catholic leanings. There was a small group of militant Liberals and at most some fifteen Republicans. There was a group of about twenty Orangests (supporters of William) and an equal group of those in favour of joining France.

In appearance, the Constitution was advanced in that it enshrined certain important progressive principles:

— executive power was to be in the hands of a government responsible to Parliament and not in the hands of the monarch, whose role was reduced to that of a constitutional head of state;
— unity of the nation in the national interest: members of Parliament represented the nation as a whole and not Provinces or other local entities.
— legislative power was invested in two elected Houses of Parliament;
— government was democratic, at least in the bourgeois-liberal sense, in that it was responsible to the middle class, who were therefore given the right to vote; and
— individual rights were constitutionally guaranteed.

However, there were important restrictions. It was stated that the King 'appoints and dismisses his ministers', a provision which Leopold I insisted on taking at face value. The Senate, its powers equal to those of the Chamber of Representatives, was elected by voters with the same qualifications as for the Chamber, but only those over forty years old. The tax qualification for eligibility for the Senate was so high that no more than 400 were eligible, and even the electorate for it remained severely restricted. No one in the Congress proposed universal suffrage. An annual tax obligation ranging, according to place of residence, from 20 to 80 florins was required, giving a total electorate in 1831 of some 55,000. The constitution was drafted in a French version only, and the high qualifications for election ensured that the political class would be drawn almost exclusively from the Francophone bourgeoisie, who had made the 1830 Revolution. Indeed, despite the popular character of the early revolts in September and the strong reservations over the national movement felt by the Francophone bourgeoisie in the early stages, it was the latter which rapidly took control of the Revolution, converting it into purely national channels rather than social ones which might then have challenged bourgeois interests. The result was a state made in the image of the liberal Francophone bourgeoisie. At least two groups, the Walloon industrial workers and the Flemish masses, were outsiders in the new state and remained alienated from it, and indeed were not to be involved in political life till late in the nineteenth century.

Political life in the nineteenth century

In the first ten years after independence, the dominant political issues related to the establishment of the new state and education. Laws were passed setting up local government (the Provinces Act 1836 and the Local Government Act 1836); two free (non-Catholic) universities were established (1835) in Brussels and Mechelen (Malines), and a new law on higher education was passed. The first railway between Brussels and Mechelen was opened in 1834, and in 1858 the Maas-Scheldt canal was completed. Customs treaties liberalising trade were concluded with France and the German *Zollverein*.

It is difficult to talk of party politics at this period, but Catholic and liberal tendencies are clearly identifiable. However, the 'Unionist' alliance, which had made the Revolution possible after 1828, remained in existence till 1847, although after 1840 it was in decline. In this Unionist period, Belgium was ruled by nine governments of which that of Count de Theux lasted longest – for more than five years.

The period 1847-57 can be considered as transitional. After the first Liberal party congress in 1846, party government began to develop,[16] and Belgium had a succession of Liberal governments, with the exception of the two-year Unionist government under Deckers. This return to Unionism was part of a personal attempt by Leopold I to block the advance towards party government – which proved unsuccessful. Over the period 1857-70, a series of moderate Liberal governments held office, to be followed by two years (1870-2) of Catholic government. From 1878 a radical Liberal government under Frère-Orban held office and introduced controversial measures in the minefield of education policy. These measures were reversed after the Catholic election victory of 1884, which ushered in a period of Catholic rule lasting without a break till the First World War. After 1893, and even more with the introduction of proportional representation in 1899, the Liberals lost their position as the major opposition party. In several elections the Socialists, who had first entered the Chamber in 1894 with twenty-eight seats out of 152, overtook the Liberals.

The election system was an important issue throughout the period between Independence and the First World War. The first reforms were made in response to the 'events' of 1848 throughout Europe. The qualification was reduced to its constitutional minimum – 20 florins in annual taxes – which increased the electorate to 79,000, or by 71%. Only small minority groups supported the introduction of universal suffrage, but they did so with growing insistence. The first bill to that end was introduced in 1870, but failed even to be debated. After 1885 the Belgian Workers' Party (Socialists) demanded the introduction of universal suffrage. Initially they were not supported even by the breakaway progressive wing of the Liberals under Janson, whose founding congress in 1887 rejected universal suffrage, and demanded the vote only for those who were literate. After the strikes of 1886 an active group of Socialists, Progressives (Liberals) and Social Catholics began to mount a concerted campaign for some degree of reform. Under pressure, the Catholic cabinet accepted a proposal, presented by Janson, that the Constitution be amended, but the Chamber elected in 1892 to carry out that amendment no longer had the Catholic two-thirds majority necessary to carry the amendment sought by the Catholics (a householder qualification). There was also the extra-parliamentary pressure of the Socialists. A compromise was reached and approved by 119 to 14 votes. Universal suffrage was introduced, but it was tempered by plural voting for the more highly qualified electors who would have up to three votes. 853,628 voters would have one vote, 293,678 two votes and 223,381 three votes. Thus the electorate was enlarged from 136,755 to 1,370,687, and at the same time voting was made compulsory. The secret ballot had been ensured by an Act of 1877. Despite continued activity by the Socialists on the issue, it was only after the sacrifices of the First World War and under strong pressure from King Albert that in 1919 universal male suffrage was introduced by the Delacroix government constituted immediately after the war.

The development of political parties was another important theme in the period up to the First World War. As we have seen, there were already distinct liberal and Catholic political tendencies in evidence at the foundation of Belgium, but it was not till 1846 that the first political party was founded. On 14 June that year a congress of 384 delegates of the Liberal Electoral Associations was held in Brussels under the chairmanship of E.E. Defacqz. It established the Confédération Générale du Libéralisme en Belgique and adopted a six-point programme: reduction of electoral qualifications as far as was permitted by the Constitution; independence of the civil power from the Church; organisation of a state system of education at all levels; increase in the number of senators; repeal of reactionary laws; and immediate improvements in the condition of the working class. But already at the time of this Congress, the divergences within the Liberal movement were visible. The 'Alliance', the Brussels branch of the Liberal party and the radical Union Libérale from Liège were pressing for more radical positions on social matters, some of which indeed found their way into the programme. In Brussels, the Alliance split, when the doctrinaire Liberals' proposal on suffrage was rejected and a moderate group under Verhaegen was set up for the 1847 elections. These early battles prefigured the Liberal splits of the 1880s. With the greater modernisation of Belgian society in the 1860s and '70s and the development of scientific positivism in the middle of the century, the radicals in the Liberal Party gained ground, especially on the issue of clericalism and suffrage. After the Liberal election defeat of 1884, the Liberals were in opposition for thirty years. The traditional 'doctrinaire-bourgeois' Liberal group showed no indication that it was prepared to accept the Radicals' proposals on the suffrage issue and on social questions. In 1887, a new Progressive Party came into being under Paul Janson. This party, though rejecting universal suffrage, had many points of convergence with the Parti Ouvrier Belge (POB). The Liberals were reunited in 1900, with many concessions to the Radicals.

The Catholics were much slower in creating a party. The need for some organisation was recognised, but there were divergences about the validity of linking the fate of the Catholic cause to any one particular party. A centre or conservative party seemed preferable. Only the later 'provocations' of the Liberals on the schools issue ensured the creation of a Catholic party. Meanwhile, Catholic conferences,[17] such as those at Mechelen in 1863-4 and 1867, and organisations such as the Société de St Vincent de Paul created the ideological basis for the Catholic movement and enabled difficulties between moderates and ultramontanes to be resolved. Both the Flemish movement and local Antwerp Meeting Partij (anti-militarist, Flemish nationalist) reinforced pressure for a more organised Catholic opposition. From the 1850s, Catholic election committees were set up in the constituencies under the title of Union Constitutionelle et

Conservatrice – forged into a national federation in 1864. At the same time, some fifty *Cercles Catholiques* were formed, again with a federal committee: these were more actively involved in policy-making, whereas the former were merely electoral agencies.

Throughout the 1870s, the political battle became more bitter. The ultramontane group under Charles Périn went as far as to reject the Liberal constitution and criticised the Catholic governments of the period 1870-8 as excessively moderate. The internal debate was swept aside by the Liberals' educational legislation after 1878, and in 1889 a Catholic party was formed by the fusion of the Fédération des Cercles Catholiques and the Fédération des Unions Constitutionnelles et Conservatrices. Within the new body under Beernaert (prime minister 1884-94) the main issue was about social questions in the light of the papal encyclical *Rerum Novarum* (1891). The Christian Social tendency began to emerge and, by means of such umbrella bodies as the Ligue du Suffrage Universel, made common cause with Radicals and Socialists.

Belgian Socialism[18] was also in the process of entering the arena. The Association du Peuple of César De Paepe joined the First International in 1865. The severe internal tensions between Socialists and Anarchists, which marked the First International, were mirrored in Belgium. In Wallonia the Anarchist tendency was dominant, whereas in Brussels and Ghent the less radical Socialists, such as De Paepe and Anseele, were in control. The Flemish Socialists supported the reformist Gotha Programme of the German SDP (1875) and after negotiations with the Walloons, the Flemish Socialist party and the Brabant Socialist parties were founded in 1877. These fused in 1879 into the Belgian Socialist Party. Practical support by the new party for the Borinage strikers in 1884 created the conditions for a genuinely national party. Sixty-nine delegates met to found the party at *'De Zwaan'* in Brussels in April 1885, and the first Congress was held in Antwerp in August 1885. The new party, the Belgian Workers' Party (POB), joined the second International on its formation in Paris in 1889. The basic programme for the party, the so-called 'Déclaration de Quaregnon', was adopted in March 1894. Its basic philosophy was that all material riches should belong to all citizens. As a practical political programme, it was to strive for universal suffrage and proportional representation, and a number of social measures. The POB first entered Parliament in 1894 with twenty-eight members.

One of the main political battles of the nineteenth century was over education and the role in it of the Church. The Convention Nationale had already been obliged to come to terms with Catholic demands for freedom of religion and education. However, when the vicar-general Sterckx reported to the Vatican, as required by it, on some aspects of the 1830 Constitution, papal condemnation was only just avoided. As we have seen, it was this issue which provoked the formation of the Liberal Party in 1846 and, later, a Catholic party. Until the First World War it also meant that, unlike today, the Liberals and Socialists stood closer to each other than the Socialists and the Christian Democratic wing of the Catholic party. Frequent clashes arose over such issues as the maintenance of churches and churchyards, scholarships, the work of charitable institutions, and the organisation of the school system, culminating in the controversies of 1879-84, which saw the adoption of strongly anti-clerical school legislation by the doctrinaire Liberal cabinet of Frère-Orban and its reversal after the Catholic election victory in 1884.

Another important issue which emerged from time to time was that of the Flemish language. As we have seen, the Revolution and the state which it created were in a real sense appropriated by the Francophone bourgeoisie. The Flemish people were outsiders. Laws of 1831 and 1845 stipulated that the French-language versions of Acts of Parliament and of royal decrees were to be the only official texts. Flemish could be used neither in Parliament nor in the courts, nor was it used in the school system.

Gradually, in the period leading to the First World War, the growing Flemish movement[19] won important concessions. An '*arrêté royal*' (royal decree) on the correct spelling of Dutch in Flanders was issued in 1844, and in 1851 a royal commission was set up to examine the Flemish question. This was a clear response to the nascent Flemish movement which had found expression through actions such as the 1840 General Petition to Parliament. The Commission proposed, in Flanders, the exclusive use of Flemish in primary education, equality with French in secondary schools, and the use of Flemish in administrative and legal procedures. The government of Charles Rogier totally rejected this report. Then, after 1859, more Flemish activists entered Parliament, and a series of court cases, in which Flemish-speaking defendants were even sentenced to death in French, moved opinion. The Antwerp Meeting Partij was also Flemish-minded, and in 1866 declared Flemish to be the official language of Antwerp; in 1863, Jan De Laet, one of its Deputies, had taken the oath in Flemish. From 1879 parliamentary proceedings were printed in both languages, and from 1888 speeches could be made in Flemish.

Considerable progress was made over the use of Flemish in the courts. An Act of 1873 provided for the use of Flemish in criminal assizes; in 1893 the problem of the appeal courts in Brussels and Liège was settled, but only in 1908 was a Flemish assize court set up in Brussels for Brabant. In 1878, a law was passed providing for the use of Flemish in administrative correspondence and documents, where the citizen opted for that language. However, it was only after the reform of the suffrage in 1893, when the Flemish people were at last enfranchised, that real pressure built up for equality between the languages. The 1894 Congress of the Katholieke Vlaamse Bond came out for such equality. The 1894 election, the first under the new law, saw the entry into Parliament of a considerable number of Flemish activists such as Corremans, Daens and de Vriendt, who in 1898 finally obtained the passage of a law guaranteeing the equality of the two languages. However, the Flemish version of the Civil Code only appeared in 1961. A 1913 law went some way toward giving Flemish its proper status in the army, but orders still had to be given exclusively in French, which was to become a serious issue during the 1914-18 war.

Another area of pressure was that of education and literature. A series of laws in 1883, 1890 and 1914 gradually extended the use of Dutch in schools in Flanders. The 1913 language law adopted the 'mother tongue' principle, but the amendments of Flemish activists in favour of the 'territorial principle' were rejected by Parliament. The Royal Flemish Academy for language and literature had been set up in 1886, and with other Flemish cultural bodies and societies (Willemsfonds, Davidsfonds) it became a permanent source of ideas and pressure. In the period immediately before the First World War, the key issue was that of a Flemish university and its 'Flemishisation'. A mass movement related to this issue emerged, led by politicians from the three parties – Van Cauwelaert (Catholic), Huysmans (Socialist) and Franck (Liberal) – and a petition with 100,000 signatures maintained pressure after 1910. However, no positive results had been obtained that year. The last victory came in another area with the use of Flemish being introduced in Catholic schools under a law of 1910.

There was by that time a certain backlash in Walloon opinion, especially in the Senate, which made each successive step in any area increasingly difficult. The Senate had caused major problems over the law on the equality of the two languages. On the university question, the episcopate added its opposition to that of others.

Through the personal initiative of Leopold II, Belgium became a major colonial power in Africa.[20] The King was recognised as the sovereign ruler of the Independent Congo State by the Berlin Congress of 1884-5, and the Belgian Parliament authorised this by the necessary two-thirds majority. However, the Congo was still not a Belgian colony. In 1886, 1887 and 1890 laws were passed authorising loans to the Congo State, both for railways (Matadi Stanley Pool) and to enable Leopold to meet his obligations under the 1890 Brussels anti-slavery convention. This loan of 25 million francs was backed by the right of the Belgian state to take over the Congo in the event of default after ten years. When new private loans became necessary in 1895, the government sought to take over the territory immediately, but met too strong an opposition both in Conservative circles, which feared the financial consequences, and in Radical Liberal and Socialist circles opposed to the colonial ethic. A second and more serious attempt by the Catholic Cabinet to take over the Congo occurred in 1901 when the ten-year loan expired. Under strong attack from the Socialists and Liberals, and internationally (from Britain, France and Germany), Leopold reacted strongly, posing unacceptable conditions for the take-over. A compromise was difficult but was finally reached in 1907 by which time the affair had caused Leopold considerable unpopularity. After a controversial election campaign in which the Catholic party lost two seats, the bill for the annexation of the Congo was passed in August 1908. Social questions came increasingly to the fore at the end of the period. The serious economic crisis of the mid-1880s, unlike earlier crises, met an active trade union and labour movement. In 1866, the previous legal prohibition on 'combinations', as trade unions were designated, was partly removed, although the right to strike remained severely limited by restrictions on necessary secondary activity such as picketing. In the spring of 1886, there were a greater number of serious strikes than earlier, although severe strikes had already occurred as early as 1839, 1849, 1857 and 1861 in the Ghent textile industry, and in 1861, 1868 and 1869 in the coal mines in the Charleroi area.

Immediately after the 1886 strikes, a series of laws (1887-9) was passed following the recommendation of a royal commission on the condition of workers. At long last, after many years of pressure, these laws regulated wages and the working conditions of women and children, and established conciliation machinery to deal with disputes. The doctrinaire Liberals and conservative Catholics – perhaps for different reasons – opposed such state intervention in economic matters.

In 1907-9, a new ideological battle broke out over the right to regulate working hours. In legislation on the mines, amendments were passed, against the wishes of the conservative Catholic government, by a coalition of Socialists, Radicals and Social Christians. The doctrinaire Liberals remained opposed. The fall of the government interrupted the passage of the bill, which was later passed in a milder form but still contained important measures of social progress: underground work for women and for boys under fourteen was forbidden, the working day was limited to nine hours, and miners were to receive a pension at the age of sixty.

After Independence, foreign policy assumed less political importance than domestic issues. Exceptions were perhaps the drive for free trade (largely attained by 1860), the colonial question, and defence policy, with its obvious foreign policy implications. The status of Belgium had been regulated by the great powers, which guaranteed its neutrality and territorial integrity. Gradually her relations with the Netherlands were normalised, although throughout the nineteenth century there was a tendency – sometimes criticised in Flanders – to lean towards France. Before 1914 the serenity of Belgium's foreign relations was only disturbed by the ill-advised support given by Leopold II to the Mexican adventure of Maximilian of Austria; the pressures from Napoleon III and later Bismarck to control agitators operating from Belgian soil; the future of Luxembourg when the North German Confederation was dissolved in

1866; and the ideologically motivated support of the Liberal governments for Italian unification against the Vatican, which led to a short-lived breach of diplomatic relations with the latter. Belgium remained out of all nineteenth-century wars.

Belgium in the First World War

When war broke out in the Balkans in July 1914, Belgium expected to remain neutral, and indeed the powers initially indicated their acceptance of its neutrality. However, the long-prepared German plan for the invasion of France – the Schlieffen plan – required passage through Belgium. As a precaution the Belgian government ordered mobilisation on 31 July; on 2 August Germany presented an ultimatum to Belgium and on 4 August invaded.

It falls outside our scope to consider the course of the war in any detail;[21] it is only necessary to say that, despite Allied aid, the greater part of the country was rapidly overrun and occupied by the Germans. Brussels fell on 20 August, by mid- September the country south of the Meuse was in German hands, and Antwerp fell on 20 October. After the great German offensive on the Ijzer river from 18 to 30 October, which failed, the war of movement was over. Only a small strip of territory in the north-west, bounded by the coast and the Leie river, the Ijzer and the French frontier, containing the town of Ypres, remained in Belgian hands and was to do so throughout the four long years of trench warfare on the Western front. The Belgian front became part of the vast Allied front stretching from the Swiss frontier to the Channel coast. It remained relatively calm, and an army of 170,000 men was built up which took part in the offensive of September 1918. However, by the Armistice in November the line had only moved east as far as Ghent and Mons.

During the war the government of de Brocqueville, formed in 1911, remained in office, operating from Sainte-Adresse near Le Havre in France; in July 1918 de Brocqueville was replaced by Corremans. At the outbreak of war, the Socialist Emil Vandervelde and the Liberals Paul Hymans and Goblet d'Alviella were brought into the government, initially as ministers without portfolio. The most important question to exercise the government during the war years related to foreign policy – whether the pre-war neutrality of Belgium should be preserved, as the King and some ministers sought, or abandoned in favour of a frankly pro-Allied stance with territorial demands on Germany. The latter viewpoint largely prevailed after various attempts to test the German peace terms had shown that these were unacceptable to Belgium, since they would have involved loss of territory and the acceptance of German military bases in Belgium. The other important question was the attitude to be adopted towards the growing Flemish movement. In March 1918, commissions were set up to study the closely related issues of the Flemish movement, universal suffrage and the schools question.

The war itself and developments in occupied Belgium had important post-war consequences. The war had seen the Socialists integrated into government, and created pressures for universal suffrage which could no longer be ignored. The occupation had also led to developments in Flanders which strengthened the Flemish movement,[22] but at the same time it had set off hostility at a new and hitherto unknown level against it in Brussels and Wallonia. In the same way as many Irish nationalists, such as Roger Casement, supported the German cause in the First World War in their own national interest, so to varying degrees the Flemish nationalists saw the German occupation as an opportunity for themselves. The most radical group, *Jong Vlaanderen* (its main leaders were Nieuwenhuis and Borms), based in Ghent with its newspaper *De Vlaamse Post*, worked for an independent Flemish state. The Unionists supported a federalist solution. Within this group, the exiles in Amsterdam (mostly 'Monarchists', i.e. supporters of a monarchical union between Flanders and Wallonia, such as Anton Jacob and Frans van Cauwelaert), though radicalised after 1915, feared that excessive reliance on German support would damage the Flemish cause. However, some important results were obtained. In March 1916, a German decree made the University of Ghent a Flemish 'institution', and the collaborationist Ministry of Arts and Science was split in the same year. In February 1917, the Vlaams Nationale Landdag (Flemish National Assembly) set up a Vlaamse Raad, representatives of which went to Berlin and obtained the total administrative separation of Flanders (capital Brussels) and Wallonia (capital Namur). In November 1917, the Vlaamse Raad declared the Le Havre government removed from office and Flanders independent (on 22 December). This last move caused the resignation of moderates and led to a radical second Raad van Vlaanderen whose representatives sat in a German administrative commission, responsible only to the German Governor and in reality established to control the nationalists. The Le Havre government naturally condemned all these measures and declared them void, but it was forced to promise a Flemish university.

Economic and political conditions under the occupation became more and more severe. Basic freedoms were suspended, unemployment rose to 500,000 and food was extremely scarce; also, 120,000 workers were deported to Germany in addition to 90,000 who went there more or less voluntarily. This situation provoked resistance and a flourishing illegal press, such as *La Libre Belgique*. Many personalities such as Cardinal Mercier of Leuven, Burgomaster Adolphe Max of Brussels and the Supreme Court judges, who resigned *en bloc* in 1918, set an example. A number of people who took action against the occupiers, such as the

English nurse Edith Cavell, were shot. Not unnaturally, relations between such circles and the Flemish movement deteriorated irreparably.

Between the world wars

With the introduction of universal suffrage the Socialists definitively eclipsed the Liberals as the second largest party, and in Wallonia became the largest party. However, the expectations of the Socialists were not to be fulfilled insofar as their steady rise was not sustained. They won thirty new seats in 1919, making a total of seventy, and in 1925 reached a peak of seventy-eight seats, equal to the Catholics; but their representation then declined throughout the 1930s to a low point of sixty-four seats in 1939. The 1925 election, when the Poullet-Vandervelde Socialist progressive Catholic cabinet was created, seemed to offer the Socialists the springboard to majority status, but this was not to be. The period was one of considerable instability. Between 1830 and 1918 there were twenty-seven governments, and in the inter-war years alone there were eighteen. Despite previous co-operation and affinities on the schools question, there were no Liberal-Socialist governments.

The first period (1919-21) saw a series of historic reforms carried out by three tripartitie progressive *'Union Sacrée'* governments (a 'government of national unity' is the closest Anglo-Saxon equivalent of this peculiarly Gallic concept). As we have seen, governments in which the Socialists played a major role introduced universal suffrage, reformed the Senate, brought in the eight-hour working day, and obtained at Versailles the abolition of the compulsory neutrality imposed by the 1831 Treaty and the incorporation of the Eupen-Malmédy area into Belgium, thus creating a German-speaking community alongside the Flemish and Francophone ones. Belgium failed to obtain Luxembourg (or Maastricht) as it had hoped, but entered an economic union with the Grand-Duchy.

All the political parties underwent some reorganisation and internal turmoil[23] between the wars. The Catholic party took the name 'Union Catholique Belge' and organised itself as more clearly representative of various 'estates' in society. The old Fédération des Cercles Catholiques was joined by the Boerenbond (farmers' organisation), ACW (Catholic trade union) and the Fédération Chrétienne des Classes Moyennes. The General Council was made up of six representatives of each body. After the 1935 elections, at which the Flemish nationalists did well, separate Walloon and Flemish wings – the Parti Catholique Social and the Katholieke Vlaamse Volkspartij (KVV) – joined in the Bloc des Catholiques Belges.

The Socialists (POB) became increasingly reformist, at least till 1931. In that year, a radical group formed around Paul-Henri Spaak and Hendrik De Man, which favoured planning and a generally more radical stance. A split was avoided by De Man's compromise *Plan de Travail;* however the *Plan* led to Emil Vandervelde's resignation in 1939; the post of Party President had officially been created in 1933, and Vandervelde was elected as its first occupant. The Socialist trade unions, which since 1898 had merely been a Commission Syndicale, gained some minimal autonomy when they became the Confédération Générale du Travail de Belgique in 1938.

The Liberals strengthened their organisation. They now clearly occupied the third place in Parliament, but their influence in this period was actually greater than numbers alone would suggest. The National Council was their leading body, which elected the Party Chairman and Bureau; here the Party's parliamentary Deputies played a dominant role. There were continual divergences on doctrinal purity, with some, such as Devèze, wanting to moderate the Party's economic liberalism, and Heymans and Janson anxious to moderate its anti-clericalism. Despite the efforts of figures such as Louis Franck, the Party remained hostile to Flemish demands.

Some smaller new parties developed in this period. The Frontbeweging gave rise to the Frontpartij, a small Flemish party which supported Flemish self-government and was anti-militarist. It won five seats in 1919, four in 1921 and six in 1925. The party later developed into the Vlaams National Verbond (VNV), which won seventeen seats in 1939 (8.27% of the national vote). Throughout the period, important divisions remained within the ranks of the Flemish nationalists, making it difficult to present a united front.

The depression, the falling prestige of Belgian parliamentary democracy and the rise of Adolf Hitler in neighbouring Germany created the conditions for Rexism led by Léon Degrelle (later a volunteer in the SS). This movement, which began as a Catholic rightist-populist movement, inclined more and more towards Fascism as the 1930s progressed. It brought to Belgian politics the personal abuse, crude propagandistic lies, verbal and physical violence and open contempt for democracy which were the hallmarks of National Socialism in Germany. The Rexist Party won 11.49% of the vote and twenty-one seats (in the 202-member Chamber) at its first election in 1936. In the Walloon Provinces and Brussels, its vote rose to 21%, and in parts of Wallonia was nearer 30%. However, a common front against Rexism by the traditional parties was symbolised in the 1937 by-election in Brussels, when the Prime Minister Paul van Zeeland defeated Degrelle with the support of all the main parties, and received 76% of the vote as against Degrelle's 19%. At the 1939 election, the Rexists suffered a sharp decline to 4.43% and a mere four seats – two in Brussels (five in 1936) and two in Wallonia (thirteen in 1936). In Flanders they won no seats at all.

In 1920, a left-wing group in the Parti Ouvrier Belge (POB) called '*Les Amis de l'Exploité* ' was excluded from the Party and went on to form a separate party under F. Jacquemot. Under pressure from the International, it fused in December 1921 with a pre-existing party led by Van Overstraeten to form the Belgian Communist party (PCB). It first entered the Chamber in 1925 with two seats and 1.64% of the vote. At the 1936 election it gained nine seats and 6.05% of the vote, a level which it maintained in 1939.

As we have seen, the Flemish question became more and more important, and conflict over it sharper. A new climate had developed: Flemish demands could no longer be ignored, yet they were not easily accepted either. As early as 1921, a new law was passed, after considerable resistance in the Senate, on the use of languages in local government administration. Despite concessions over Brussels – a bilingual area, which was extended to cover seventeen as against fourteen Communes – the principle of territoriality, and hence the exclusive use of Flemish in Flanders, was established.

The issue of a Flemish university in Ghent remained very much alive, although of course the creation of such a university by a German decree in March 1916, which had in any case divided the Flemish movement, could not be accepted. The speech from the throne in 1918 promised the establishment of such a university, but gave no details. Divisions in all parties ensured that no rapid action ensued. The parliamentary commission set up to examine the matter proposed in late 1922, by a very small majority, the gradual transformation of the existing university into a Flemish institution (*vervlaamsing*). Opponents of this proposal saw that they could not reject the principle of a Flemish university and so argued for the retention of a French university in Ghent as well. The Chamber passed the proposal by a majority of four, but it was rejected by the Senate. The government was forced to introduce a compromise proposal. Ghent University would be essentially Flemish, but would have Flemish and Francophone sections within it. This compromise passed both chambers and became law in August 1923.

Another serious issue which reached a climax in 1928 was that of an amnesty for the so-called 'Activists', which had become an insistent Flemish demand going well beyond the extremists. The most celebrated case was that of August Borms who, from prison, won a by-election in Antwerp against a Liberal, with the Catholics and Socialists calling for a spoiled ballot. This gave the issue an altogether greater impact than in earlier years (1924-6) when amnesty bills were heavily rejected. A typical Belgian compromise was reached: for sentences of less than ten years' imprisonment a special review commission was established, but other more serious sentences, including that of Borms, were considered irrevocable (i.e. not subject to further review) but also to have become null, a very strange judicial conception.

The Christian trade unions (ACW) and the Socialists declared themselves in favour of a linguistic frontier defined by law, each region then being unilingual, possibly with a special regime for Brussels. The gains of the Flemish nationalists in the 1929 elections made action even more urgent. As a result, the government pledged itself to propose solutions. An immediate response was a bill making the university in Ghent fully Flemish (with some transitional provisions), which became law in April 1930. The Liberals still wanted to retain some concessions for the French-speaking minorities in Flanders, but this was now almost impossible to achieve on any permanent basis.

Progress continued towards the complete application of the 'territorial' principle, with a minimum of exceptions. In 1932, after a false start in 1930, a new law was passed covering both private and state schools; under it, the 'mother-tongue principle' was limited exclusively to Brussels. In 1932, a unilingual administrative regime in each of the two regions was enacted, with concessions to minorities of 30% in *communes* (urban administrative units) in Brussels. In 1935, a new law was passed on the language to be used in legal proceedings. From then on, with minor exceptions (still contested), Flemish was to be used exclusively in Flanders. In 1937, a new amnesty law was passed, but did not give civic rights back to those who had been convicted.

This was where the 'Flemish question' rested at the outbreak of the Second World War. The movement had made important advances along the road to complete equality in the eighty years during which it had been campaigning. But the collaboration of some Flemish nationalists with the Nazi occupiers was to set the movement back considerably, and the advance was only fully resumed in the late 1950s.

Social and economic problems were increasingly important in this period. As we have seen, the post-war governments *'de l'Union Sacrée'* were progressive in character and introduced important social reforms. After 1921, apart from the short-lived Socialist-Catholic progressive government of 1925-6 and the second Van Zeeland government in 1936-7, which took office after the serious strikes in June 1936, the successive governments were mostly concerned to reduce public expenditure and maintain confidence in the franc. The measures of the post-war National Unity cabinets – the eight-hour working day, universal suffrage, a reform of the 'reactionary' character of the Senate and some improvement in the rights of trade unions – were to remain as almost the only significant social achievements.

The 1925-6 Poullet-Vandervelde government intended to introduce wide-ranging social reforms but it was overtaken by a financial crisis arising out of the escalating national debt, which led to a serious weakening of the franc from 107 against the British pound to 162 in early 1926. The government was forced to resign on 8 May 1926. Its successor was able to stabilise the franc by issuing shares in Belgian railways to reduce the public debt. The period 1927-30 saw considerable economic progress. External trade went from 15 billion francs in 1925 to 32 billion in 1932. Despite important public works such as the Albert Canal, the national debt fell from 52 billion francs in 1926 to 32 billion at the end of 1930. Laws of 1928 and 1930 introduced and extended a system of family allowances for workers.

Between 1930 and 1932, the world recession made its impact in Belgium. Trade fell back to 15 billion francs in 1932, the budget deficit rose to 1 billion, share values fell by one-third, and the cost of unemployment relief rose by a factor of eight. The number of unemployed reached 225,000. Action was required, but the parties failed, despite elections in both 1932 and 1933, to agree on any solution, and faced a series of strikes by workers whose wages were actually being reduced, especially in the Charleroi industrial area. The government obtained from Parliament a delegation of full power to act. Wages and pensions were reduced, taxes were increased, credit facilities and public works were planned. Price and production controls were imposed.

These measures were largely ineffective.[24] The Socialist opposition put forward its *Plan de Travail*, produced by Hendrik De Man and Paul-Henri Spaak, who soon came into conflict with the traditionalist Vandervelde, who resigned as leader in 1937. The plan departed from both the Marxist notion of class struggle and that of proletarian internationalism. It sought national solutions to economic problems by 'Keynesian' means: more public spending and state intervention, and an active and enlarged public sector alongside the private sector – in short a mixed economy with the state setting basic macro-economic targets. The plan failed to gain the support of the Catholic unions, which reduced its immediate practical importance. However, it was forward-looking in that it embodied a coherent alternative economic strategy to neo-classical orthodoxy.

By 1935, it was clear that the measures of the Catholic-Liberal government were inadequate to meet the increasingly serious economic situation, with unemployment, bankruptcies, financial scandals, falling exports and an overvalued currency. Serious strikes were in prospect. Without Socialist support the royal commission on employment failed to produce viable results. In the classic manner, the response was a tripartite (Catholic-Socialist-Liberal) government, the first led by Van Zeeland (1935-6). Rapid measures were taken to devalue the franc by 28%, balance the budget, control interest rates and set in train measures for public works on a limited scale under the Office de Redressement Economique. Unemployment fell to 100,000 – a considerable success which, however, was far from satisfying the Socialists, who sought a more complete application of the De Man plan.

After the 1936 election, as we have seen, the country became increasingly ungovernable. The formation of the Van Zeeland tripartite government coincided with a serious wave of strikes, which developed into a general strike involving 320,000 workers. On the model of the 'Matignon Agreement' in France, a national conference of unions, employers and government was held. Only when a comprehensive social programme, backed by the employers and government, had emerged did the strikes come to an end. The programme stipulated a forty-hour week and a seven-hour day in heavy industries, six days' paid holiday a year, increases in wages and family allowances, and compulsory sickness and invalidity insurance. Political agreements sought to improve the working of Parliament and to ensure greater stability for the Executive. A study centre for the reform of the State was set up to act as a 'think tank'. The social measures were all enacted by the end of July and a rapid start was made on the political ones, but most of these were not realised before the government fell in October 1937 after unfounded but damaging allegations of financial impropriety had been made against Van Zeeland, from which the Rexists and VNV derived important propaganda advantage in their campaign against the 'rottenness' of the parliamentary system. It then became increasingly difficult to form a government, and internal strains in all parties increased. As a result, no effective measures were taken to deal with the renewed economic crisis resulting from increasing world protectionism after 1938. The only response of the first (21-27 February 1939) and second (April-September 1939) Pierlot governments was to propose a 5% reduction in public expenditure and a vague promise to improve the unemployment benefit system.

A major issue throughout the inter-war period was foreign policy.[25] As we have seen, Belgium was only relatively successful at Versailles. Its demands on Allied Luxembourg and neutral Holland were not accepted. It did however obtain the *'Cantons de l'Est'* (Eupen-Malmédy), trusteeship over the African territories of Rwanda and Burundi, reparations from Germany, and the removal of the neutrality clauses of the 1839 treaty. But the victory of the anti-neutrality party by no means in itself solved the problem of Belgium's future foreign policy orientation, although for many the implication was clear: an alliance with France, if possible supported by Britain. This orientation was strongly contested by the Flemish movement.

This issue was to play a considerable part in the controversy over the secret Franco-Belgian military agreement of 1920, whereby the parties were pledged to assist each other in the event of aggression. This pact made possible the conclusion of the economic union with Luxembourg, and rejected the Luxembourg referendum in favour of union with France, in the interest of the Franco-Belgian alliance. The projected military union between Belgium and Luxembourg failed to materialise. The pact made Belgian participation in the occupation of the Ruhr in 1923 morally obligatory. The related increase in the length of compulsory military service provoked serious domestic controversy, as did the ratification of the Franco-Belgian agreement; the latter was made an issue of confidence by the Theunis government, which fell when the House rejected it.

Belgium was forced to accept the Dawes plan, which limited reparations to BF 400-500 million; this hardly exceeded the renegotiated (and reduced) Belgian debt to the United States of some BF 300 million. The plan ended the occupation of the Ruhr and improved the political climate. In this new atmosphere the Locarno pact (1925) was signed, whereby Italy, Germany, France, Britain and Belgium guaranteed, among other things, the Franco-German and Belgian-German frontiers. Over and above the guarantee itself, Belgian foreign policy was placed in a wider multilateral framework, which could more easily attain consensus in Belgium. The Kellogg-Briand pact and the disarmament conference which began in Geneva in 1932 were hopeful signs that the post-Locarno spirit was bearing fruit. However, the world depression and above all Hitler's accession to power in Germany in 1933 shattered these hopes and led to a new troubled period which culminated in the outbreak of war in 1939.

This new situation was underlined by the patent failure of the League of Nations to act against Germany's re-occupation of the Rhineland and the Italian invasion of Abyssinia (Ethiopia). Belgium, like other small countries which had placed their faith in the League and the 'Locarno spirit', adopted a suicidal position. In 1936, in solemn statements, Leopold III and Paul-Henri Spaak, the foreign minister, postulated a new sort of neutrality. The 1920 military agreement with France was virtually abandoned, and Belgium declared that she would defend herself against any threat from any quarter. This was tantamount to refusing any effective coordinated action against Germany, which in the conditions of modern *Blitzkrieg* was to make the Franco-British aid promised in April 1937 largely ineffective. When war broke out in September 1939, the government was obliged to include the Socialists, who had previously been in opposition. A declaration of neutrality was issued and the army mobilised.

Belgium in the Second World War

Methods of waging war had changed since 1914, but the strategic and tactical conceptions of Germany's enemies, including Belgium, had stood still. Belgium resisted for a mere eighteen days after the German invasion of the Low Countries on 10 May 1940. Germany immediately obtained a decisive advantage, and Allied help was too little, too late and misconceived. The *Panzer* divisions broke through the French positions at Sedan and by 20 May reached the Somme at Abbeville. By 27 May the British evacuation from Dunkerque had begun, and on that day Belgium sued for peace.[26]

In wartime, according to Belgian custom, the King assumes effective command of the army, and it was in that capacity that Leopold III, acting in his personal capacity and without consulting his government which was in France, ordered the surrender. The government had requested the King to leave with them, but he had refused to do so. From Poitiers the government condemned his action and assumed his executive power. After the fall of France the majority of the cabinet, deputies and senators abandoned any active role and returned to Belgium, or remained in the unoccupied zone of France, having resigned. Only Pierlot, Spaak, Gutt, De Vleeschauwer, and later Delfosse, De Schryver and Balthazar, went to London and constituted an exile government. The government only gradually broke with all the German satellites and Italy, and not till 1942 did it become a full ally of Britain, the United States and the Soviet Union by signing the Atlantic Charter. It also signed the Benelux economic union agreement with the Dutch and Luxembourg exile governments in September 1944. Belgians outside Belgium and in the Congo played an important economic and military role in the war.

Internally there were many parallels with 1914-18, but the reality was much more severe. Nazi Germany was a barbarian state obsessed with its evil racist totalitarian ideology which would tolerate no dissent or opposition. Its main aim was to weld the conquered territories into a 'New Order' in the service of Germany. Any apparent concession or co-operation, for example with Flemish movements, was based on the most total cynicism and opportunism. In contrast to 1914, the trauma of such rapid defeat in May 1940 and the subsequent defeat of all Germany's enemies except Britain, whose survival hung by the thread of the indomitable 'Few' of the Royal Air Force Fighter Command, induced a state of shock, disorientation and passivity, which served the German cause well. Many thousands of Belgians had left their homes, the economy was in chaos and the army was in German prisoner-of-war camps; all internal leadership had dissolved; and the dispute between King and government increased the general confusion.

At first, as in 1914-18, the Germans established a military government headed by General von Falkenhausen, with a civil administration under his command. In addition, of course, the various 'ideological' agencies such as the Gestapo and SS operated in Belgium against the Resistance and the Jews. The secretaries-general of the Belgian ministries remained in office and constituted a subordinate Belgian administration, which established numerous special agencies in the field of food supply and control of industry. A corporatist type of organisation was introduced for many key economic sectors (coal, metallurgy and textiles) and by the replacement of the trade unions with the Union des Travailleurs Manuels et Intellectuels. At the same time Hendrik De Man dissolved the Parti Ouvrier Belge (POB).

As the initial stupefaction wore off, reaction to the occupation developed along three main lines. The majority of the population accepted, unwillingly, the new situation as a necessary evil, seeking merely to survive. No doubt in the early war years, with the memory of the failures of the parliamentary system fresh in their minds, and presented with the apparent invincibility of German arms and, for some after June 1941, the attraction of the assault on Soviet Communism, a few leaned towards support for the 'New Order' rather than mere acquiescence in it. However, as the war progressed, rationing bit deeper, German barbarism revealed its true face, and the battles of Stalingrad and El Alamein and the 1,000-bomber raids offered a glimmer of hope, the vast majority leaned increasingly towards the Allied cause.

However, a small group both in Flanders and Wallonia openly embraced collaboration. In Flanders two groups, the nationalist but fascistic Vlaams National Verbond (VNV) under Staf De Clercq and later Elias saw collaboration as a means of realising their dream of a *Groot Nederland* (Greater Netherlands), embracing Flanders, northern France and Holland as part of the 'New Order'. Germany certainly encouraged these aims, but took much less concrete action than in 1914-18. The Nazis preferred the less nationalist and more clearly National Socialist 'De Vlag' under Vandewiele. Both groups provided contingents for the German armies on the Russian front. As elsewhere in Europe, German tactics towards such movements lacked any subtlety and led to a crisis within the VNV. In Wallonia, 'Rex' under Léon Degrelle, was the main collaborationist organisation. The VNV had 86,000 members. In all, over 340,000 persons were accused of collaboration after the war, of whom 58,000 were found guilty and 241 were executed. That excludes 60,000 who volunteered to work in Germany, and who were not brought to trial.

Resistance rapidly grew. By the liberation six major organisations had some 120,000 men under arms, and double that number of other active members. The most important were the Armée Secrète, the military organisation run by the exile government (about 50,000 members), the left-wing Front de l'Indépendance (40,000) and the Mouvement National Belge (20,000). Belgium was liberated rapidly. British troops crossed the frontier on 2 September 1944 and entered Brussels on 4 September. By 3 November all German troops had left Belgian territory. However, the country had to suffer two more trials: 'V1' and 'V2' rockets fell in Liège and Antwerp, and the Ardennes counter-offensive between 16 December 1944 and the end of January 1945 almost brought the Nazis back to the Meuse.

Belgium after the war

The events which have marked post-war Belgian history have been varied and controversial: the repression of collaboration to which we have already referred; the '*Question Royale*'; the remarkable economic recovery; Belgian membership of NATO and the European Communities; the decolonisation of the Congo in 1960; and the rise of the language and 'community' issue, especially after 1965. Many of these issues will be discussed in later chapters, particularly the 'regional' question and the major changes in the party system which occurred during the 1960s.

Compared with earlier periods, political stability has been as elusive as ever. There have been thirty-eight governments since the liberation up to the time of writing. Of these only seven lasted longer than three years and only one the full four years of the legislature. There have been sixteen elections since the first one after the war in 1946, giving the average legislature a life of barely three years. Almost all possible types of government have been formed: homogeneous CVP/PSC; homogeneous Socialist; CVP/PSC-Socialist; CVP/PSC-Liberal; Socialist-Liberal; classic tripartite PSC/CVP-Socialist-Liberal; governments including all the regional parties (RW, FDF, VU) or only some of them (FDF, RW, FDF or VU only) and between 1944 and 1947 four governments including Communists, and a few governments without the Catholic party (now IUP/PSC) in 1945-7. However, since 1947 the Catholic party has only been in opposition during four years (1954-8). There have been governments headed by both Socialists (eight) and CVP/PSC (twenty), but none by Liberals. Most governments have fallen as a result of their internal dissensions rather than by defeat in Parliament.

Between 1945 and 1951, three questions dominated political life: the *Question Royale*,[27] reconstruction and the reorientation of Belgian foreign policy in response to the onset of the Cold War after 1947. When Belgium was liberated in September 1944, the Germans removed Leopold III to Germany and he was only freed by Americans forces in May 1945. Parliament, therefore, elected his brother Prince Charles as regent on 20 September 1944. Statements of that time gave no hint of the animosity that was to develop against the King when he was freed, but in the face of Socialist, Communist and some Liberal reservations he was asked by the government not to return to Belgium but to stay in Switzerland.

In June 1945 a law was passed to the effect that the Regency could only be ended by a vote of both Houses of Parliament in joint session; a proposal by the CVP/PSC for a referendum was not then accepted. The Spaak-Eyskens government (PS-PSC/CVP) agreed to disagree on the issue. The 1949 election – the first in which women were able to vote and the first to take place after the Communist take-over in Czechoslovakia, saw a significant rightward swing, which greatly modified the situation. The PSC/CVP almost had an absolute majority in the Senate. Logically, a

Liberal-CVP/PSC government was formed, which agreed on a referendum on the future of Leopold III. This was held on 12 March 1950. Overall, 57.6% voted 'yes' (in favour of the King's return), but in Brussels only 48% did so and in Wallonia only 42%, whereas in Flanders the 'yes' vote was 72%. After the 1950 election, in which the CVP/PSC alone gained a secure absolute majority in both Houses, Parliament voted for an end to the Regency as prescribed by Article 82 of the constitution and the law of June 1945.

The referendum result was not accepted in Wallonia, and the opposition – Socialists, Communists and others – organised meetings and demonstrations, including a march on the royal palace at Laeken, just outside Brussels. On 15 August 1950, in order to avoid further violence, unrest and division, Leopold abdicated in favour of his son Baudouin. So the *Question Royale* ended, but the bitterness it had generated lived on, not least in Flanders where it was felt that a minority had gained its will by the use of violence and civil disorder in the face of a clear vote of the people.

In defence of the opponents of King Leopold, the very strong emotions aroused by the *Question Royale* should be understood. This substantial minority considered their action justified on the grounds of Leopold's behaviour during the war. In the first place, he had taken it upon himself to surrender the Belgian army without the approval of the government, and had refused to follow his ministers into exile. His remarriage (his first wife, the popular Queen Astrid, had been killed in a car accident in 1935) also fuelled controversy, because it seemed inconsistent with his declared intention to share the lot of his troops as a prisoner-of-war, and because of the Flemish and Catholic origins of his second wife, Liliane Baels. A more serious grievance might seem to be his relatively extensive dealings with exponents of the 'New Order'; these are only now coming fully to light, but they were already at that time exemplified by his meeting with Hitler at which he purported to discuss the future of Belgium within a Europe dominated by Nazi Germany. Perhaps it was not surprising that his opponents, most of whom were from the ranks of the Walloon Resistance, considered that he had forfeited his right to reign.

Post-war reconstruction was also a key issue. Housing was an immediate priority: 200,000 new houses were needed. Laws of 1947 and 1948 made grants of up to BF 22,000 and loans at the low interest rates of 2 and 2.75% for house-building. The law on the National Bank (6 October 1944) 'sterilised' a considerable part of the inflationary money supply; at the same time, tight controls were placed on prices and incomes. The economic measures taken initially by the returning Pierlot government were ill-adapted to the actual situation and were only partially successful. The Van Acker government gave priority to the immediate reopening of the coal mines, which provided the best available source of export revenue. With the liberalisation of world trade and the inflow of Marshall aid, Belgium benefited from the general view of growth which began in the early 1950s. The resulting prosperity made possible a relatively painless solution of major structural problems brought about by technological change. The Sambre-Meuse coal mines were almost all closed, causing almost 200,000 jobs to be lost, directly or indirectly. Even in Flanders considerable numbers of jobs disappeared. But apart from the strikes against mine closures in early 1959 and the severe but almost totally unsuccessful strike in the winter of 1960-1 in protest against the so-called '*loi unique*', which reduced public expenditure and social benefits, the 1950s and early 1960s were a period of social peace.

In the period 1945-60, foreign and colonial policy was a major preoccupation. With the Brussels treaty directed at Germany and then with the onset of the Cold War after 1947-8, Belgium for the first time committed itself to a system of preventive alliance by becoming a founder-member of NATO in 1949. It was an early supporter of European integration, joining the Council of Europe (1949), becoming one of 'the Six' to join the European Coal and Steel Community in 1952 and later playing a major role in the establishment of Euratom and the European Economic Community (1957). In a wider setting, it was a founder-member of the United Nations, and joined the IMF, GATT and the OEEC established under the Marshall Plan.[28]

Towards the end of the 1950s, the anti-colonial movement gathered strength and many former colonies of Britain and France were in the process of achieving independence. In the Congo itself an urban proletariat had come into existence and was increasingly unionised, and the educated Africans began to organise nationalist movements such as UNISCO. A triumphant visit of King Baudouin in May-June 1955 served to conceal the growing nationalist reality. Parties were formed by such figures as Kasavubu (ABAKO) and Lumumba (Mouvement National Congolais). Events perhaps moved too rapidly, for as late as November 1958, when the Eyskens-Lilar government was formed, there was still no clear policy towards the Congo.

A timid beginning was made in late 1958 when a group of Belgian politicians went on a mission to the Congo. A statement on future policy was promised, but this was overtaken by riots in Leopoldville in January 1959. These events led indirectly to the resignation in September 1959 of the minister for the colonies, van Hemelrijck, and his replacement by the more decisive August De Schrijver. The latter accelerated the trend towards re-evaluation already in train, and organised the famous *Table Ronde* between Belgian and Congolese political leaders in January-February 1960. The conclusion was that the Congo should become independent on 30 June 1960. The rapidity of the move towards independence probably contributed to the later tragic events; there were several military interventions by the Belgians to save lives and to safeguard the still enormous Belgian economic interests, which were further threatened in the civil war caused by the breakaway of the copper-rich Katanga province. A massive peacekeeping operation by the United Nations followed, which lasted till 1964.[29]

In the 1950s, the old 'school question',[30] which had proved so divisive in the 1880s, returned to the forefront of actuality. In 1947 and 1950, problems arose over state subsidies to 'free' (Catholic) technical education and general secondary schooling. Up till 1954 the PSC/CVP was in power either as the major component in coalitions or, as in 1950-4, with an absolute majority; and during these years it regulated the problem in a way which could not be acceptable to the opposition – involving considerable increases in subsidies to Catholic schools (more than BF 3000 million under a law of 1951). The education minister Pierre Harmel sought a permanent solution: by the law of 17 December 1952 permanent increased subsidies were introduced, together with full freedom of choice of parents between 'free' and state education. On educational methods and curricula these laws also increased the influence of the Catholic education sector by means of 'mixed advisory committees', which thus gained a right of intervention in the state sector.

In the elections of 1954, the PSC/CVP lost its absolute majority, and the school question was a major factor in the formation of the unusual coalition of Socialists and Liberals, under A. van Acker (Socialist), which resulted. A new law was prepared which would both reduce subsidies and increase the number of state schools. Subsidies were also to be conditional upon greater control of curricula and the qualifications of teachers in Catholic schools. Despite vast demonstrations, a petition with 2 million signatures and episcopal condemnation, the law was approved by both Houses in July 1955.

The 1958 election showed that such an extreme policy was not desired by the electorate. The outgoing coalition lost its majority, and a CVP/PSC minority government came to power. The new situation required a peace or at least a truce in the 'school war'. The national school committee was formed consisting of the presidents of the three major parties, and a compromise, incorporated in the 'school pact', was concluded for twelve years (it was later renewed). A Commission du Pacte Scolaire was set up to monitor its operation. This was an early example of Parliament being bypassed by 'corporate' *ad hoc* bodies, since Parliament's role was limited to approval – unanimous except for the Communists – of the results of the negotiations. However, peace was restored and has barely been disturbed since.

Although considerable ill-feeling was aroused in Flanders when *incivisme* (a latter-day euphemism for collaboration with the Nazis) was repressed with particular severity there, 'the community question' was not a major political issue in the 1950s. However, it was to become the dominant political issue of the 1960s and '70s, breaking up the old party structure and making the state almost ungovernable. We shall look at this issue in greater detail in Chapter 4, hence it will be sufficient here to point to the main milestones along the way.

With the recession of the post-war Communist tide (twenty-three parliamentary seats in 1946 and only five in 1961), the three traditional parties dominated political life. The new Volksunie appeared in 1954 with one seat; by 1961 it had five. The first deputies from the Brussels-based Front Démocratique Francophone (FDF) and Front Wallon – three from the FDF and two from the Front Wallon – were elected in 1965. Until then the 'community' parties had been totally marginal, but 1960-1 saw a general radicalisation which would completely change the picture. The strikes of 1960-1 were midwife to a new Walloon consciousness. Wallonia was now on the defensive economically; this created a new situation and new nationalist reflexes, which found expression in the Mouvement Populaire Wallon and the Front Wallon, which later fused into the Rassemblement Wallon. The same defensive reaction in Brussels led to the formation of the FDF in 1964. By 1968, the 'federalist' parties (Volksunie, RW and FDF) had made a decisive breakthrough, gaining respectively twenty (9.79% of the vote), seven and five (5.90% of the vote) seats.

At the same time, the three 'national' parties were feeling the pressure of community problems, which in time led to each dividing into two; the 'pairs' of ideologically similar parties on either side of the community divide having different positions from each other. As early as 1968, the PSC and the CVP were clearly two separate parties. The Liberal 'family' soon followed, and in 1978 the PSB/BSP became the PS and SP.

The community issue[31] could not longer be ignored. Palliatives such as discussions about the linguistic frontier (fixed in 1932) – arising out of the language census of 1960, especially in relation to the *communes* in the Brussels suburbs – were no longer enough. Attempts to alter the status of several *randgemeenten* (Flemish *communes* near Brussels) during 1961-3, basically to include new *communes* in the bilingual capital area and create facilities for French speakers in otherwise Flemish areas, led to increased conflict. At the same time, no change in the distribution of seats in Parliament had taken place since 1947 due to Walloon opposition, but the distortions had become so flagrant (Wallonia should properly have lost four seats) that action was now inevitable.

More radical measures required changes in the country's political structure, which presupposed a constitutional reform. After a round-table conference in January 1964, agreement was reached on limited changes, and the Parliament elected in 1965 was '*constituant*'. But, as the situation worsened, the agreement was not implemented. The Harmel-Spinoy (1965-6) and Vanden Boeynants-De Clercq governments fell without being able to steer any amendment through Parliament; the latter did so over the issue of a French section being created at Leuven University. So the 1965 Parliament was dissolved. The federalist parties made large gains in north and south. The problem of regionalisation had now forced itself on to the political agenda. However, the forces in favour of a unitary state, especially the CVP and certain economic groups, remained very strong.

A CVP/PSC-PSB/BSP government was formed under Mr Eyskens (1968-71) with the revision of the constitution as its main task. An initial proposal met so much opposition that it was withdrawn, and a 'Committee of Twenty-Eight', including opposition members, was set up in September 1969. Although it achieved no results, it succeeded in clearing the ground, and led to a compromise proposal from the government in February 1970. Some articles were passed with the aid of the Volksunie, giving the necessary 142 votes, which the coalition lacked (128 seats). Just before Christmas 1970, the last major amendments were approved by both chambers. The basis was now laid for a 'semi-federal system':

— Article 59 *bis* established two (Flemish and Francophone) Cultural Councils and a council for the German-speaking community, with law-making powers in cultural matters;
— Article 107 *quater* established regional councils for Wallonia, Flanders and Brussels with important powers in the socio-economic field;
— a *sonnette d'alarme* (alarm-bell) system (Article 38 and 38 *bis*) gave two-thirds of a linguistic group the right temporarily to suspend the adoption of certain language laws; and
— it was required that laws implementing Articles 59 *bis* and 107 *quater* be approved by two-thirds majority *and* a majority in each linguistic group in Parliament.

The following election in 1971 saw even more drastic gains for the federalist parties: FDF/RW gained twelve, and the Volksunie gained one. These gains were consolidated, but not expanded at the following elections (1974, 1977, 1978, 1981). The community problem thus remained a permanent feature of the political landscape, not least because the solutions of 1970 created new problems and required considerable legislation to be implemented. Some of the least controversial of this legislation, such as the laws on the functioning of the community councils (1971 and 1973) and the reform of local government, creating five *agglomérations* (Brussels, Liège, Charleroi, Ghent, Antwerp), were passed.

However, the elections of 1971 and the election to the council of the new Brussels *agglomération*, of which the FDF seized control, sharpened conflict and made progress on the implementation of the key Article 107 *quater* on the regions impossible. Neither the second Eyskens government (January-November 1972) nor the Leburton government composed of the three traditional parties (1973-4) was able to make any significant progress.

After the 1974 election, Mr Tindemans formed a PSC/CVP-PLP/PVV government, while attempting to find a broader-based solution to the community problem. 'Provisional' regionalisation laws, falling short of the degree of devolution required by Article 107 *quater* but representing a degree of decentralisation, were envisaged, and for the first time the inclusion of the 'federalist' parties in government was a serious option. The conclave held at Steenokkerzeel failed to reach a global solution, and in any case excluded the Socialists, but it led to a narrowing of disagreement and to the entry of the RW into the government. This coalition was divided – as the RW moved leftwards in 1976 and lacked the 'special majorities' needed to execute 107 *quater*. It fell in April 1977. However, the 'inter-community dialogue' had started, and the ground was prepared for the Egmont-Stuyvenberg pact, which was the basis of the second Tindemans government in which the community parties (PSC/CVP-BSP/PSB-FDF-VU) were included.

The continued resistance to regionalisation inside the CVP sabotaged this brave effort at an elegant, coherent global solution (see Chapter 4), and led to a new election and a prolonged crisis in 1978-9. The four governments of Wilfried Martens (CVP), who personally enjoyed the confidence of the other parties, fell in turn between 1979 and 1981 because of the suspicion of the CVP engendered in the other parties both over community questions and over its economic policy aims, especially reductions in public expenditure.

However, the 1978 legislature, unlike that of 1977, was *constituant*, and the Martens III government, made up of the three traditional parties, succeeded in the summer of 1980 in passing a package which – apart from the Brussels issue and the reform of the Senate – completed the programme embodied in the Egmont pact. Although the final result was more patchy and less coherent than the Egmont pact intended, the community issue could nevertheless at long last cease to be treated as overwhelmingly urgent.

In 1980 and 1981, the main economic and social issues (and sources of controversy) were unemployment, public expenditure, the indexing of wages to the cost of living, issues relating to the role of the police and the maintenance of public order against private militia (mostly of the extreme right), and 'Cruise' missiles. With eight governments since 1973, Belgium had become increasingly ungovernable. The recession has created a vicious circle: coalition governments 'across the middle' (i.e. PSC/CVP and PS/SP) have become ever more necessary to ensure social peace, but have become ever more unwieldy and immobile at a time when divisions between right and left were being exacerbated by the crisis and a whole range of issues among which the indexing of wages, public expenditure and defence policy are the most visible.

Despite the best efforts of the FDF and the upheavals in the RW, leading to a breakaway by its historic leader P.-H. Gendebien, community issues were in the background at the election in November 1981 but they have since returned to centre-stage. New small parties – the Ecologists and the UDRT (the anti-tax party) – appeared to have some impact in a general 'anti-politician' mood, but then their electoral impact remained modest. While the electorate largely resigned itself once again to its relative powerlessness to bring about change, returning a parliament whose basic structure differed only slightly from that elected in 1978 and offered few new possibilities, it would be wrong to conclude that there was no change, at least in the mood of the electorate. That mood was quite unequivocally autonomist in both Flanders and Wallonia, and generally pessimistic and resigned.

In the early 1980s, Belgium entered a new political phase. With the reforms of 1980 in place, there was a sense that socio-economic problems had been neglected in favour of the communitarian ones. Economic problems were becoming pressing: the restructuring of the steel industry, the cost of regionalisation, the growing public sector deficit and pressure on the Belgian franc. Clearly, the 'tripartite' governments needed to reform the state, and the CVP/PSC and PS/SP coalitions of 1981 could not grasp the nettle of economic reform by adopting austerity programmes.[32]

Influential decision-makers and opinion-formers began, during 1980, to promote the view that a coherent package of measures was needed involving devaluation, de-indexing of salaries, and cuts in public expenditure to reduce the public sector debt – but that at the same time such a package had to be socially acceptable. It was felt that the political precondition for such a package was a change in coalition. Tensions with the red/black coalition over the impending deployment of Cruise/Pershing missiles in Belgium under the NATO twin-track decision, especially with the SP, also pointed towards a new coalition. During 1981, this strategy matured and its existence was probably a factor in the collapse of the short-lived, almost transitional Eyskens government and the early election held on 8 November 1981.[33] The major winners in both communities were the Liberals. The CVP lost six seats and the PSC seven. The Socialists also gained three seats. The CVP/PSC and PVV/PRL could muster a majority (113 seats) in the House.

After a short period in which some, especially in the PSC, considered going into opposition, the new model CVP/PSC and PVV/PRL was formed. This government, led again by Wilfried Martens, saw a swing back to a situation in which power was located in the cabinet and not in the hands of the party presidents; most of the latter became vice-premiers, being replaced as party presidents by younger figures without comparable experience or profile, thus refuting – at least on the surface – the charges of a growing '*particracie*' trend.

The new legislature was able to revise the Constitution because a 'Declaration' had been passed in the outgoing Parliament, but the new team did not have the necessary two-thirds majority and was decidedly weak – indeed, it had only a minority among French-speakers. In any case, it was perhaps time for a pause and consolidation in institutional reform, which was not the main priority of the new coalition. Furthermore, as Belgian politics entered a more confrontational phase, there was no prospect of any broader co-operation on reforms outside the coalition parties.

For this, the first independent community and regional executives (sitting outside the national government, which was one of the elements in the 1980 reform), the rule of proportionality was applied, which naturally meant that the PS and the SP, now in opposition nationally, sat in the Flemish executive and in the two Francophone executives (region and community). The Brussels executive, of course, remained within the national government, because no definitive regionalisation of Brussels had been agreed upon in the 1980 reform package. Some tidying up measures did find broad agreement. Thus, in 1983, a special law was adopted according the small German-speaking community in the *Cantons de l'Est* equal status with the two other communities, including its own three-member executive, and equal legislative and financial powers, including important areas of 'personable matters' such as health and education. In one way, the German community, with its own Parliament (a 25-member council) elected separately and not composed of national MPs, was ahead of the other communities and regions. The arbitration court was also established by special law; its members were appointed and it began to function. The executives began to put flesh on the bare bones of the constitutional arrangements. The ministries of the regions and communities were established and officials were transferred to them. However, the independence of these new bodies still remained limited.[34]

The main priorities of the two centre-right Martens governments of 1981-8 that were based on the CVP/PSC and PVV/PR were economic reforms.[35] The Belgian budget deficit, which had reached 13% of GDP, was to be cut back to 7% over the term of the legislature. A devaluation of 8.5% (against an initial request of 12%) was authorised within the EMS, and measures were taken to cut public expenditure and de-index wages and salaries for one year. In order to avoid difficult parliamentary votes on these measures, especially for PSC deputies, the government obtained special powers to pass the necessary measures by royal decree for the same period of a year.[36] This method, which involved virtually side-lining Parliament from all key areas of policy-making, was strongly attacked, not only by the opposition but also by Jean Defraigne (PRL), president of the House of Representatives. Those measures led to waves of strikes, especially in Wallonia and in the public sector, in 1982 and 1986. Given the strength of trade union opposition, not only in the FGTB but also in the Walloon CSC, special powers were probably essential to prevent defections by PSC Deputies close to the trade union movement.

The other polarising issue was the deployment of forty-eight Cruise missiles in Belgium under the NATO twin-track decision of December 1979.[37] The first track was to offer the carrot of negotiations with the Soviet Union on mutual reductions of intermediate nuclear weapons. The Cold War was by now in a new ice-age and the Soviet leadership saw the prospects of splitting NATO as peace movements gathered momentum. Socialist parties moved that deployment should be phased out in all smaller NATO countries, including Belgium, and even in larger ones like Britain and Germany, by 1983. Opposition to deployment was much stronger in Flanders, where the peace movement could count on support from the SP, the Volksunie and even from large numbers of CVP MPs. The key political consequence was that in reality the SP and hence the Socialists in general were not possible coalition partners after the 1985 elections, since the SP was not willing to compromise on this issue. There were several mass demonstrations in Brussels, mobilising over 150,000 people in the 1982-4 period. The former PS foreign minister, Henri Simonet, left the PS and joined the PRL, his motive being the anti-NATO stance of the Socialists.

In the two major political families, CVP/PSC and PS/SP, opposition to deployment was much less marked in the Walloon parties. The SP, under its dynamic young chairman Karel van Miert, was a leading force in the peace movement, and the party campaigned hard against deployment in both the 1984 European elections and the 1985 elections. The PS kept a low profile on the issue, and even rank and file PS activists were less involved in the protest movement. Up to ten CVP deputies took part in the various demonstrations (as did the Volksunie), whereas the PSC was not involved. One immediate consequence was to make a change of coalition parties to a '*rouge romaine*' centre left CVP/PSC and PS/SP coalition in 1985 unviable; even if the electoral arithmetic had in any way encouraged such an outcome. It made the SP and hence the Socialist family as a whole an impossible partner. This also widened the north-south split that was already considerable.

The tragedy of the deaths of a number of spectators at the Heysel stadium during a football match in May 1985 and the apparently poor policing and safety that had led to it acted as an external catalyst for the collapse of the government slightly prematurely in the early autumn of 1985. Although the decision of the PRL to withdraw support from the coalition was ostensibly directed at interior minister Charles-Ferdinand Nothomb's (PSC) failure to resign over criticisms of him by the parliamentary inquiry into the Heysel disaster, it is more likely to have been a classic case of the PRL looking for an issue on which to steal a march on their coalition partners in launching the election campaign, and thus limit their losses – which they succeeded in doing.

This coalition did not have a two-thirds majority, and there was no thus significant progress in the 'community' issue. Yet after the local elections of 1982, the issue came back with a vengeance, due to the Fourons problem. The French-speaking Action Fouronnaise won ten of the fifteen seats in the Council. Its leader, José Happart, was nominated as mayor, which led to a virulent Flemish reaction, since he refused to demonstrate that he spoke Dutch. Behind the seemingly ridiculous problem of some scattered French-speaking villages in the Flemish Limburg province – to which they were unwillingly joined in 1963, a sort of Belgian Clochemerle – was a serious issue. It was a conflict between two almost equally respectable but irreconcilable principles: the democratic rights of the local inhabitants and respect for the integrity of the Flemish nation. Both felt they had right on their side. Various creative Belgian compromises were sought: attachment to bilingual Brabant, replacement of the too visible Happart, nomination of various government commissioners. But all after being only considered, failed. The issue became increasingly politicised, to the irritation of the Liberals, especially the PVV, which wanted to concentrate on pushing Belgium on to a long-term neo-Liberal economic course. José Happart became a Walloon hero, and the PS opted for the federalist card, running him on their list for the Euro-elections in 1984. He was triumphantly elected, with the record number of 234,996 preference votes. The PS 'recuperated' the old Walloon movement.[38]

The 1985 Parliament was no longer constituent. The outgoing coalition declared its intention of continuing if the electoral arithmetic permitted it to do so. The coalition parties actually made a net gain of two seats. The PVV lost six seats, losing much of the ground it gained in 1978 and 1981, and the PRL maintained its position. The CVP gained six seats and the PSC two. For the first time, the regional and community executives were formed according to normal parliamentary principles. The coalition parties at the national level agreed to form similar coalitions of all levels despite their wafer-thin majority in the Walloon and French community councils. Formation of the national government and the executives was by Belgian standards quite rapid: the election was held on 13 October and the cabinet was sworn in on 28 November. The team remained almost unchanged, except for the arrival of the PVV 'young Turk', Guy Verhofstadt, as vice-premier and budget minister in place of Willy DeClercq, who had been nominated to the EC Commission earlier in the year.

Despite the government's electoral victory and the continued problems of the opposition, the Martens VII government was never as comfortable as its immediate predecessor. Nothomb remained, but his position was weakened. However, the PRL had failed to evict him. Radical neo-Liberal Verhofstadt had difficult relations with the CVP and, above all, with the PSC, which had close relations with the Christian trade unions. During its less than two years of existence, the government was beset with economic and community issues which tended to divide it and which it failed to resolve. Under the impulsion of Guy Verhofstadt (PVV), the budget minister, the government held a budget conclave in April 1986 and imposed savage and unpopular spending cuts, which were met by strikes. Cuts in the education budget led the PRL education minister to resign.

Later, in 1986, the Fourons issue resurfaced. Mr Happart was disqualified as mayor and the CVP demanded his immediate removal. The government tended its resignation but it was refused by the King. A series of solutions was tried: nomination of a mayor from outside the communal council, shifting nominations of mayors and commissioners – but all failed. Nothomb, the interior minister, resigned. Tensions rose between the PSC and CVP on the issue, and at the same time the debate on an abortion bill, introduced in the Senate by a Liberal, led to conflict between the CVP in particular and their Liberal allies. On 19 October 1987 the government was forced to give up and resigned, unable to find a solution to the Fourons problem. Elections were held on 13 December 1987.[39]

The outcome did not preclude continuation of the outgoing coalition, but made it difficult and unlikely. The pressure for change came most clearly from the Walloon region. Here, the Socialists (+4.5% and +5 seats) gained most. At the regional and probably the community levels, the PS could no longer be excluded. The PSC also wanted change. For the CVP and its leader Mr Martens, who had made continuation of the centre-right coalition and its economic policy almost a point of honour with its slogan *'Geen Ommekeer'* (no turning back), a reversal of alliances to return to the centre-left model was extremely difficult. Yet in the end that was what happened. The dominant parties seized the initiative at the supposedly autonomous regional and community levels to try and pre-empt the national coalition talks. The CVP and PVV already confirmed their centre-right Flemish coalition on election night. The PS made overtures to the Greens and the FDF in the French-speaking community and the Walloon region in order to put the PSC under pressure to push for a national reversal of alliances.

After six weeks of inconclusive talks and several *'informateurs'* (persons named to explore coalition possibilities), the King nominated not Mr Martens but another CVP insider, Jean-Luc Dehaene, who was mandated to form a centre-left government with a broad policy for reform of the State and some additional social measures, while preserving the thrust of the outgoing coalition's economic policy. This was a tall order. But Mr Dehaene almost met his goal, encapsulated in his now famous demand to the King, *'Sire*, give me a hundred days'. Within 103 days, he had put together a five-party centre-left coalition (PS/SP and CVP/PSC and VU) with a broad agreement on the next stages of the reform of the State and enjoying the necessary special majorities. At the last moment, there was a *coup de théâtre*: Mr Martens returned to become prime minister of the coalition put together by Jean-Luc Dehaene, who was pushed aside to take the posts of vice-premier and minister of communications. The Institutional Reform portfolio went to vice-premier Philippe Moureaux (PS). It seemed that the palace felt Mr Dehaene to be too 'provincial' and to lack standing on the wider European and international scene; more important, perhaps, he was too federalist. Mr Martens was also perhaps better, in Lyndon Johnson's immortal phrase, 'inside the tent pissing out than outside pissing in'.[40]

Yet the construction worked. The government survived both the 1988 communal elections and the 1989 Euro-elections with only minimal erosion, and lasted almost the full term of the Parliament, a distinct rarity in Belgium. It carried through the majority of its programme, including solutions to both the Fourons and Brussels problems. Yet its collapse was both ignominious and tragicomic, creating a serious reaction at the election of 24 November 1991.

What were the achievements of one of most successful and stable Belgian governments in the post-war period? The most spectacular results were achieved in the Reform of the State. Within barely more than a year of taking office, there had been significant progress towards creating a federal Belgium. The problem of the Fourons and other communes close to the linguistic boundaries were resolved by providing for the direct election of '*échevins*' (members of the local executive) by a proportional system and the right of voters to register in neighbouring communes for parliamentary and European elections. This package deal was sufficiently balanced to obtain both PS and Volksunie backing. Provision was made for the full devolution to the communities of education and, with that, appropriate protection of minority rights. More power was devolved to the regions (transport, public works etc.). An independent executive and council (elected in June 1989) was established for Brussels, at long last making Brussels a full region almost with the same powers and status as the other regions. At the same time, a complex system of protection was instituted for the Dutch-speaking minority in Brussels. The government was unable to make progress on the so-called 'third phase' which would have reformed the Senate, making it a regional second chamber, dealt with the treaty-making powers of the various layers of government and devolved new areas such as agriculture. Yet, even so, the results achieved were considerable and seemed to have created a degree of community peace.

The new centre-left coalition continued the policy of restoration of competitiveness, but with more flexibility and social concern. The government acted to introduce a series of supply-side measures, a tax reform, a reform of banking law, and measures to improve the efficiency of the public sector utilities and corporations. The policy of keeping public expenditure under control and reducing the public sector borrowing requirement (PSBR) as a share of gross domestic product (GDP) remained as key policy goals, but with the return of the PS/SP, there was, as implied in the PS slogan '*Le Retour du Coeur*', some additional support for those on basic pensions and state benefits and for the unemployed. The economic policy of the government was, at least until the Gulf war, quite successful. The rate of inflation remained below 3.5%, the franc was aligned with the Deutsche Mark in 1990, growth was healthy and the public sector deficit fell by 1991 from 8.7 to 6% of GDP.[41]

However, by the summer of 1991 there was some restlessness in the coalition. The Volksunie especially feared that unless it broke ranks and left the coalition before the election, it would suffer, especially as the third phase had effectively been shelved. The SP may also have considered similar tactics. This was the background to the autumn crisis – ostensibly about arms exports – that led to the premature collapse of the government in circumstances that tended to obscure its quite favourable balance sheet. There was also the failure, particularly serious for the Volksunie, to make progress on the 'third phase' of the Reform of the State. At the same time, the government had barely survived the damaging strikes of teachers in the French-speaking school system which brought to the surface the problem of finding additional resources for the French-speaking community to meet the pay settlements and demands for more investment in schools.

In June 1991, the SP and the Volksunie demanded the suspension of arms exports to the Middle East. Their tactical considerations led them to press the issue through the summer. On its own, this issue would probably not have been decisive, but difficult community issues were also accumulating. The arms issue was crucial for the survival of Walloon companies, which inevitably made the Francophone parties in their turn more intransigent.

It was becoming clear that there would be no agreement on a significant third phase in the Reform of the State during the life of the legislature. The proposal to finance the education policy, now devolved to the communities by according to them the revenue from television licences, ran into trouble. It was only acceptable to the Flemish side if new competences were devolved, and here social security was mentioned. This however was totally rejected by the PS and PSC. Eventually, the government found a 'creative solution' to the problem of export licences: two regional communities within the national government were set up. This typically Belgian pragmatic solution was rejected by the Volksunie and only accepted with minimal good grace by the SP, perhaps because the French-speaking ministers were threatening to block a BF 30 billion telecommunications contract in Flanders as a counter-measure.

Following the withdrawal of the Volksunie, a small coalition of the four centre-left parties was formed to push though the financing of the communities and regions, the telecommunications contract and a declaration of revision of the Constitution. But this government no longer commanded a two-thirds majority. Relations between the communities and especially between the prime minister, Martens, and the PS president, Guy Spitaels, reached boiling point. The respective regional councils adopted strong motions. There was an atmosphere of dissolution in which nothing could be achieved. In some confusion, but still after voting through a *déclaration de revision*, the government went to the country on 24 November.[42]

The election campaign was dull, but the preceding events had left a deep scar. There was a dangerous public reaction against the political establishment. All the traditional parties lost ground, with the share of the vote won by the three traditional families falling to 70.1% from 78.9% in 1987. The election clearly showed that there were two, if not three, distinct political systems. For Wallonia, the PS, the PSC and the opposition Liberals all lost ground, whereas in Flanders, the CVP and the SP lost more heavily than their Walloon sister-parties and the PVV made a slight gain (+0.5% of the Flemish vote). In Brussels, the PS and the PRL lost quite sharply and the PSC gained slightly. There was also a regional divergence in the beneficiaries, although they were all anti-system parties. In Wallonia and Brussels, the Greens doubled their vote (in Flanders they made almost no gains). The beneficiaries were the far-right Flemish nationalist Vlaams Blok and the anarchist-rightist protest list led by the millionaire Jean-Pierre van Rossem. In Brussels gains were made by the far-right, Front National, the FDF and the two Flemish protest parties, Vlaams Blok and the list of van Rossem.[43]

After torturous attempts to examine alternatives to the outgoing centre left coalition, mainly designed to show that no alternative existed (now of course it was without the Volksunie), the old coalition was revived under Jean-Luc Dehaene. It had preserved a narrow majority but naturally did not have the special majority necessary to revise the Constitution. The Dehaene government showed surprising survival capabilities – due, of course, largely to the patent lack of any viable alternative and the desire of almost the whole political class to avoid an early election, which would probably produce an alternative and even weaker version of the basic four-party coalition or an unwieldy and paralysed tripartite cabinet. However, beyond these essentially negative factors, the government was able to act in a relatively decisive way on both its key priorities: the 1993 budget and the continuation of the reform of the State.

Despite the collapse of the first round of the community dialogue before the summer of 1992 and the elimination of both the Liberals and the FDF as potential providers of the necessary external support enabling the government to reach the '*constituant*' two-thirds majority for its reform package, the majority's own reform package was first agreed on and then adjusted in two successive 'conclaves' to bring in first the Volksunie and then Ecolo. The adjustments were in part quite minor in comparison to the whole package. As in the past, progress was greatly eased by the previous efforts, going back to the parliamentary committee on the third phase of the 1987-91 legislature. The elements of a solution had been lying around, and needed to be collected and put together in a politically viable package. The process was again typical of the Belgian method of bringing new partners into the political decision-making process gradually. The Volksunie was not of course a new partner. The Francophone and Flemish Green parties, Ecolo and Agalev, were for many years outside the compromises that are the small change of Belgian political life. They, with Ecolo very much in the lead, first signalled a desire to come in from the cold in 1991; next, it took a constructive part in the community dialogue, and then joined the '*constituant* majority', gaining in the process concessions not only on the package itself but also elsewhere (on the creation of an eco-tax). The next logical step would be its inclusion in a government, perhaps first at regional rather than national level.

The so-called *Accord de la St Michel* represents an important further step in the process of federalisation in Belgium;[44] essentially it embodies the substance of the 'Third Phase' of the 1988 reform that was not enacted. It introduces into the Constitution a clearly federalist terminology: Belgium is declared to be a 'federal state' (Article 1). National or central authorities were renamed federal authorities, and the community and regional executives became community or regional governments. Community and regions have full international competences in those areas where they are internally competent, but they must inform the federal government and consult with it. In EC matters, there is provision for consultation, and in line with the provisions of the Maastricht treaty, regions and communities will represent Belgium in the council where they are competent for the issue concerned. Additional environmental competences are transferred to the regions, as are those for external trade, agriculture (except some aspects of price policy), and scientific research with some exceptions. Supervision of local authorities and CPAS (social services administration) is transferred to the regions and communities, respectively.

The bilingual Brabant province, whose institutions had in recent years been virtually paralysed by linguistic problems, was split from 1995 into a Flemish Brabant and a Walloon Brabant, each with its own provincial council. However, there is still only be one governor and one vice-governor for the two 'provinces', which will formally remain one. Provincial competences in Brussels are to be hived off to the various regional community and bi-community bodies.

The regions and communities are to receive a limited 'organic' or *constituant* power. They will be able, by a two-thirds majority, to alter the number of members of the councils and the number of electoral districts and the procedures of the councils. They will also be able to fix the number of members of their executives and their functioning. There is also a complex system established whereby the French community could, by a two-thirds majority, transfer (not delegate) powers to the Walloon Regional Council and in Brussels to the French Community Commission (COCOF), which would then be given decree powers. This will enable an effective functional fusion of the community and region and, via the drawing rights (up to BF 2.6 billion per year from 1995) in a ratio of 80% Francophone and 20% Dutch from the Brussels region by the COCOF and COCON, guarantee the financing of former community responsibilities. Thus the federalised entities will be able to establish their own independent and hence probably different structures.

This tendency towards differentiation will be given a powerful push forward by the centrepiece of the *Accord de la St Michel*: the direct election of the community/regional councils and the concomitant reform of the national parliament. Important basic principles underlying the reform, especially in this period of alienation from the political system, have been the avoidance of inflating the number of elected representatives – taking all levels together – and prohibiting excessive '*cumul des mandats*' (holding a series of offices) while maintaining existing balances between regions/communities in the national institutions.

The reformed House has 150 members elected for four years; dissolution will be possible only where a motion of no confidence passes, but no alternative prime minister can be elected. The House alone would be competent to control the executive and vote the budget, and would have the last word on ordinary legislation. The reformed Senate would have only seventy-one members. It is the weakest element in the reform. Its structures lacks intellectual coherence. A fully regionalised body was not possible, as the CVP in particular fought to retain a body of directly elected senators. Thus, there are forty directly elected senators, elected for four years at the same time as the House. There would be twenty-five Flemish and fifteen Francophone senators elected in two language colleges as for the European elections, with voters in Brussels-Halle-Vilvoorde being able to vote in either college. The community councils would elect twenty-one senators from among their members, who would remain members of both bodies (ten Flemish, ten Francophone, one German-speaker). There would be ten coopted senators (six Flemish, four Francophone). The *ex-officio* royal senators would remain. The Senate's approval would be needed for amendment to the Constitution, for special laws and treaties that transfer sovereignty (such as Maastricht). On the other bills, the Senate would have a mere thirty days to propose amendments that the House could immediately overrule (i.e. less power than the House of Lords has in Britain).

The various councils are to be composed as follows:

— *Flemish council:* 124 members. 118 will be directly elected and six elected from the Dutch-language group in the Brussels regional council, in which they will also remain.

— *French community council* (CCF): 94 members. 75 will be directly elected members of the Walloon regional council, plus 19 members elected by the French language group of the Brussels regional council will make up the council. This weak basis is another sign that the CCF is in effect on its way out.

— *Walloon region council* (CRW): 75 directly elected members. The existing House electoral *arrondissements* are to be used.

— *The Brussels region council:* 75 members (unchanged).

— *The German community council:* 25 members (unchanged).

This complex structure will give in all 493 elected national and regional parliamentarians, that is three less than now. A maximum of forty-six of those could have a national/regional dual mandate. They would not be able to hold any other elected political office (communal, provincial, House or European).

With this package, adding to the 1970, 1971, 1980, 1983 and 1988/9 packages, the reform of the State has reached a resting place. Belgium is now openly a federal state with genuine federal structures.

The various attempts by the Liberal opposition and extra-parliamentary organisations to destabilise the *Accord de la St Michel*, and with it the Dehaene government, failed, and the political agreements with Ecolo held, both in the national parliament and in the council of the French community, where it was necessary to find a two-thirds majority to approve the various delegations of competences to the Brussels region that were part of the package. The provisional end of the long march towards federalism did threaten the future of the two purely regional parties, the FDF and the Volksunie. The FDF is seeking some form of alliance with the PRL, and the Volksunie has lost much of its electorate to the new VLD (Flemish Liberals).

In August 1993, King Baudouin died unexpectedly while on holiday in Spain. This led to an outpouring of royalist sentiment and a sense that perhaps after all it did mean something to be Belgian. However, it seems unlikely at this stage, with the federalisation process all but complete, that the various unitarist efforts to exploit this public feeling will have much real or longer-term political impact on the direction of Belgium. The new King is Albert II, brother of Baudouin who had no children.

NOTES

1. The aim of this chapter is to provide a short and easily comprehensible account of Belgian history as it bears on the characteristics of the country, its people and its political culture; accordingly footnotes and unnecessary detail have been kept to a minimum. The main sources on which the chapter draws are, for the period before 1790, Frans van Kalken, *Histoire de la Belgique et de son Expansion Coloniale*, Office de Publicité, Brussels, 1954, and for the period after 1790 F. van Kalken, op. cit., and Th. Luykx, *Politieke Geschiedenis van Belgie*, Elsevier, Amsterdam/Brussels, 1977, in 2 volumes with through pagination.

2. For the pre-Roman and Roman period, see van Kalken, op. cit., 5-17 and 18-30, and F. Cumont, *Comment la Belgique fut Romanisée*, 2nd edn, Larmartin, Brussels, 1920.

3. Van Kalken, op. cit., 49-50 and 51-4.

4. On the role of the towns see van Kalken, op. cit., 110-12, and H. Pirenne, *Les Villes et Institutions Urbaines*, vol. 2, Nouvelle Société d'Edition, Brussels, 1939, and V. Friis, *Histoire de Gand*, De Tavernier, Ghent, 1930.

5. Van Kalken, op. cit., 168-74.

6. Ibid., 175-83, and P. Bonaufont, *Philippe le Bon*, Collection Notre Passé, Renaissance du Livre, Brussels, 1943.

7. For the Spanish period and the revolt of the Low Countries, see van Kalken, op. cit., 152-356; A. Henne, *Histoire du Règne de Charles V en Belgique*, 10 vols, Flautan, Brussels, 1858-60; and L. Pfandl, *Philippe II*, Hachette, Paris, 1942.

8. Van Kalken, op. cit., 375-86.

9. For the Austrian period, ibid., 422-55, and Luykx, op. cit., for the first Brabançonne revolution (1788), 31-6.

10. Van Kalken, op. cit., 450-64.

11. For the French period, ibid., 477-510.

12. For the Dutch period, ibid., 512-28, and Luykx, op. cit., 40-5.

13. For the Belgian revolution, Luykx, op. cit., 46-60.

14. For the work of the National Congress, Th. Fuste, *Le Congrès National*, Brussels 1880; and for the international context see R. Steinmetz, *Englands Anteu an der Trennung der Niederlande 1830*, The Hague, 1930, and R. Rollot, *Les Origines de la Neutralité Belge*, Paris, 1902.

15. See Luykx, 52-62.

16. Ibid., 94-7 and 100-7.

17. Ibid., 124-30.

18. Ibid., 182-4 and 205-9, for the origins of the Socialist Party.

19. Ibid., 113-20, 160-2, 163-4 and 167-8, for progress in improving the rights of Dutch-speakers.

20. Ibid., 239-43; E.D. Morel, *King Leopold's Rule in Africa*, London, 1904; and E. van der Velde, *Les Derniers Jours de l'Etat Indépendant du Congo*, Mons, 1911.

21. See van Kalken, op. cit., 662-701 for the 1914-18 war and 704-6 for the Versailles settlement.

22. On the Flemish question in the war and after, see Luykx, 254-66, and 329-3C.23. Van

Kalken, op. cit., 724-7, and Luykx, op. cit., 283-9. 24. For inter-war domestic policy, see van Kalken, 707-35, and Luykx, 298-367. 25. Van Kalken, *op. cit.*, 718-20.

23. Van Kalken, op. cit., 724-7, and Luykx, op. cit., 283-9.

24. For inter-war domestic policy, see van Kalken, 707-35, and Luykx, 298-367.

25. Van Kalken, op. cit., 718-20.

26. Luykx, *op. cit.*, 383-400, for Belgium in the war.

27. Ibid., 441-52, on the '*Question Royale*'.

28. Ibid., 460-9, 478-9 and 483-4.

29. For developments after 1960, see ibid., 498-500 and 516-19.

30. Ibid., 484-87 and 509-11.

31. See Chapter 4 and Luykx, op. cit., 585-602, 606-10 and 619-21, and A. Allen and P. Van Speybroek, *La Réforme de l'Etat Belge de 1974 jusqu'au Pacte Communautaire*, CEPESS 1977, and *Dossiers du CRISP*, no. 893-4, 'La Réforme de l'Etat', 1980.

32. Xavier Mabille, *Histoire Politique de la Belgique*, CRISP, Brussels, 1986, pp. 364-66.

33. For the background to this change, see Hugo De Ridder, *Le Cas Martens*, Duculot, Paris, 1991, 123-40.

34. J. Fitzmaurice, 'Belgium: Reluctant Federalism', *Parliamentary Affairs*, vol. 37: 4 (1984), 418-33.

35. On the work of the centre-right coalition, see Mabille, op. cit., 365-8; De Ridder, op. cit., 141-9.

36. Xavier Mabille, 'La Législature, 1981-85, *Courrier Hébdomadaire (CH) du CRISP, no. 1088, 21-8*.

37. Xavier Mabille, *CH* 1088, p. 23.

38. On the 1985 elections, see Xavier Mabille and Evelyne Lentzen, 'Les élections du 13 octobre 1985, *CH* 1095/6.

39. For the elections of 1987, see Xavier Mabille and Evelyne Lentzen, 'Les élections du 13 décembre 1987', *CH* 1179/80 (1987).

40. On the formation of Martens VIII, see J. Brassinne and X. Mabille, 'La crise gouvernementale – décembre 1987-mai 1988', *CH*, 1198-9 (1988); De Ridder, op cit., 159-203; H. De Ridder, '*Sire, donnez-moi cent jours*', Duculot, 1990.

41. On the achievements of Martens VIII, see Etienne Arcq, Pierre Blaise, Evelyne Lentzen, 'Enjeux et compromis de la législature 1998-91', *CH*, 1332-3, 6-68.

42. On the crisis, see *CH* 1332-3, op. cit., pp. 69- 74.

43. Xavier Mabille, Evelyne Lentzen, Pierre Blaise, 'Les Elections du 24 novembre 1991', *CH* 1335/6, and Johan Bijttebier *et al., 24 November 1991. Het Betekenis van een verkiezeinguitslag*, Kritak, Leuven, 1992.

44. Text of the *Accord de la St Michel* concluded on 28 September 1992, entitled 'Propositions Visant à Achever la Structure Fédérale de l'Etat' and Jos Bouveroux, *Het St.-Michielsakkoord: naar en Federaal Belgie*, Standaard Uitgeverij, Antwerp, 1993.

2

THE ECONOMY AND SOCIETY

In Belgium, more than in most countries, political and economic issues are ultimately linked. The economy is exceptionally open and therefore vulnerable. Trade links, cost structures, comparative competitiveness and the value of the franc are all of such importance that they dominate politics, except when the 'intracommunity' question is dominant. Relations between the two communities are also largely connected with economic problems, although this is not to deny the importance of linguistic and cultural differences. Belgium's history has been a continuous see-saw of economic predominance between north and south, which does much to explain their difficult political co-existence within the Belgian state. And when one adds the fact that the predominant ideological approach to economic problems – liberalism or state intervention – has also been 'regionalised', some sense of the extreme sensitivity and complexity of the issue begins to emerge.

It is not our purpose here to present a detailed economic geography or economic history of Belgium, but some indication of its vital statistics, of the trend of economic development over the past three centuries, and of the present structure of the economy – its strengths and weaknesses and medium-term problems – is essential before we can analyse economic policy-making and current economic policies.

THE COUNTRY AND PEOPLE

Belgium is a relatively small country, and it is one of the most densely populated in Western Europe. It is in essence part of the north European plain, wedged between France and Germany, and crossed by a major river, the Meuse. It has therefore always been of strategic importance and a vital economic crossroads. In its physical and human geography, the country can be divided into two zones. In the north, from the coast to the Sambre-Meuse valley, is the Flemish plain, crossed by several smaller rivers, as well as the Scheldt with its mouth at Antwerp, the country's major port. The Sambre-Meuse valley, crossing the country from west to east, is the major industrial basin, with the towns of Mons, Charleroi,

Namur and Liège. In the south and east lies the Ardennes region, rugged and thinly populated.

The greatest length (east-west) of the country is about 290 km. and the greatest width 145 km. The total area is 30,519 square km., slightly larger than Wales. Some 60% of the land area is in Wallonia and 40% in Flanders. In 1990 the total population was 9,947,782,[1] a density – of 325 per square kilometre – exceeded only in the Netherlands; were it not for the Ardennes, Belgium would have the higher population density. This is higher than the population density of Britain as a whole, but not of England. There were 5,087,683 women and 4,860,099 men.[2]

According to 1990 figures, 57.8% of the population live in the Flemish region, 32.4% in the Walloon region and 9.8% in Brussels.[3] The population of the German-speaking community is 67,007. The major cities in the country are Brussels, with 955,372 (1,015,000 in 1980), Antwerp with 470,349, Ghent with 206,543, Charleroi with 206,779, Liège with 196,025, Bruges 117,460, Namur 103,465, Mons 91,867 and Leuven 85,193. There are six towns (outside Brussels) with populations above 100,000 and twenty-one with populations of over 50,000. Together, these constitute 32.9% of the total population.[4]

It is difficult to say that the population is homogeneous, but there are no evident ethnic minorities apart from the more recent immigrants. There is little population mixture between communities outside Brussels and the Province of Brabant. The Dutch-speaking population in Brussels is about 18%. It varies from *commune* to *commune* (28% to only 8%). In the Flemish *communes* surrounding Brussels (*'communes de la périphérie/ randgemeenten'*), which are heavily populated by suburbanite commuters and have language facilities for French-speakers, the latter are in the majority or close to it, as the 1982 and 1988 local elections showed quite dramatically. This is especially true of Kraainem, Tervuren and Rhode-St Genèse. The more distant *communes* have smaller but significant French-speaking minorities (up to 25%) but they are without language facilities. Minorities in the two main communities proper are hard to measure, as no census data on this has been collected since 1947, when 2.6% of the Flemish *arrondissement* of Leuven were French-speakers only (5.7% were mainly French-speaking). For Ghent, the figures were respectively 2% and 7.4%. In Walloon areas, Flemish-speakers represented less than 1%.[5]

There has been significant immigration into Belgium, consisting of three distinct waves or types.[6] The first chronologically was of Italian and, to a less extent, Polish origin (Mr Gierek, the Polish Communist leader in the 1970s, had worked in Belgium); these people were brought in to work in the mines and factories in the Sambre-Meuse coalfields. In 1900, 212,000 non-Belgians were residing in Belgium, almost all (92.5%) from the immediately neighbouring countries. In 1938 there were 339,779 immigrants, who included 61,809 Poles, 37,140 Italians and 46, 230 Czechs. The first post-war decades (1945-64) saw the arrival of more than 100,000 Italians.[7] After 1956 the Italian immigration slowed down, and the sources diversified to include Spain and Greece. From 1964 immigration from the Mediterranean, North Africa, Yugoslavia and Turkey was actively encouraged to meet manpower needs in an era of rapid economic expansion.

A third wave or group that has greatly expanded, mostly in Brussels and to a less extent in Antwerp, is related to Belgium's role as the host to major international organisations, such as the EC and NATO, and with them interest groups and multinational companies. This group comes from EC countries, the United States and Japan, and may be estimated at about 150,000, including some 11,600 Americans, 26,400 Germans, 21,000 British and part of the total figure of 91,000 French nationals (1990 figures). It is mainly located in Brussels and its periphery and in Antwerp. It is mobile and prosperous.[8]

In 1964, there were 367,619 immigrants (4.3% of the population). By 1985, the number had risen to 897,630 (9.1%), to fall slightly to 868,757 (8.8%) in 1989. In the early 1990s, the figures are again rising slightly. In 1989, 27.4% of immigrants (4.2% of the total population) lived in Flanders and 42.2% (11.2%) in Wallonia, and made up 27.2% (30.4%) of the total population of Brussels. Of all immigrants 61% come from EC countries: Italians 27.7%, French 10.5%, Dutch 7%, Spanish 6%. Of the third-country immigrants, Moroccans led with 15.6% (55.4% in Brussels), followed by Turks with 9.1% (25.1% in Brussels and, unusually, 49.5% in Flanders), Zaïrois with 1.3%, Algerians with 1.2%, Tunisians 0.7% and Yugoslavs 0.6%. Thus, it should be noted that *all* the non-EC Mediterranean and African immigration amounted to 28.5%, barely exceeding the number of Italians.[9] These groups, targeted by anti-immigrant political forces, barely exceed a quarter of all immigration and represent less than 3% of the total population. Even in Brussels, which has the heaviest concentration, these groups only represent about 100,000 people, or some 12% of the capital's total population, though, of course, in some poorer *communes* such as Lower Schaerbeek, Molenbeek and Anderlecht the concentration is much higher and more visible, with all the explosive political consequences that this can cause.

THE ECONOMY

As we saw in Chapter 1, there has been a perpetual see-saw between the northern (Flemish) and southern (Walloon) provinces in terms of economic development. In the Middle Ages, thanks to the wool trade, a flourishing urban civilisation grew up in Flanders,[10] which ranked as one of the richest areas in Europe. English competition, political complications, internal strife and the silting up of the port of Bruges led to the decline of the Flemish economy and with it, by the end of the Austrian period, the political power of the quasi-independent Flemish towns.

Early industrialisation

The first step towards the Belgian industrial revolution came with the French occupation in the 1790s; Belgium was thus the second industrialised country after Britain. The concept of economic liberalism was gradually introduced, in place of the semi-feudalistic corporations which had earlier characterised the Belgian economy. More flexible and efficient legal, fiscal and administrative structures were put in place, which encouraged capitalist development. At the same time, the needs of the French war economy encouraged production and modernisation. Three main industrial centres developed in this period: Liège, Charleroi and Ghent. It was the steam-powered machine of the Englishman William Cockerill which modernised both the weaving industry in Verviers and the metal industry in Liège, based on nearby coal supplies and abundant high-quality labour. The mines of Hainaut, with steam pumps, produced 1 million tons of coal annually, a quarter of the total continental European production in this period.

Important improvements in canal communications were undertaken (Charleroi-Brussels) in the 1820s, and in 1835 railway expansion began. With these advantages, heavy industry in both the Liège and the Charleroi-Mons areas developed considerably in the period 1830-50. Only one industrial growth-point developed in Flanders, based on mechanised cotton-spinning in Ghent (10,000 workers in 1810), but after 1815 it suffered a severe setback in the face of competition.[11]

The golden age of Wallonia

The revolution of 1830 which gave Belgium its independence also left it with severe economic problems. There was now only a small internal market, with the loss of the Dutch colonial markets in Asia, while the loss of control of the Scheldt river limited the value of Antwerp as a major transit port. The new government reacted energetically to meet these challenges, and a major part of this policy was the creation of a railway network (593 km. in 1843, 1,730 km. in 1860 and 3,350 km. in 1870). This construction in itself stimulated industry and provided major benefits with the transport of raw materials and finished goods.[12]

Another important advantage was the policy of the Société Générale de Banque, which soon initiated long-term loans to finance industrial investment. The Walloon metal industry grew by 3% yearly in the 1830-45 period, but doubled that rate of growth in the next fifteen years to 1860.

There was a considerable industrial concentration in Liège and Charleroi to take advantage of economies of scale and the transport network.

The depressions of the late nineteenth century slowed down growth and increased concentration (in 1895 only twenty-nine large furnaces were operating, as against fifty-six in the 1840s). Also, the home market became saturated, and export opportunities were reduced. However, increases in productivity and control of costs, which caused severe labour unrest, enabled Belgian industry to remain internationally competitive in the difficult period 1875-90. The spearhead of Belgian industry was coal mining, which quadrupled its production between 1850 and 1895. It employed 116,000 workers in 1896, more than the textile, metal- working and machinery industries combined. Other major industries besides coal, steel and textiles were zinc and glass-working (glass exports grew at 9% yearly between 1840 and 1873).

By comparison, the Flemish economy[13] was meanwhile in a state of stagnation or worse. Between 1830 and 1880 the cloth industry and agriculture, the mainstays of the Flemish rural population, suffered severe setbacks, and the traditional linen industry collapsed in the 1850s creating much unemployment and misery. Also, bad rye harvests and potato blight (as in Ireland) had a severe effect on Flemish agriculture. Many unemployed or under-employed Flemish workers or evicted peasant farmers were forced into emigration; some sought work in Walloon industry, and 30-40,000 of them went to America.

In the 1870s the opening up of the American and Canadian West and falling transport costs saw serious falls in cereal prices; this made Flemish agriculture, which still employed well over half the population, uncompetitive. Already industrial concerns were dominating government; protectionist measures were rejected for fear of reprisals against Belgian (Walloon) industrial exports. From the 1890s, reconversion to less labour-intensive animal husbandry began to gather pace.

For industry, the only light in the tunnel was the relative success of the more modern textile industry based on Ghent and St Niklaas. However, the port of Antwerp became the main growth-point in Flanders; registered tonnage handled grew from 159,999 tons in 1840 to 457,000 in 1860 and 2,623,000 in 1880, placing it at the head of the European ports, ahead of Rotterdam and Hamburg. Growth continued more slowly, reaching 6,720,000 tons in 1900 and 14,140,000 in 1913. This expansion attracted many associated industries: food processing, sugar refining and some technologically innovatory industries, such as Bell telephones and the Minerva motor company (co-production). Already by 1913 these 'futuristic' activities in Antwerp were employing some 6,000 workers.

The later part of the nineteenth century and the early twentieth saw overall industrial employment growing faster in Flanders than Wallonia, and in 1901 coal mines were opened in Limburg. Flanders had an industrial future, even if its experience before 1913 had been very difficult.

Taking the 1880 level as 100, industrial production in Belgium reached 163 by 1900 and 257 by 1913 on the eve of the war. Cereal agricultural production, already standing at 79 in 1845 (against 21 for industrial production) reached only 114 by 1900 and 122 by 1913. But because, due to the Walloon industrial revolution, Belgium had become an industrial country well before 1914, industrial policy, whatever the continued importance of agriculture, would henceforth be the dominant political consideration of all governments.

The economic loss from the First World War was very large: 16-20% of the nation's assets. Production only reached 1913 levels again in 1924. In 1920, the price index had risen to 455 (1913: 100), and it continued to rise. However, especially with the help of raw materials from the Congo and a major and well-organised national effort, recovery was remarkably rapid. The main problem remained the inflationary spiral caused by the over-abundant money supply. In 1926, drastic deflationary measures were necessary, and were carried out successfully. Production continued to rise, reaching 130 (1913: 100) in 1929. It seems with hindsight that this growth was too rapid and uncontrolled.[14]

Structural change was also advancing.[15] Coal production soon recovered and reached a peak in 1925, but the Walloon mining regions were no longer expanding. Hopes were now pinned on the (Flemish) Limburg mines. The apparently unbounded growth in other key sectors – steel, textiles, glass – hid important structural and cost problems, which the 1926 devaluation partly and temporarily resolved, at least in restoring international competitiveness. Now industries such as electricity, represented by ACEC of Charleroi, and specialised metallurgical industries based on metals from the Congo (copper, gold, radium) were also becoming more important. However, no significant Belgian motor industry was able to survive even in the 1920s.

This then was the state of the Belgian economy at the onset of the great depression which in effect lasted until the Second World War. With competitive devaluations, falling demand, generalised cutbacks and protectionism, Belgian industry, with its over-expansion and high cost structure, was in a poor position to meet the crisis and ride it out. This was particularly problematical for the older Walloon industrial areas. Between 1929 and 1933, Belgian exports fell by half. Textile and steel production fell by 60%. In agriculture, herd sizes and cereal production also fell after 1930. Unemployment rose massively from a mere 9,000 in 1929 to 22,000 in 1930 and 79,000 in 1931, peaking at an annual average of 165,000 in 1935. The highest recorded figure was 223,000 in the winter of 1934/5. By 1939, the yearly average figure was still 160,000. At times, as many as 40% of the workforce were unemployed. Bankruptcies and bank failures were numerous. The Van Zeeland 'national unity' government held the line with a 28% devaluation and some 'semi-Keynesian' measures inspired by the Socialists' *Plan de Travail* (the '*Plan De Man*').

Flemish industry had, as we have seen, already begun to catch up before the First World War, and the process continued between the wars. The Flemish share in total national industrial employment rose from 31.05% in 1910 to 38.7% in 1937. The advance of Flemish industry was spread over a broad front. In Wallonia, such limited growth as there was fell below the national average, and many traditional industries suffered decline – partly because wage costs in Flanders were 25-30% lower. Transport costs were also vital. Thus by 1937 16% of mine workers were in Flanders as against 0.2% in 1910; and the share in metallurgy was 26% (18.5) and in glass 18% (2.0). Of all the workers in Flanders 37% now worked in industry as against 31.51% in 1910.

Contrary to almost all expectations, the three decades after the Second World War saw continuous expansion and optimism.[16] By 1948, production had reached its 1938 level. In the early post-war years, average growth at 2.5% was lower than the OECD average (5%), but in 1960-73 real growth was up to 5.1% and throughout the 1970s was up to 5.4%. Unemployment fell steadily to reach a low point of 1.6% in 1965, but showed some relatively high temporary increases.

The movement out of agriculture continued apace, as the accompanying table shows. This has meant a total loss of 300,000 jobs in the primary sector (209,000 in Flanders and 100,000 in Wallonia), which the industrial growth of the 1950s, '60s and early '70s could readily absorb, either in manufacturing industry (+ 70,000 jobs in Flanders by 1960) or in the tertiary sector (Flanders + 59,000 jobs and Wallonia + 34,000 jobs in 1953-60). Regional policy measures have created 375,000 jobs since 1959.[17]

WORK FORCE IN AGRICULTURE (%)

	Flanders	Wallonia
1947	19.8	11.8
1960	10.7	9.2
1970	5.1	5.0
1978	3.6	3.3
1980	3.0	3.0

Source: Annuaire Statistique, 1980.

There have been other significant structural changes. Industry in Wallonia has faced serious difficulties: coal mining is in severe decline (103,000 jobs in 1950, 39,000 in 1960), and in the same period there was a net global loss of 76,000 jobs in manufacturing industry.[18] Flanders saw a reverse trend. There has been a significant move away from commuting to work, with the creation of jobs in the localities – Ghent, Antwerp, Bruges and many smaller towns – where labour was available on a much more decentralised basis. The Flemish industrial revolution is based on 'new' industries: e.g. electronics, and petrochemicals, with highly skilled labour, foreign investment and diversification. Like all new industry it has shown some initial vulnerability to the world economic situation. The increasing involvement of multinationals both in Flanders and Wallonia has brought investment, but at the high price of seeing control of sensitive investment and employment decisions pass out of Belgium.

This period saw Flanders catch up with and overtake Wallonia economically.[19] In 1955-60, its GDP grew spectacularly faster – by over 16.5% (in Wallonia the rate was 5.5%). In 1966-71, GDP in Flanders grew by 6.1% per year and only by 3.9 in Wallonia. The Flemish share in national GDP rose from 47% in 1955 to 49% in 1965 and 55 in 1974. *Per capita* income in Flanders overtook Wallonia in 1966.

Unemployment in Flanders remained more significant than in Wallonia until 1970; indeed as late as 1961, 64% of all Belgian unemployment was in Flanders. In 1959, for example, it was 8.3 as against a national average of 6.7%.

The structure of the economy today [20]

Agriculture now represents only 2.8% of the workforce, giving Belgium with Britain (2.2%) one of the smallest farming sectors in the EC. Belgium has a small net agricultural trade surplus. Agricultural production represents 2.2% of total value added in the economy, 8.0% of imports and 8.5% of export by value in 1989. Some 58% of all cultivable land is down to grass and 27.2% to arable. Nearly 40% of holdings are less than 5 hectares (13.5% in Britain) and almost none are over 50 hectares (5.8% in Britain). There is rough equality between land in tenancy and owner-farmed. Overall, only pig production has grown significantly in recent years. Other meat production has remained fairly static. Total agricultural output grew 3.5% in 1984-8, faster than the economy as a whole. Belgium makes a significant contribution to overall EC production only for sugar (6.8%) and pork (almost 6%). It is self-sufficient in sugar, vegetables, butter, pork and almost all meat, but has a deficit in cereals, potatoes, cheese and fats.

Belgium has few raw materials except some coal, which is only mined in Limburg. In 1980, she produced 4 million tonnes of coal annually, but this had fallen to 2.5 millions of tonnes by 1989. Production had been 21 million tonnes in 1961. Now it imports large quantities of oil (7.7% of all imports by value in 1989), but exports electricity, mostly nuclear-produced (8% of EC production and more than all except for France, Germany and Britain).

Despite the lack of raw materials, 23% of the value added in the Belgian economy comes from manufacturing, 5.7% from construction and 3.1% from energy. There is some significant steel-making production. In 1980, Belgium produced 11% of the EC pig iron, 9.5% of crude steel (more than in Britain), 9.5% of finished steel for the EC. But the steel industry suffered a serous crisis and cutbacks in the 1980s from which it is now recovering. The production trends were as follows (x 1,000 tonnes):

1974	20,486
1982 (*floor level*)	17,300
1988	19,991

Similarly, the shipbuilding capacity (x 1,000 tonnes) was 212.2 in 1983 and only 129.2 in 1985. The production index (1980 = 100) was 143 in 1983, 45 in 1987 and 118.5 in 1988. Belgium's shipping fleet has always been small and was fairly stable over a long period, but it declined from 2.4 billion tonnes in 1939, to 1.869 billion in 1980 and 1.680 billion in 1990. Its share of world maritime traffic was less than 0.5%. It has no significant oil-refining capacity, but does have significant production of basic chemicals such as sulphuric acid, caustic soda, fertilisers, plastics, bricks and cement. There is no significant motor vehicle production as such, but some local vehicle assembly, a field where it holds a virtual monopoly in the EC. Processing of copper from Zaïre (the former Belgian Congo) gives it an important position in that sector (nearly 40%) such as it has for zinc and tin processing. Textiles remain in severe decline.

The fishing industry based at Ostende, Zeebrugge (the largest centre) and Nieuwpoort grew from an annual catch by value of 32 million BF in 1980 to 65 million BF in 1987 after which there was a slight fall to 57 million in 1989.

There has been a steady loss of jobs in the industrial sector: from only 6,000 in 1964 to 17,869 in 1974 and 32,898 in 1977 as the crisis set in. Even more severe losses followed in the early 1980s, but the situation stabilised again in the late 1980s before the Gulf war. By 1979, 62.2% of the workforce were employed in the service sector; this has since risen to 65%. Various forms of services provided 63% of value added in the economy. There has also been an important expansion of sophisticated high-technology industries, especially in Flanders where multinationals have established themselves in large numbers since 1965, especially in petrochemicals and electronics. On the other hand, small firms continue to provide a significant proportion of employment in the private sector (31% in industrial sectors and 48% in non-industrial sectors).

Belgium is a very open economy. Trade, which represents over 50% of GDP, is vital to its economic health. There have been constant swings in the trade balance, with a very large surplus in its best year (293m. ECU in 1973), chronic and growing deficits through the 1970s, and a return to surplus in the 1980s and early 1990s. Both exports and imports have grown fast since the mid-1980s, but Belgium's share of overall world trade, never more than 0.003%, has drifted downwards. The accompanying table shows the pattern of its trade in 1991.

	Exports	*Imports*
EC	75.8	73.3
Non-EC Europe	7.5	7.6
East/Central Europe	1.9	2.0
USA	5.6	5.8
Japan	1.2	1.6
Africa	1.3	1.2
Other	8.7	8.5

There had been a significant growth in the EC share of exports since 1980, when it took only 72%. For imports the rise was even more dramatic, from 63.1% in 1980 to 73.3% in 1991. Belgium's main trading partners were its immediate EC neighbours: Germany took 20.3% of exports and provided 23.5% of imports. Trade with the united Germany grew by a startling 5.7% in 1990. France, followed by the Netherlands and Britain, were the next most important trading partners. These four neighbours together represented over 60% of Belgium's trade. Its exports are mainly manufactured goods (33%), machinery (25.3%), chemicals (13.7%) and food and drink (9.8%). Imports are mainly fuel and raw materials.[21]

The state of the economy

Since 1975, Belgium has felt the impact of the crisis. Problems of the rural exodus, high wage costs and outmoded declining heavy industry – masked earlier by the beneficent effects of steady growth, which created new jobs to replace those lost – could be masked no longer. The uninterrupted rise in production after 1958 was brutally broken in 1975, recovering only slightly in 1976. From 1975 there was a fall in the absolute number employed in industry. Real growth in GDP was negative in 1975 (-2%) and marginally positive in 1976, 1977 and 1978.

Unemployment rose to 6.7% in 1975, reaching 7.0% in 1976 and 11.6% in 1981. Business closures rose from 305 in 1974 to 671 in 1975 and 1,127 in 1977. In 1974, 17,879 jobs were lost, and there were dramatic rises to 21,123 in 1975 and 32,898 in 1977. The largest losses were in metallurgy (18.8%), construction (17.5), clothing (12.9) and textiles (10.8). Belgium's budget deficit rose to 15% of GDP in 1980. Its external indebtedness was already 1,419 ECU in 1979 and rose dramatically in 1980.[22]

After the severe crisis of the early 1980s with a large balance of payments deficit, severe sectoral problems for heavy industries such as steel, textiles and shipbuilding, soaring unemployment, stagnant growth, dangerously low competitiveness and a public sector deficit of 13% of GDP in 1982, the economy began to return to a more healthy situation in the late 1980s.

In the late 1980s and early 1990s, before the Gulf war, the Belgian economy returned to a trade surplus and a more rapid rate of growth than the OECD average, with 4% growth in 1989 and 3.5% in 1990. Even so, employment was still falling as jobs were lost in industry, and the rate of unemployment remained high at 9.1% in 1989 and 8.6% in 1990. Inflation stabilised at 3.5% and falling, in the middle range for the EC. The public sector deficit, Belgium's most serious problem of economic policy, began to come under control, falling from 6% of GDP in 1990 to 5.7% in 1990. The Gulf war slowed growth in Belgium, as did the post-unification economic problems in Germany. By 1992/3, the deficit was climbing again to 6.9% of GDP and public expenditure was again rising as a share of GDP.

Monthly gross wages in industry (1990) stood at 83,529 BF for men and 53,530 BF for women, but taking 1980 = 100, the index for men stood at 138 and for women at 145.3. There is a small catching-up element for women. Again, on an index of 1980 = 100, Belgian wages stood at 133 (1988) having increased more slowly than in Germany (136.5) and France (172.8), but faster than in the Netherlands (122). Hourly earnings have been rising significantly since the 1980s. In 1975, Belgian rates were in fifth position after Denmark, but in 1982 had reached second position after Denmark. Hourly labour costs in industry by 1980 had reached 10.20 ECU, the highest in the EC (e.g. in Germany it was 9.30 ECU). In 1990, wage costs rose by 5.7% in Belgium, but rose by only 3.9% in its seven main competitors. Direct costs represented 75.2% in 1989 (76.1% in 1978). Social security represented 23.7% (21.9% in 1980). Wages in agriculture compared favourably with those in industry; hours worked on average were 36 (36.9 in 1980), compared with 37.7 in Britain and 36.7 for the twelve EC member states.[24]

On almost any indicator – including, as we have seen, earnings – Belgium has one of the highest standards of living. GDP per head in 199 was US$15,828 (8,300 in 1979); the average is 15,971. Belgium has a high level of quality consumption. For example, meat consumption was 23 kg per head below the EC average, energy consumption and steel stands second to Germany. With 355 telephones per 1,000 population Belgium is above the EC average but with 320 televisions per 1,000 is below the EC average of 329.

Health services are good but patchy. Medicine is private, but financed through the complex system of *mutualités*, a compulsory insurance scheme. The ratio of doctors and pharmacists – professions constituting a powerful and highly conservative lobby which governments have rarely challenged – to the population is higher than in any other EC country. On the other hand, Belgium is less well endowed with hospital beds than the EC average. Sickness and pensions are the greatest charges on social security: 28.4% of GDP goes on social expenditure (27.1% in 1978), which places the country second in the EC. Taxes and social contributions took 41% of GDP (43% in 1979).[25]

Problems of the economy and economic policy

Belgium is an advanced industrial nation, with a high standard of living and well developed social network, and with all the characteristics of a post-industrial economy: negligible agricultural employment, and heavy industries and large-scale enterprises of the first industrial revolution in severe decline, especially in Wallonia. Recent expansion has been in smaller, more flexible industries and services, based on advanced technology.

The Belgian economy is by any measure very open and dependent on trade, and therefore vulnerable to movements in the European and world economies. The country's trading partners are mainly its immediate EC neighbours, and its economic position therefore depends on a narrow range of relativities. It must maintain competitiveness with a narrow group of EC countries, whose economic development will, as a result of EC convergence policies, follow a very similar pattern. In one sense this facilitates diagnosis and response, yet the very openness of the Belgian economy and the absence of alternative policy options mean that there are no compensatory effects in any policy failure. The tuning needs to be extremely fine. This, in turn, calls for considerable flexibility, which in the Belgian context is made difficult by some corporatist institutional rigidities, structural functionalities and regional variations.

Belgium depends on energy imports and raw materials that are re-processed and exported, and thus needs access to raw materials at steady prices and to export markets. It must therefore be a proponent of free trade, stabilisation of raw materials prices and economic and political integration in the EC. The single EC market and the nearest and most developed parts of it are its national hinterland, to which it needs equal access. Conse-quently, Belgium has strongly supported EC monetary co-operation and integration, since that would guarantee monetary stability in its economic space. Thus it supported the Werner Plan, the 1970 'Snake', the EMS and Economic and Monetary Union as prescribed in the Maastricht treaty. Not only is Belgium in the EMS narrow rate band, but it decided in 1990 to tie the Belgian franc to the strongest currency of the EMS, the German mark. Defence of its stability has often had to take priority over other desirable policy objectives, and as part of the austerity measures of the early 1980s, devaluation of the franc by 8.5% was necessary as part of an EMS realignment mainly provoked by France. Since then, up till the time of writing, the franc has remained stable. Thus the discipline of EMS rate alignment and the necessary maintenance of competitiveness in the economic relation to its key economic partners are the central concerns of Belgium's economic policy.

From 1974 onwards, as we have seen, the international crisis hit Belgium severely, and its intensity increased right into the 1980s. Unemployment rose dramatically from 104,720 in 1974 to 228,537 in 1976, to 321,895 in 1980 and 512,400 in 1985, when it began to decline. Investment, which was already below that of its main economic partners as a share of GDP, dried up. There was also considerable regional impact: the decline of the coal industry continued in the Borinage and in Limburg, with that of the textile industry mainly affecting Flanders (75%). However, Wallonia was worst hit by industrial decline and factory closures, and unemployment grew much faster there than in Flanders.[26]

By the early 1980s, structural difficulties were real, but were most severe in Wallonia. Heavy investment by multinational companies (MNCs) had given them 49% of sales and 40% of value added in the economy (as against 25% in France and Germany and only 14% in Britain) and they had come to dominate (75%) high-tech industries. They employ 1.8% of turnover in Research and Development compared with 1.5% for Belgian firms. Their productivity per worker is 50% higher than 'national' firms, and their record in creating jobs was also considerable (net 130,000 jobs) in the period 1968-75; this represented a growth rate of 5.1% compared with a fall in 0.43% in pure domestic undertakings. This rate could not be maintained in the recession, although in its first phase (1975-8), they accounted for a 0.41% rise in employment, which subsequently fell. On the regional level, the cost of job creation was far higher in Wallonia (234 million BF in public and 2,460 billion BF in private investment) than in Flanders (111 million BF in public and 1,435 billion BF in private investment).

There were also political differences in diagnosis and policy prescriptions between Walloon and Flemish parties and social partners, and these introduced serious blockages and paralysis in both the social dialogue and political decision-making in the early 1980s. Consensus became impossible over the future of the Walloon steel industry, and over measures to increase the competitiveness of Belgian industry and reduce the public sector deficit that had reached 13% of GDP. The PS and FGTB rejected the demands for a draconian austerity programme and re-indexation of wages put forward by the *patronat*, the opposition PRL/PVV and part of the PSC and CVP.

The reversal of alliances by the PSC/CVP after 1981 to form a centre-right coalition with the Liberals put these hardliners in the driving seat. The new government introduced special powers in 1982, 1983 and again in 1986. Under these laws, more than 200 royal decrees were adopted. The key purpose was to increase the competitiveness of the economy, limit wage costs, promote exports, encourage investment and reduce the public sector deficit. The instruments were many and varied: a devaluation of 8.5% in 1982, a price freeze, de-indexation of wages for a period of time, cuts in public expenditure, measures to control social security costs, measures to promote exports and encourage new productive investment while reducing subsidies, preparation for deregulation, and even forms of privatisation of the public sector.[27]

As we have seen, these measures began to have some effect by 1986, but they provoked serious trade union opposition. Following the 1987 election, the PSC notably was unwilling to engage in a new and more radical phase of cuts in public spending and of deregulation and even privatisation, which would inevitably have resulted from a new centre-right coalition led by Mr Verhofstadt. For the PS a return to power, even if the party had to accept at least in principle the basic continuity of the post-1981 economic policy, was vital to break the dynamic of the centre-right and prevent its extension to the public services, social security and industrial relations before it was too late.

Thus, the new social measures introduced by the new centre-left coalition were quite modest; however they were welcome, since they involved upgrading pensions and other benefits and measures to promote employment. The law on competitiveness adopted in 1988 contains most of the former objectives and instruments; even de-indexation is included as an option, but crucially it is not a special powers law. Therefore there must be prior attempts by the social partners to reach agreement on measures to restore competitiveness before any government intervention can take place, on which Parliament would have been consulted.[28] Last, but crucially, with the Socialists in power, acting as in 1982-3 would be impossible.[29]

At the time of writing the most difficult economic issue is compliance with the Maastricht treaty targets on the public sector deficit (3% target by 1997) in time to enter the third phase of economic and monetary union. For the first time, a real debate on Europe has been opened. Europe under EMU is not just a vague general concept but would have a price.[30] The financing of community services such as education is also causing severe strains, and this led to strikes in 1994.

THE BELGIAN POLITICAL SUBCULTURE: SOCIETY

The nature of Belgian society has been constantly changing, becoming more fragmented and pluralistic. At the start, public affairs and opinion formation were totally in the hands French-speaking 'unionist' (Liberal and moderate Catholic) élite, who had provoked the 1830 revolution and fashioned the new state in their own image and interests. In the nineteenth century new social groups arose which came to play an important role in

Belgian society and politics, although this role was often purely embryonic at the time. These were the labour movement – originating in the industrial proletariat which the industrial revolution brought into being, above all in urban Wallonia – and, parallel to it, a new class of industrial entrepreneurs and financiers involved in trade and colonial development, which came to have an increasing role in public affairs. Lastly, the Flemish cultural and political movement began to take shape and to find its voice, although this was to become more significant in the twentieth century.

Within the framework of Belgium, there has been a generalised tendency towards fragmentation, with elements supportive of 'Belgian consciousness' or national unity tending to diminish over the course of time. Subcultures have developed, of which the Socialist working-class movement in Wallonia, with its many manifestations – trade unions, '*mutualités*' (non-governmental health insurance schemes, peculiar to Belgium and a few other smaller European counties), co-operatives, clubs – and its traditions making it self-contained and almost self-sufficient, was a prime example. Likewise the Christian trade unions, *mutualités* and sociocultural organisations were enclaves, self-contained and often isolated from or hostile to their Socialist counterparts.

The Flemish movement has matured and come of age, having surmounted the handicaps it suffered in the aftermath of the two world wars. It is multi-faceted, having cultural, political and economic manifestations, each dimension enriching and reinforcing the other. The cultural foundations belonging to the Flemish movement – Davidsfonds, Willemsfonds, the Ijzerkomitee – and the Flemish universities and press contribute a permanent source of consciousness and pressure on the political parties other than the Volksunie, which already shares their ideals. This has produced a fragmented society or two societies, each of which has tended to turn in on itself, maintaining its own traditions and cultural development. Since the mid-1960s there has also been a defensive reaction in Wallonia to the Flemish movement: the tendency was for Walloon reaction, under the impulse of the Mouvement Populaire Wallon, the Rassemblement Wallon and the FDF, to shift radically first towards a defensive position and then – as the position of the PS in the 1981 elections shows – towards a position not unlike the Flemish attitude, in which each part of the country can and should be able to exercise considerable autonomy in a wide range of cultural and economic areas of policy. This had led to the two communities developing in separate directions, sometimes in confrontation and often ignoring each other, which has made national unity ever more elusive and difficult.

The rise of a Belgian entrepreneurial class[31] (great captains of industry such as Baron Solvay, Coppée, Bunge, Anseele, Empain) based on rapid innovation, foreign trade and exploitation of the mineral wealth of the

Congo did much to stimulate the golden age of Belgian industry. This is turn created the basis for the high and continuing level of material prosperity in Belgium, the passing of which many are psychologically unable to accept, thus explaining the difficulty of the dialogue between the two sides of industry in the present crisis. At the same time, a structure of industry has been created based on interlocking trusts, often with the strong participation of banks such as the Société Générale. This has tended to concentrate economic power in a very small number of hands or institutions, which can cause severe problems of control and accountability. It has created an economy in which there is probably less competitive behaviour than in most western economies, which in turn leads to greater rigidities and poor adaptability.

The decline of ideology in the 1950s and 1960s, which has been a feature of western societies, has also been evident in Belgium. The accelerating social change, the changes in social and economic structure, have tended to undermine the 'collectivist' tendencies in Belgian associative life and reinforced inherent tendencies towards introverted individualistic materialism. These tendencies have always been in conflict. This latter tendency has also no doubt done much to ensure that the broad movements which have influenced Europe and the world – the international fascist movement of the 1930s, the anti-war movement inspired by Vietnam, the student movement in the 1960s – only had a limited echo in Belgium, as if there were shock-absorbers on the boundaries of the country. For example, the French events of 1968 found only pale echoes in Belgian universities in the following three years.

There has been little or no sign of a significant *kulturkampf* between the generations in Belgium, but that is not to suggest that there has not been alienation and disaffection from traditional patterns and values. The sense of unease and of a society in a state of crisis and fragmentation, while certainly present, has tended to be incoherent and not clearly defined. Certainly, it is only in the recent past that it has found channels of expression of any significance. There are now signs that the recent reform of the education system, which created the '*école renovée*', has begun to bear fruit in the creation of a more questioning and independent generation. Belgium, with its strongly conformist and materialist tendencies and its high share of nuclear energy, seems an unlikely candidate for having the first ecologist members of any national Parliament (since the 1981 elections). Perhaps the most immediately obvious explanation for this is that the phenomenon owes less to 'new leftism' or a latent 'green movement' than to the concept of alienation canalised into protest. Young voters – eighteen-year-olds now vote – and others reacted to the increasing inability of the Belgian political system to manage society and to produce solutions to even the most pressing problems by seeking refuge in protest parties and rejecting the traditional political parties and the consensus of post-war 'large is beautiful' growth-oriented policies fuelled by an ever larger and more bureaucratic public sector. Divergences between the three traditional parties have, after all, only concerned the degree and extent of these developments and not their reversal.

The arrival of large numbers of immigrant workers in Belgium in the 1960s and 1970s also had a considerable impact on society. There have always been immigrants to work in the mines, especially from Italy, France and Poland, but these came over a relatively long period and have become integrated into Belgian society without excessive difficulty. However, the situation became different with the arrival of large numbers from the Mediterranean. These migrants have not been able to integrate into Belgian society and have often not wished to do so, preferring to maintain their own customs, religion and way of life in Belgium. Having been imported to undertake menial work, for which in the 'golden sixties' there were no Belgian volunteers, they are usually poor and confined to areas of inferior housing in the inner city, especially in Brussels where in some *communes* (especially Schaerbeek and Anderlecht) they have come to represent nearly 30% of the population. This has given rise to serious and even racist reactions, especially with the increase in unemployment during the recession. With well over 800,000 immigrants (up from 450,000 in 1961), the majority of whom came at first from Italy but subsequently from Spain, Yugoslavia, Turkey and North Africa, immigration has already become a serious political issue.

That the façade of relative stability and conformism of Belgian society is deceptive was clearly shown in the elections of November 1991. As well as the Green tendency in Belgian politics that had been developing since 1981 and which almost doubled in Wallonia, another new and more worrying tendency emerged, with the Vlaams Blok and the Front National leaving their stable ghetto of marginality. Analysts have seen some common causes in these developments, although naturally the proposed remedies of Ecolo/Agalev and the Vlaams Blok and Front National are diametrically opposed. The causes have been seen less as a response to a specific issue such as the environment or the perceived increase in immigration or the threatening nature of immigrants, and more as forms of anomie or alienation from the existing social order.

Belgian society has become more individualistic, more critical – though not always positively or constructively so – and less willing to accept traditional structures and organisations or forms of authority. Only 25% think politics are very important or important (19 per cent in Wallonia), according to a recent survey.[32] Few institutions inspire trust or confidence. Only 15% consider religion 'very important', although in Flanders 48% still consider it to be 'very important' or 'important'. Religious practice fell from 42.9% in 1967 to 18.7 in 1989. Only 15.09% think that the church should intervene in politics; the figure is 16% even in the PSC and CVP. The church inspired confidence in 49% and no confidence in 21% in 1990 (in 1981 the ratio was 60:13). Large enterprises only inspire confidence in 49%; trade unions in 37%, Parliament in 42%, the army in 33%. For most the balance is positive and for some their rating has improved since 1981, but the trends are not healthy. Only the social security and educational systems, with 73%, achieve a genuinely positive rating.

A number of scandals, some of them linked and involving the security services, the judicial system, organised crime, political terrorism, and corruption in political parties have done much to increase public alienation from politics. There was the murder of the former PS leader André Cools in 1991, perhaps by the Mafia in league with some local PS politicians.[33] Then there was the possibly arranged kidnapping of the mayor of St Josse, Guy Cudell, and the kidnapping of the former prime minister Paul Vanden Boeynants, and his conviction for tax evasion. In the 1980s there were the terrorist ravages of the supposedly far-left Cellules Communistes Combattantes (CCC) and the Tueurs du Brabant,[34] a paramilitary gang that committed several bloody holdups and murders in the early 1980s, murky links in the 1970s between the Security Services and groups on the extreme right such as the Frond de la Jeunesse, the revelation of an occult international anti-Communist group linked with the CIA (Gladio) that operated in Belgium in the 1970s and '80s[35] despite the country's centre-right government, are a long but by no means exhaustive list of strange events. Some would explain them in terms of the Italian far-right theory of tension creating the conditions for public acceptance of authoritarian government. The Cools affair re-surfaced dramatically in 1993, as there were allegations of corruption involving PS ministers receiving kickbacks for party funds for giving preference to an Italian consortium for the supply of helicopters to the Belgian armed forces. This led to several resignations (Spitaels and the Federal defence minister) and some indictments. Up to the time of writing no one has been convicted. Judgement must remain suspended, but certainly these events have not made Belgium more governable, or increased confidence in the democratic institutions. As it is, the Belgian political class knows that it has to repair its image and that of many institutions. The 'checklist' of expectations raised by political parties needs realistic revision; a clearer understanding is necessary of what the political system can reasonably be expected to deliver. That alone would do much to restore credibility.

NOTES

1. *Annuaire Statistique* no. 109 (1990).
2. Ibid.

3. Ibid.

4. *Source*: Bibliothèque Royale (1990).

5. K. Macrae, *Conflict and Compromise in Multilingual Societies*, Wilfrid Laurier University Press, Waterloo, Ont. (1986), table 1, 293-321.

6. For a history of immigration, see *Intégration. Une Politique de Longue Haleine*, vol. 1., Commissariat Royale à la Politique des Immigrés, Brussels (1989), pp. 17-21.

7. Commissariat Royal, op. cit., 17.

8. Commissariat Royal, op. cit., 30.

9. 1989 figures, Commissariat Royal, op. cit., 27, 28.

10. H. Haems *et al., De Belgische Industrie. Een Profielbeeld*, De Nederlandse Boekhandel, Brussels, 1981, 14-16.

11. The development of the Walloon industry is described in Haems, op. cit., 17-22.

12. Haems, op. cit., 23-6, for the Flemish situation in the nineteenth and early twentieth century.

13. For a discussion of the economic recovery, see van Kalken, op. cit., 707-12.

14. Haems, op. cit., 31-2.

15. Ibid., 38-43, and van Kalken, 837-47.

16. Haems, op. cit., 39.

17. Ibid., 39-40.

18. Ibid., 42.

19. Ibid., 45-7 and table XXIV (210-11).

20. Economic data taken from *Annuaire Statistique de la Belgique*, vol. 109 (1989) and *Basic Statistics of the European Community*, Eurostat 1991, tables 1, 9 and 10.

21. Trade data taken from 'L'économie belge en 1991', Synthèse Annuelle, Ministère des Affaires Economiques, Brussels, 1992, 36-40.

22. Eurostat, table 9.

23. *L'économie belge*, op. cit., table 54.

24. Basic statistics, op. cit.

25. Social Face of the European Community, Eurostat, 1991.

26. For the onset of the crisis, see X. Mabille, *Histoire Politique de la Belgique*, CRISP, Brussels, 1986, 361-4.

27. J. Moden and J. Sloover, *Le Patronat Belge*, CRISP, 1981, 11-14.

28. X. Mabille, op. cit., 364-8.

29. E. Arcq, P. Blaise, E. Lentzen, 'Enjeux et Compromis de la Législative 1987-1991', *CH* 1332-3 (1991), pp. 37-8.

30. Prime Minister Dehaene, speaking on the television discussion programme 'Faire le Point', 21 June 1992.

31. For an analysis of the individual entrepreneurs, see F. Baudhuin, *Histoire économique de la Belgique*, Bruylant, Brussels, 1946, vol. 2, 205-58, and for financiers, 259-86, where a colourful account is given of many leading personalities.

32. L. Voye, B. Bawin-Legros, J. Kerkhofs, K. Dobbelaere, *Belges, heureux et satisfaits: les valeurs des Belges dans les années 90*, De Boeck Université/Fondation Roi Baudouin, Brussels, 1992, 10.

33. 'Politique et Mafia. L'énigme du Guêpier Liégeois', *Le Vif-Express*, 26 June 1992.

34. H. Gijsels, *L'Enquête. 20 années de déstabilisation en Belgique*, La Longue Vue, Paris/Brussels, 1989, 33-80.

35. Gijsels, op. cit., 119-41.

3

CENTRAL GOVERNMENT

The Constitution of 1830 created a unitary state and a hereditary constitutional monarchy within a parliamentary system; it was liberal for its time.
The structure of the state was simple: a central government, with a
bi-cameral Parliament, provinces and *communes*. Political power was
centralised in the hands of a small Francophone élite, based in Brussels.
Gradually the unilingual character of the state gave way to a bilingual
regime at the national level and eventually to a combination of unilin-
gualism in each community and bilingualism in Brussels and in the
national institutions. From 1918 universal manhood suffrage was
achieved, and from 1970, the date of the first major constitutional revision,
Belgium began to move towards a more complex structure of a federal
type. The process is still going on and is far from complete, but already
the Belgian state has taken on important federal characteristics with
devolution of significant powers to the communities and regions. The
most recent constitutional revision declares Belgium to be a federal state
(Article 1).

THE EXECUTIVE

The Crown

Belgium has been a hereditary constitutional monarchy since the founding
of the state, with descent being restricted to the male line until a revision
of the Constitution in 1991 enacted that the heir to the throne would be
the first-born child of the reigning monarch, irrespective of sex. As we
saw in Chapter 1, the great powers insisted on a king from a small German
royal house, without connections to the dynasties of the major powers.
There have been six Belgian kings: Leopold I (1831-65), who was mainly
responsible for building up the new Belgian state and ensuring its
neutrality; Leopold II (1865-1909), best known for acquiring the Congo;
Albert I (1909-1934), the valiant symbol of resistance to the Germans in
the First World War; Leopold III (1934-51), forced to abdicate after the
Second World War; Baudouin (1951-93); and Albert II (1993-), who
succeeded on the sudden death of his brother Baudouin, although it had

been expected that the succession might pass immediately to one of Albert's children.[1]

All Belgian kings have been activist, using their formal and informal powers to the full. Leopold I took a literal view of Article 65 of the Constitution, which states that 'the King appoints and dismisses his Ministers'. Leopold II acquired and ran the Congo as a personal venture. Both Albert I and Leopold III actually commanded the armed forces, and indeed Leopold III ordered their surrender in May 1940 without the approval of the Cabinet. Albert imposed universal suffrage and other reforms on reluctant politicians in 1918. Baudouin, after a slow start, came to assume a much greater political role.[2] He supported gradual reform and helped political figures agreeable to him such as Mr Martens, and hindered others such as Leo Tindemans and Jean-Luc Dehaene. Belgian kings have also taken an active interest in defence and foreign policy, carrying on correspondence with their prime ministers and other ministers[3] and even speaking out from time to time in public. In theory, the Crown is 'irresponsible': all its acts must be countersigned by a Minister, and the Minister concerned then assumes responsibility. This requirement is even seen as covering official royal speeches.[4] However, it has not prevented the Crown from exercising very real influence behind the scenes. The monarch must formally sign and promulgate all bills and royal decrees and the dissolution of Parliament.

Until recently, the royal signature was seen as a mere formality, a kind of notary's signature. Even before the crisis over the 1990 Abortion Act, there was evidence that the palace objected to publicity being given to decrees that had been agreed in cabinet but not yet signed. King Baudouin also sought to monitor closely through his cabinet (personal staff) matters passed for signature by a caretaker government that has resigned and is only responsible for day-to-day administration ('*expédiant les affaires courantes*'). Here the monarch may insist on delaying measures such as appointments until a new government is appointed.[5]

The crisis surrounding the 1990 Abortion Act rocked the monarchy. A 'lay' parliamentary majority of Socialists, Liberals and Greens had come together to pass an abortion law (the so-called Michielsen-Lallemand Bill, after its Liberal and Socialist sponsors), despite opposition from the CVP/PSC government parties. The question arose in March 1990 whether King Baudouin, who was known to oppose the bill on religious grounds, would sign the bill into law or exercise his undoubted formal right to refuse to sign it, despite its having been passed in Parliament. He declined to sign, setting out his reasons in a letter to the prime minister, Mr Martens (CVP), but also stated that he did not desire to thwart the will of Parliament and asked the government to find a solution to the impasse. A senior official invented a creative if somewhat dubious way out. The King was declared 'unable to reign' for thirty-six hours, during which time the cabinet assumed his functions and signed the bill. Thereupon Parliament, in accordance with Article 82 of the Constitution, declared the 'inability to reign' at an end. Quite clearly this procedure was an abuse of the constitutional provisions intended for quite other cases, such as long-term illness or mental breakdown, but no one wished to object and so make the crisis worse. The King and the institution of monarchy did not emerge from this affair with their credibility enhanced.[6]

The most important function of the King, where in the nature of things he has least guidance, is the formation of governments. Indeed, this is one area where the greater political fragmentation and institutional complexity of modern Belgium has made government formation more difficult, so that the real ability of the King to influence the course of events has actually tended to grow. Formally, the Constitution merely states: 'The King appoints and dismisses his Ministers' (Article 65) and 'No act of the King is valid unless it is countersigned by a Minister who thereby takes responsibility for that Act' (Article 64). This provision naturally also applies to the act of nomination of a prime minister and the other members of the government. The incoming prime minister countersigns his own nomination to avoid the problems that could arise if the outgoing prime minister were required to sign. The countersignature requirement only applied formally to the actual act of nomination and not to the preceding intermediate decisions and consultations, although those are formally 'covered' by the outgoing prime minister.

Of course, the King is by no means as free in his appointment of a government as the text of Article 65 implies. Clearly, as in any parliamentary system, he must form a government which has the confidence of Parliament. In Belgium, this is taken as a positive requirement. A government will be expected to control an absolute majority in the Lower House, at least nominally, and by tradition seeks an immediate vote of confidence on its programme. There is no tradition of minority government which might be 'tolerated' or supported externally; indeed, governments that lose their formal majority resign even without a vote in Parliament, as happened for example when the RW ministers left the Tindemans government in 1977, thus depriving it of a majority in the House, although it might well have survived a no-confidence notion if one had been tabled. This requirement is of course a limitation on the range of options available in the formation of a government. Beyond that the process of regionalisation, coupled with the custom (it is no more than that) of forming what are called 'symmetrical' governments in which only whole political families, in blocs of two (PS/SP; CVP/PSC; PRL/PVV) are included in governments, has limited freedom of choice in forming governments.

Almost every government since 1968 has been faced with the 'community issue'. The Reform of the State – the process of federalisation of Belgium – has been a central priority for most governments. This has meant that governments have had to command the special majorities that are necessary to revise the Constitution and pass the special laws mandated by its Articles 59A and 107 *quater* establishing the powers of the communities and regions. Thus, on the formation of such governments, the search was on for coalitions able to command a two-thirds overall majority and a majority in both language groups in both Houses. That again has reduced the range of choice available to the King.

Government formations might be considered according to the degree of change involved as either 'routine' or 'watershed'. The most difficult formations are those involving changes in partners from, say, CVP/PSC and PS/SP to CVP/PSC and PRL/PVV (as in 1981) or back again as in 1988; or moves to 'classic' tripartite coalitions as in 1973 or 1980; unusual combinations such as the only recent red-blue coalition (1954-8); or the inclusion of 'community parties' as in the Egmont pact government (1977-8), embracing both the VU and the FDF. Continuation of the same basic formula, even after elections, will be easier, such as in 1985 and 1992. Much of course depends on expectations. Has a given formula made its way, behind the scenes and in the *air du temps*? This was the case with the change to the centre-right coalition in 1982. Indeed recent revelations show that the change was long promoted by the King and was prepared for many months behind the scenes by Mr Martens. His abandonment of the premiership in early 1981 to Mr Eyskens (CVP) was merely a case of '*reculer pour mieux sauter*'.[7]

The wide variety of possible scenarios that can arise in the modern Belgian political situation has led to the development of much more complex procedures for government formation.[8] In what follows we examine these various procedures, although naturally not all of them may be cumulated in any given government formation process. First of all, the King will consult the outgoing prime minister, who may of course still be a candidate to succeed himself. He will consult the presidents of the House of Representatives and the Senate and possibly elder statesmen in the party that has made gains in the election. He has also come to consult party leaders at this stage. These steps are not an obligation, but develop a force of their own once they have been repeated on several occasions. Within a few days, he will hand the consultation process on to an *informateur*, rather than as in the past going straight to the appointment of a *formateur*. The person chosen will be somewhat detached either by being an elder statesman, such as Mr Segers (PSC) in 1968, Mr De Jaeger in 1972 and Mr Vanderpoorten (PVV) in 1981, or be unlikely to become prime minister because of the party he comes from, such as Willy Claes (SP), who has been *informateur* on several occasions (1978, 1980, 1987). There have been several occasions when more than one *informateur* has followed after another (Mr Spitaels and Mr Claes in 1987). More complicated and imaginative constructions, such as the appointment of two co-mediators in 1979 (Mr Claes and Mr Nothomb [PSC]) or, as in 1979, receiving all the party presidents of the outgoing coalition, have also been tried.

The task of the *informateur* is strictly only to hold soundings and report to the King, recommending if possible a possible *formateur*, who may then be charged with actually forming the new ministry. Yet he mostly goes further, clearing the ground, eliminating various possibilities, suggesting the coalition format or, as in 1988, laying down the parameters of a policy agreement.[9] An *informateur* may of course fail or even, as in the case of Mr Verhofstadt (PVV) in 1992, be intended to fail to make any progress. Once the *informateur* has reported and a *formateur* has been named, the path to a government may be long and far from smooth, but the direction will usually be clear. The *formateur* may also occasionally fail and be replaced. Mostly, however, he manages to put together a coalition along the lines set out in his mandate. The task of the King is then complete, except for formally appointing the prime minister and the other members of the government.

There is evidence that in more recent years King Baudouin actively supported Mr Martens as a moderate unionist as against the old unitarian Tindemans or the more federalist Dehaene.[10] He mostly tended to favour the traditional '*rouge romaine*' centre-left Socialist/Christian Democratic coalition as binding the Socialists into the system, although in 1981 he favoured a non-Socialist centre-right cabinet to impose an austerity programme which clearly could not be carried through as long as the PS/SP remained in power. The King also attempted to prevent the appointment of justice ministers with strong pro-abortion views and closely scrutinised appointments to the defence and foreign affairs portfolios. From time to time, he also attempted to block the appointment of individuals, mostly Socialists or Liberals, who had been critical of the monarchy during the '*Question Royale*' or whose personal lifestyle had too openly not accorded with the King's strict moral views.[11]

More generally, the King can intervene in public affairs by writing to his ministers and calling them in to criticise policy and demand action. His robust defence of Sabena as an independent national airline against sell-off, merger and cuts in subsidies is an example of this.

All in all, the Belgian King seems to have more real power than almost any European constitutional monarch and perhaps as much as a constitutional monarch may decently exercise. According to a judgement on the late King in 1991: 'Baudouin has more political power than any other European monarch. His power has a nineteenth-century extent.'[12]

The government

Having looked at the role of the King and the basic procedural aspects of government formation, we have to consider the formidable political constraints and difficulties that have contributed to an image of ungovernability. The formation of a government is often the outcome of a lengthy process taking up to five months. The end-result may bear little resemblance to the trends which emerged from a by then quite distant election. The large number of parties and the emergence of distinct subregional political systems in Flanders, Wallonia and Brussels can mean that no clear national trend can be read into the election result. In 1992, for example, the PRL lost ground whereas the PVV gained slightly. Did the Liberals gain or lose? This gives politicians ample opportunity either to give their own interpretations of the results or to ignore them as unclear in their intent. This tendency was clearest in the formation of the Dehaene I (CVP/PSC & PS/SP) coalition in 1992: in this case it was clear from the start that there was no viable alternative to continuing with the existing centre-left formula, but that could not be stated too baldly because of the violent discontent expressed by voters in the election of November 24, 1991.

As we have seen, there are a number of significant limitations in the available options for any given cabinet formation. These are: the fragmentation of parties and hence the need for extensive multi-party coalitions; the political need for majorities in both communities, deriving from the constitutional rule that, with the possible exception of the prime minister, there must be parity between Flemish and French-speaking ministers in the Cabinet (Article 86 *bis*); the search for the special 'double majorities' (two-thirds overall and majorities in each language group) in order to continue the institutional reform process; the custom of only forming 'symmetrical' governments; and the strong pressure for another kind of symmetry, in equivalent coalition at every level of government – national, regional and community.

Classic coalition theory suggests, at the very least, a preference for the formation wherever possible of closed, minimum winning coalitions, i.e. the minimum combination able to muster a majority in Parliament. However, this has little relevance to Belgian government formation. As we have seen, the key decision rule in Belgium is often not the simple majority but the so-called special majority, and since 1970 a coalition with this greater majority has been found wherever possible. A closed coalition is one in which the partners are ideologically contiguous. Ideological distance is measured usually in classic right-left terms, but in Belgium, especially where a special majority coalition is under active consideration, this aspect may be considered secondary. Some of the community parties are difficult to place in the right-left spectrum: thus the more left-leaning RW was in the centre-right (CVP/PSC & PRL/PVV & RW) Tindemans I cabinet, while the more right-leaning Volksunie has only served in core centre-left coalitions (1977-8 and 1988-91). The other factor blurring left-right differences is the development of linguistic fronts, which are adhered to formally or informally by all government parties in each community (PS/PSC/FDF in 1977 or PS/PSC or PSC/PRL in different coalitions or CVP/SP/VU) or even by all parties in a community.

Before the 1970s the Belgian system had illustrated some characteristics of the coalition theory. Since the development of the modern party system after the First World War, the CVP/PSC had been a pivotal party. Political alternation has been ensured by the Catholic Party (later CVP/PSC) changing partners between the Socialists (centre-left) and the Liberals (centre-right). In crisis situations, as after 1918, with the rise of Rexism and the external threat from Nazism in the 1930s, or immediately after the Second World War (1946-7), other models such as a tripartite grand coalition or, in 1944-7, an anti-clerical (Socialist-Liberal-Communist) alliance were attempted for brief periods. With the one exception of the 1954-8 anti-clerical coalition formed over the issue of religious schools, the Socialist-Liberal model was not viable because in the left-right spectrum the Christian Democrats lay between the Socialists and Liberals. Only where a non-socio-economic conflict became of primary importance could the SocialistLiberal model be preferred. By the 1970s, another non-socioeconomic division – the community issue – with its attendant structural constraints (special majorities) was emerging introducing new coalition models.[13]

When socio-economic change predominates, the choice of coalition will be between the centre-left CVP/PSC & PS/SP or the centre-right CVP/PSC & PRL/PVV. This assumes that the parliamentary arithmetic would permit both possibilities, but it is not always so. Indeed, in the 1991 legislature the centre-right option did not command a majority, whereas it has always done so in recent years. Where the community division is uppermost, the alternatives will be a grand coalition of the six traditional parties or the addition of one or more community parties (RW, FDF or Volksunie) to the basic centre-left or centre-right construct. The Tindemans II government had a centre-left core with the addition of the FDF and the Volksunie. The subsequent Martens I had the centre-left core with only the FDF. Martens VIII (1988-91) had the centre-left core with the addition of the Volksunie only.

Coalition theory also tends to consider parties as monolithic actors. This is clearly a simplification of a complex reality. In Belgium it is a false assumption when applied to the CVP/PSC and, especially, to the CVP.[14] These parties are pivotal in the political system, making choices between a centre-left coalition with the Socialist parties or a centre-right coalition with the Liberals. This choice is influenced if not determined by the balance between the almost institutionalised '*standen*' in the CVP or tendencies in the PSC. There are three of the former: the Catholic workers (ACW), the farmers (Boerenbond) and the so-called middle class of small businesses, shopkeepers and liberal professions. The strong ACW, in which both Martens and Dehaene but not Tindemans were active, has leant towards co-operation with the Socialists. The Boerenbond and the middle-class groups, have tended more in the opposite direction, towards coalitions with the Liberals. In the PSC there have not been *standen* but two organised wings. Leaning to the left is the union-based Démocratie Chrétienne which, though a minority, expanded its position in the party during the 1970s. It was counterbalanced by the rightist anti-union Mouvement Chrétien des Indépendants et des Cadres (MIC), which joined the militant Centre Politique des Indépendants et Cadres Chrétiens (CEPIC) in 1972. When the CEPIC became discredited through far right associations in 1978/9, the new PSC president, Gérard Deprez, disbanded party factions. However, a new body which officially did not breach that ban was then set up – the Rassemblement du Centre (RDC). These wings play the same balancing role as the CVP *standen*, providing the catalyst for periodic changes in partners for the PSC/CVP.

There has been a tendency since the 1960s for the coalition pacts to become even more detailed and technical, covering a wide range of issues, some of them uncontroversial. Often they are carried over from previous governments.

Before 1961 it was only the then unitary PSB/BSP that required ratification of the coalition pact and hence participation in government by a special party congress, but this has become general. However, it is largely a formality. A congress has only rejected the pact on one occasion– the Brussels Liberals in 1974.[15]. However, in 1988, 40 per cent of delegates in the PS opposed the pact, and the powerful Charleroi *fédération* cast a negative vote.[16] Parliamentary approval is virtually a formality, rarely with more than the odd maverick negative vote or abstention in the ranks of the government party MPs.

Once the principle of forming a government coalition between different parties to implement a given programme has been agreed, the distribution of portfolios must be considered. Certain posts may tend over the years to become the fiefs of certain parties or individuals. The foreign and defence ministries, agriculture and finance were a CVP or PSC fief with only occasional exceptions. However, in the Martens VIII government, the defence portfolio went to Guy Coëme (PS) and in the 1970s foreign affairs went to Henri Simonet (PS). In the Dehaene I coalition it went to Willy Claes (SP), who was earlier minister of economic affairs in several governments. The more 'noble' portfolios such as defence, justice, interior, finance and foreign affairs have never been accorded to minor coalition partners, such as the PCB in the 1940s or later to the community parties (RW, FDF, VU).[17]

There must be a balance (excluding the prime minister) between Flemish and Francophone ministers, but not between State Secretaries (junior ministers) who do not sit in the cabinet,[18] as laid down in article 86 *bis* of the Constitution). Usually, every coalition partner will nominate one vice premier. The vice premiers can form a collective inner cabinet, meeting to resolve key political issues; they also have a portfolio, usually a weighty one. Indeed, in the Martens VIII cabinet even the Volksunie vice premier Hugo Schilz held the Budgets portfolio. Ministers need not be parliamentarians, but in fact almost all are. Governments are sometimes composed of second-tier personnel, while real power remains in the hands of the party presidents outside the government. This was especially true of the Tindemans II (1977) government, in which the college of party presidents played a quasi-institutional role in arbitrating key issues.[19] This continued until the Martens V government, which saw all key party presidents enter the cabinet (Gol, De Clercq, Tindemans), leaving junior caretaker party presidents in their place. Since then, the weakened authority of the cabinet has been restored to a degree, but when Guy Spitaels was PS party president outside the cabinet (1988-91), it was clear that his authority was greater than that of any PS minister.

Until the full impact of the Reform of the State was felt, there was a tendency for the size of the cabinet to grow, due to the increasing functions of modern government, the creation of temporary regional executives within the national government, and the needs of regional and party balance in the very broad coalitions that were formed in the 1970s and 1980s.[20] Thus, there were five ministers in 1831, seven in 1878 and nineteen in 1946. The number of ministers has since expanded even more. The Eyskens government (1968) had twenty-nine ministers, the Leburton government (a tripartite) had twenty-two ministers and fourteen state secretaries. The Tindemans II (1977) government had twenty-three ministers and seven state secretaries. The first regionalised legislature, the Martens V centre-right coalition (1981), saw a reduction to sixteen ministers and eight state secretaries. Since then, the number of ministers has remained lower. Martens VI (1985-87) had fifteen ministers and thirteen state secretaries. Martens VIII, formed in 1988, originally had nineteen ministers and thirteen state secretaries, but when the latest phase of the Reform of the State was in place, the national government was slimmed down to seventeen ministers and ten state secretaries. The posts of minister of education and public works disappeared since these functions were fully devolved. Under the most recent Reform of the State package (the *Accord de la St Michel*, enacted in early 1993), the maximum size of the federal cabinet will be reduced to fifteen, with parity – excluding the prime minister – being retained.

State secretaries were first appointed in 1960, and have since been given formal constitutional recognition (Article 91 *bis*), but they do not belong to the cabinet and may not always be authorised to countersign bills or royal decrees. They are always placed under a specific minister.

Often, they are in a certain sense the eyes and ears of a different coalition partner in the ministry, but more recently have been appointed from the same party as the ministers whom they serve.

There are also a number of cabinet committees, all chaired by the prime minister, and on which all vice premiers and other relevant ministers sit. The most important of these are the *Comité de Politique Générale* (CPG) and the *Comité Ministériel de Coordination Economique et Sociale* (CMCES). In the Martens VIII government there were seven such committees. Their task is to prepare the decisions of the cabinet.[21]

The Belgian prime minister, like the British institution, grew initially through tradition. In the early years of Belgian independence the 'strong man' of a ministry, after whom it was named, might hold one of various key posts, usually foreign affairs, interior or finance. The *formateur* was head of the government, but was at best a *primus inter pares*. Gradually, in the twentieth century, the term 'prime minister' came into use. G. Theunis (Catholic), appointed in 1934, was the first to bear the title officially, but even then the post was not recognised constitutionally; this only happened in 1970. In our media age the position has grown in importance. Not only is the prime minister the animator and coordinator of the team, who chairs the cabinet and directs the work of the government, but is also its front person in the media as well as in Parliament, personifying the government at home and abroad, in the EC and internationally. He must be by nature a diplomat, a conciliator who resolves conflicts over policy and personalities within the government. Because it is crucial to gain the confidence of key ministers and party presidents from other coalition parties, he cannot be a strident party man. The power of the office has grown, but the constraints of coalition government and the fact that he is not the leader of his own party make him less powerful than his British counterpart.[22]

The Belgian government, like the British, does not vote but operates by consensus. The aim is to avoid conflict in the cabinet. Cabinet committee work, talks between the parties and between the prime minister and his vice premiers in the inner cabinet, the involvement if necessary of the party presidents all work for compromises that can be endorsed in cabinet without confrontation. The prime minister, also in the British style, will sum up the 'sense of the meeting'. The cabinet members must then in general support agreed government policy, as the cabinet has become a collective body. Theoretically, ministers can exercise considerable individual autonomy, presenting royal decrees for signature to the King in many cases without deliberation having taken place in cabinet. However, the political reality is that ministers must operate within cabinet policy, as that has been laid down in the government declaration. Indeed, many matters such as draft bills, foreign policy decisions and even royal decrees of importance and appointments must be submitted to the cabinet for final decision. There is more latitude for a degree of divergence among ministers, since forcing ministers from another coalition partner to resign would probably lead to the withdrawal of that party from the government and hence its fall. Indeed, internal divergences are the most frequent cause of Belgian governments breaking up, and the prime minister must guard against them, if necessary by loosening the reins.[23]

The central administration

On the French model, each minister appoints a 'cabinet' of personal advisers who do not form part of the civil service. These cabinets, which may include up to twenty members, are important as a go-between in negotiations between parties, ministers and 'social partners' (the two sides of industry) on one side and government on the other, as well as being influential in policy formulation within a ministry. These appointments are of course political and personal to the minister concerned. Cabinet advisers often come from the same party background as their ministers, and may have worked with them for many years.

There has been a tendency for at least senior appointments in the civil service and what are called in Belgium *organismes parastataux* (state enterprises or bodies) to become increasingly politicised, with coalition governments practising a '*proportz*' (or share-out) system between themselves.[24] There has also been the problem of achieving linguistic equilibrium in appointments, at all levels, especially in some areas such as development co-operation, where for obvious reasons French is a much more practically useful language than Dutch. This is the case, for example, in dealings with Francophone Africa.

The power of appointment to posts in the central administration and diplomatic service is expressly given by the Constitution to the King (Article 66 [1]). The right to make other appointments may only be given to the King by express legal provision. This gives some safeguard to the autonomy of regional, provincial and local government in the appointment of their personnel. For example, Articles 87 and 88 of the special law on the Reform of the State 1980[25] provide that the executives shall appoint their own personnel but that the conditions of employment in each category shall be the same as those applying to the national administration. The basic statute of all national civil servants is laid down in a royal decree of 1937, although more recent laws of 1965 and 1972 have updated some of the earlier provisions.[26]

Contrary to popular belief, the number of civil servants and of other public officials has not gone on rising, after peaking in the mid-1980s, but has actually fallen, as the following Table shows.[27] Furthermore, the state corporations have been transformed into state-owned but independent and

market-oriented corporations, with some minority infusion of private
capital and a degree of competition.

Ministries	31.12.1992	30.6.1982	30.6.1970	1964
Federal	60,667 (6.85%)			
Community/regions	24,432 (2.73%)			
Total	85,099 (9.60%)	91,290 (10.2%)	108,074 (17.49%)	99,198 (18.91%
Special bodies (police, military)	77,747 (8.79%)	87,194 (9.74%)	70, 596 (11.42%)	199,806 (38.11%) (incl. *onderwijs*)
Public corporations				
Federal	155,048 (17.52%)			
Community/regions	46,781 (5.28%)			
Total	201,829 (22.80%)	201,310 (22.50%)	115, 969 (18.77%)	126.292 (24.09%)
Teachers	281,225 (31.77%)	314,983 (35.21%)	202,088 (32.7%)	
Local/Provincial	237.368 (26.81%)	198,664 (22.20%)	120,299 (19.47%)	98,010 (18.7%)
Parliamentary staff	1,959 (0.22%)	1,317 (0.15%)	969 (0.15%)	1,000 (0.19%)
Total	885,227 (100%)	894,758 (100%)	617, 995 (100%)	524,306 (100%)

PARLIAMENT

The Constitution states that 'all power emanates from the nation' (Article
25[1]). Article 26 provides that legislative power be shared between the
executive and the legislature. This is the classic nineteenth-century
Liberal-Democratic model. Power emanates from the people, but is constitutionally delegated to Parliament and other organs. Thus, there is no
provision for referendums in the Belgian Constitution. Since in reality
executive power is exercised by the cabinet, which is responsible to
Parliament, Parliament becomes in theory the central body in the state,
representing the sovereignty of the people. However, Parliament itself is
not sovereign in the sense that the British Parliament is; it is bound by the
Constitution, which it can only amend by a special procedure (two-thirds
majority) after recourse to the electorate.

Belgium has not escaped the tendency in modern Western democracies
for this classic schema to be eroded. Power is more and more concentrated
and exercised outside Parliament – in the cabinet, in the parties, through
'corporatist' arrangements between the state and the two sides of industry
– making Parliament little more than a *'chambre d'enregistrement'* (a
rubber-stamping body) which gives its formal approval and therefore legal
effect to decisions already taken elsewhere. Parliament, however, retains
its function as an 'electoral college' from which the executive emerges,
although even here election results are often so ambiguous that the
political parties can create coalitions which seem almost to defy the verdict
of the electorate. One should not, however, overstate this case; Parliament
is and will remain an important actor on the Belgian political stage.

As we have seen, bi-cameralism was originally introduced to provide a blocking mechanism against the (already limited) 'dangers of radicalism in the Lower chamber'.[28] Gradually both chambers were democratised by changing the electoral qualifications, the electoral system and, for the Senate, qualifications for membership. In more recent years, with the emergency of parties as the dominant feature of political life, the Senate's composition has become almost a carbon copy of that of the House, with a slight advantage to the large 'national' parties. For this reason conflict between the two chambers is now almost excluded. The Senate's role as a 'revising' body has never seemed important, since its political independence is non-existent, but with the Reform of the State it is to find a new vocation.[29] The most recent stage in the Reform of the State, enacted in 1993, provides that eventually the Senate will be completely transformed into a body with almost no collective national role except in revising the Constitution and in framing special laws.

Parliament is elected for four years, but the King may dissolve it earlier. In recent years, few legislatures have come near their full term. Under the Constitution (Articles 7 and 56 *quater* [4]) the King – naturally only on a proposal from the cabinet – may dissolve one or both chambers. When the Senate is dissolved, he may also dissolve the provincial councils which elect a proportion of it. In fact, the dissolution of only one chamber is in modern terms very rare. The power of dissolution is the *quid pro quo* of cabinet responsibility to Parliament, avowing an appeal to the electors whereby a government has been censured. Since the mid-nineteenth century (cases occurred in 1833, 1851 and 1864), it has been almost impossible, although it can be argued that the 1977 election was caused by the Tindemans I government having lost its majority. Most dissolutions occur (as in 1981) because of internal dissensions in the ruling coalition.[30] As we shall see, the new Reform of the State limits the dissolution power.

The House of Representatives

The House of Representatives now has 150 members elected by universal suffrage for four years by proportional representation (PR). The original text of the Constitution provided for a minimum of one deputy (technically '*représentant*', although '*deputé*' is normal usage) for every 40,000 inhabitants, which led to a growth of the House's membership from 102 in 1831 to 212 in 1949, reduced to 150 in 1995. Since 1949, despite the increase in population, the various electoral laws have held the number of members static at the same level, and this norm was written into the Constitution (Article 49) in 1971. Each electoral district (*arrondissement*) is accorded a number of seats proportional to its population revealed in each census (not its number of voters), which includes foreigners (300,000 in the Brussels-Halle-Vilvoorde *arrondissement*). At the 1991 election this gave the distribution shown in the table below (with comparative figures for 1950 and 1978).[31]

Since the late 1960s, there has been a tendency for the representation of the Flemish provinces to be increased and representation of the Walloon provinces and Francophone Brabant to be reduced. There has also been some redistribution within Flanders and Wallonia. Limburg and Antwerp are growth areas, and Namur has increased its relative weight against the declining weight of the Hainaut and Liège provinces. Each province is split into between two and five *arrondissements*. The largest are Brussels-Halle-Vilvoorde (33 members), Antwerp (20), Liège (13), Ghent (12), Charleroi (10) and Leuven (9). The smallest, Neufchâteau-Virton in the Luxembourg province, retains only two members. In the final distribution of seats, the system of '*apparentements*' (alliances) at province level may replace one seat for arbitrary reasons.

	1991		1978		1950	
Brabant (Brussels)	48 (33)		48		44	
Antwerp	34		32		33	
East Flanders	28	} 101	29	} 98	30	} 98
West Flanders	23		23		24	
Limburg	16		14		11	
Hainaut	28		30		32	
Liège	21	} 63	22	} 65	24	} 71
Luxembourg	5		5		6	
Namur	9		8		9	

The electoral system

Since the European elections in June 1979, the citizen obtains the right to vote at the age of eighteen years; this first applied to parliamentary elections in 1981.[32] Candidates, on the other hand, must be at least twenty-five years old. Since 1893[33] voting has been compulsory – fines, albeit derisory (1–25 francs), may be levied on those who do not comply – and as a result the number of non-voters is very small: 5.22% for the whole country in 1978, with a high-point of 7.42% in Brussels.[34] Voters must vote in their *communes* but can do so in certain cases by proxy.

Article 48(2) of the Constitution lays down that elections to the House and Senate shall take place by 'a system of proportional representation as laid down by law'. This does not tie Parliament to a particular form of PR, but it makes a majority system unconstitutional. Since the introduction of PR in 1899, even before universal suffrage, there has been little variation in the basic system used: the D'Hondt list system, invented by a Belgian professor in the nineteenth century. Initially, Article 48 imposed the *arrondissement* and the province as the basic electoral units, which introduced very high *de facto* thresholds in smaller provinces. This was long contested by smaller parties as preventing full proportionality, as for example in the Netherlands. The law has reduced this disadvantage by permitting alliances between lists of the same party between *arrondisse-ments*, the so-called '*apparentement*', and a second distribution of seats for lists that obtain 66% of the quota for the House and 33% for the Senate. From 1978 onwards there was an intention to revise Article 48 to eliminate the province as an obligatory electoral area, and this was actually done in 1988. However, up till the time of writing no new electoral law has made use of this wider constitutional latitude.[35]

The Belgian system is a list system.[36] Parties or political movements may table lists. To do so they must be supported by between 200 and 500 electors (depending on the size of the *arrondissement*) or by three deputies. The list may contain candidates up to the maximum number of seats to be filled in the *arrondissement* and an equal number of candidates as '*suppléants*' (alternates who replace an elected candidate whose seat becomes vacant). The order of candidates is decided by the party in whatever manner it may determine (we shall look at this later). Voters may cast a valid vote in four ways. They may vote:

— for the list as a whole;
— for a given candidate by preference;
— for a given candidate and alternate by preference; or
— for an alternate by preference.

A vote for the list implies acceptance of the order established by the party.

Each list then receives a number of seats allocated in accordance with the D'Hondt system. The electoral law allows lists to conclude *apparentements* at the provincial level. Naturally lists of the same party do so. Sometimes 'cartel' lists are formed (as between the PS-RW in some provinces in 1974). These are not *apparentements*, but 'mixed' joint lists. The distribution of seats and the election of candidates is arrived at by the following four basic steps:

1. In each *arrondissement* of a province an electoral divisor is calculated:

$$\frac{\text{Total vote cast}}{\text{Seats to be filled}} = A$$

For each party an electoral quotient is calculated:

$$\frac{\text{Votes cast for that list}}{A} = B$$

The first distribution allocates a seat or seats to each list having an electoral quotient of one or more.

2. After this distribution, some seats will remain to be filled. Only those

lists with an electoral quotient of at least 0.66 in one *arrondissement* may participate in the second division. This reduces the value of *apparentement* to small parties (e.g. to the Ecologists or the Walloon list in Hainaut in 1981). For each qualified list, the number of votes cast in the whole province is divided successively by the number of seats already won plus one, then two, three (e.g. 1, 3, 5, ...), and so on. The quotients thus obtained are classified in descending order, until all the remaining seats are allocated.

3. It remains to allocate the second distribution of seats to an *arrondissement*. Local quotients are calculated for each list as follows:

$$\frac{\text{Electoral quotient in the } arrondissement}{\text{First-distribution seats} + 1, 2 \ldots}$$

The seats for each party are then allocated to an *arrondissement* in accordance with the size of the local quotients of that party in descending order.

4. The final stage is the election of candidates to fill the seats allocated to each list. A 'list quotient' is calculated:

$$\frac{\text{Votes obtained}}{\text{Seats to be filled} + 1}$$

The votes given to the list as a whole are used as a 'pot' to top up the preference votes given to candidates, but the preference votes can upset the order of the list established by the party. In this case they tend to do so in the middle of the list, rather than at the top which is rarely affected. There has been a growing tendency to give preference votes.

Example List X obtains 100,000 votes and five seats. List quotient = 20,000. List votes = 50,000, preference votes = 50,000.

Candidates	Topping-up of preference vote	Order of election
A 20,500	–	(1)
B 8,000	+ 12,000	(2)
C 3,000	+ 17,000	(3)
D 3,500	+ 16,500	(4)
E 2,000	+ 4,500 (remainder)	
F 3,500		(5)
G 8,000		
H 1,000		
I 400		
J 600		
50,000	50,000	

Candidates E and F are thus elected. It should be noted that a higher preference vote does not ensure election in order of 'merit'; for example, D is elected after C. This example is typical in that a relatively modest preference vote for a 'middle-order' candidate can reverse the order of the list, which is why certain popular figures accept a 'marginal' position on the list, often called '*la position de combat*'.

The parties determine the order of candidates on their lists according to their statutes and internal procedures. There are various types of procedure, some of which are relatively centralised and others more democratic. In the Socialist Party, especially in the Charleroi and Borinage Regions, there is a lively tradition of 'polls', i.e. votes by all party members, whereas in Brussels the PS Federation leadership has always avoided them. In some *arrondissements* the CVP also has a tradition of holding such polls;[37] the party statute generally provides for them (para. 37), but it allows the national executive to provide for exceptions where they are not held: small *arrondissements*, elections at short notice and, in all cases, if there are amendments to the list by a three-quarters majority.[38] The FDF, on the other hand, provides (by Articles 23 of its statutes) for a '*commission électorale élargie*', mostly chosen from the executive, to fix the list after receiving candidatures from the sections, over and above the outgoing FDF deputies and senators.[39]

Under the most recent phase of the Reform of the State, the size of the House is reduced to 150 members to be elected by the D'Hondt system in the previous senatorial electoral *arrondissement* (see below).

Election of the Senate

Originally, as we have seen, the Senate was intended to be a conservative counterweight to the more democratic House.[40] Both its electorate and, even more, the reservoir of those eligible for membership were very restricted. It was hoped that at a later stage the introduction of senators elected by the provincial councils and by cooption would enable the Senate to represent the various regions of the country, as well as economic and social interests, and to introduce some political personalities outside the cut and thrust of day-to-day partisanship, in much the same way as is done with the cross-bench element in the British Upper House. However, this has not worked. The Senate has become as politicised as the House, whose composition it almost exactly mirrors. Party discipline is also just as strong. It never happens now that independents are elected or even co-opted to the Senate. Only in 1958, when the CVP/PSC won an absolute majority in the Senate but not in the House, was there a serious divergence. With the smaller *arrondissements* for directly-elected senators, the small parties are at some slight disadvantage.

The 1921 compromise that introduced higher educational and financial requirements for election to the Senate while eliminating restrictions on the electorate (such as a minimum tax payment of 3,000 BF!) had become meaningless in modern times. These restrictions have now been abolished. Only the age-limit of forty has been retained. The Senate has four categories of members elected in three stages (this too will be radically altered under the *Accord de la St Michel*):

Directly-elected senators. There are 106 directly-elected senators, half the number of members of the House of Representatives.[41] They are elected at the same time as the House, according to the same basic system, in *arrondissements* with *apparentement* at province level for lists that reach 33% of the electoral quota (average number of votes needed to elect a senator) in at least one *arrondissement* in a given province. There is usually very little variation at the national level between the share of the vote obtained by House and Senate lists: in 1991 the widest variation was +0.3% for the PVV Senate list, although at local level divergences were much wider.

Provincial senators.[42] This category, introduced in 1893, is elected by the provincial councils by proportional representation. Normally, the provincial councils are elected on the same day as the House and the directly-elected senators, hence their political composition is almost identical. Each province elects at least three senators; there is one senator for every 200,000 of their population and one for any 'remainder' above 125,000 inhabitants. Those elected may not be members of the provincial council that elects them. The distribution by province is less than perfectly proportional to population:

	1970	*1987*
Antwerp	8	8
Brabant	11	11
Hainaut	6	6
Liège	5	5
Limburg	3	3
Luxembourg	3	3
Namur	3	3
West Flanders	5	7
East Flanders	6	5
Total	50	51

Co-opted senators. The first two categories meet and elect a number of additional senators, again by PR, equivalent to half the number of provincial senators. At present there are 26 co-opted senators.[43]

Ex-officio senators. Royal princes are *ex-officio* members, but take no part in political life.

Thus, at present, the Senate has 183 members. Its full composition only becomes known some two weeks after the election following intense bargaining within and between parties. The positions of provincial and co-opted senators are used by parties as 'correctives' to rescue defeated candidates for the House or direct Senate seats and to cut deals with small partners. In this way the PS has often co-operated with the RW and Ecologists. A politician whose star is waning may be successively deputy, elected senator, provincial senator and co-opted senator before disappearing into oblivion. Of course the co-opted or provincial senators are more beholden to the party leadership for their election.

There are no by-elections in Belgium, but there is a separate list of '*suppléants*' (replacements). The *suppléant* is taken in order from that list and not from the list of non-elected candidates, although some candidates also appear on the *suppléants* list. This is the only way to 'move up' during the course of the legislature's term. Some politicians prefer to seek election only as *suppléants* in view of the increasingly strict legal and party rules about '*cumul des mandats*' (multiple office-holding). For example, it is legally forbidden to be a Member of the European Parliament (MEP) and a national deputy at the same time. Election as a *suppléant* while serving as a mayor, EC Commissioner or MEP increases a politician's range of choices.

As we see below, the composition and powers of the Senate have been radically altered by the most recent Reform of the State, enacted in April 1993 and to be applied after the 1995 elections.

The powers of the two chambers

With certain minor exceptions, the two chambers have equal powers and functions,[44] and legislation must be passed in the same form by both of them. Financial appropriation acts must pass both chambers: however, financial measures must be introduced in the House of Representatives first. The latter alone may impeach ministers before the *Cour de Cassation* (supreme court). The Senate proposes candidates for appointment to the *Cour de Cassation*. The Senate may not meet when the House is not is session. Broken down into its two linguistic groups, the directly-elected senators form the regional assemblies, which have important legislative powers in their own regions and communities under the provisions for the Reform of the State.

For matters relating to the succession to the throne, e.g. the declaration under Article 82 (applied in 1945 to Leopold III) that the King is 'unable to reign' (*impossibilité de régner*), the two chambers meet and vote in joint session.

Because, at least till 1893 if not 1921, the Senate formerly had no real democratic basis, the tradition had developed to regard the House of Representatives as the true representative of the people and the Senate as an upper house, a revising or 'blocking' chamber. This tendency still survives. New governments first seek the confidence of the House, which virtually binds the Senate although it in turn is called upon to approve a new government. Conflict has been rare. A study has shown that in the 1977-81 period the second chamber to vote on a bill amended it in only 5.42% of cases.[45]

Following the recasting of the Senate under the 1993 *Accord de la St Michel* to make it a regionally-based second chamber, there will be a clear functional division of labour between the two chambers. The Senate will no longer be co-equal with the House. It will still be required to pass constitutional amendments by a two-thirds majority and special laws by the same special majority as in the House. It will have no role in relation to giving a vote of confidence to governments or approving the annual budget. Over ordinary bills it will have a right to propose amendments within a tight time-limit of thirty days. Its delaying power is less than that of the British House of Lords.

The House of Representatives will be the basic legislator. It will invest governments and it alone will be able to remove the cabinet, but only by a so-called constructive motion of non-confidence, which must propose a new prime minister to replace the censured holder of that office. This actually makes a censure motion almost impossible to achieve under Belgian conditions. The House will also be solely responsible for passing the annual budget.

The dissolution of the House and Senate (relevant only to the part which is directly elected) can only occur under the new arrangements before the end of the four-year term if a government should lose the confidence of the House, and where a new prime minister cannot be elected under the constructive no-confidence motion system. This is the German model and should made early elections rare.

The future of the Senate

As we have seen, there has always been debate about the role of the Senate. Indeed, during the National Congress in 1831, there was considerable debate about the Senate and a large minority that regarded it as useless. The nineteenth-century Senate avoided conflict with the House, playing a relatively minor role in political life. Initially its role was seen as acting as a conservative check on the lower chamber, but this has disappeared . Then there was the idea of making it a regional and expert chamber, freed from narrow political partisan control, which lay behind the reform of the 1920s introducing co-opted senators and looking to elected senators for certain educational qualifications or experience of business or government, but his never made headway. As Belgium moved towards a federal structure in the 1970s, the question of the role of the Senate was raised again. A reform to make the Senate a federal-type upper chamber was first raised in the Egmont pact (1977), and revision of the articles of the Constitution relating to it was contained in the 1978 and 1981 revision declarations, but no progress was made.

The 1980 special law appears to see the community and regional assemblies as being composed of national directly-elected senators and representatives, but only transitionally; it speaks of directly-elected senators in the final phase of the Reform of the State. The 1988 government declaration refers to the third phase of the Reform of the State, in which, among other matters, the direct election of the community and regional assemblies and the composition of the Senate would be dealt with. These issues of direct election and reform of both the composition and role of the Senate are seen as closely interlinked. The Brussels regional council (since 1989) and the German community council (since 1973) are directly elected and it is intended that the other assemblies shall be so.

The 1989 proposals remained vague. The government put forward two options. Either the reformed Senate would be 'an emanation of the regional and community assemblies', i.e. its members would be chosen by and perhaps among the members of those assemblies, and would then only exercise reserve powers to protect at the federal level the interests of the regions and communities where constitutional revision and institutional matters are concerned. The government would certainly not be responsible before the Senate; the latter's powers over other legislation might be limited to the right to propose amendments which the House could reject. The second option sees a Senate with a directly elected base and wider powers over all national matters. No progress was made on the third phase. The issue remains very much open.

As we see in Chapter 5, the so-called third phase was not achieved during the 1987-91 legislature and the joint parliamentary commission reached no meaningful consensus on the Senate. In the *Accord de la St Michel* (September 1992) enacted in 1993, the composition and powers of the Senate were radically revised. The new Senate, from 1994, will be mixed body, not corresponding wholly to either of the 1989 options. Like its predecessor, it too will have four categories of senators:[46]

Directly-elected senators. There will be 40 of these, and the same system will be used as for the European elections. There will be a Flemish collège with 25 seats and a Francophone one with 15. In Brussels-Halle-Vilvoorde, voters may vote for either the Flemish or Francophone list.

Community senators. The community councils will elect 21 senators from among their members. Ten will be elected by the Flemish council, ten by the French community council and one by the German community council.

Co-opted senators. There will be ten co-opted senators (six Flemish and four Francophone).

Ex-officio senators. The Royal princes, as at present.

This would give a total of seventy-one members, excluding the *ex-officio* senators. The CVP insisted on retaining at least some directly-elected senators. The Senate will become essentially a body with reserve and revising powers. The reform of the Senate remains the least coherent and satisfactory part of the whole structure of the Reform of the State, but no coherent design, in any direction, could find broad support. There is a significant regional/community input, but with twenty-one out of seventy-one members remains less than a clear blocking third, although the co-opted members will have to be acceptable to the communities.

The organisation of Parliament

There is considerable similarity in the internal organisation and functioning of the two chambers, though this may now change. We concentrate here in more detail on the House of Representatives (abbreviated to 'House') and indicate where the Senate has special characteristics. The main bodies[47] established in each chamber are the president, the vice-presidents and secretaries, the bureau, the conference of presidents, the college of quaestors, the committees and political groups. There are also several working parties for internal administrative matters, some of which are joint bodies with the Senate. Each chamber elects its president for the term of the legislature. In reality, these posts are part of the negotiations surrounding the formation of the government. This was well illustrated in 1988 when the Senate elected Roger Lallemand (PS) as president during the long crisis, only to replace him with Mr Kelchtermans (CVP) when the government was formed in May. The president has often been an elder statesman or former prime minister (Van Acker, Huysmans, Leburton in the House; Struye, Harmel in the Senate). He is assisted by a number of vice-presidents (six in the House and three in the Senate) and secretaries (eight in the House and six in the Senate). The bureau[48] in both chambers is composed of president, vice-presidents, secretaries, quaestors, and the chairs of political groups with more than twelve members in the House but not in the Senate. The bureau is responsible, with the college of quaestors (made up of deputies, who deal with members' facilities), for administrative, financial and staff matters. In both chambers there is a conference of presidents.[49] These bodies are responsible for the political organisation of parliamentary work as distinct from administrative matters. They are composed of the president, vice-presidents, former presidents and group leaders. The government is represented by the prime minister or another minister, and committee chairmen attend. The conferences meet in principle once a week, on Wednesdays at 11.30, and in the 1990/1 session the conference of presidents in the House of Representatives met forty-six times. It is a forum for discussion between the official groups; it proposes the agenda of sittings and deals with the procedure to be followed on such matters as oral questions and interpellations. The bureau makes a proposal to the full House on the order of business. The government or a minimum of twelve members (in the House) may propose amendments.

Originally the two chambers used to divide into sections – six in the House and four in the Senate – which were a sort of sub-Parliament. However, in recent years they have not been active: for example, between the 1976/7 and 1980/1 sessions only one section met at all. These sections were abolished in a major reform of procedures in 1987 since they in fact duplicated the work of the committees.

Until the 1960s each chamber tended to have a restricted number of permanent committees, with one per government department and some purely parliamentary ones such as that responsible for rules of procedure. Then there was a certain proliferation of committees in both chambers, reaching twenty-three in the House and twenty-two in the Senate in 1980; there was then an effort to reduce their number. There are at the time of writing eighteen committees in the House, as against thirteen in 1982.[50]

House committees have twenty-three members and a number of alternates. In the 1987-91 legislature, the FDF and Vlaams Blok were not represented because they were too small. Each committee has a president, vice president and secretary. Several committees are chaired by opposition members (PRL and PVV). Nine are genuine permanent committees. The others are special committees with a narrow remit or a temporary character, or a purely parliamentary function. Several sub-committees have been set up, and a special budget committee, created from the standing finance committee and the chairmen of the other committees. In the Senate there are sixteen permanent committees, a rules committee and a credentials committee. Senate committees also have twenty-three members and, as in the House, a fixed number of seats per group. In 1987-91 three committees were chaired by opposition (PRL-PVV) members. Even the smallest government party, with one seat in each committee, held a committee chair. The most important committees in each chamber were finance, external relations, justice, defence, infrastructure and economic affairs.

The activity of the House of Representatives (at the 1990/1 session) is summarised in the Table:[51]

All Committees

| | 1985/6 | | 1990/1 | |
	Meetings	Length (hrs)	Meetings	Length (hrs)
Public sessions	159	423	346	562
Closed sessions	255	n.a.	368	622
of which hearings	n.a.	n.a.	17	n.a.
Total	414	750 (est.)	714	1,184

Breakdown by Committees (Top Six)

	Meetings	Length	Interpellations	Bills
Justice	87	165	14	39
Finance	68	112	21	35
Interior	71	96	14	42
Economic	55	95	18	20
Infrastructure	55	86	24	22
Social Affairs	60	85	28	24

The role of committees is to consider in detail bills that fall within their remit and report them to the full House, with or without amendments.[52] In the course of working on a bill they call for written submissions and hold auditions with interested parties. All deputies can submit written observations even if they are not on a particular committee. Committees also exercise control functions on behalf of parliament as a whole, considering less important interpellations, oral questions and ministerial explanations. The government always takes part in committee work. Staff of political groups (also those not represented in committees) attend meetings and report back to their groups.

Each chamber has two linguistic groups (French and Dutch), which can exercise specific functions such as activating the so-called 'alarm bell procedure' (Article 38 *bis*) that suspends consideration of an item where the interests of one community appear to be adversely affected. These have no real structure, but can and do meet when the occasion so demands.

The rules of both chambers recognise political groups, but the conditions they impose for their recognition are minimal. In the House a group must have three members, hence in the 1987-91 legislature the two Vlaams Blok deputies could not be recognised as a group. The groups elect a president and a small bureau of up to five members. Several groups set up small specialised working groups (PVV, VU etc.). Groups organise study days or conferences on special themes, and most met between twelve and twenty-five times during the 1990/1 session. Several groups have meetings with their counterparts in the other House. The CVP group in the House has established coordinators in each committee and appointed a staff member to follow its working. The coordinator and staff members hold prepatory meetings of CVP members in their committee.[53]

There seemed to be no organised coordination between political families (CVP/PSC, PS/SP and PRL/PVV). The PVV introduced a British-style innovation: a PVV 'shadow cabinet' under Guy Verhofstadt. This however is an alien concept in Belgium, and has not caught on. The style of Belgian parliamentary politics is consensual rather than conflictual; groups do not seek to pose as 'the opposition'. The music changes and partners change. Over-violent criticism might be regretted later. Furthermore, there is no single opposition. The PVV shadow cabinet did not even contain PRL members. There are always several opposition groups. At present there are Greens, FDF, Liberals, Vlaams Blok and the Van Rossem members (those on the list led by the idiosyncratic anarchic millionaire J.P. van Rossem, often referred to simply as Rossem). These cannot offer a coherent alternative and would not associate with each other, except (without the Vlaams Blok) on some procedural matters relating to the rights of Parliament.

The complexity of the parliamentary calendar, with deputies and directly-elected senators also sitting in the Vlaamse Raad, and in the Walloon regional council, and with the French community council and council of the Brussels region also using the building, has made it necessary to coordinate activities at least in relation to the dates of sessions. Hence, the *Conférence des Cinq Présidents* (the Senate, the House, three regional/community councils) has been established to coordinate the work of the various assemblies.[54] It met three times during the 1990/1 session.

Both chambers normally hold an annual ordinary session from October to October when elections or extraordinary sessions have been held. On average, the Senate holds eighty sittings (mornings and afternoons) per session. In 1979, the House of Representatives met on seventy-one days (410 hours). In 1985/6 it held sixty-three sittings (266 hours) and in 1990/1 seventy-one sittings (252 hours). There has not been a tendency to increase sittings or at least not the total sitting time – rather the contrary. Ordinarily, neither chamber sits on Saturday or Monday, but with the hectic pressure of the Reform of the State, both have sat during the weekend in recent years. Night sessions are rare.[55]

Parliamentary control is one of the main functions of both chambers, in addition to legislation. Both receive the government's policy declarations and can vote on motions of confidence or no-confidence, both in relation to these declarations and following interpellation debates or some aspect of government policy.[56] Interpellations, which are questions followed by debate, and which can lead to a motion (*'ordre du jour'*) being tabled and voted on, are the heavy parliamentary artillery. Only the most important interpellations are debated on the floor if the Conference of Presidents so decides, all others being debated in committee only. The opposition may table a 'reasoned motion' (a motion setting out reasons for a given position) or even a censure motion, although this is quite rare (about one per session). When this happens, the majority parties counter by tabling a simple *ordre du jour* which is voted on first, and if it is carried, as it always is, it makes the reasoned motion void. In the 1990/1 session, 378 interpellations were tabled, but only thirty-three were debated on the floor of the House of Representatives and 284 were discussed in committee; the remaining sixty-one were referred.[57] Those discussed in plenary ranged far and wide, covering immigration policy, Zaïre, economic policy, the third phase of the Reform of the State, the teachers' strike and agricultural policy.[58] The largest number of interpellations in committee were debated in the committees for foreign affairs (45), the interior (32), and social affairs (25). In thirteen cases these resulted in motions tabled on the floor of the House, raising the political profile of the issue.[59]

Members may also ask oral questions on the floor of the House. There is provision in both chambers for a 'question time' at least once a week for the first hour of business, normally on Thursdays. There is no provision for supplementary questions, and no debate takes place, nor can a motion be tabled. Ministers are restricted to a maximum of three minutes for their replies. In 1985/6, there were 144 oral questions, which rose to 206 in the 1989/90 session and 247 in 1990/1. The number of questions has declined since the early 1980s, when, for example, there were 299 in 1979/80 and 258 in 1980/1. The same trend can be seen in written questions: 4,900 in 1979/80; 5,326 in 1980/1; 4,353 in 1985/6; 2,546 in 1989/90 and 2,318 in 1990/1.[60] Written questions must be answered within fifteen days. There are fewer questions in the Senate, both oral and written. Speaking time is always severely limited, except for *rapporteurs* on bills and ministers. The longest time allocation is thirty minutes for an intervention in a general debate on a bill. Interpellations are allotted fifteen minutes.[61]

As we have seen, there is to be a division of labour between the two chambers. The control function will in future be the sole prerogative of the House of Representatives.

Legislative work. The technicialities of the legislative process are, of course, the same for every bill: proposal, three readings and committee stage in each chamber and, if necessary, a *'navette'* (shuttle) between House and Senate until an identical bill is approved by both chambers and then signed by the King, counter-signed by a minister and published in the *Moniteur Belge* (official journal). Yet no bill is exactly like any other. There are several types of bills. There are the routine, uncontroversial ones, which make up the mass of legislative work; and there are those which are politically controversial, such as Reform of the State measures, which require a special majority and represent central planks in the government's programme, and, for example, economic, fiscal and social measures or ones that deal with the structure of local government or state enterprises. Such measures are usually approved, with the government majority voting for, and the opposition parties all voting against. The influence of Parliament on Reform of the State measures may be significant but its influence on socio-economic legislation is limited and may be less than that of important groups.

Special power bills. There are two types: extraordinary powers and special powers. Both types in effect delegate the power to legislate by decree to the government for a limited period and in limited areas. The more extreme form, which has only been enacted in times of the most severe crisis (1939 and 1944), allow government to enact decree-laws that can themselves be implemented by decrees. Such laws cover a broad area and refer to measures needed to 'ensure the security and independence of the national territory, public order and the country's financial and economic interests'. There could hardly be a broader remit. No special majority is needed to adopt such laws and the decrees are not subject to judicial review under Article 107 of the Constitution.[62] It should be noted that decrees are executive instruments signed by the monarch (equivalent to orders-in-council in Britain).

The more usual special powers acts have become ever more frequent (1914, 1932, 1935, 1937, 1939, 1944-7, 1957, 1961, 1967, 1978, 1980, 1982, 1983, 1984, 1986). Indeed, during the 1982-7 period, such powers were in force for thirty-two months and 545 individual royal decrees were enacted. However, although such special powers acts are more limited both in time and in material scope, the royal decrees can amend prior law where the parent act so provides, and after the expiry of the parent act, they can only be amended by a law. Thus, in 1982, it was possible for indexation of wages to be suspended by royal decree. There has been some criticism of this procedure, especially by Parliament, but no action has resulted.

The presidents of the House in 1982-6, Jean Defraigne (PRL) and Charles-Ferdinand Nothomb (PSC), both frequently complained about the procedure, and both had been members of governments that had recourse to special powers. However, in the 1982-6 period there was perhaps excessive use of the procedure, and it was not used in the 1987-91 legislature. The advantage for the centre-right coalition of 1981-7 was that PSC and CVP deputies from their parties' trade union wing were spared from having to vote on anti-trade union measures, and indeed the procedure may well have been used at the insistence of the PSC/CVP. Certainly its excessive use has not enhanced the reputation of Parliament.[63]

The use of various other broad, general forms of legislation that delegate wide rule-making power to the executive has also developed over the last thirty years. These 'framework' or 'programme' laws have greatly enhanced the power of the executive and reduced the detailed power of amendment of Parliament, which is merely called on to approve very general long-term infrastructural plans and the like. These laws are no more than broad directives, and they are meaningless without implementing decrees. Programme laws often come close to mixing budgetary and legislative provisions in the same law, which is not permitted. All in all, these types of legislation represent a very broad interpretation of those provisions in the Constitution (Articles 29, 67 and even 78) that permit a degree of delegation.[64]

Bills originate either with the government (*projets de loi*) or with deputies (*propositions de loi*). The *projets de loi* (government bills) have absolute priority and, short of a government crisis, almost every one of them passes. The *propositions de loi* that come from members or groups, often opposition groups, have little chance of passing and must be considered as propagandistic or kite-flying efforts to get an issue aired. Such proposals are never taken up for consideration and do not pass the '*prise en considération*' stage. In 1989/90, 120 government bills were tabled and 113 passed. None were rejected or withdrawn. In 1990/1, 139 bills were tabled and 140 were passed (one from a previous session). Government bills can be defeated or withdrawn – this happened to seventeen in 1986/7 and one in 1985/6. In 1985/6, 509 *propositions de loi* were tabled and only fourteen adopted. In 1990/1, 229 were tabled, thirty-four were adopted and seventy-three rejected or withdrawn. The rest were never even considered. All these figures refer to the House;[65] in the Senate the position is generally similar.

When a bill is tabled by the government, it must in most cases be examined by the *conseil d'état*'s legislation section, which gives an advisory opinion on its legality according to the Constitution, the distribution of competences and the technical issues raised. The presidents of the two chambers, the government or a majority in either chamber can refer to the *conseil d'état* for an opinion any bill, whether it be a *projet*, a *proposition de loi*, or an amendment. Such a referral automatically suspends Parliament's deliberations on a bill.

The *conseil d'état*, which was established in 1946, is modelled on the equivalent body in France. It has twenty-four members appointed for life by the King on a proposal from the House of Representatives and the Senate alternatively.[66] It examines preliminary draft bills prepared by the government and its opinion is annexed to them. Its opinion is not binding but is extremely influential with Parliament, especially where it considers a proposal to be unconstitutional. The government frequently modifies bills following the *conseil's* opinion. Government bills are automatically '*prise en considération*'. Other bills (which cannot be financial bills) require five sponsors and a majority vote if they are to be taken up for consideration.

If taken up, the bill then goes either to a permanent committee as the main committee or, in the case of the European elections bill or Reform of the State bills, to a special committee, as the main committee and other committees may be asked to give an opinion to that main committee. Each committee appoints one or more *rapporteurs*. The committee discusses the bill with the sponsoring minister, may hear evidence in hearings, although this is rare, and may receive observations from interested parties. Sub-committees may be formed to examine bills and hold hearings – examples have been those on tobacco advertising or the reform of the '*mutualités*' during the 1990/1 session. Amendments may be tabled by members and by the government. It is not unusual for government bills to be amended following inter-party agreement. The committee votes on the amendments and reports the bill out to the full House or Senate. The report contains observations on the bill, a revised text if one has been agreed, and the voting on amendments.

The plenary proceeds to a general debate, then votes on each amendment (for which five signatories are needed) and each article. The 'alarm bell procedure' (Article 38 *bis* of the Constitution) can suspend consideration of the measure at this stage, but it has only been used once. Minor matters can be dealt with directly without a committee report in the Senate. Otherwise, the legislative procedures are identical. For a bill to pass, both chambers must agree on identical versions. There is no conciliation committee procedure, and neither chamber has the last word. Deadlock is rare, and in practice it is the Senate that tends to give way. Those procedures have now been revised, with the House having the last word on all ordinary and financial legislation.

Financial legislation. Several articles in the Constitution are devoted to public finances (Articles 110, 111, 112, 113, 115 and 116) and financial control. The supremacy of Parliament is clearly established. No tax or other levy may be imposed except by legislation and the courts have clearly established that it is the substance of a measure and not its name that determines whether it falls under this provision. If a measures is really a tax, then it is covered. Taxes must be voted or renewed annually, and for no more than a year at a time (Article 111). However, in complex modern times it is permissible for tax rates to be altered by a royal decree. State expenditure (appropriations) must also be determined by law every year (Article 115). It is also necessary for the budget to include income and expenditure.[67]

The increasing complexity of government and the need to plan expenditure over a period of several years have led governments to treat the constitutional rules as formalities to be met by use of provisional appropriation bills when the deadline of September 30 has not been met for tabling the budget, enabling the thirty bills or so which have not been passed by the end of the year to come into force in time for the new financial year. Frequent supplementary appropriations are pushed through each year, using the government's docile majority. As a result, Parliament was tending to become a financial rubber-stamp, losing political oversight of expenditure since it could never form a clear and comprehensible view of the overall situation.

Previously Parliament gave priority to budgetary bills between September and December, with a deadline for the main ways and means budget of December 25, and March 30 for all others. Budget bills were examined in the finance committee of House and Senate, and each ministry's budget was also examined in the relevant committee. There is a rapid procedure in committee, and floor debate remains quite general and speaking time limited, although there are votes on individual items. Budget bills may not have non-budgetary items included in them. A budget is usually only examined in detail in one chamber, the other passing it on the nod. For certain types of expenditure multi-annual commitment appropriations can be voted, and transfers between items are possible. The level of approved appropriations can be overspent in cases of manifest urgency, provided the court of auditors and Parliament are informed and the additional amount is included in a supplementary appropriation bill. In reality, public expenditure was increasingly under little real parliamentary control.

As a result, Parliament, through a joint committee of both chambers, set in train a serious reform of budgetary procedures, which led to the adoption of a new budgetary procedure law in June 1989. The main aim was to ensure timely adoption of the budget after adequate scrutiny.[68] In 1990, the reform was extended to require each government department to make a budgetary policy statement each year at the outset of the procedure (by September 10). A general budget – one single budget – was established, broken down into a clear programme structure. The right of the government to exceed appropriations and to draw on advances was restricted, and parliamentary control over implementation during the year was reinforced. The budgetary policy statements were reviewed in each standing committee as background to the budget debate. The 1990 and 1991 budgets were tabled in time (before September 30) and, for the first time since the war, approved in time.[69]

Parliament exercises control over the implementation of the budget. As part of the 1989 reform, the court of auditors produced a projection of the accounts for the 1990 financial year in June 1991 and the House voted a resolution on July 6. The government must present the accounts of the previous year by August with the observations of the court of auditors. Parliament must then pass a discharge law, and failure to do so would amount to a motion of no-confidence. The court of auditors, which has ten members with financial expertise appointed by the House for a renewable term of six years, examines the legality and soundness of expenditure and can impose financial penalties on officials responsible for misusing public funds; its rulings can be appealed to the *Cour de Cassation*. The court of auditors is the long arm of Parliament in this very complex area.[70]

Parliament and foreign policy. Parliament exercises powers of oversight in the field of foreign policy through its treaty-making and budgetary powers.[71] In modern times, the complexity and intensity of foreign relations has tended to reduce the real influence of Parliament and strengthen the executive. In Belgium this tendency has been reinforced by the increasing role of the European Community where the government may agree to, or else be outvoted on, far-reaching measures, with direct effect without any prior parliamentary control. We look at the more recent efforts to improve co-operation between the Belgian Parliament and the Belgian MEPs through the creation of a joint consultative committee ('*comité d'avis*') in Chapter 8. The transfer of treaty-making powers to the communities has also reduced the role of the national Parliament in foreign policy.

Amendments to the Constitution. Under Article 131 of the Constitution, amendments must be explicit. A complex and difficult procedure is laid down, with the implied aim of limiting the number of amendments and creating constitutional stability. Indeed, in the nineteenth and early twentieth centuries, amendments were few and mostly concerned with extension of the franchise and the electoral system (1893, 1920, 1921). Since 1969, an increasing number of important revisions have been undertaken (1969, 1970, 1971, 1980, 1983, 1988, 1993) in connection with the Reform of the State.

Revision cannot take place when Parliament cannot meet freely on Belgian territory or in time of war. The first step is for Parliament (both chambers) to adopt by a simple majority a '*Déclaration de Révision de la Constitution*' (declaration of intent to revise), indicating the articles that require revision. The draft is referred to a special committee and amendments may be moved on the floor in either chamber. On several occasions before 1991, amendments were proposed to include the right of foreign residents to vote in local elections, but up till that year these were defeated. In 1987 several alternative Reform of the State proposals were put forward (by the Volksunie, FDF, PS, SP, Ecolo/Agalev and Vlaams Blok), as well as those agreed between the four coalition parties of the time (CVP/PSC and PVV/PRL).[72] Sometimes, as in 1985, the outgoing Parliament fails to vote on a declaration and hence the next legislature cannot revise the Constitution. The declaration need not state in detail *how* a given article should be revised, but only that it should be revised. Sometimes it is merely stated that 'Article 113 should be revised' or, more precisely, 'It is necessary to revise Article 113 to provide for the annuality of budgets of the regions'. On the other hand, the revision of Articles 59 *bis* and 17 in 1987 were a package involving a detailed agreement to devolve education to the communities. Adoption of the declaration automatically leads to the dissolution of Parliament and new elections. The newly-elected House may, but need not, revise all or some of the articles designated, but it cannot revise any others.

Actual revision requires adoption of revised articles in both chambers in identical form by a two-thirds majority of those voting, provided two-thirds of the total membership is present. However, there is no requirement for majorities in each linguistic group. Governments therefore often seek a two-thirds majority when they are formed. It is rare, but not impossible, for the government to find additional votes from the opposition benches when it lacks a two-thirds majority on its own. That happened over the major Reform of the State revision of 1971, where some Liberal support was available, and for less controversial articles in 1983/4, and in 1992/3 over the *Accord de la St Michel*, which was supported from outside by the Volksunie, Ecolo and Agalev.

The Influence of Parliament

The Belgian Parliament has always had less real influence than in some other northern European countries. Since the late 1950s, the crisis of confidence that has affected all western democracies has not passed Belgium by, and in this period Parliament's real influence has declined: it has been seen more as a rubber-stamp for decisions effectively taken elsewhere than as the nerve-centre of political life. Governments are made and unmade outside Parliament. Rival power centres in the parties and pressure groups have proliferated.

Parliament is neither a forum of confrontation as in Britain nor one of consensus as in the Nordic countries, and as an element of the political system it has been discredited. Opposition is weak and divided. Government deputies are there to support the government and often may not propose bills, amendments or interpellations without the prior authorisation of their groups. There are discussions in progress of plans to revitalise and rationalise Belgian bi-cameralism; these involve some useful reforms of modest scope generated by a joint committee of House and Senate.[73] The more radical provisions of the *Accord de la St Michel* will also greatly alter the functioning of the Belgian Parliament in future.

THE JUDICIARY

The judiciary in Belgium has traditionally never played a major political role in the way it has done in countries like the United States, Canada and Germany, where there is a tendency to expect the courts to deal with issues that are as much political as judicial. It is perhaps no accident that the countries in which courts play a major political role are all federal in structure. With the Reform of the State, creating several tiers of government and the attendant possibility of conflict between them, some change in this area has taken place Belgium. Up till the present, Belgium has more closely resembled Britain in the deliberate cultivation of judicial restraint, showing a tendency to avoid judicial involvement in what might be political issues and equally to accept at face value the decisions of the country's political institutions. For example, the Constitution states that only the legislator (national, community or regional) can interpret the law (Article 28). This implies a greatly restricted role for the courts in determining the constitutionality of legislation.

The Constitution gives the judiciary all the classic guarantees of independence,[74] such as exclusive competence to hear cases dealing with citizens' civil or political rights (Articles 92 and 93). The creation of special or administrative courts outside the ordinary judiciary is expressly forbidden (Article 94). The right to jury trial is expressly provided for in criminal cases. Judges receive permanent appointments, but a fixed retirement age may be laid down. Appeal court judges are appointed by the Crown from a list proposed by provincial councils in each circuit and the courts themselves. The *Cour de Cassation* (supreme court) is appointed by the King on a proposal from the court itself and from the Senate, the latter ensuring a minimum democratic element in judicial appointments.

Organisation of the judiciary

In each *canton judiciaire* (judicial area) one or more *juges de paix* (magistrates) deal with small claims litigation (up to 50,000 BF) and, where there is not a *tribunal de police* (local criminal court), also hears minor criminal cases. At the higher level of the *arrondissement*, there is the *tribunal de première instance*, with sections for civil, criminal and juvenile cases; it also hears appeals from the *juges de paix* or the *tribunaux de police* in its area. There will also be labour and commercial courts with specialised competences as allowed by the Constitution (Article 105). More serious criminal cases, defined as such by law, are tried before an *assise*, a court in which a president and two assessors sit with a jury. There is one in each province. There is a quite separate system of military justice with a number of permanent courts martial and a military appeal court in Brussels. There are five courts of appeal – in Brussels, Ghent, Antwerp, Liège and Mons – each with a civil, criminal and juvenile section. These courts hear appeals from all lower courts, except for labour courts, which have their own separate appeal court, and military courts.

The *Cour de Cassation* hears appeals from all these lower courts, both ordinary and special (commercial, labour and military), but it can only consider legal questions and may not reconsider the facts of a case (Article 95). It does not have the same right to establish precedents *erga omnes* (i.e. applicable to all future cases) as do the British or American courts. The Constitution (Article 28) reserves to national, regional or community legislation the right of general interpretation, hence a judgement only concerns the case for which it is sought (a ruling merely refers the matter back to the trial court). The *Cour de Cassation* has original jurisdiction in cases involving the removal of judges from office and the impeachment of ministers brought by the House. Only one impeachment case has ever been brought, in the nineteenth century.

The basic criminal system closely resembles that of France. The prosecution, generally called the *'ministère public'*[76] is represented before each court and in each judicial district. The *'parquet'* (prosecutions authority) is composed in each *arrondissement* of a *'procureur du Roi'* with several *'substituts'* (assistants), who prosecute cases in that district. A *procureur général* is attached to each appeal court, and a *procureur général* and assistants to the *Cour de Cassation*. For the specialised courts, there are *auditeurs*. The police refer investigations to the *procureur du Roi*, who may refer cases either to a *'juge d'instruction'* or directly to a *tribunal correctionnel*. The minister of justice may only intervene to order the *procureur* to proceed, never to drop proceedings. Under the basic legislation of 1867, many criminal charges in which there are mitigating circumstances are referred to the *tribunaux correctionnels*, which impose lower sentences than the assizes but which from the prosecution viewpoint are more reliable since juries at assizes are notoriously unpredictable.

The *parquet* received about 250,000 complaints in 1930, 658,000 in 1970, 884,558 in 1975 and 1,063,158 in 1986. There are 489 judges in the whole judicial system and 8,685 lawyers. The highest courts (appeal courts) hear some 6,500 cases per year and allow as a whole or in part about 55 per cent of them, which seems a high proportion. The *juges de paix* deal with almost 250,000 cases per year. Assize courts acquit only about 10 per cent of the cases (about 100 per year) that they hear. The death penalty can still be pronounced, but since 1918 it has been a formality and is always commuted by the King. Between 1944 and 1950 there were executions of collaborators with the German occupation forces.[77]

Administrative justice

Administrative justice, i.e. the hearing of appeals against the acts of administrative bodies, is the province of the *conseil d'état*, which was discussed earlier in this chapter in another guise, in relation to its advisory functions regarding legislation. It is the administrative section of the *conseil d'état* which concerns us here. When Parliament passed the law of 1944 setting it up, it carefully examined the constitutionality of such a step in relation to the jurisdiction of the normal courts, and concluded that the *conseil d'état* operating as part of the executive branch, did not interfere with the competences of the courts. At the same time, since it does in effect exercise a judicial competence, the law seeks to ensure by a series of measures the independence of its members. The latter are appointed for life by the Crown from two lists proposed by the *conseil d'état* itself and by the two chambers of Parliament (Article 70 of the law on the *conseil d'état*). The 1978 declaration of constitutional amendment (repeated in 1981) proposed to devote a section of the Constitution to administrative justice and the role of the *conseil d'état*, but up to the time of writing no action has been taken on this. The *Cour de Cassation* is competent to decided disputes over the boundaries of competence between the courts and the *conseil d'état*.

The function of the *conseil d'état* is to consider the legality and validity of acts of the administration in relation to the law. This may lead it to pronounce on what in British parlance would be called delegated legislation – royal decrees and ministerial orders. This function, though based on other criteria of an administrative character, is more thoroughgoing than that accorded to the courts under Article 107 of the Constitution. A decision by the courts that a given decree is not in conformity with the law implies only that it should not be applied in the case before the court. In other words, the judgement only applies *inter partes*. A judgement of the *conseil d'état*, on the other hand, may (under Article 14 of the law on the *conseil d'état*) annul a decree. A request for an annulment must be made within sixteen days of the decision complained of. However, the right to ask courts not to apply an administrative act is unlimited in time and may be based on broader criteria such as the legal consistency of the actions of the administration. The scope of the *conseil d'état* has now been extended to the legality of administrative acts of the regional and community executives.

In 1973-4, the *conseil d'état* rendered fifty-nine judgements on appeals from other administrative bodies and 414 judgements on appeals for annulment, which were accorded in 166 cases. In 1982, this had risen to 1,160 rulings and 305 annulments. There is a serious backlog of cases to be head, and measures are being considered to deal with this.[78]

The constitutionality of laws

Belgium never had a constitutional court, and, as we have seen, the Constitution in Article 28 clearly sets its face against allowing the courts to examine the constitutionality of laws. They are only permitted, under Article 107, to examine the legality of the acts of the executives and of subordinate bodies such as the provincial and local authorities. This tend to a doctrine of sovereignty of Parliament, similar to that prevailing in

Britain. Yet the Belgian Parliament is not sovereign in an absolute sense, unless it is *constituant* for the article of the Constitution in question and can find the necessary two-thirds majority. An ordinary law cannot routinely override the Constitution. The Constitution itself does not deal with this paradox; the issue has certainly been debated, but both Parliament and the courts themselves have excluded the courts from such jurisdiction. Indeed, in a judgement of 23 July 1849, the *Cour de Cassation* held: 'It is not the function of the courts to examine whether a law is in conformity with the Constitution'.[79] This view was confirmed in a 1974 case, and the *conseil d'état* has further concurred with it on several recent occasions. Yet the position in Belgium is increasingly complex, with an EC legal order enforced by the European Court which overrides Belgian law; interventions by the European Court of Human Rights, which has condemned Belgium on several occasions; the creation of new community and regional legal orders within the country; and increased public concern over the state's attitude towards human rights. Hence the traditional view embodied in the 1849 judgement has become untenable and some kind of constitutional jurisdiction is required only for practical reasons.

The sensitivity of the issue was shown by the fact that a new institution to deal with it only made a late appearance, being introduced into the Constitution in 1980 and taking concrete form in 1984. It was deliberately kept separate from the ordinary courts that were excluded from the constitutional function. Its jurisdiction was at first strictly limited and its very name, 'arbitration court', was an uneasy compromise, deliberately eschewing lofty pretensions. There was also a marked preference for political arrangements and procedures to prevent and resolve conflicts without litigation. The arbitration court was intended to be the last resort.[80]

NOTES

1. D.I. Llegems and J. Willems, *De Kroon Ontblooft*, Kritak, Leuven 1991, 87-100.
2. A. Molitor (former secretary to the King), *La Fondation Royale en Belgique*, CRISP, Brussels 1979, 7-8.
3. See Llegems and Willems, op. cit., 19 and 78-80.
4. See A. Mast, *Overzicht van het Belgisch Grondwetettelijk Recht*, E. Story, Ghent, 1981, 335-6.
5. Molitor, op. cit., 78-80.
6. See X. Mabille, 'Le débat politique d'avril 1990 sur la sanction et la promulgation de la loi', CH 1275 (1990).
7. See Llegems and Willems, *op. cit.*, 26-28; Hugo De Ridder, *Le Cas Martens*, Duculot, Paris/Louvain-La-Neuve 1991, 141-59.
8. On cabinet formation, see Mast, op. cit., 333-5 and Molitor, op, cit., 31-4; A. Mast, 'La nomination et révocation des Ministers' in *Journal des Tribunaux*, no. 649 (1949). On

the 1978 crisis, see L. Neels, 'Het leven van de grondwet: kabinetskrisis', *Rechtskundig Weekblad*, 1977, 508-604.

9. Llegems and Willems, *op, cit.*, 29-30.

10. *Ibid.* 77-8.

11. For the complex process in 1988, see J. Brassinne and X. Mabille, 'La crise gouvernementale de décembre 1987 à mai 1989', *CH* 1198/9 (1988).

12. Llegems and Willems, *op. cit.*, 71.

13. On coalition theory and Belgian coalitions, see Chris Rudd, 'Coalition formation and maintenance in Belgium: a case study of élite behaviour and changing cleavage structure, 1965-81', in G. Pridham (ed.), *Coalition Behaviour in Theory and Practice*, Cambridge University Press, 1986, 117-44.

14. Rudd, *op. cit.*, 127-35.

15. *Ibid.*, 134.

16. J. Brassinne and X. Mabille, *op. cit.*, 33, gives a table for voting in the congresses of all five coalition parties.

17. W. De Wachter and E. Clijsters, 'Belgium: political stability despite coalition crises' in E. Browne and J. Dreijmanis (eds) *Government Coalitions in Western Democracies*, Longman, New York, 1982, 187-216. Point made at 212-13.

18. On the role of the state secretaries, see C. Ysebaert (ed.), *Mémento Politique 1988*, Kluwer, Antwerp, 1989, 75.

19. J. Brassinne, 'La Réforme de l'Etat: phase immédiate et phase transitoire', CH 857-8 (1979) for this 'Particratic' tendency.

20. A. Mast, op. cit., 392.

21. *Mémento politique*, op. cit., 97-8.

22. *Mémento politique*, op. cit., 73-5.

23. A. Mast, op. cit., 373-6 and R. Urbain, *La fonction et les services du Premier Ministre en Belgique*, Librairie Encyclopédique, Brussels 1958.

24. Patterson and Thomas (eds), 394-5.

25. *Moniteur Belge*, 15 August 1980.

26. Mast, op. cit., 314.

27. *Annuaire Statistique de la Belgique*, vol. 109 (1989).

28. Luykx, op. cit., p. 55: 'Un corps aristocratique...et un pouvoir modérateur'.

29. Mast, op. cit., quotes the policy statement of the Martens II government to this effect (p. 193). See also Jos Bouveroux, *Het St.-Michielsakkoord: Naar en Federaal Belgie*, Standaard Uitgeverij, Antwerp, 1993, pp. 20-1 on the new role of the Senate.

30. See F. Velu, *La dissolution du Parlement*, Bruylant, Brussels 1966.

31. X. Mabille, E. Lentzen, P. Blaise, 'L'élection du 24 novembre 1991', CH (1991), 40-1, table 24.

32. Constitutional amendment of 28 July 1978.

33. Mast, op. cit., 165.

34. *Annuaire Statistique*, 110.

35. 'Révision de la Constitution 1988', *CH* 1207, 12-13.

36. The account of the election system is based on information supplied to the author by the Service des Elections of the interior ministry.

37. *Dossier du CRISP* no. 10, 'Les parties politiques en Belgique' (1978), 20.

38. CVP, *Statuten en Reglementen* (last amended 1979), rules 36 and 37.

39. Statutes du FDF as amended by the Congress of 5 November 1977 and 1981, paragraphs 23 and 24.

40. For the historical development, see summary in Mast, op. cit., 182-9.

41. Ibid., 185-6.

42. Ibid., 187-8.

43. Ibid., 188.

44. On powers, see ibid., 189-93 and 286-7.

45. Marc Uyttendaele, 'Le Sénat et la Réforme des Institutions', *CH* 1196/7 (1986).

46. Bouveroux, op. cit., p. 20.

47. For details of internal organisation of both houses, see Chambre des Représentants *Rapport Annuel*, Session 1990/1, hereafter RA and for the Senate, *Mémento Politique*, op. cit., 52-70.

48. RA, 121-2.

49. Ibid., 124-5, Rules of procedure, para. 28.

50. Ibid., 47-9, for data on committees in the House; 65-70 for the Senate *Mémento*.

51. Ibid., 49.

52. Ibid.

53. Ibid., 96-119, for reports on the activities of groups in the 1990-1 session.

54. Ibid., 132.

55. Data on sessions in ibid., 10-11.

56. Ibid., 36-7.

57. Ibid., 37.

58. Ibid., annex B3-B4.

59. Ibid., annex B3-B4.

60. Ibid., annex B5-B38.

61. Ibid., 39.

62. Mast, op. cit., 224-7 on constitutional issues.

63. For use of special powers in 1981-5, see X. Mabille, 'La Législature 1981-85', *CH* 1088 (1985, 21-23).

64. Mast, op. cit., 222-3.

65. RA, 11-13.

66. *Mémento Politique, op. cit.*

67. Mast, op. cit., 449-559.

68. The finance committee in the House is 'enlarged' into a budget committee during the annual budgetary round by the addition of representatives of the spending committees. See RA, 76.

69. For the 1989 budget reform, see R.A., 40-1 and Rules 74-84.

70. Mast., op. cit., 460-4 and *Mémento*, op. cit. 204.

71. Colloquium on Parliamentary Foreign Affairs Committees, Florence, April 1981.

72. For the 1988 revision see 'La Révision de la Constitution: Juillet 1988', *CH* 1207 (1988).

73. RA, 80 and 92.

74. H. Van Impe, *Le Régime Parlementaire en Belgique*, Bruylant, Brussels, 1968.

75. See Mast, op. cit., 397-417.

76. See article 104.

77. *Annuaire Statistique*, 184-6, for statistics of cases.

78. Mast, op. cit., *Annuaire Statistique*, 192.

79. Mast, op. cit., 432-44.

80. Pas 1849 I 449.

4

THE REFORM OF THE STATE

This chapter examines how Belgium gradually changed from being a centralised unitary state to a decentralised and finally a federal state. The Constitution of 1830 envisaged a strong centralised national government. The provinces and local authorities (*communes*) enjoyed a constitutional right to exist, but their powers, financial resources and legal instruments were limited and their actions subject to administrative oversight by the central power. The Constitution recognised neither regions nor language communities. Initially, the state was effectively unilingual. Gradually, in the course of the nineteenth and early twentieth century, the equal status of Dutch came to be recognised and its use permitted. This, however, did not in any sense imply the federalisation of the state, although it was a precondition of this later development.

The process has been gradual and has gathered pace since the 1960s. Pressure for extensive autonomy has almost exclusively come from those who were objectively (i.e. numerically and/or economically, or even psychologically) in the minority. At first the pressure came from Flanders, but later, as Walloons and French-speakers gradually lost their economic and psychological dominance, they took up the cause of federalism, at first defensively then more radically and proactively.

In the first phase, the Flemish community developed a radical consciousness and raised demands first for equality, and then for serious forms of autonomy. From 1873 a series of language laws extended the use of Flemish, and by 1923 the key demand for a Flemish university in Ghent had been achieved. The language laws of 1932 enacted the idea of language regions and a 'linguistic frontier' applying the long-standing Flemish demand for application of the territorial principle. This was of immense psychological importance since it created two unilingual regions, with the mother-tongue principle being restricted to Brussels. As we have seen, the events of the Second World War discredited the Flemish movement and retarded further advance till the 1960s. After the war, with most of its linguistic aims met, the Flemish movement shifted into a qualitatively new gear, raising structural political issues that would eventually lead to federalism.

Early expressions of Walloon federalism, such as the votes of the Walloon congresses of 1945 and 1946 and attempts to revise the Constitution in a federal direction in 1953 were premature and led nowhere. But, from the time of the *Question Royale*, the '*guerre scolaire*' and the strikes of the winter of 1960/1, clear regional cleavage lines were developing.[1]

In the 1960s, regional political parties for the first time threatened the hegemony and indeed the unity of the three traditional political families. The regional issue at last forced itself on to the political agenda.

The Reform of the State should be seen as a cumulative process, taking place hitherto in four distinct stages, each of which in turn has fallen into distinct phases.[2] The basic method has been similar: enactment of a package of constitutional changes and then a number of implementing laws; leading on to consideration and preparation for the next stage. One can identify a first stage between 1970 and 1979. Here, constitutional amendments were enacted in 1970-2 and implementing laws in 1971-9. The second stage followed in 1980-7, with constitutional amendments being voted up till 1983 and implementing legislation every year. The third stage began in 1988-90. In this stage, constitutional amendments were voted in both phases 1 and 2 and implementing legislation mainly in phase 2. Phase 3 was intended to complete the process with the reform of the Senate, and dealing with competence in international relations was not completed by the end of the term in 1991. The *Accord de la St Michel*, which took over these unresolved issues, is a significant fourth stage.

Definitions

Regions are a geographic concept and *communities* are a cultural/linguistic concept. There are three regions in Belgium:

– *Flanders*, consisting of four Flemish provinces (Antwerp, Limburg, East Flanders, and West Flanders);
– The *Walloon region*, consisting of the four traditional Walloon provinces (Hainaut, Liège, Namur and Luxembourg) and part of Brabant (basically the *arrondissement* of Nivelles); and
– The *Brussels region*, consisting of 19 *communes* (municipalities).

There are three communities in Belgium. They do not have a geographic competence as such, but are responsible for linguistic and cultural policy, education and so-called personalisable matters (health, social provision) for speakers of French, Dutch and German. Given the application of the territorial principle, their 'territory' in effect covers the areas in which their language is spoken and for the French and Flemish communities in bilingual Brussels as well.

– The *Dutch-speaking community* consists of all Dutch-speakers in the Flemish provinces and Brussels. The Flemish region and community have been fused and, though deriving their competences from separate articles of the Constitution (59 bis and 107 *quater*), have only one set of institutions and are seen as one unit.

– The *French-speaking community* consists of all French-speakers in the Walloon provinces, part of Brabant and Brussels.

– The *German-speaking community* consists of 70,000 German speakers living in the Eupen-Malmédy-Sankt Vith area near the German border.

– The *Brussels region*. Some community matters in the capital are handled by the Brussels regional executive and council, split into its two linguistic components.

The now small French-speaking minority living in Flanders, outside Brabant, belongs to no community at all. The official language of Flanders is Dutch, but is often referred to as Flemish – Flemish in fact being a series of Dutch dialects spoken in Flanders. Dutch-speakers are referred to either as '*Nederlandstalige*' or '*Vlaamstalige*'. However, the official name of the Flemish community is '*De Vlaams Gemeenschap*'.

The remainder of this chapter looks at the progress of the Reform of the State through its various phases up to the time of writing. Chapter 5 examines the present federalised structure of Belgian government.

The community question has become the dominant political issue in Belgium. By the 1960s it was clear that the unitary structure of the state, created in 1831, had ceased to be viable. By the early 1970s, it appeared – deceptively, as it turned out – to have matured sufficiently to be susceptible to a global and far-reaching solution. Simple 'geographical federalism' was clearly inadequate to meet the complicated reality of the Belgian situation. Such a solution would imply four 'states' – Flanders, Wallonia, Brussels and the German-speaking *cantons* – all exercising the same devolved powers over both cultural and socio-economic matters. But Brussels is not a third linguistic community; it is bilingual, and therefore can not exercise powers in the cultural domain. Furthermore, from a socio-economic and cultural (but not historical or political) point of view, the French-speaking people in the commuter suburbs should belong to Brussels, but this is politically impossible. No geographically tidy solution can therefore be found: to bring them into Brussels is politically unacceptable to the Flemish-speaking parties, and to ignore their specificity and leave them as part of Flanders is unacceptable to the French-speaking parties.

Secondly, the German-speaking community in the five eastern *communes* is not a socio-economic unit, and its institutions could not usefully combine 'cultural' and 'socio-economic' powers. For these reasons, a more complex and differentiated pattern of institutions had to be found; this was the aim of the Egmont pact (1977). The latter is important as the first politically realistic attempt at a coherent and intellectually consistent solution to the problem. Although it was never implemented as such, much of its inspiration – watered down and fudged – found its way into the less elegant solutions finally adopted. Under the pact Belgium would eventually have comprised the central state (government and bi-cameral Parliament) and three communities (Flanders, Wallonia and the German-speakers), each with an elected assembly and executive, and three regions (Flanders, Brussels, Wallonia), each with an elected assembly and executive. There would be special guarantees of Flemish minority rights in Brussels and for French-speakers in the suburbs.

The roots of the problem go very deep. Indeed, they go right back to the origins of the Belgian state, but for a long time they lay buried, only to re-emerge with increased virulence in the 1960s.[3] What is today Belgium had already broken with the United Provinces over religious differences in the course of their common struggle against Spanish domination (Belgium is mainly Catholic). The French Revolution and the subsequent period of French rule in the period 1790-1810 saw the rise of a liberal French-speaking middle class, not only in Brussels and Wallonia but also in some of the larger Flemish towns, for whom the solution imposed by the great powers at the Congress of Vienna – incorporation into the Netherlands – was intolerable. The revolution of 1830 against this imposition opened a long period of domination by the French-speakers. The very idea of a Belgian state was theirs, and it was they who made the revolution and determined the nature of the political institutions and the system of administration. Since the late Middle Ages economic power had passed from Flanders, and with the industrial revolution it moved decisively to the areas of Mons, Liège, Namur and Charleroi situated on the Sambre-Meuse coalfield in Wallonia.

In the twentieth century, as we have seen, Flemish nationalism began to emerge. At first it did so largely on a cultural level, only finding political expression for the first time after the First World War.[4] Indeed, the war itself had proved a powerful catalyst to the movement. The two world wars have on the one hand given the Flemish movement greater consciousness and even a certain impulsion, but on the other hand they greatly handicapped its wider political action. Rightly or wrongly, it became identified as anti-patriotic (which it may have been in the sense that it rejected the Belgian state) and pro-German and prepared to collaborate with the enemy. This was partly unjust, since in the Second World War many Flemish nationalists were anti-Nazi. Nevertheless, these sentiments provided the French-speaking establishment with a convenient alibi for refusing to respond to the grievances of the Flemish movement.

The 1960s were a watershed in Belgian politics. It became clear that profound reforms were necessary. First, there was a reversal of the balance of power. Not only was the Flemish community the national majority in numerical terms, but it was no longer on the defensive. The new economic dynamism of the country was in Flanders. The Walloon industrial base was in decline: coal, steel, ceramics, glass, chemicals. The Flemish movement became more self-confident and militant. Manifestations of this were the Flemish march on Brussels and the expulsion of the Francophone university from Louvain.

These changes led to something new: Walloon defensive movements. These on the whole tended to be ideologically left-wing, whereas Flemish nationalism is more right-wing. This of course responded to the Walloon working-class radical tradition, which was one of the Walloon particularisms which the new movements sought to defend. The movements were launched around the bitter strikes of the winter of 1960-1. They eventually fused first into the Parti Wallon (1965) and then the Rassemblement Wallon (RW) in 1968.

Brussels was the cauldron of linguistic politics, and in the late 1960s was the front line. Many questions were raised. Was Brussels, as the Flemish movement proclaimed, 'Flemish soil'? Or was it a coequal third region? What should be the rights of the Flemish minority in the city? On the other hand, what should be the rights of the French-speakers living in the Flemish *communes* just outside the city? These issues were the battleground. With the rise of a more militant Flemish movement, the French-speakers of the capital felt increasingly vulnerable and feared that they would be the victims of any settlement between the two communities. This led to the formation of the Front Démocratique des Francophones de Bruxelles (FDF) in 1964.

In the 1965 election, the three regional parties obtained 8.7% of the vote between them, and by 1968 their combined share of the vote had almost doubled to 15.7%,[5] and reached its peak in 1971 with 23.5%. The vote for the community parties (FDF + VU) fell back in the elections of 1974 (21.1%) and 1977 (17.0%),[6] but not dramatically since their combined vote remained well above their level in the breakthrough year of 1968. In any case, the fall in 1977 was almost entirely due to the break-up of the RW. This global result also hides the fact that in Brussels the peak combined vote for the community parties was not reached till 1974, but the FDF no longer being in a cartel with the small Brussels Liberal Party makes comparison difficult. Even if by 1977 the community vote had ebbed slightly, it was clearly now a permanent phenomenon in Belgian politics of which account would have to be taken. Furthermore, by 1977 the community parties had achieved a major objective: to show that the Belgian unitary state was ungovernable and to participate themselves in the implementation of the necessary reforms.

It has been a long process. The constitutional revision of 1971 had done no more than establish general principles and procedures which subsequent legislation was to implement.[7] In the new Article 59 *bis*, it established the cultural councils for the three communities. In Article 107 *quater*, it established the principle of regional councils with powers in the socio-economic field. The implementation of these constitutional provisions was left to the legislator, but under conditions almost as onerous and complicated as constitutional amendment itself. Laws under Articles 59 *bis* and 107 *quater*, as has been stated elsewhere, have to be adopted by a two-thirds majority in each chamber of the legislature and a majority in each linguistic group in each chamber. These special majorities have dominated negotiations for the formation of a government and have often made one form of coalition preferable to another. This was the rationale behind the short-lived Leburton government of 1973-4. It was a 'classic' tripartite government (PSB/BSP-CVP/PSC-PLP/PVV), with the necessary 'special majority' but suffering from internal tension on other issues (Socialists versus Liberals) and from the external pressure of the community parties, which greatly reduced its freedom of manoeuvre.

The first Tindemans government (1974-7) attempted to avoid these defects, narrowing its ideological dimension by excluding the PSB/BSP (which gave it only the barest parliamentary majority) while seeking broad agreement among all parties on the community issue through inter-party talks carried on outside the framework both of the government and Parliament (the Steenokkerzeel meeting).[8] When this approach failed, Tindemans sought to enlarge his majority by taking in some of the community parties, especially in Wallonia, where his government was weakest. He succeeded only in part, and in the summer of 1974 he added the RW alone. This gave him greater strength in Wallonia and some protection against the threat of the community parties, but no 'special majority'. Indeed, this mini-enlargement had other negative consequences: the RW was initially to the left of the government's centre of gravity and was to become more so.

Participation in a centre-right government without the FDF imposed severe ideological and regionalist strains on the RW, leading ultimately to a rupture between the increasingly leftist party chairman, Paul-Henri Gendebien, and the more moderate RW ministers. At the same time, the Tindemans government was open to attack by the PSB/BSP and the trade unions for its economic policies, which also strained RW loyalty. Further-more, the CVP faced VU criticism on its Flemish flank. The Tindemans I government seems to have collapsed more under the accumulated weight of these contradictions than because of the break-up of the RW – the ostensible reason.[9]

Meanwhile, the positive spirit of Steenokkerzeel had not been com-pletely forgotten. In all the political parties, in inter-community study groups, in various organisations and associations and through individual action, an enormous amount of positive work[10] had been going on outside the formal framework of the government to increase mutual understanding, narrow areas of disagreement and build up areas of agreement and a non-binding basis to test various solutions to the most serious problems. Since 1976 the Socialists of all three regions had agreed a common position. The CVP/PVV/VU had also attempted to reach a common approach (October 1975). Two well-known figures, Mr Claes (BSP) and Mr Moureaux (RW), published a plan.

A conference on the theme was held in Antwerp on 10 January 1976. The minister for institutional reforms, Mr Périn (RW), published on a personal basis a political report on the institutions. None of these various plans gained universal approval, but they made a positive contribution to the debate and prepared the ground for the official inter-community dialogue between all the parties represented in Parliament, with the government present as an observer.[11] This dialogue, under the joint chairmanship of Mr De Keersmaeker (CVP) and Mr Hurez (PSB), lasted from 30 November 1976 to 3 March 1977 and was just entering a new phase of negotiations as distinct from 'dialogue' when the government fell. Its results[12] were available for the Egmont negotiations. Furthermore, as a result of these discussions, relations between the PSB and the FDF and the CVP greatly improved.

The 1977 elections saw gains for the CVP, the PSB and the FDF. The RW were the main losers. Above all there was a real simplification. One party was clearly dominant in each region: the CVP in Flanders, the PSB in Wallonia and the FDF in Brussels. When it came to stating negotiations for a new government, two points were clear. First, the PSB should be in, and secondly, the parties supporting the community pact and those forming the majority should this time be the same. Tindemans' first preference was for a classic tripartite coalition. Others still hoped to exclude the Socialists (the PSC/CVP and Liberals had a bare majority). The tripartite was rejected by the PSB, and even the Flemish PVV was not enthusiastic. Moreover, it would not outflank the community parties. The exclusion of the PSB would weaken the government in Wallonia and mean that it would enjoy no special majority, and furthermore the socio-economic issue would not be resolved. Thus these coalitions were rejected in favour of the preference of André Cools (PSB) and Wilfried Martens (CVP) for a broad majority: CVP/PSC-PSB/BSP-FDF-VU.[13] This combination had the 'special majority': 172 seats out of the 212 in the House and firm majorities in all regions. Politically, too, it contained the leading parties in each region and a socio-economic consensus. These parties then both entered the government and negotiated the community pact (the Egmont pact). These arrangements initially had a remarkably easy passage, obtained wide agreement in the community parties, and could even count on some support from the Liberal opposition and the RW. Even in the VU defections were minimal.[14]

The pact was to be implemented rapidly; indeed, speed was essential if the dynamism and impulsion of the original political will – the spirit of Egmont – was to be maintained. Just how costly any delay could be was shown only too clearly when the objections of the CVP came to the surface in October 1978. The pact was annexed to the government declaration and approved by the House of Representatives on 9 June 1978, by 165 votes to thirty-four with three abstentions. On 14 June, the declaration was also approved by the Senate by a large majority (139 votes to twenty-four with five abstentions).[15] As the pact made clear, many of the final arrangements would require a revision of the Constitution, which was not immediately possible since the 1977 Parliament was not *constituant*. This defect, which had perhaps played a not unimportant role in the demise of the Egmont pact, was rectified in later attempts at a solution since the 1978 Parliament was *constituant*.

The government's immediate task was to prepare the first phase of the pact, which required three bills: one to implement Article 107 *quater*, one to extend the 'cultural matters' forming the powers of the cultural councils, and one amending the laws on the administrative use of languages. Many details of the pact were unclear, or problems had been exposed in the parliamentary debates or in the copious public discussions of the pact and its implications. Above all, the pact had to be translated quickly into legislative texts. The 'Committee of Fifteen' (the six party presidents of the majority, the prime minister, the two ministers for the reform of the institutions and some other advisers and party representatives) met at the Château de Stuyvenberg between 24 September 1977 and 17 January 1978. Its deliberations led to an annex to the government declaration being tabled in February 1978. It was then the task of the two responsible ministers – Mr Hoyaux (French-speaking) and Mr De Bondt (Flemish-speaking) – to add the finishing touches to the texts. This was not easy and required frequent interventions by the party presidents. Even at this stage CVP ministers were dragging their feet, especially Mr De Bondt. The texts were finally approved by the cabinet and presented to Parliament on 11 July 1978.[16] This was Bill no. 461.

Looking beyond the difficulties of the moment, what were to be the main provisions of the institutional reform? What sort of institutions would Belgium have had in the 1980s if the pact and the bill had been fully implemented, including the necessary constitutional amendments? Certainly it would no longer have been a unitary state. Powerful regional institutions were to be set up with wide powers which could not have been revoked; these institutions were in some cases to have power to impose taxation and to conclude international agreements. There were to be elected assemblies and executives which were to have their own administrations, and not be subject to the tutelage of the central government. The political majorities in the regions and at the centre were likely from time to time to be different. At any rate, it was not to be a form of simple 'geographical federalism' with one central government and several co-equal regional governments.

There would be two kinds of devolved authority with either geographical or personalisable competence. It could be called a mixture of cultural and geographical federalism, and perhaps just this realisation was what provoked the eleventh-hour opposition by the CVP – on the ostensible grounds of constitutional problems. It was always clear, and indeed agreed, that even if politically the Egmont pact[17] constituted an indissoluble whole, it could only be implemented in stages.

First, some parts only required the 'special majority' in order to apply either Article 59 *bis* or Article 107 *quater* of the revised Constitution of 1970. These provisions of the pact were to be enforced rapidly – before 1 January 1979. There would still be some transitional arrangements: the members of the regional councils would not yet be specially elected, but would be existing members of the House of Representatives.

Secondly, other parts required revision of the Constitution (reform of the Senate, direct election of members of the regional councils, financial provisions etc.). For these matters, a *Déclaration de révision de la Constitution* (Article 131) would be required, followed by new elections and adoption of the amendments. The pact provided for this, but only at a later stage. Hence this was a crucial watershed in Belgian politics, and it was inevitable that opposition would arise. At first, however, the bill made reasonable progress in the special committee of the House chaired by the then CVP president, Wilfried Martens. It was approved, with amendments after crisis interventions on specific points by the party presidents, on schedule at the end of September. By then, however, CVP senators and the CVP congress had begun to raise doubts about the constitutional validity of the first phase.

It is a commonplace of Belgian politics, which has been shown time and again to be true, that what is not gained now tends never to be attained at all. Bargains are rarely fully kept. Given the need to defer some aspects of the pact until a revision of the Constitution could be carried out, it was one of the most ingenious features of the Egmont-Stuyvenberg agreement that enough reciprocal guarantees and concessions were contained in the first part of the pact to satisfy both the French and Flemish parties of the majority.

It was for these reasons that the constitutional objections raised late in the day by the CVP (in September 1978)[18] set off alarm-bells in the other parties – both Flemish- and French-speaking – of the majority, which saw in the attitude of the CVP a thinly disguised effort to sabotage the pact. Previous rumours of Prime Minister Tindemans' limited attachment to the pact were only confirmed by his precipitate resignation. It is true that the advisory legal body, the *conseil d'état*, had given an opinion that certain articles of the bill providing for 'various institutional reforms' to implement the provisional phase of the pact were in fact unconstitutional. But at the time the government, through no less person than Mr Tindemans himself, had rejected these criticisms.

It became clear that the objections were essentially political. Indeed, 'unitarist' sentiment had always remained strong in the CVP, and it now saw the chance of making even greater electoral gains by blocking the implementation of the pact on three grounds: first, defence of the constitution; secondly, defence of the Belgian state; and thirdly, defence of Flemish rights in the periphery of Brussels. The other parties of the majority, especially the French-speaking ones, thereupon insisted on the full and rapid implementation of the pact.[19] Mr André Cools (PSB chairman) was particularly insistent on this. On the CVP demand for more discussions, he was totally dismissive: 'Everything that could be negotiated has already been negotiated.'[20] In this new climate, a crisis was inevitable, and it was not long in coming. The other five parties of the majority demanded an immediate vote on Bill 461 and insisted that the prime minister make the vote an issue of confidence to force the CVP into line. Mr Tindemans preferred to resign, which he did dramatically on 11 October 1978.

His successor was Mr Vanden Boeynants (PSC), with the same coalition and the same team. The task of this 'interim' government was to agree a *Déclaration de révision de la Constitution*, to be followed by elections within a few months. The new Parliament would be able to amend the Constitution, which would presumably mean that the transitional phase could be dispensed with. Otherwise Mr Vanden Boeynants considered that the Egmont framework remained valid.

At this point, it is perhaps worth standing back before we resume the Byzantine narrative, and looking in more detail at the ingenious intellectual heritage of the Egmont pact and of Bill 461 which was based upon it, since this structure was largely to form the basis of the solution adopted four years later. The pact proposed to set up three community councils and three regional councils, to provide for their financial autonomy, to set up arbitration machinery to settle conflicts of competence, and to transform the Senate. We shall look at each of these aspects in turn.[21]

The communities

The three existing community councils – the Dutch cultural council established by the law of 21 July 1971 under Article 59 *bis* of the Constitution, the French cultural council set up by the same law, and the German cultural council set up by the law of 10 July 1973 – were to be changed into community councils with new powers over what are called 'personal' matters such as hospital services, local welfare services and vocational training – in addition, of course, to the existing powers over culture, the use of languages, local aspects of education and international cultural co-operation.

Each community would have had a directly elected assembly in the sense that this was to consist of regional councillors, to be directly elected. The two larger community councils would have been composed of the Flemish or Walloon regional councillors plus, for the French-speaking community, half of the French-speaking group of the Brussels regional council. The German community council was to continue to have twenty-five members directly elected for four years. Under existing apportionment, that would give 121 members for the Flemish council (118 + 3) and ninety-one for the French-speaking council (70 + 21). The Egmont pact and Bill 461 proposed that for a transitional period the councils should continue to consist of deputies and senators as now, but that later they would be separately elected.

Bill 461 proposed a provisional executive composed of a minister and three state secretaries (Article 75). These executives would be responsible for preparation of proposals for the councils, execution of decrees voted by the councils, execution of the budget, and general administration. They would be responsible before their community council, but also members of the national government. This rather difficult arrangement was perhaps made necessary by the fact that the Constitution could not be modified. The German council was to continue as it was without an executive.

In the definitive stage, after the constitutional revision, the community councils (except for the German community) were to have their own independent executives (*collèges*) with a president and three members, with one member from Brussels. The *collège* was to be responsible to the council, but the censure procedure was to be the 'constructive no-confidence' system found in clause 66 of the Basic Law of the German Federal Republic: a motion must replace the whole *collège* or the individual member censured.

Members of the regional executives would have been able to take part in meetings of the community executives, but without the right to vote.

The regions

There wre to be three regions, as specified in Article 107 *quater*: Flanders, Brussels (the nineteen *communes* only) and Wallonia. Each region was to have a directly-elected regional council and an executive elected by the regional council and responsible to it. The Flemish and Walloon regional councils would have a number of members equivalent to the number of deputies elected in each region (now 118 and seventy respectively). The Brussels regional council was to have forty-eight members, or double the number of deputies elected in that region. The Brussels members were to be elected on unilingual lists and form (as in Parliament) two linguistic groups (on present figures, six Flemish-speakers and forty-two French-speakers). The councils were to be elected for four years, but if they failed to elect a new executive within twenty-one days of rejecting a motion of confidence in the existing one, they could then be dissolved. There were special provisions for the Brussels regional council in that censure motions and elections of the bureau had to obtain a majority in each linguistic group.

In the transitional phase, Bill 461 proposed that the regional councils should be composed of senators and deputies from each region until the revision of the Constitution. Obviously, these transitional councils could not be dissolved (and would be automatically renewed at each national election). The bill set out the procedures to be followed by the councils, which closely paralleled normal parliamentary procedure.

Even in the transitional period, the regions were to have an executive of seven members, to be elected by the regional council in a separate election for each seat. The executive was to elect its own president who would then be formally appointed by the King. The executives were to act as a *collège*, each member being obliged to bear collective responsibility. It would be responsible to the council, which could adopt a 'constructive motion of no-confidence' against the whole *collège* or against one member. Decisions were to be taken by consensus (neither by majority nor unanimously), and if a member could not agree with the consensus, he had to resign. The *collège* would assign 'portfolios' to its members, as in government. It would have the right to initiate *ordonnances* (the regional equivalent of a bill) in the council and execute them, to issue regulations (the regional equivalent of an AR), and to draw up and execute the budget; in short, it was to have all the normal powers of a government.

Brussels was as usual a special case. Its executive had to include two Flemish-speakers elected separately by the Flemish linguistic group in the council. Censure motions were to be adopted by both linguistic groups if they were against the whole *collège*, but motions against individuals needed only to obtain a majority in the linguistic group of that member. The distribution of portfolios in the Brussels executive was subject to special rules. If political agreement was not reached, there was an automatic procedure for assigning among its members six portfolios (finance, economic policy and employment, housing, public services and undertakings for the French-speaking members, and urban planning and local government for the two Flemish-speaking members).

The regions and central state were each given exclusive competences. The state alone remained competent for foreign affairs, defence, justice, elections, macro-economic policy, taxation, credit policy, monetary policy, national health policy, social security, infrastructure and national transport undertakings. The region alone was to be competent (by way of *ordonnances*) for planning, housing, local transport, supervision of local government, licensing of mineral exploitation, regional economic development (state intervention, investment etc.), water policy (vital in Wallonia) and agricultural land holding policy. The Brussels region inherited the local government powers (fire service etc.) of the council for the 'Greater Brussels' area (*Agglomération bruxelloise*), which was to be abolished.

Naturally, neither the state nor the regions could intervene in matters devolved to the communities under Article 59 *bis* of the Constitution. The residual matters in the exclusive competence of neither, which are given to the communities, are in the competence of state and regions concurrently. As in Germany, the regions could have intervened in these 'concurrent' matters but *only provided that* the state did not do so.

The regions were to have several sources of finance. They were to be accorded a global grant by the state, to be apportioned between them according to a special formula. On condition that they acted in accordance with overall national policy, the regions might seek loans. They could have been accorded a proportion of certain taxes, but this was not fixed in detail. Under the Egmont pact they were to have their own tax revenues, but only after the revision of the Constitution. The communities were to be authorised to take up loans, but were otherwise, as at that time, to continue to be financed from the state.

These new structures would have introduced a new and complicated '*hiérarchie des normes*'. Clashes between the law (the state), decrees (communities) and *ordonnances* (regions), all of which had the same legal force within their respective spheres of competence, were inevitable. In the transitional phase, all these norms were to be subject to the control of the ordinary courts and of the *conseil d'état*. In the 'definitive phase', an arbitration court was to be set up, appointed by the King for a period of eight years.

Special provisions were to be made for Brussels and its periphery (where there were already facilities for the French-speaking minorities). As we have already seen, there were special provisions giving protection to the Flemish minority in Brussels. In addition, cultural committees (one for each community) were to be set up in each of the nineteen *communes* of Brussels and in the six *communes à facilités*, where the French-speakers were to receive some local services in French. These were to be guarantors of minority rights in each case. French-speaking minority voters in the six peripheral *communes* and in some other peripheral quarters were to be able to exercise the right of a 'fictive' electoral and administrative domicile in one of the nineteen (bilingual) *communes* of the capital. This provision was hotly contested, and the Flemish parties sought to minimise its fiscal and electoral impact (e.g. the taxes to be paid back to the *commune* of effective residence), but it was imaginative in that it gave French-speakers rights without extending the boundaries of Brussels.

The Senate was to become a regional chamber composed of the members of the regional councils. The government would no longer have been responsible before the Senate nor would it have co-equal legislative powers with the House of Representatives. It was to be able, within thirty days, to propose amendments to ordinary laws, which the House could disregard. It would retain equal rights (two-thirds majority vote required) over constitutional amendments and laws, requiring a special majority (e.g. those under Articles 59 *bis* and 107 *quater*). It would also have the power to pronounce on motions from community councils on the protection of ideological minorities (in cultural/educational matters).

The provisions of the Egmont pact seem at times excessively complex but this was required to deal with the very real complexity of the situation. Indeed, the structure of the pact corresponds in its main outlines to the structure proposed over the previous two years by almost all the different plans published by parties, organisations and individuals. The transitional period was necessary both because the 1977 chambers were not '*constituantes*', and because it was thought useful to 'test' the whole edifice in a preliminary period; also in order that a start could at least be made, exploiting the positive climate after the 1977 elections.

The breakthrough

The pact was an imaginative synthesis or distillation of what was desirable and possible. It failed not because of its own weaknesses but through a failure of political will. Much of the detailed work was rescued from the debris and, except for its Brussels provisions, thus formed the basis for the reform of 1980 which telescoped into one phase the two phases of the Egmont pact. Indeed it is amazing how closely the present arrangements, after three rounds of reform, resemble the pact.

We return to the point after the shock elections of December 1978, which had taken place in an atmosphere of mutual recrimination and distrust. We are not concerned with the general political aspect of the elections, which are treated elsewhere, nor with the acrobatics which marked the unpredecentedly long government crisis after the election.[22] The Volksunie suffered a severe setback; the CVP did not obtain its expected advance, but rather a marginal decline, as did the Socialists; the FDF made very slight progress. The PSC increased its vote. Among the opposition parties, the PVV advanced, but the Walloon Liberals declined and the RW made a slight recovery.

No clear trend was evident, except in the case of the Volksunie, which withdrew into its shell. Anyway, no lesson emerged for the future Reform of the State. It was the collapse of the front of the French-speaking parties of the majority (PS-PSC-FDF) – which made possible the solution of the problem without Brussels, making the reform acceptable to the Flemish parties – which led to the breakthrough. The front came into existence during the crisis to ensure that no new government, of whatever character, would do as some, especially in the CVP, wanted – namely put the community question on a back burner.[23]

This, certainly, was not the case with the Martens I government whose declaration underlined the necessity of the Reform of the State. From its appointment in April 1979 it began work on a number of fronts.[24] First, there was an intermediate phase. This involved in effect what had earlier been called a preparatory stage. It required a law (of 5 July 1979) and forty-two royal decrees. Those matters which were to be within the competence of the communities were increased, by the inclusion of some *personalisable* matters (aid to the aged, public health, some research matters) and fixed regional competences in nine areas (employment, housing, refuse disposal, water policy, energy policy and so on). At the same time a very complex system of executives *inside* the national government was created; these were in effect cabinet committees under a minister but with their own regionalised administrations and with budgets, to be voted by the community and regional councils and legislatures, again in the form of the various councils. These executives, being part of the national government, were of course not responsible to the councils. For the first time an old CVP demand was taken into account: there was only one executive for both community and regional matters on the Flemish side.[25]

Secondly, after a lengthy dialogue with the *conseil d'état* over the constitutionality of the fusion of the two Flemish executives and councils, the responsibility of the executives,[26] and the need for a constitutional revision to enable the communities and regions to raise their own financial resources (most of which the government accepted), drafts of revised Articles 3 *ter* (communities), 59 *bis* (community competences), 100 and 113 (finance) were prepared. So too was a special law fixing the competences of the regions (the nine matters of the July law and some new matters such as tourism, powers of *tutelle*, borrowing powers and natural resources) and of the communities (*personalisable* matters), and the functioning of both. Finally, an ordinary law was prepared basically on finance and conflicts of competence. These bills were tabled on 1 October 1979 in the Senate.[27]

A special Senate committee began work on 24 October 1979 and held twelve meetings before Christmas. It soon become clear that many difficulties lay in the way of success.[28] The Flemish position – that nothing should be approved in this phase which would prejudice the final and definitive phase, especially over Brussels, which the CVP sought to reduce to a lower status than the other regions – was an early warning of problems. These pressures grew as the CVP congress of 16 December 1979 approached. In fact, the special committee became increasingly paralysed, which provoked a virulent reaction from the PS by J.M. Dehousse, who in a speech at Bossu on 2 December demanded in trenchant terms '*la régionalisation à trois*'.[29] The crisis was brewing. The CVP congress adopted motions which threw the continuance of the present debate into doubt.[30] It refused to 'prejudice' future stages of the reform; it rejected the notion of Brussels as an equal third region; and it demanded that the regional *ordonnances*, unlike the decrees of community councils, should not have the status of laws and thus (vital for Brussels) be subject to revision by law.

Brussels was to be 'city region' only. More significant was the tone employed. Eric van Rompuy, chairman of the CVP youth wing and often kite-flyer for Mr Tindemans, said at the congress: 'We intend to retain a free hand in the third phase and amend the second phase accordingly.'[31] The crisis could not now be avoided. The French-speaking parties with their united front reacted strongly. Mr Martens presented several series of proposals, and held meetings with all those concerned in an attempt to reach a compromise. His first proposals of 7 January 1980 sought to reduce the number of articles of the constitution to be revised, to 59 *bis* and those providing for financial autonomy for regions and communities.

The vexed status of the *ordonnances* would thus be solved as desired by the CVP. Brussels would not have the same competences. The measures were to end at the latest on 31 December 1982, and if no solution had been found the régime of 1979 would be reintroduced. The PS, which above all wanted assurance about a rapid and definitive (hence the issue about the 'life' of the proposal) regionalisation, did not reject these proposals; neither, at this stage, did the FDF.[32]

On 9 January a mini-package was put forward, with almost no constitutional revision in the short term.[33] The PS accepted in order at last to obtain regionalisation. After seeking Francophone solidarity, the FDF did not accept, and its ministers were forced out of the government. A new agreement on a bipartite PS/SP-CVP/PSC cabinet was reached on 18 January on the basis of the 'mini-package'.[34] The FDF had broken the Francophone front, as the PSC-PS had done before. André Cools argued that the FDF had entered a trap sprung by the CVP in seeking too many guarantees which would be of little use. The political fact was there. The 'significant majority' basis for the government fell and with it not only its two-thirds majority but also the need to include Brussels in any solution. With hindsight it is possible to see that the way was now open for a solution.

The new bills were extremely modest; difficult matters were excluded. Regional authorities were not placed on the same level as the communities. The *personalisable* matters would not be included. The regions and communities would not have their own tax resources, having to rely on grants, and Brussels would have a secondary status. It seemed a small advance. Even this provoked CVP opposition and on 2 April 1980 one article (117 *ter*) failed to obtain the two-thirds majority in the Senate due to CVP opposition, resulting in the fall of the Martens II government.[35]

Meanwhile, the committee of twenty-eight, with representatives of all parties under the co-presidency of Mr Blankaert (CVP) and Mr Brouhon (PS), had been set up on 4 February 1980 to draft proposals for the definitive Reform of the State,[36] and was making progress. It therefore became possible to form a 'tripartite' government – Martens III – on 7 May 1980 with the CVP/PSC-PS/SP-PVV/PRL. Ironically, while the CVP revolt had aimed at slowing down reform, all it had done was spectacularly to accelerate it. There was now movement, and the stage was set.

The new government returned to the more ambitious 1979 formula of Martens I, a solution not so far from the spirit of the Egmont pact, except on the status of Brussels. This involved:[37]

— revision of a series of articles of the Constitution: 3 *ter* and 59 *bis*, to add *personalisable* matters; 28, giving the decrees of the communities and regions equal status with laws; 107 *ter* setting up the arbitration court; 110, 111 and 113 on finance; and 108 on the *tutelle* of provinces and *communes* which is given to the communities and the regions. The new 59 *bis* also authorised the fusion of the Flemish community and region into one body.
— a special law, setting out the organisation, functioning and competences of the communities and regions.
— an ordinary law on finance matters and the settlement of conflicts.

It was agreed that the constitutional revision was a precondition of phases 2 and 3, as the earlier opinion of the *conseil d'état* had indicated. These amendments to the Constitution were passed rapidly and with relatively little difficulty, the only real opposition coming from the FDF, VU and some CVP and Brussels Socialists. On 21 May 1980 the proposals were tabled and all were passed by 28 July that year and some as early as 4 July.

Parallel to these discussions the two bills were being examined. The government rejected the opinion of the *conseil d'état* that the omission of Brussels made the law unconstitutional[38] as an incorrect application of Article 107 *quater*; the government's view was that the intended progressive solution was not opposed to the sense of the Constitution. With some relatively minor amendments (the only important one relating to the creation of 'Title 4' in the special law on co-operation between the communities) the bills passed Parliament as follows:[39]

	Senate		Conseil régional	
	vote	*date*	*vote*	*date*
Bill 434 (Special Law)	137:22:0	27 July	156:19:5	5 August
Bill 435 (Ordinary Law)	132:23:2	7 August	152:21:2	3 August

This partial solution left many issues unresolved, most notably the position of Brussels, the problem of mixed municipalities near the language border (such as the Fourons), residual powers, international relations, finance and judicial control. However, it was a start. The regions could be finally established and the executives could be set up outside the national government. This happened already in November 1981. The first executives (1981-5) were also proportional, which meant that the smaller parties in each region (SP and PRL) could still be represented. Indeed, despite the creation of autonomous regional and community authorities, with at least superficially significant developed powers, the extent of the reform was more apparent than real. The predominance of the central government was reduced less than seemed to be the case. Its pre-eminent fiscal power and spending power; the complexity of the distribution of competences, which often restricted a general devolved competence with reference to national norms or principles, or subordinated their exercises to national policy objectives, such as monetary policy or distribution of responsibility between all three national/regional/community levels, as well as the international competences of the central authorities – all tended to reduce the extent of effective federalisation.[40]

In addition, or perhaps partly because of that situation, the community and regional authorities were also kept politically subordinate. They had no independent legislative assemblies, and elections were called for national reasons; they were affected by the national political cycle. The executives were at first proportional, but then, in 1985, 1987 and 1991, the parties insisted on linking the formation of community and regional executives to the national government formation process and thus even cancelled prior regional arrangements. In 1985 the PSC and PRL insisted on forming the narrowest possible coalition (52 seats out of 104 in the Walloon regional council and 67 out of 133 seats in the community council) because that coalition was maintained at the national level.[41]

In 1987 the PVV and CVP had agreed to continue their alliance in the Vlaams Raad if it was arithmetically possible, and confirmed this on election night. This prior arrangement eventually had to give way to national coalition needs, underlining the political dependence of the regions at that stage. Thus, this arrangement was torn up and the special law revised to revert to a proportional executive for four years to associate the SP and the VU, which were national coalition partners. In other federations, such as Germany, there may be many forms of *Land* coalition that differ from national arrangements, which reinforces the position of the regional layer of government.

Clearly, the 1980 reform was merely one further step along the way, and much remained to be done. The government that took office in 1981 did not have a two-thirds majority, or even an assured majority in the French-language group. Through its economic policy it polarised opposi-

tion. Hence, although the 1985 legislature was *constituant*, its achievements in the fields of the Reform of the State were meagre. Indeed, the
Martens-Gol team deliberately marginalised the issue in order to concentrate on its austerity economic programme. A government without the
Walloon Socialists and with no prospect of gaining their external support
could not expect to make progress with the reform process.

Article 59 *bis* was revised to give the German community near-equal
status. A special majority law was adopted in June 1983 setting up the
arbitration court, and another law clarifying the effect of the court's
judgements was passed in June 1985. Some additional laws dealing with
the financing of communities and regions or abolishing some powers of
the Brussels *agglomération* were passed in August 1987, but these were
relatively minor matters. Following the local elections of 1982, the problem of the Brussels suburbs – large French-speaking minorities in
Flanders and, above all, the Fourons – and economic and fiscal conflicts
between the regions faced the cabinet. However, the PRL/PVV refused to
be distracted from their greater priority, which was economic policy.

Yet the community question came back with a vengeance and led to
the premature collapse of the government in 1987 even after it had
survived the 1985 election, which in turn had been brought about by
internal disunity. Indeed, in some ways the 'revolving door' issue of the
mayor of the Fourons and his ability to speak Dutch was, as its relatively
easy solution in 1988 showed, no more than a symptom of a wider and
deeper malaise caused by the attempted benign neglect of the community
problem by the Martens-Gol team.[42]

So it was that the wheel came almost full circle with a search, reminis-
cent of the Steenokkerzeel, Egmont and Stuyvenberg days, for a global,
comprehensive pacification. At a very early stage, indeed on 4 January
1988, the second *informateur*, Willy Claes (SP), was instructed to report
on a possible programme 'which could offer solutions to the various
community problems and prepare a new reform of the State'. The third
informateur and later *formateur*, Jean-Luc Dehaene (CVP), established a
complex negotiating structure of a central negotiating group (party presidents and two other representatives per party), numerous working groups
and a system of consultations between Francophone (PS and PSC) parties
on the one hand and Flemish and other parties of the future coalition (CVP,
SP, VU) on the other. As the coalition agreement later put it, there was
general recognition that 'application of the laws of 1980 over the past
seven years has shown there are deficiencies in the distribution of competences between the central government, regions and communities...'[43]

Hence there was a double aim: to deal with problems left unresolved
in 1980 and to correct the deficiencies in the 1980 reform. The coalition
agreement signed on 2 May 1988 contained over 100 pages, excluding
appendices that were also voluminous.[44] There were very detailed

provisions on the Reform of the State measures with precise deadlines; the third phase was less detailed. Once again, the iron law of Belgian coalitions was to be confirmed: namely that only the early period of a coalition, with a precise timetable and adequate dynamism, is fruitful. The first and second phases were completed with great speed, and indeed the new Brussels regional council was elected on schedule in June 1989, but the third phase was effectively abandoned.

The agreement meant considerable compromises and provoked strong opposition in the two Francophone coalition parties. The PSC, which had of course wanted a reversal of alliances, saw ratification by only a 66.4% majority at its special congress. The main problem was localised and was to do with concessions over the *communes à facilités* near the language border. Indeed, of the two PSC 'No' votes in Parliament, one came from a deputy from Comines.[45] The other came from a recent PSC ally, the former RW president and Walloon activist, Paul-Henri Gendebien. The opposition in the PS was even more extensive and on a broader front, despite trade union pressure to return to government and the personal weight of Guy Spitaels behind the agreement. The agreement was only ratified by 60% and the two major federations, Charleroi and Liège, cast negative votes.

The opposition was based on an inadequate change in the socio-economic policy and a 'sell-out' of Walloon and Francophone positions in general and of José Happart in particular.[46] However, in Parliament there was only one PS negative vote from a deputy from Mouscron, near the language border. The high level of support for the agreement at the CVP Congress (641:41:23, 91.2% in favour)[47] and the return of Mr Martens as premier reassured the other parties which otherwise might have feared an Egmont scenario with the government later being sabotaged by the CVP right wing with the tacit of encouragement of Martens.[48]

The main elements of this wide-ranging agreement were:

— full communitarisation of education;
— devolution of additional powers to the regions (public works, transport, economic policy etc.);
— powers of the communities and regions in international relations (they had already had some such powers since 1980);
— establishment of the Brussels region and 'community commissions' to exercise some community competence in Brussels;
— extension of the competence of the arbitration court;
— special measures in relation to municipalities near the language border: the Fourons, Comines/Mouscron, and '*communes à facilités*' near Brussels,
— reform of the Senate.[49]

Backed by the detailed nature of the coalition agreement and a series of explicit and implicit linkages, the government moved fast to take advantage of the new dynamism created by the agreement. Responsible for pushing the process forward were the vice premiers of the two major coalition partners, who had also staked their prestige on their role as key negotiators of the agreement: Jean-Luc Dehaene (CVP) and Philippe Moureaux (PS). They worked with a cabinet committee on institutional reform, chaired by the prime minister and including all five vice premiers (one per party).[50] For a year intense activity was maintained, and where less important issues could not be resolved they were deferred to the so-called 'third phase' (of which the main issue was reform of the Senate and, with it, direct re-election of various councils). This was, for example, the case of international competences.[51]

In July and August 1988, the necessary constitutional revision was undertaken, involving Articles 59 *bis* (education devolved), 17 (educational guarantees), 47 and 48 (*communes à statut spécial*), 107 *ter* (arbitration court powers), 108 (Brussels) and 115 (financial provisions). At the same time, there was a radical revision of the 1980 law, extending the powers of the regions and regulating co-operation and consultation between the different levels of government. The necessary legislation on the special status of municipalities near the language border was enacted. The 'second phase', which ran from January to June 1989, saw the revision of Article 59 *ter* (German community) and the adoption of legislation by special majority on the arbitration court, and the establishment of regional authorities in Brussels and on financial matters. In the two phases eight articles of the Constitution were revised, and six special majority laws and five ordinary laws were adopted.[52]

The so-called 'third phase' was then to deal with the difficult issue of the exclusive competences of the central government; residual competences for the regions and communities; direct election of all regional and community councils; reform of the Senate; international competences of the regions and the proposed system of 'constructive no-confidence' and appointment of governments for the full fixed term of the legislature (this was borrowed from Germany and was already applied to the regional and community executives).[53]

However, except for the Volksunie, there was less energy behind the 'third phase' and a certain desire to consolidate the previous year's frenetic progress. At a political level, there was, to put it crudely, a desire to do only just enough to maintain the coalition. Two parallel approaches followed: one involved giving the initiative to Parliament, a sure sign in Belgium of a desire for a pause. In the past, such parliamentary initiatives have proved useful in terms of long-term consensus building, but have not been generative of immediate solutions and so it was to prove in 1989/90.

The presidents of the two chambers set up a joint parliamentary committee on institutional reform on December 22.[54] It had twenty-six members (thirteen from each chamber) from all political groups. It sat in two phases: until April 1990 in its original composition and from June to its winding-up in July with only members of the majority. In the first phase four reports were produced: the first, on parliamentary reform, produced only a very limited consensus on the Senate's future; the second, on residual competences, produced no agreement; and the third, on international competences, was able to agree that the regions should also receive international competences and on measures to ensure coherence among the various levels of government. The fourth report was little more than a catalogue of issues to be included in the 'third phase'.[55] During the second period, two additional reports on the Senate and international issues failed to break any significant new ground.

When the committee was being wound up, the government began, under Volksunie pressure, to look at the 'third phase'. Dehaene and Moureaux reported to the prime minister and the vice-premiers on 21 September 1990. Essentially, they noted the difficulties and recommended that the existing working party under Mr Alen, the cabinet secretary, should be given the task of taking up the one issue on which there was some agreement in Parliament: the matter of international relations. The cabinet agreed on this limited step.[56] There the matter rested till the spring of 1991, which turned out to be an election year. The Volksunie demanded a substantial third phase.

In March 1991 there appeared to be limited agreement on two aspects: international relations competences and direct election of the regional/community councils, separate from national elections. This pre-agreement fell apart under conflicting pressures and demands, but a full third phase was still demanded by the Volksunie. The PS and PSC wanted devolution of TV licence revenue, but this was opposed by the Flemish parties unless new matters, such as social security, were devolved; this in turn was opposed by the PS and PSC although they demanded devolution of agricultural policy. The right of Francophones living near Brussels to vote in the French community was opposed by the Flemish parties, which however demanded the splitting of the Brussels-Halle-Vilvoorde electoral district.

Mr Martens proposed a compromise, based on the work of the Alen group. He recommended that a limited 'third phase' package should be put forward dealing only with the matter of international competences and the principle of direct election and the reform of the Senate. This last point would not be achieved in the existing legislature. At the same time, the rules of the two chambers would be modified to achieve a 'specialisation' of the two chambers, a fully regional Senate reducing duplication. For the moment, the Volksunie accepted.

The PS/PSC demanded that the devolution of TV licence fees should also be added. There the matter rested as the government collapsed in September 1991.[57]

NOTES

1. For this post-war period, see Xavier Mabille, *Histoire Politique de la Belgique*, CRISP, Brussels, 1986, 313-23.
2. For this useful analysis, see J. Brassinne, 'Les Nouvelles Institutions Politiques de la Belgique', *Dossier du CRISP* no. 30 (1989), section 1: 'La Réforme de l'Etat 1970-1989', 1-2.
3. See A.R. Zolberg, 'Les origines du clivage communautaire en Belgique', *Recherches Sociologiques*, VII, 2, 1976, 150-70, and M. Ruys, *De Vlamingen. Een Volk in Beweging, en Natie in wording*, Tielt, 1972. For the parties see also Rowies, *Les Partis Politiques en Belgique*, CRISP, 1977, no. 10.
4. See M.P.
5. For analysis of these elections and results, see N. Delruelle, R. Evalenko and W. Fraeys, *Le comportement des électeurs belges (1965 et 1968)*, Editions de l'Institut de Sociologie de l'ULB, 1970.
6. For later election results, see *Dossiers du CRISP* no. 10, *Les partis politiques en Belgique*.
7. For background, see J. Grootjans, *La Révision de la Constitution: l'évolution des idées et des textes jusqu'en juillet 1970*, *CH* 518 and 519 (1971).
8. A. Alen and P. van Speybroeck, 'La Réforme de l'Etat belge de 1974 jusqu'au Pacte d'Egmont', CEPESS 1977 (hereafter cited as 'CEPESS'), 7-9.
9. CEPESS, 23-28. Also *L'évolution du R.W. d'avril 1974 à mai 1977*, *CH* 736, (1978), 12-18.
10. For the contents of these schemes, see CEPESS, 48-66.
11. For the position of the parties before the Dialogue Communautaire, see CEPESS, 68-110.
12. CEPESS, 111-24.
13. *CH* 783/94 (1977), 3.
14. CEPESS, 12.
15. CEPESS, 144 and 154.
16. See *CH* 857/8, 7 and 8.
17. See text of the pact, preamble quoted in CEPESS, 289.
18. On the CVP objections, see *Le Soir*, 7 October 1978, 1 and 2.
19. Statements by André Cools and Mme Spaak in the RTB discussion programme 'Faire le Point' on 8 October 1978.
20. Editorial by André Cools in *Le Peuple*, 7 October 1978.
21. For full text of the pact, see CEPESS, 289 and 299. For a description of the Egmont and Stuyvenberg Agreements and for an analysis of Bill 461, see *Les nouvelles institutions de la Belgique*, CRISP 1978.
22. For full election results, see *CH*, 826/7, 'Les élections législatives du 17 décembre 1978', 4, 18 and 32.
23. Pact signed 14 November 1978, see *CH* 874/5, 'La Réforme de l'Etat' (II), 51, 52 and 53.
24. For an explanation in detail of these phases, see *CH* 857-8, 'La Réforme de l'Etat: phase immédiate et phase transitoire', 9-11.
25. For the preparations and the legislation on the 'immediate' phase, see *CH* 857/8, 12-24.
26. Ibid., 25-33.
27. Ibid., 34-7, for an analysis of these texts.
28. *CH* 874/5, 'La Réforme de l'Etat' (II), 6-21.
29. Cited in ibid., 21.
30. Ibid., 22-5.
31. Cited in ibid., 874-5, 25.

32. For the crisis, see ibid., 26-41.
33. Ibid., 27.
34. Ibid., 47-9 and annex 6.
35. For parliamentary consideration and the fall of Martens II, see *CH* 893-4, 'La Réforme de l'Etat' (III), 8-14 and 16-19.
36. Ibid., 14 and 15.
37. Ibid., 19-23.
38. Ibid., 24.
39. Ibid., 26-42, for details of parliamentary discussions.
40. F. Dehousse, 'Apparences et réalités de la Réforme de l'Etat belge', in *CH* 1138 (1986) for an exposé of this theory.
41. X. Mabille et E. Lentzen, 'Les Elections du 13 octobre 1985', *CH* 1095/6 (1985), 52.
42. Xavier Mabille, 'La Législature 1981-85', *CH* 1088 (1985), 23-31.
43. Cited in E. Arcq, P. Blaise, E. Lentzen, 'Enjeux et Compromis de la Législature 1988-91', *CH* 1332/3 (1991), 12.
44. Arcq, Blaise, Lentzen, op. cit., 7.
45. On the PSC Congress, see J. Brassinne, X. Mabille, 'La Crise Gouvernementale: décembre 1987-mai 1988', *CH* 1198/9 (1988), 31.
46. Brassinne and Mabille, op. cit., 29-31. Portion of the P.S. Federations, 30.
47. CVP Congress, Brassinne and Mabille, 31.
48. On the importance of Martens, see Guy Dalozem, *La Libre Belgique*, 30 April 1988.
49. J. Brassinne, *Dossiers du CRISP* no. 30, op. cit., section 1, 7-8 and Accord du Gourvenement: Section II, 'Une nouvelle phase de la Réforme de l'Etat'.
50. Mémento, op. cit., 98.
51. Brassinne, op. cit., section 1, 11.
52. Arcq, Blaise, Lentzen, op. cit., tables on pp. 11 and 16.
53. *Documents Parlementaires*, Chambre 516-6 (SE 1988), 65 *et seq*.
54. Arcq, Blaise, Lentzen, op. cit., 17-23.
55. The four reports can be found in Documents Parlementaires Chambre 11167-1 (1989-90); 11167-2; 11167-3; 11167-4
56. Arcq, Blaise, Lentzen, op. cit., 23-4.
57. *Ibid.*, 69-71.

5

THE STRUCTURE OF THE NEW BELGIUM: FEDERALISED GOVERNMENT

Belgium has now by general consent travelled a considerable and irre-versible distance towards a federal structure. Indeed, the revision of the Constitution implementing the 1992 *Accord de la St Michel* declared Belgium a federal state and introduced clear federalist terminology into the Constitution. Thus the central government is now called the 'federal government'. The reforms of 1970 established that principle, and those of 1980 and 1988 have given the devolution of power and the autonomy of the communities and regions sufficient solidity. The process, as we have seen, is far from complete but it has travelled far enough to put the regions and communities firmly on the map. The debates on the exact nature of the Belgian institutional structure that were characteristic of the 1970s have lost their vigour. Few would now contest that Belgium's institutions are evolving in a federal direction and that they show many *sui generis* features that, while not found in other federal systems and while lacking some features normally found in federal systems, certainly do not dis-qualify Belgium from being considered virtually a federal state.

This conclusion is confirmed by the 1988 coalition government which stated: 'The government considers it opportune to take another step towards a federal state structure.'[1] Referring to the package on the table in 1988, the then prime minister Martens told Parliament: 'When this proposal is in force, our country can take its place, from the point of view of is structure among states that are called federal.'[2] The King, in his National Day speech of 1988 given just after the first phase had been adopted, referred to Belgium as a federal state. In the parliamentary debates on the various proposals, Prime Minister Martens spoke of *'fédéralisme d'union*, that is to say greater autonomy of the regions and communities, associated with mechanisms reinforcing the central state'.[3]

In short, this was federalism but a very Belgian form of it, designed to save rather than destroy national unity. It was a form of federalism that contained many ambiguities and permitted different readings. However, unlike the early reforms, the sheer weight of cumulative change has made a more federal reading not only possible but even inevitable, and the *Accord de la St Michel* drew that logical conclusion.

There are five levels of government. Of these only the federal level, the regions and the communities have legislative powers. The other two layers – the provinces and the municipalities (*communes*) – are subordinate authorities, subject to oversight and without legislative powers. The structure is set out in the Table opposite.[5]

The different levels should not be seen as watertight – there is considerable porosity between levels. For example the judiciary is 'national'. Regional and community MPs are national MPs, elected nationally, wearing community and regional hats, except for the Brussels regions and the German community. This is of course intended to be temporary, and to be changed as from the next general election. There are mixed, shared and concurrent competences, and mechanisms for co-operation between different layers. The system being put in place corresponds to what is often called 'co-operative federalism'. The different levels exercise checks and balances and must mesh in and work together. This is less difficult in what is already a consensual political culture than it would be, say, in Britain.

We will now look at the powers, organisation and financing of each level and then at the mechanisms for conflict prevention and resolution, co-operative action and judicial review, which have resulted from these successive reforms, culminating in 1993.

The distribution of competences

Competences in Belgium have not been distributed according to a planned scheme. The central state, which has existed since 1930, holds all power. Then, from 1970, powers have been devolved in successive slices out to the communities and then to the regions in 1971, 1980 and 1988. In the still awaited third phase, abandoned with the collapse of the Martens VIII government in 1991, it was intended that all residual competences should go to the communities and regions and that the central state should only retain ones that were explicitly attributed.[6] As a first step, it had been intended that the regional economic competences should be general and be limited only by the reserve powers retained by the central state. Such an approach was considered inconsistent with Article 107 *quater* of the Constitution and abandoned.[7] So for the moment residual competences are left with the state, and the regions and communities have only those explicitly devolved to them either by the successive amendments to the Constitution or by special laws implementing Articles 59 *bis* (communities) and 107 *quater* (regions). The main competences of the three types of authority are set out below. It should be noted that while the competences of the Flemish and French communities and the Flemish and Walloon regions are equal and identical, the Brussels region and the

Level	Institutions			
Federal	FEDERAL GOVERNMENT (House and Senate)			
Communities	German community	French community / Joint community commissions (in Brussels): French community commission | Dutch community commission		Flemish community and region
Regions	Walloon region	Brussels region (F) (NL) — Bilingual		Dutch region
Language regions*	German | French-language region	Bilingual		Dutch region
Provinces (9)	Namur, Hainaut, Liège, Luxembourg	Brabant | Brabant (split into 2 provinces) | Brabant		Antwerp, Limburg, W. Flanders, E. Flanders
Municipalities (589)	Unilingual (F) *communes and communes à facilités*	19 Brussels *communes*		Unilingual (NL) *communes and communes à facilités*

THE STRUCTURE OF BELGIAN GOVERNMENT

Source: Adapted from J. Brassinne, 'Les Nouvelles Institutions de la Belgique', *Dossiers du CRISP*, no. 30 (1989), Section 4, p. 2 and the dossier published by *Le Soir* on 15 Dec. 1992.

* These are areas established by the Constitution and not institutions as such.

German community are not identical to the other regions and communities.

At the federal level [9]

Limits to the competences of the central state cannot of course be set out, since that level retains all residual competences. Basically it has those national competences that have not been devolved; reserved national competences in areas where competences belong mainly to the regions or communities; and concurrent competences in two specific areas.

NATIONAL COMPETENCES

– external relations (except those devolved to the regions), including European Community (EC) policy.
– defence
– the Gendarmerie
– justice (the court system, prisons etc.)
– social security and pensions
– public health
– public debt
– public services administration
– Economic and Monetary Union
– residual powers.

Economic and Monetary Union is a concept going beyond a reserve or residual power. The national authorities are required actively to safeguard the unity of the Belgian economic and monetary space and to guarantee the application of EC laws and norms in Belgium. Belgium is thus to remain a single economic area within the wider EC. Of course this concept is borrowed from the EC single market concept into which to an extent it merges. To that end the central authorities retain twelve key economic competences and the right to set general norms and conditions necessary for ensuring the unity of the economic and monetary space and free movement and access of factors of production. The central government is thus exclusively competent for internal and external monetary policy.

Other national competences are: financial policy (banks and credit policy); prices and incomes policy; competition policy except local norms. commercial and company law; access to professions; industrial and intellectual property except artistic property; foreign trade licences and quotas (but not trade promotion); norms and legal units of measurements (the metre, etc.); statistics. The Société Nationale de Crédit à l'Industrie (SNCI), which is responsible for large-scale industrial investment, remains national despite regional economic and industrial competences; labour law and social security.

FEDERAL RESERVE POWERS AT THE COMMUNITY LEVEL

On *education*:
– school-leaving age
– minimum (but no other) conditions for having qualifications
– pensions of teaching staff.

On *cultural policy*:
– the right to broadcast government statements on radio and television
– advertising (formerly a reserved national competence, now 'communitarised')
– national cultural bodies
– some professional retraining.

On *'personalisable'* matters:
– basic legislation on health care
– basic legislation on the CPAS, on the handicapped, on the rehabilitation of prisoners, and on youth policy.

NATIONAL RESERVE POWERS AT REGIONAL LEVEL

These include:
– environmental norms
– basic norms for distribution of water and treatment of used water
– species conservation
– the national electricity grid
– the nuclear fuel cycle
– energy pricing
– limited reserve competence on employment policy
– infrastructure and transport, civil and military defence, the Brussels national airport (Zaventem), protection of the environment in territorial waters, access to the professions
– administrative supervison of the two provinces of Brabant
– special measures arising out of the international role of Brussels.

CONCURRENT COMPETENCES

– scientific research
– export promotion.

National measures authorised in parallel with regional measures where, for example, international co-operation is a dimension.

The communities [9]

The communities have three basic competences:
– *Education*. With the few exceptions that are reserved to the national

level, the communities alone are competent for all educational policy, including higher education. There is thus no longer a national education ministry.

– *Cultural matters*. These include cultural policy, subsidies to cultural organisations, libraries, language policy and, most important, all aspects of broadcasting. There are now three separate and autonomous broadcasting authorities. The matters of advertising and support for the written media have also been communitarised since 1989.

– *'Personalisable' matters*. These include health and social assistance, including hospitals, family policy, but with the exceptions reserved to the central authorities that we have already noted.

The communities have all the necessary legislative powers by decree and administrative powers necessary to exercise those competences. They have also been given the power to conclude international treaties in all areas of their competences. The executive concerned negotiates the treaty and presents it for ratification to its council.

The competences of the communities reach their respective language regions: the French-, Dutch- and German-language regions and, for the French and Flemish communities. They also cover institutions and services in the bilingual region of Brussels that are clearly unicommunitarian. In addition there is in Brussels a form of decentralised community authority exercised by the community commissions and the *commission réunie* (joint commission) with the corresponding executive *collèges* and the *collège réuni*. These bodies can exercise functions delegated by the parent communities and also exercise various implementing functions within the scope of community legislation. Those commissions and *collèges* are formed from the elected members of the Brussels regional council splitting into its two language groups and the regional executive splitting into its linguistic components.[10]

In principle the German community has the same powers as the other two, but it has not yet received the extra competences devolved in 1988. Therefore in education and broadcasting its powers remain more limited than those of the two others. This will eventually be remedied.[11]

The regions

The regions derive their competences from laws adopted by special majority under Article 107 *quater* of the Constitution. There is a separate Walloon region with its own institutions, whereas there is one single set of Flemish institutions exercising both regional and community competences. The German community area is part of the Walloon region, but by agreement it may exercise some of the Walloon region's competences in the German area by delegation, which has in fact been agreed for some environmental matters relating to the protection of the Hautes Fagnes area.

The Brussels region, both as a city region and as the capital of Belgium and seat of European and international bodies, is also treated differently in some ways. Due to a theoretical, almost theological quarrel over the status of Brussels as an equal third region, opposed by the Flemish, the Brussels council legislates by *ordonnances* and not decrees.[12] The practical significance is minor. The Brussels council is directly elected from the start. As we shall see, it has many linguistic checks and balances. It also has, as we have seen, some involvement in the exercise of community competences in Brussels and there is a joint national-Brussels region coordination committee to agree on measures relating to the status of Brussels as a national and international capital. It can by consensus deal with planning, transport, and infrastructure issues, but only in relation to the city's special status. Where there is no consensus, the central government can impose measures at its own expense. The Brussels region has also absorbed the competences of the former *agglomération* (Greater Brussels council).

The basic common regional competences are:[13]

– *town and country planning* and land use
– *environmental matters*: protection of the environment, waste disposal, hunting, fishing, forestry, water management
– *housing*, including public health aspects
– *economic and industrial policy*: natural resources, promotion of exports, economic and industrial expansion and investment, restructuring of the five so-called ex-national sectors (steel, glass, chemicals, textiles, mining) credit policy (all these are of course subject to the limitations resulting from the remaining national reserve powers in the economic field).
– *financing, organisation and supervision* (*tutelle*) of the provinces (except Brabant) and municipalities (except those of the Fourons, Comines and the German-language area)
– *energy policy*: gas, new energy sources, low-tension (up to 70,000 volts) electricity grids, energy distribution and transport (however, there are important national 'reserve' powers in this area)
– *employment policy*: labour exchanges and employment creation programmes
– *transport and public works*: all transport except Zaventem airport and rules on access to the professions; infrastructure policy
– *agricultural policy*, with some national reserve powers
– *external trade promotion.*

A key provision of the *Accord de la St Michel* is that the powers of the French community can be transferred to the Walloon and Brussels regions, where they will be exercised by the French language groups and the French community commission, which have been given decree powers and a financial drawing right on the region. The delegator, the *Conseil de la Communauté Française* (CCF), must decide such transfers by a two-thirds majority and the recipient by an absolute majority. This will be exercised to a considerable extent, thus virtually *de facto* abolishing the CCF. This was a controversial provision, but it proved necessary for financing education, where the Walloon and Brussels regions have had to 'refinance' the community's education policy.

Organisation and structure

The structure of the national level has been covered in Chapter 3. All the communities and regions have a similar structure with a legislative/parliamentary organ and an executive responsible to it with the power of legislative initiative and of executive and administrative functions. The Flemish region and community, being combined, have a slightly different organisation. The Brussels region and the German community differ from the others in that their legislative organs are already directly elected outside the national Parliament. Unlike some federations such as the United States, Canada or Germany, the Belgian regions and communities do not have a '*constituant*' power of their own, although that has now been partly remedied. The communities and regions are now competent to fix independently the number of members of their governments, their working methods and the procedure for the election of the councils. Over time, some distinct features may emerge. The structural arrangements are set by the Constitution and in very great detail by the various national special laws, down to such matters as portfolio distribution in the executives, although this will be eliminated by the *Accord de la St Michel*, to give more freedom to the communities and regions. This is in part justified, at least in the Flemish and French communities and the Brussels region, by the need to ensure special provision for Brussels, and in Brussels itself to guarantee minority protection that cannot subsequently be removed. Judicial power – ordinary courts, *conseil d'état* and *cour d'arbitrage* – is in any case purely national, although the community and regional assemblies can establish penalties for violation of their legislation.

Legislative/parliamentary bodies[14]

The *Accord de la St Michel*, now translated into constitutional and special laws, provides that the councils will all be directly elected for a term of five years, as the German community council and Brussels regional councils already are. The elections will be held at the same time as European elections (June 1999 etc.). These measures are to be phased in with the 1995 general election. The number of members will be as follows:

The Flemish council. 118 directly elected, plus six chosen by the Dutch-language group of the Brussels regional council.

The Walloon regional council (CRW). 75 directly elected.

The council of the French community (CCF). The 75 directly elected members of the CRW, plus 19 chosen by the French-language group of the CRB from among its members.

The council of the Brussels region (CRB). 75 directly elected.

The council of the German community. 25 directly elected.

The Flemish council. There is a single parliament (Vlaams Raad) for both community and regional matters. When Flemish regional matters are discussed, the members elected in Brussels may not take part or vote. Initially, the special law provides that the council is composed of elected senators. This has been changed with effect from 1994. Currently, however, by way of derogation from what might be called the semi-definitive solution, the council is composed of all deputies and directly-elected senators (not provincial or co-opted senators) elected on Flemish lists in both Flanders and Brussels – in other words, all those deputies and directly-elected senators in the Flemish linguistic groups in the House and Senate. These members have a 'dual mandate' or two hats. They sit both as national parliamentarians and as members of the Vlaams Raad; the latter meets in the building of the national Parliament but at other times. Following the 1991 elections, there were 188 members of the Vlaams Raad (a small increase on 186 in 1988 and 182 in 1981). Of these, only four (deputies and senators) come from Brussels. In its political composition the council is weighted to the centre right. The CVP and PVV have an absolute majority (98 out of 188) and the Volksunie, Vlaams Blok and the Rossem list, all leaning to the right, hold another 35 seats. The left (SP and Agalev) only has 44 seats.

The Raad is organised much like the national Parliament. It elects its president and bureau. It has political groups and fifteen committees with fifteen members each, which do not distinguish clearly in their competences between community and regional matters. As in the other assemblies, there is a committee on co-operation, i.e. co-operation with the other communities and regions.

Like the other assemblies, the Vlaams Raad exercises legislative power in its area of competence (in its case, in both community and regional matters) by decree which has the same normative value as laws. It elects the executive (when it is not composed by proportional representation as before 1985 and between 1988 and 1992), it exercises the various powers of parliamentary control including censure, interpellation, committees of inquiry, and parliamentary questions (written and oral). Each assembly may establish its own rules, but these cannot alter the detailed provisions of the special laws. The session begins in October and lasts for forty days. Decrees are promulgated by the executive and not by the King.

The Walloon regional council (CRW). The CRW is composed only of the deputies and senators directly elected in the four Walloon provinces and the *arrondissement* of Nivelles in the province of Brabant. Following the 1991 elections, it has 104 members (106 in 1981). Here, the PS has 47 members (51 in 1987), close to an absolute majority. The PS/Ecolo constitute a clear '*majorité de progrès*' with 60 seats. The PS has the same strategic options of alliances as in the CCF. In 1985, the PSC and PRL had just half the seats.

The CRW, which meets in Namur and not in Brussels, exercises only regional functions and like the other assemblies legislates by decree, and elects and controls the Walloon executive. It has seven committees each with fifteen members. Some committee chairs are held by opposition PRL members. Members have (at least) three hats: national deputy or senator, member of the CCF and member of the CRW.

The council of the French community (CCF). Since the 1991 elections the CCF has had 130 members (it had 132 in 1988) of whom 104 are Walloons and 26 from Brussels, who can of course vote on all matters there. Demographics have led to a decline in membership though the weight of the Brussels members is much greater than in the Vlaams Raad. Politically, the CCF leans to the centre-left: the PS and Ecolo have 69 seats and with the FDF 73 out of 130. It is hard to put together a majority without the PS. The PSC and PRL, at their height in 1985, had a bare majority of 67 out of 133 seats. Here, the PS has the most strategic options: a centre left PS/Ecolo (FDF) coalition, the traditional *rouge-romaine* (i.e. Socialist-Catholic) coalition with the PSC (a comfortable 80 seats) or even a PS–PRL coalition (82 seats).

The CCF has the same functions in community matters as the Vlaams Raad and is similarly organised. It has nine committees, including separate ones for co-operation with the other regions and communities. Like the Vlaams Raad it has a committee for international relations and one for radio and television.

The council of the Brussels region (CRB).[15] The CRB is separate from the national Parliament, and since its election for the first time in June 1989 it has been unaffected by national government crises and by national elections. It is therefore more autonomous than the other assemblies, except the council of the German-speaking community (CGC). It is elected for a five year term (June 1989, 1994 [prolonged to 1995], 1999, etc.) and cannot be dissolved. Its elections are held on the same day as those to the European Parliament. Lists are unilingual and candidates may not change their language group, which is fixed once and for all on the basis of their identity cards. The council's 75 seats are distributed first to the two language groups and then subsequently to the lists in each language group. This ensures that groups will be fairly and, for the Dutch group, adequately represented in the CRB. A limitation has been placed on the *cumul des mandats* (multiple office-holdings): members of the CRB cannot also be municipal councillors and national deputies or senators (which could of course also mean membership of the Vlaams Raad or the CCF). They can have two but not three elective offices. *Suppléants* (alternates) sit in the CRB but cannot vote unless the full member is absent, but sit in the committees with full voting rights, when a member becomes a member of the executive in order to avoid excessive depletion of the small Dutch linguistic group.

In the elections of June 1989, sixty-four members of the French-speaking group and eleven Dutch-speakers were elected. The political composition of the assembly was as shown in the Table below. The numerous guarantees for the minority Dutch-speaking community make necessary the formation of very large coalitions, as the executive must contain two members from the Dutch community and must in reality have majority support in both linguistic groups. Thus the 1989 executive was composed of six parties (PS/SP, CVP/PSC, FDF and Volksunie). The Liberals, Ecolo and the FN represent a divided and disparate opposition.

French-speakers		*Dutch-speakers*	
PS	18	CVP	4
PRL	15	VLD	2
FDF	12	SP	2
PSC	9	Volksunie	1
Ecolo	8	Vlaams Blok	1
Front National	2	Agalev	1
Total	64	*Total*	11
Global total	75		

The principal minority guarantees are: the election of a vice-president of the council; at least one (currently two) members of every committee; certain recognised rights of the language groups as such to convoke sessions, known as the *sonnette d'alarme* (alarm-bell); one-third of the seats in the bureau; complex 'double majority' provisions for elections to posts; minority guarantees for two ministers in the executive; and the facility for political groups to be formed by members representing lists that obtained 10% of the seats in their linguistic group (hence only unilingual groups can be formed). This currently means two members for the Flemish groups as against seven for the French-speakers.[16]

The CRB organises its work in a similar way to the others. It has a *bureau elargi* (president, vice presidents, group chairman). It has six committees and two for the *commissions réunies* for community matters. There can be joint meetings and temporary committees for special tasks. As in the national Parliament, many interpellations are heard in committee.

For community matters the council divides into its linguistic groups which each act as the legislative assembly for matters falling in their competence and also sit jointly (all seventy-five members) as the *commission réunie* (joint committee) for matters concerning both communities.

The CRB was very active in its start-up period, indeed much more so than the other regional councils had been in their equivalent period. The extent of this activity can be seen in the Table below.[17] Nineteen private members' bills and nineteen government bills were tabled. Of government bills 89.47% passed and of private members' bills only 19.15%.

	1989/90		*1990/91*	*1991/92*
Plenary sittings	41		42	46
Committee meetings	68		141	135
Interpellations		77		
Topical questions		206		
Oral questions		167		
Written questions		1,130		

The council of the German community (CGC). Since its inception in 1973 the CGC, which has its seat in Eupen, the capital of the German-language area, has always been directly elected. It has twenty-five members elected for four years (every fourth October) by proportional representation. An election took place in October 1994. German-speaking national MPs and provincial councillors can attend, but may not vote. The council has six committees, each with nine members. The largest party is the PSC, but second-largest party, with five members, is the local Partei der Deutschsprächigen Belgien (PDB).

The German-language community consists of about 66,000 people living in a rural, wooded, isolated and strongly Catholic area south-east of Liège, against the German border. The area, which consists of nine *communes*, of which Eupen and Sankt-Vith are the most important, was awarded to Prussia in 1815, having previously been part of the principality of Liège and as such part of the Holy Roman Empire. It was awarded to Belgium unconditionally by the treaty of Versailles after a so-called test of opinion, but the latter was hardly genuine and the area would undoubtedly have opted for Germany if given a genuinely free choice in 1920. In the 1930s there was considerable Nazi agitation although many citizens remained loyal to Belgium. In 1940, following the occupation, the area was annexed to the Reich. As German citizens some 8,700 men were enrolled in the *Wehrmacht*, whereas others went underground. The prevailing outlook was not necessarily Nazi but many felt they had been wrongly incorporated into Belgium in 1920 and were German in sentiment. Their situation was tragic. At the liberation some 3,000 were convicted of various collaboration crimes and for some years the area was regarded with suspicion.

The 1932, 1935 and 1963 language laws gradually established the right to use German in administrative and judicial matters as well as in education, not only within the area but for communication with the provincial, regional and central authorities. There remains some provisions for local French-speakers.[18]

The executives

Each community/region has its own executive. Thus, alongside the national government, there are the Flemish community, Brussels region, French community, Walloon region and German community executives. The rules governing the appointment and functioning of all those executives are very similar, although the Brussels regional executive has special rules to ensure that the Flemish minority is represented.

Basically, each one is elected by the council for the same term as the council itself. The system is that if a list of nominees signed by a majority of members of the council is presented, it is deemed to be elected. Otherwise each place on the executive is filled by election by an absolute majority in the council. The executive can be collectively or individually removed by a so-called constructive no-confidence motion on the German model: Such a motion must at the same designate a successor, preventing purely negative and circumstantial coalitions arising and so reinforcing the stability of the executive.

The executive of the Flemish community has eleven ministers, the French community four, the Walloon region seven, the German community three. In the Brussels region, besides three state secretaries who are not part of the executive, there are five ministers, two are French-speakers and two are Dutch-speakers, as at the national level; the minister president is linguistically neutral but as he will be a French-speaker, there is *de facto* a 3-2 Francophone majority. The executive power for special Brussels community matters is exercised by the two French-speakers and two Dutch-speakers sitting as separate *collèges*; for joint matters, the four sit together as a *collège réuni*. The mode of appointment of the Brussels executive is also more complex than for the others. Unless an agreed slate is presented with the support of majorities in both linguistic groups, election of the minister president is by the whole council and of the two ministers in each linguistic group by absolute majority. The executives of the French and Flemish communities must include one Brussels member. That of the German community, unlike the others, need not be elected from among council members.

The executives are organised like the cabinet, with their members distributing portfolios and taking decisions by consensus. They propose legislation, steer it through the councils, draw up budget proposals, implement legislation and run the administration. With the present degree of devolution, they are now politically important. This was symbolically shown by the decision of Guy Spitaels, then PS president, to take the presidency of the Walloon regional executive in 1991.[19]

The financing of the regions and communities

The weakest part of the Reform of the State has been the financial provisions.[20] The regions and especially the communities have been provided with adequate short- and medium-term financial resources but serious restrictions have been placed on their autonomous revenue-raising capacity. As a result, the theoretical autonomy of the new devolved authorities has been at least partly undermined and the French community faced a serious financial crisis over education in 1990/1.

In the early phase of the Reform of the State, the regions and communities were financed by block grants called '*dotations*' from the central government. The aim of the 1989 reform was to bring the resources accorded to each region and community into line with the latter's share of the *impôt sur les personnes physiques* (IPP) or income tax. Thus the current Walloon share of overall grants is 38%, which has to be reduced to 31% by the year 2000. The Constitution and the 1980 and 1989 special laws established a series of sources of revenue for the communities and regions. These are for the regions in the definitive period (after 2000):

– *regional taxing powers*. The regions may levy taxes, but only on goods, services or persons *not* already taxed. Here the regions may within these limits devise their own taxes and set the rates.
– so-called *regional taxes* that have been transferred to the regions (taxes on gaming machines, on gaming itself and on the licensing of bars, death duties, property taxes, stamp duties on property transfers, vehicle excise tax). These represent the major resource for the regions. For some of those taxes, for example vehicle excise, the rate is set nationally, but for others the region can very both the tax-base and the rate.
– *non-tax revenues*, e.g. revenue from forestry and tolls on waterways
– *loans*, which may be taken up both in Belgium and abroad, but are subject to supervision by a national body (*Conseil Supérieur des Finances*)
– *specific federal grants* (job-creation programmes and aid to municipal finances)
– an *IPP-based transfer* linked to old (1980) and new (1988) competences transferred
– *national solidarity*, based on a contribution for the region that receives the lower transfer based on the IPP. It would cushion the fall in the

Walloon share of the IPP compared with the higher block grants existing now.

For the communities the financial resources are fairly similar, though with significant variations:

– *radio/TV licences* to be progressively transferred to the two communities on the basis of a 'key' (20% for the Flemish community and 80% for the French community in Brussels)

– *a share of VAT revenue distributed* on the basis of a 55-45% key between the Flemish and French communities

– *a share of the IPP*. The communities, unlike the regions, cannot impose an additional per cent on the IPP.

– There is no *solidarity contribution* as such, but there is an educational needs contribution which will effectively act as a transfer to the French community.

– *loans for financing*, in particular capital investments.

In the transitional period there is a global resource transfer based on estimates of the loss of the old and new transferred competences, distributed by the usual way. The German community will also be financed through a share of the IPP, VAT and TV licences (about 0.63%).

The 1989 budgets for the various bodies (in millions of BF) were as follows:[21]

	Flemish community	French community	Walloon region	Brussels region	Flemish region
Current expenditure	212,591.5	165,596.1	68,940.9	22,237.1	102,387.1
Capital expenditure	9,551.4	10,176.6	568.0	4,602.2	14,718.3

Overall, some 30% of public spending capacity is to be transferred to the regions and communities by the end of the transitional period.[22] The main problems likely to arise are the solvency of the French community if it is not fused with the Walloon region, municipal deficits, and the lower financial capacity of the Walloon region even when the 'solidarity' and 'educational needs' elements are taken into account. The Flemish view is that each region/community should largely have financial autonomy, that is to say live from its own means, with either national or community solidarity being strictly limited.

Administration[23]

Each region and community has its own administration, admittedly quite small but nonetheless autonomous. The basic system was one of transfer of staff from the national level, corresponding to devolved competences rather than permitting the new bodies to build their administration from the ground up. However, the 1988 special law authorises the executives to fix staffing levels, recruit, appoint and fix the terms and conditions of employment, including remuneration, but not pensions which remain a national responsibility. Recruitment must still take place on the basis of merit (at least at lower levels) through the Secrétariat Central de Recrutement du Personnel de l'Etat, a sort of civil service commission. The original legislation provided for one single ministry for each region and community, but these may be split. For example, the Walloon region has already set up two separate ministries: one for transport and the other for all other matters.

The Walloon region has a staff of 6,256. The staff of the Brussels region is about 500 and must follow the requirements of bilingualism laid down in the national language laws. The Flemish community (region and community combined) has a total staff of 3,327 and, like the other regions and communities, expects this to increase with its increase in competences to about 6,500. The French community has a staff of 1,394. The German community for its part has a staff of thirty-six. Overall, the staff of the communities and regions represents no more than 2% of all civil service employment.

Prevention and resolution of conflicts

The framers of the reforms were well aware that their unavoidable complexity provided the potential for conflict,[24] and that considerable co-operation between the various layers of government is necessary if the whole system is to function, not least because the Constitution placed them all on an equal footing within their own spheres of competences. There is no '*hiérarchie des normes*', hence the intricate interlocking of competences and international responsibilities and the complex financing system clearly require a high degree of co-operation. Although in the design concept of the new institutions there is provision for judicial settlement of conflicts through the court of arbitration, this is seen as a last resort. A range of instruments of co-operation exist at different levels with the aim of limiting the number of damaging conflicts requiring a judicial remedy.

Certain forms of co-operation have been laid down as legal obligations, failure to follow them is a procedural violation that can make a law, decree or executive act null and void,[25] and results in legal sanctions. At the same time co-operation committees and, more important, the conciliation committee (CC) between the government and executives have been established. A complex system of mutual information, of consultation, requirements for assent, 'association' and joint decisions covers areas where the national government is competent (reserved powers and energy policy, loans, agricultural loans and grants, EC decisions) but must associate the regions/communities with it in the decision-making; areas where there is mixed competence or where coordination (railways, buses) is required and between regions and communities themselves. In other cases, there is a requirement that regions and communities should be represented in various national administrative bodies (and vice versa), especially in relation to culture, transport, agriculture and energy. There are also provisions for agreements between federated bodies (regions and communities) and the state, and between the federated entities themselves, e.g. to provide for joint administration or provision of services (tourism). In some cases (ports, hydraulic works and public works going beyond regional frontiers) agreements are compulsory.

Conflicts can also be avoided by the use of various devices during the legislative procedures in the various assemblies. The legislation section of the *conseil d'état* can be asked for a ruling by the presidents of the various legislative bodies and the executives, and where the *conseil d'état* considers that there is a conflict of competences; then the matter is referred to the conciliation committee which has forty days, during which the measure is suspended, to find a solution by consensus. The same applies to delegated legislation.

Where one assembly considers its interests to be seriously harmed by a bill or proposed decree under discussion in another assembly, it can by a three-quarters majority require the suspension of the measure for sixty days for a conciliation procedure to take place. If there is no solution the House of Representatives (in future the new Senate) delivers an opinion in thirty days to the conciliation committee, which takes a decision on the matter within sixty days. Those procedures are little used, being more in the nature of a deterrent. They only have suspensive effect, but their invocation would cause a severe political crisis and a search for a Belgian-style compromise. The government and executives can also inform the conciliation committee of measures proposed or decided by other executive bodies, with suspensive effect for sixty days.

As we have seen, the conciliation committee is an important lynchpin in the whole system of co-operation.[26] It is the main forum for consultation and coordination as well as for the prevention of conflicts being formally declared. It is composed of the prime minister and five national ministers; the president and a member of the Flemish community, the president and a Dutch-speaking member of the Brussels executive, and the presidents of the Walloon region and the French community. Thus there is a double parity – linguistic and national/regional and community. The president of the German community attends as a full member when his community is involved. The prime minister takes the chair. Working parties can be set up. Since 1989, there has been a small central secretariat and co-operation has been intensified and extended through specialised inter-ministerial conferences, of which there are now fifteen (public services, energy, education, public health, agriculture, international affairs etc.).[27]

Where prevention and conflict resolution fail or where individual interests are involved, there can be recourse to the courts. Delegated legislation can be ruled *ultra vires* by the ordinary courts (as can Brussels region *ordonnances*) and by the *conseil d'état*. Co-operation agreements can establish arbitration bodies.[28] The arbitration court hears cases concerning competences and violation of procedural requirements. Cases can be raised by the government, executives, presidents of the various legislative bodies, individuals and corperate bodies whose interests are directly affected by the measure complained of, within six months of the law, decree or *ordonnance* concerned being published. Other jurisdictions must refer such questions of competences to the arbitration court for a preliminary ruling that is binding on the ordinary courts.[29]

The provinces

Belgium is made up of nine provinces which are given a recognised existence by Articles 1, 2, 3 of the Constitution. Article 108 guarantees them certain basic functions and recognises them as representing, with the municipalities, forms of decentralisation of the state.[30] In 1830, of course, the provinces were the only level of government between the mass of small *communes* and the central authorities in Brussels. The provinces also represent a link with Belgium's historic past, corresponding to medieval areas and having survived the 'departmentalisation' of Belgium during the period of French occupation. The original provinces laid down in 1830 have not had either their number or their boundaries altered and thus represent the only level of Belgian government to have survived without serious reform. Under the Egmont pact, the provinces were to disappear as redundant in a federalised Belgium. In 1980 they lost their fiscal competence but recovered it again in 1982.[31]

Since 1970, the provinces can only be subdivided, their borders altered or new ones created by a law passed by a special majority. There are four 'Flemish' provinces – Antwerp, Limburg, East Flanders, West Flanders; four 'Walloon' provinces – Hainaut, Liège, Luxembourg and Namur; and the 'mixed' bilingual province of Brabant, which is in many ways an anachronistic complication in a communitarised Belgium. Brabant has been split administratively into a French-speaking and a Dutch-speaking area, each with its own institutions. The population of the provinces in 1989 is shown in the following Table.[32]

	Population	No. of seats in provincial council	
Brabant (to be split)	2,240,362	{ Flemish	75
		Walloon	56
Antwerp	1,592,437	84	
East Flanders	1,329,830	84	
Hainaut	1,278,255	84	
West Flanders	1,099,384	84	
Liège	997,864	80	
Limburg	740,974	65	
Namur	418,885	56	
Luxembourg	229,587	47	

Provincial elections are highly politicised. In 1988, only one provincial councillor was elected who did not belong to a party represented in the national Parliament (he was a far-left AMADA councillor in Antwerp); in 1994 none was elected. Coalition alliances in the provincial executives (*députations permanentes*) of six members may well not follow the wider national or regional pattern. Thus, for example, in 1987 the PRL in Luxembourg province formed a coalition with the PS, despite the eight-year PSC-PRL regional/community coalition pact concluded in 1985. One could even say that this was a pattern of PS-PRL coalitions at provincial level. In 1991 there were three in the Walloon provinces with a PS-PSC *députation* in Hainaut. In Flanders, there are one CVP-SP, one CVP-PVV, one grand tripartite coalition CVP/PVV/SP and one PVV/SP/VU coalition. In Brabant there was a form of 'grand coalition' of CVP/PS/PSC/SP/PRL/PVV members of the *députation*, refined in 1991 to exclude the PSC, thus making it a first asymmetrical coalition.[33]

The provinces are a subordinate authority. The Walloon and Flemish ones are subject to the administrative supervision (*tutelle*) of their respective regional councils.[34] The position of Brabant, with both French-speaking and Flemish-speaking inhabitants inside and outside Brussels, is somewhat more complex. Here *tutelle* remains in national hands. In addition to a governor, as in all other provinces, there is a vice governor charged with ensuring the application of the special language laws that apply to the six *communes à facilités* in the Brussels suburbs, and exercising the function of governor in the nineteen *communes* of Brussels. He will normally be a French-speaker if the governor is a Dutch-speaker. This has been replaced by the split of the province into two administrative areas.

Provinces also have their own executives. In each there is a royal governor, appoint by the King on the proposal of the minister of the interior. He is the representative of the central authority, with considerable direct executive authority, and he can reserve decisions to the central government.[35] There is also a political provincial executive of six members (*députation permanente*) elected for four years by the provincial council. The *députation* is the result of coalition negotiations, unless – as in Hainaut – one party has an absolute majority. Once elected, the *députation* is not subject to a vote of censure by the provincial council. The provincial council is the 'parliament' of the Province. It holds a session in July or October each year lasting fifteen days, although with the permission of the governor, it can be extended to four weeks. While the members of the *députation* are full-time officials, the councillors will have other jobs and often combine their positions in the provincial with local or national office. The Crown or the governor may call a special session for a specific purpose.

The main tasks of the council are to elect provincial senators (which will now be abolished), elect the *députation*, approve the provincial budget, propose nominees for provincial courts of appeal, oversee funds for roads, waterworks, assistance to local authorities, and matters of provincial interest, such as public works. It may enact provincial regulations on these matters, which must respect national laws or regional or community decrees (these laws and decrees may confer their implementation on the provincial authorities). The *députation*, as the executive, prepares and carries out the decisions of the council. It must table a budget, an annual report, and such other proposals as it may think necessary for the council's consideration. It may issue regulations (*arrêtés provinciaux*) and fix penalties for their breach. Provincial staff now number 14,615, a mere 1.8% of the total government staff, a fall on the figures for the 1970s.[36] The provinces are financed by a provincial fund raised at national level but due for devolution to the regions, and by fees, loans and provincial taxation; this resource accounts for less than 30% of the expenditure of the provinces. The main areas of expenditure are further education (50%), roads (10%) and aid to small business (10%). Total provincial expenditure was 26,885 million BF in 1978 and rose to 39,000 million BF in 1988.

The provinces seem increasingly to be an irrelevant anachronistic tier of government between *commune* and region and create a syndrome of overgovernment in what is after all a quite small country. Yet they are survivors whose demise is frequently predicted yet never quite seems to happen.

Local government

The most decentralised level of government and the one closest to the people is to be found in the *communes*, which may be urban inner city areas such as the nineteen in Brussels or rural ones as in Luxembourg province. There are in all 579 *communes*. The largest group (172) has between 3,000 and 10,000 inhabitants; 277 have less than 10,000 inhabitants; only eight have more than 100,000 inhabitants, most of these being in the large conurbations: Charleroi, Antwerp, Namur, Brussels.[37] One of them has less than 500 inhabitants.

Amalgamation has caused a significant decline in the number of *communes*. In 1920 there were 2,668 and by 1958, at 2,359, the figure had declined by only a little over 10%. But a major reform brought in by the 1976 elections reduced the number to 596. These amalgamations are not always successful and are certainly not popular, especially in rural areas – or in Brussels, where discussion on fusions has never made any serious progress. An alternative way of providing for wider planning and transport coordination is the constitutional provision introduced in 1970 for the creation of *agglomérations* in Brussels, Antwerp, Charleroi and Namur. However, such an *agglomération* was only ever established in Brussels. The Constitution also offers an alternative model, the *fédération de communes* (association of municipalities), especially in suburban areas. Five were established in the outer Flemish suburbs of Brussels in 1972 but then abolished again in 1977. *Agglomérations* and *fédérations* have their own elected councils and executives. A less formal and more successful form of co-operation between *communes* has been the system of *inter-communales* (inter-communal corporations) established to run certain services such as utilities or transport jointly. This possibility is also directly mandated by the Constitution.[38]

The *communes* are accorded a general constitutional guarantee of local self-government (Article 108), but the various forms of *tutelle* imposed on them and the close regulation of their powers set by the various municipalities acts since 1836 in fact greatly limit their real independence.[39] They can only act within the powers accorded them by the various laws regulating their activities. The *tutelle* is not merely a formal or legal control; it can also quash or alter their decisions on grounds of broader public interest. Often this can mean that the supervisory authorities – now the regions, but earlier the central minister of the interior – consider that municipal decisions breach regional or national policy or spending limitations. This is especially likely where there is a political divergence between the municipal majority and the supervisory authority. In the 1981-5 period, when there was still no Brussels regional authority outside the central government, PS *communes* in Brussels often came into conflict with the centre-right national coalition. Some matters must be submitted directly to the supervisory authority for approval; these include loans, town and land-use planning, by-laws and even recruitment. All other matters, whether decisions of the executive *collège* or the municipal council, can be suspended for up to forty days in which they may be annulled.

The mayor has a dual role, he is both a representative of the national authorities in the *commune* and in that capacity he is responsible for public order and controls the police force in the *commune* and may even in an emergency requisition the assistance of the *Gendarmerie* or the army. In that task he is not responsible to the council. Secondly, he is head of the communal executive and leader of the political majority in the *commune*. This dual status is reflected in the manner of his appointment. Mayors are appointed by the King on the proposal of the minister of the interior, who normally acts on a recommendation from the majority in the council. With the approval of the provincial *députation*, a mayor may come from outside the council. In the nineteenth century, these measures were designed to weaken the democratic elements and prevent the appointment of radical mayors. Today the 'reserve' powers of the central authorities and *députations* are more or less a formality, although, as the Happart problem in the Fourons showed, in special cases this may not always be so.

The 'parliament' of the *commune* is the council, elected by proportional representation for a fixed six-year term (1988, 1994, 2000 *et seq.*) in October of election year. The Municipalities Act regulates its size: the minimum is seven members and the maximum fifty-five for *communes* with over 300,000 inhabitants. The most usual size is 15-25 except in Brussels where 30-40 is the norm. In Brussels there is a guarantee for the Flemish minority that if no Dutch-speakers are elected, the first non-elected Dutch-speaker sits on the CPAS committee and has access to council papers. The council's main functions are to nominate the mayor, elect the *échevins*, oversee the executive *collège*, vote on the annual budget, set local taxes, approve loans, and approve local by-laws and plans for building and land use. In that sense it is the local legislature.

The mayor will be the head of a single party majority, and inevitably that party will be either the CVP, the PS or the PSC since only those can achieve overall majorities, local list majorities or coalitions. A mayor who is from the PS will be that party's *tête de liste* at the election and, if a vacancy occurs, the second on the list. Other parties are more flexible. Where coalitions are required, negotiations will determine the distribution of posts – that is mayor, *échevins* and CPAS administrators – among the coalition parties. The *collège* is like the cabinets at the national, community and regional levels and the *députations permanentes*; its member is from the majority only and does not include opposition members. There are usually about six *échevins*, who like a cabinet divide up portfolios (finance, social affairs, registrar of births, marriages and deaths, education and culture). In Brussels an additional *échevin* can be added from the language minority, and this inevitably means a Dutch-speaker. In the eight *communes à facilités* (six near Brussels, Comines and the Fourons), the *collège* has been elected since 1989 directly by proportional representation, to ensure minority representation. The *collège* meets collectively like a cabinet and prepares proposals for the full council, whose decisions it administers. It cannot be censured by the council. Coalitions are often local, since in many councils there may be purely local lists. Often they cross the national government opposition divide with many

PSC-PRL coalitions. There were also PS-RW or PS-FDF coalitions well before these community parties were national coalition partners. The 1994 local elections saw the first significant breakthrough by the Francophone far right.

What are the functions of local government?[40] It is responsible for planning, land-use and licensing, the school system, amenities, roads (but not highways), and welfare administration through special bodies: a *centre public d'aide sociale* (CPAS) is established in each *commune*.

Every *commune* must appoint a secretary, a *receveur* (treasurer) and a police commissioner, although this last appointment is formally made by the King. All other staff are appointed by the council. *Communes* employ a total of 93,648 staff (11.5% of all public employees) the CPAS 58,463, the *agglomérations* 2,393, and *intercommunales* 15,863. For all categories except the CPAS, this represents a fall compared with the early 1970s, since the severe spending squeeze imposed on local authorities has forced rationalisation.[41] Indeed, local government finances have been in something of a crisis since the early 1980s, often with severe cash-flow problems in cities with severe social problems such as Antwerp and Liège. The *communes* have only limited autonomous revenues, many of which have not proved elastic. They receive the receipts from certain charges and fees such as vehicle and dog licences, and they may levy so-called '*centimes additionnels*', a form of precept on some other taxes. However, in 1974 these raised barely one-third of revenue, which fell to 21.3% by 1978 and now stands at 20%. The most important sources of revenue are grants from the *fonds des communes*, directly from the state, regions and provinces. Education (28%) and social purposes (21%) account for nearly 50% of expenditure. Total expenditure in the *communes* was 177,068 billion BF in 1978 and 388.4 billion BF in 1989.

Local politics remains local. Although local councils have been penetrated by the national parties, there is still a significant place for purely local lists usually called 'local interests', 'the mayor's lists' or sometimes by a more pretentious title such as '*Nivelles 2000*'. In 1982, for example, 417 of 1,446 councillors in East Flanders province did not belong to national parties. In some of the Walloon provinces the proportion was higher (749 out of 1,530 in Liège province), 403 out of 710 in Namur, and 452 of 632 in Luxembourg). As we have seen, heterodox coalitions are also possible at local level. However, local authorities are part of the wider consensual political networks, with many local councillors working in social organisations such as trade unions, Boerenbond, *mutualités* and ministerial *cabinets*, which of course enables them to do favours for their local voters. Many are office holders at other levels such as provincial councils, or the national Parliament. This again provides potential for networking and wider political recruitment that is such a vital part of Belgium's consensual and '*proportz*' system that begins in its highly politicised local governments.

NOTES

1. Coalition Agreement of 8 November 1988, 5.
2. *Documents Parlementaires* (SE 1988) 516/1, 4.
3. B. Houbert and P. Vandernoot, 'La Nouvelle Loi des Réformes Institutionnnelles du 8 août 1988', *Administration Publique*, T. 3/1988, 213.
4. The remainder of this chapter draws on the CRISP dossier published in 1989 after the latest round of reforms. J. Brassinne, 'Les Nouvelles Institutions Politiques de la Belgique', *Dossiers du CRISP* no. 30 (1989), cited as *Dossier*, and on 'La Belgique fédérale', *Socialisme*, no. 239 (October 1993).
5. *Dossier*, section 1, p. 2.
6. See E. Arcq, P. Blaise, E. Lentzen, *Enjeux et Compromis de la Législature 1987-91*, *CH* 1332/3 (1991), 17, *Dossier*, section 3, 'L'Etat Central', p. 8.
7. Opinion of the *conseil d'état*, *Documents Parlementaires* SE 1988, no. 516, p. 32.
8. *Dossier*, section 3, 8-24.
9. *Dossier*, section 4 (communities), 16-22.
10. *Dossier*, section 4, 22-4, and S. Loumoye *Les Nouvelles Institutions Bruxelloises*, *CH* 1232/3 (1989), 32-53.
11. A. Méan, *Comprendre la Belgique Fédérale*, La Libre Belgique, Brussels, 1990, 25-6.
12. S. Loumaye, op. cit., 9-11.
13. *Dossier*, section 5, 12-23.
14. For details, see *Dossier*, section 4 (counties), 2-16; section 5 (regions), 5-9.
15. On the CRB, see S. Govaert, *Le Conseil de Région Bruxelles Capitale*, *CH* 1351/2.
16. Govaert, op. cit., 25-6.
17. Data from Govaert, op. cit. (committees); 32-4 (plenary); 35-6 (legislation); p. 43 (questions).
18. Méan, op. cit., 43-60, for details on financing.
19. On the executives, see *Dossier*, section 1, 31-9, and X. Mabille and J. Brassinne, 'La Formation du Gouvernement et des Exécutifs', *CH*, 1356 (1992), 12-15.
20. Méan, op. cit., 43-60 for detail on financing.
21. *Dossier*, section 4, 24-43.
22. Méan, op. cit., p. 10.
23. On staff and administration, see *Dossier*, section 4 (communities) 44-6; section 3 (regions), 43-5.
24. For procedures on conflicts, see *Dossier*, section 6, 'La Coopération, la Prévention et le Réglement de Conflits entre l'Etat, les Communautés et les Régions' and G. Nagels, *Communautaire Conflicten in Belgie. Systemen voor Beheersing van Conflicten tussen de Staat, de Gemeenschappen en de Gewesten*, Die Keure, Brussels 1986.
25. See Article 124 *bis* of the law on the court of arbitration, *Moniteur Belge*, 7 January 1989, and *Dossier*, section 6, 20.
26. Nagels, op. cit., 49-112 and *Dossier*, 17-19.
27. *Dossier*, section 6, 18-19.
28. Ibid., 14.
29. Organisation and procedure of the court of arbitration, in Nagels, op. cit., 31-47, especially procedural flow charts on p. 37 and 39. For new 1988 competences, see *Dossier*, section 6, 20.
30. *Dossier*, section 2, 8-9.
31. Ibid., 8, fn. 8.
32. *Annuaire Statistique* (1990).

33. *Mémento Politique* (1988), 184, on composition of provincial councils and coalitions, and *CH* 1356 (1992), 5 for 1991 coalitions.
34. *Dossier*, section 5, 17-18.
35. *Mémento Politique*, op. cit., 182-4, on the competences of provinces.
36. Ibid., 165.
37. *Annuaire Statistique* (1989), 5-7.
38. *Mémento Politique*, 194 and 198-202.
39. Published in *Codes Larcier*, Brussels, 1987.
40. *Dossier*, section 2, 9.
41. *Mémento Politique*, op. cit., 190-8, for details.

6

THE POLITICAL PARTIES AND
THE PARTY SYSTEM

As we have seen, the political parties are the lynchpins of the political system. But although they are central actors in the political process, they do not have a complete monopoly. Here we look at the political parties themselves, their origins, evolution, organisation, membership, electorates and policies. Having thus placed them on the political chessboard, we turn to their interaction, which constitutes the party system, and finally examine the growing criticism levelled at them and at the party system generally that has emerged strongly in recent years, notably at the 1991 elections.

Any analysis of the modern Belgian party system must also take into account the basic fact that there is no longer a single national political system nor merely national political parties. Indeed, the two wings, Flemish and Walloon of the three traditional political families (Christian, Socialist and Liberal) have become increasingly estranged from each other in the process of rapprochement within each community to defend common community standpoints. This might suggest that an asymmetrical coalition, without one linguistic wing of a given political family, is now possible. Hitherto this rubicon has not been crossed. Different federal and regional coalitions are likely to come first and open the way. There are now quite distinct and potentially autonomous politics in Flanders, Brussels and Wallonia. Some parties, such as the PS, are major players in several political systems (national, Brussels and Wallonia) while others, such as the FDF, are only important in one system (Brussels). These parties, with significant involvement in several systems, may have to set priorities and make choices.

The Belgian party landscape remained remarkably stable up till the mid-1960s, but then a more complex system took shape, with the emergence of significant community parties alongside the traditional political families and, with that, of interlocking regional/national systems. That new structure, during its existence lasting nearly three decades, acquired a certain stability of its own, but that stability is in turn under threat from new political forces that have emerged from marginality, such as the

Greens (Ecolo/Agalev) and the various strands of the far right (URDT, Vlaams Blok, Front National and the van Rossem list).

Before plunging into the inevitable minutiae of the complex history, organisation and policy of each of the Belgian parties individually, it is worth stepping back and taking a comparative overview of party membership, both in absolute terms and in relation to the electorate of each party and at the sociological make-up of the electorate of the main parties (see Table).

TOTAL PARTY MEMBERSHIP 1960-91

	1960	1965	1970	1975	1980	1985	1990	1991
CVP/PSC	213,751	132,396						
CVP			103,158	120,730	125,141	114,716	131,719	132,070
PSC			39,336	52,042	57,904	43,372	43,322	43,283
BSP/PSB	199,000	205,485	225,073	253,993				
SP					113,922	108,223	99,235	99,919
PS					154,798	140,462	153,400	155,100
PVV/PLP	48,200	86,250	77,654					
PVV				43,794	58,625	73,631	71,051	72,283
PLP/PRL				42,237	45,000	70,154	40,000	40,000
VU	2,500	12,630	36,326	52,420	49,563	50,890	40,779	36,474
FDF			?	?	10,990	10,000	10,200	10,000	?
Agalev						925	2,130	2,038
Ecolo						1,248	1,280	1,375
Vl. Blok					1,231	3,698		6,500

MEMBERS AS % OF EACH PARTY'S VOTERS

	CVP	PSC	BSP	PSB	PVV	PRL	VU	FDF	ECO	AGA	VB
1961	9.6		10.2		7.3		1.4				
1965	8.5		14.0		7.7		3.6				
1968	8.5		13.9		9.1		4.9				
1971	8.9	11.8	16.4	18.2	6.0	9.6	7.1				
1974	9.4	9.9	16.8		7.1	13.8	9.5	5.4			
1977	9.0	10.3			11.5	12.8	9.3	4.4			
1978	8.7	10.9	16.3	20.5	10.1	14.5	3.7				1.4
1981	10.7	12.8	15.7	21.8	7.8	9.2	8.0	8.0	0.7	0.6	2.4
1985	9.0	8.8	12.3	18.1	12.0	11.8	10.7	14.1	0.8	0.4	4.3
1987	11.7	8.2	11.6	15.1	10.4	13.2	10.1	18.9	0.8	0.5	3.6
1991	12.7	9.2	13.4	18.5	10.2	8.0	12.1	11.0	0.4	0.7	1.6

Although in their detailed structure Belgian political parties obviously vary a great deal, they are remarkably similar in their organisational structure.[1] There is a party president elected by the congress who will usually be a member of the national Parliament (Gérard Deprez of the PSC is an important exception: he is a MEP), but never a minister (national or

regional). The highest authority is an annual or biannual congress composed of delegates, except in the FDF where all party members are voting
members of the congress. Beyond that there is a party council, usually
consisting of delegates elected by the congress, representatives of local
sections and a large number of *ex-officio* members (ministers, parliamentarians, representatives of party youth and women's organisations and *zuil*
– i.e. ideologically associated – organisations). These party councils are
the party's 'parliament' between congresses. Day-to-day management is
in the hands of a much smaller executive and a party secretariat. All parties
provide for various more or less binding forms of minimum representation
of party youth and women in their decision-making bodies. All provide
for the possibility – in fact rarely used – for some kind of local primary
election for electoral lists. All provide for an extraordinary congress to
confirm participation in government. None provides for any organised
affiliation as such, although both the CVP and the PS, for example, do
provide for representation of 'their' *zuil* organisations.

The Christian Social family (CVP/PSC)

The CVP/PSC family has dominated Belgian politics since the 1880s,
governing alone for an unbroken period till 1914. Since then they have
governed in coalitions either with the Socialists or Liberals or in tripartite
or other broader coalitions up till the present day. Apart from a short period
following the Second World War (1945-7) during the *Question Royale*
and again in 1954-8, the Christian Social parties have never been in
opposition. Apart from 1925 and 1936 and more recently in 1987 and
1991, the CVP/PSC has been the largest – though not the oldest – of the
three political families.

The Mechelen Catholic congresses of 1863, 1864 and 1867 gave the
philosophical impulses for the organisation of the Catholic party.[2] Up till
1884, Catholic political forces were relatively disorganised and localised,
obtaining support from such diverse organisations as the Antwerp Meeting Party, but essentially based in local *unions conservatrices et constitutionelles* – the first founded in Ghent in 1852, to be followed by
Leuven (1854), Antwerp and Brussels (1858) – which were in fact little
more than election committees. In 1864 they were federated into the
Fédération Nationale des Unions Constitutionelles et Conservatrices.

A parallel development was the establishment of *Cercles Catholiques*
with a more spiritual and pastoral aim (Bruges, 1853). By 1868 there were
some fifty of these, and they joined up in the Union des Cercles Catholiques, which increasingly concerned itself with political issues. These
bodies represented the most conservative Catholic tendencies.[3] On the
other hand, bodies such as the Society of St Vincent de Paul (1845) and
the Fédération des Sociétés Ouvrières Catholiques (1867), influenced

later by the papal encyclical *Rerum Novarum*, formed the Christian Democratic tendency which was also important in the Union Nationale du Redressement des Griefs; this organised 'social congresses' in Liège in 1886, 1887 and 1890, which led to the foundation in 1891 of the Ligue Démocratique Belge, precursor of the Mouvement Ouvrier Chrétien (MOC).

The Union des Cercles Catholiques and the Fédération des Unions Constitutionelles et Conservatrices merged in 1864, to be joined in 1888 by most of the Christian Democratic tendency, forming the Catholic party under the leadership of Beernaert as chairman. Some of the Christian Democrats formed the Parti Populaire Chrétien under Daens, but this group never obtained more than two seats (Catholics averaged about ninety-six seats) and 3% of the vote. From then till 1919, when universal suffrage was introduced (despite proportional representation from 1899), the Catholic Party retained an absolute majority in both chambers of the legislature. In 1919, its share of the vote fell to 38.8% and remained relatively constant till the Second World War, with its high point of 41.3% in 1921 and low point of 28.8% in the unique election of 1936, recovering to 32.8% in 1939. Apart from the years 1925-9 and 1936-9, it was the largest group in Parliament and always formed part of the varying coalitions: CP, Socialists and Liberals (1919-21; 1926-7; 1935-9), CP and Socialists (1925-6; 1939) and CP and Liberals (1921-5; 1927, 1935, 1939). There was one Catholic minority government in 1925, which lasted one week.

The pressures of universal suffrage and the growth of the CSC (Christian trade unions) forced a reform in the old Catholic party: it had to recognise more clearly that it was a pluralistic party appealing to diverse social groups. Thus, in 1921 the old Catholic party was reorganised as the Union Catholique Belge, a federation of four '*standen*' (lit. 'estates'): the *associations constitutionelles* (the political '*stand*'), the Boerenbond (farmers); the Ligue Nationale des Travailleurs, and the Catholic middle-class organisation, the Fédération des Classes Moyennes. In 1936, the party was renamed the Bloc Catholique, and two distinct wings, the Flemish Katholiek Vlaamse Volkspartij and the Walloon Parti Catholique Social (PCS), appeared.

After the Second World War, the *standen* system was abolished in favour of a 'classless' approach based on Christian '*personalisme*'. As before, the unitary structure was tempered by the recognition of two wings, which grew in autonomy after 1965, but in 1968 a rupture (called '*distancement*') came about over the Leuven University affair (when the CVP wanted to transfer the university out of Flemish territory). Since then two distinct parties, the Parti Social Chrétien (PSC) and Christelijke Volkspartij (CVP), have come into being, maintaining only minimum mutual coordination. With time, their positions on both 'community' and economic and social issues have tended to diverge, especially with the greater and more radical trade union influence in the PSC.[4]

The Parti Social Chrétien (PSC). The PSC is the junior wing. It operates only in Wallonia, Nivelles and Brussels, but has never had the strong position in Wallonia that the CVP enjoys in Flanders. In Brussels, like other parties, it competes with CVP lists and leaders such as Mr Martens who stood in Brussels for the Senate in 1991. In that year the party had about 55,000 members, about 10% of them in Brussels.[5]

The basic level of party organisation, as for all the parties except the Communist party (PCB), is the section based on the *commune*. It is at this level that members are recruited into the party, and where associations are formed for electoral purposes (districts for the provincial elections). At the *arrondissement* level, at which parliamentary candidates are chosen, the party has a structure parallel to that existing at the national level, with a congress, a *conseil permanent* (made up of representatives of the *sections* and *ex-officio* members, such as deputies) and a *comité directeur* for day-to-day administration. At the national level the congress, which holds several preparatory seminars before the main congress, is the supreme body. Apart from the statutory congresses held annually, *ad hoc* ones may be held to decide on current political issues such as participation in government, although this is rarer in the PSC than in the other parties. The *conseil permanent*, with 150 members (delegates of the *arrondissements*, *ex-officio* members, members elected by the congress), meets from time to time and usually decides on participation in government. The *comité directeur*, chaired by the party president, meets frequently, often once a week, to deal with current matters. The leader of the party – the president – is elected by all PSC members, voting by post. After the party's defeat in 1981, Mr Vanden Boeynants resigned and was replaced by the Christian Democrat leader (on the left wing of the party), Gérard Deprez.

The PSC and the CVP share the CEPESS (Centre d'Etudes Politiques Economiques et Sociales), a political research institute linked to both parties, which provides research back-up for the party and its deputies. The parliamentary groups in the House, the Senate and community and regional councils elect their own chairmen and leadership, which are subordinate to the party leadership and president.

The PSC structure is shot through with conflict between its two '*tendances*' (wings). The right is generally organised by the Centre Politique des Indépendants et Cadres Chrétiens (CEPIC) and the left, the Démocratie Chrétienne, is closely linked to the CSC and the Mouvement Ouvrier Chrétien (MOC).[6] The Seraing congress in 1976 recognised these tendencies, but required them to support party policy. However, the activities of the rightist CEPIC discredited and divided the PSC in the early 1980s, as we shall see, and the new party president Gérard Deprez (who became a MEP) obliged the organised tendencies in the party to cease their activities. The CEPIC was remodelled and became a 'centrist tendency' in the party.

The MOC was founded in 1945, to link the various branches of the Christian Workers' Movement. In more recent years it has not identified exclusively with the PSC but with a broader union and progressive movement. This led to Démocratie Chrétienne (DC), under André Magnée as chairman, being set up in 1971. Its leading figures are Alfred Califice, Philippe Maystadt and Gérard Deprez, the current PSC President, and its nerve-centre has been in the Charleroi area. Its main concern has been to maintain and develop the progressive strands in PSC policy and avoid the party's isolation in Wallonia, where it is a minority occupying third place. The MOC is now in the process of setting up a new political movement which would be independent of the PSC. It was in reaction to the establishment of DC that the right wing, formerly active in the Mouvement Chrétien des Indépendants et des Cadres (MIC), set up in 1955, set up CEPIC in 1972.[7] At the same time, the MOC sought to set up an independent political movement (the SEP party), but this failed because the PSC and unions accepted the discipline of the centre-right coalition.

The size of the PSC electorate traditionally depends largely on the level of religious practice in an area.[8] It is strongest in the south of the Sambre-Meuse industrial valley. For the whole Walloon region, it was 19.8% in 1981 and 26.7% in 1978. Its post-war peak was 34.2% in 1958, and its low point 20.3% in 1968. Its strongest positions in 1978 were in the province of Luxembourg (average 44.6-48.5% in the *arrondissement* of Neufchâteau-Virton). In the province of Namur, it obtained an above-average 29.9%, but only 11.1% in Brabant (16% in Nivelles) and 23.4% in Hainaut, its worst score in a wholly Walloon province. In 1981, it obtained only 33.1% in the province of Luxembourg and 18.0% in Hainaut. In 1985, the PSC rose to 22.8% still behind the PRL in Wallonia (+2.0%) and 9.3% in Brussels where it was the fourth party. Its best result was 50.5% in the canton of Ferrières and Hervé (48.1%). In 1987 it was also second in Wallonia, reaching 23.2%. In 1991, it almost held its vote with 22.5% in Wallonia and 8.8% in Brussels. Its won 50.5% in the canton of Herve and over 40% in seven others.[9]

The PSC electorate[10] is about 57% female and therefore more predominantly female than the electorate as a whole. Only about 20% of its electorate is under forty years old; 29% are workers, 22% white-collar workers ('*employés*'), 19% farmers, 13% owners of one-man or very small businesses ('*indépendants*'), and 8.6% middle and senior managers; 83% considered themselves to be practising Catholics. The PSC has an older and more 'bourgeois' electorate than its sister-party, the CVP. Of all workers, only 17% voted PSC, whereas among farmers the proportion was 54.3% for men and 62.9% for women. Among male practising Catholics, 53.1% voted PSC, which only 6.2% of non-practising Catholic men did.

The basic determinants of PSC voting are therefore in order: religious practice (although this is clearer among men than women, and less clear among working-class voters) the occupation of farming, age and sex (more women PSC voters).

The PSC, with its minority position and the divisions between its strong CEPIC and DC wings, has always been a pragmatic party, a party with a governmental vocation. It has been in power uninterruptedly in various coalitions (CVP/PSC-PS/SP; CVP/PSC-PRL/PVV; CVP/PSC-PS/SP-PRL/PVV) and the broader coalitions including the RW (1974-7) and the FDF and VU (1977-80). Since the war, it has been in power for all but two short periods in 1945-7 and 1954-8. It has, however, progressively become the junior partner to the CVP, and has not provided a prime minister since 1968. Indeed, its subordination to the CVP led it to overcome its instinct to go into opposition after the November 1981 elections.[11] It has always sought to avoid both ideological and community isolation in Wallonia hence its coalitions with the PS/SP and its participation in the Front des Partis Francophones in 1978.

The policy options of the PSC are the traditional concerns of Christian Democrats. A Christian 'personalist' ideology, based on reconciliation of class interests, has involved measures in favour of the less privileged without involving major structural changes in society. The key issues have been support for the Catholic education system and the family and opposition to abortion and the permissive society. In foreign policy, the PSC has favoured a strong defence posture and more rapid European integration. In more recent times, despite pressure from the Démocratie Chrétienne wing, it has tended in its economic policy to move to the right on issues of the indexation of wages, state support for industry and public expenditure cuts.[12]

The PSC has remained prudent in its approach. It was reluctant to coalesce with the Liberals in 1981 and represented a brake on the radicalisation of that coalition. It feared isolation in left-leaning Wallonia.[13] In 1987 it was a bell-wether, sensitive to PS advances, insisting on the reversal of alliances and using its position and the stability of its vote to obtain important guarantees for the Catholic school network when education was communitarised, both from the PS and from Flemish parties. The pragmatism and moderation of the PSC with its well-balanced government team led by Melchior Wathelet and Philippe Maystadt (MOC), have amply succeeded.

The Christelijke Volkspartij (CVP). The CVP, long dominant in Flanders, is the leading party in that region, and as a result has a pivotal role both regionally and nationally, although its vote is in long-term decline.

It operates in the four Flemish provinces and in Brussels and Brabant, where it competes with the PSC. In 1978 it obtained 43.5% of the Flemish votes but in 1981 was defeated when it polled only 36.9% (representing 26.1% of the national vote in 1978 [PS: 13.1%] and 19.3% in 1981). Since the late 1960s it has dominated its sister-party, the PSC, and as the main component of the largest political grouping in the country it has further-more dominated both Flemish and national political life, giving rise to the criticism of the 'CVP-state'. Except for the Leburton government of 1973-4, it has invariably provided the prime minister since 1968 and now also commands four out of the nine seats and the presidency in the Flemish executive. Like the PSC, it has been in government in shifting coalitions continuously since 1958, and apart from 1945-7 and 1954-8 since the liberation. Its electoral high-point in Flanders was 60.4% in 1950 and up till 1981 its lowpoint was 39% in 1968. Since the '*distancement*' of the PSC and CVP in 1968, its high has been 43.9% in 1977. In Brussels, where since 1968 there has been competition between the PSC and the CVP, the high for the CVP was 10.1% in 1977 (PSC: 14.1%) and its low was in 1981 with 5.5%.

The best areas for the CVP are Antwerp province – 32.5% in 1981 (45.6% in 1978), but its results have been less good in the city of Antwerp with 28% in 1981 – (a fall from 42% in 1978). Its second-best province Limburg (47% in 1978). In 1978 its lowest were in East Flanders with 45%; even in Ostende its score was 28.3%. Thus the CVP vote is fairly evenly spread throughout Flanders. After its heavy defeat in 1981, its lowest score remained 20.9% in Ostende, and it still obtained more than 60% in many *cantons* (subdivisions of *arrondissements*).[14]

Since then, the party's electoral long-term decline has continued. In 1985, when all the centre-right coalition parties except the PVV did well, the CVP recovered some ground to 34.6%, a gain of 2.6%, but remained well below its 1978 level. In 1987 it fell slightly again to 31.4% and in 1991 to 26.9%, its historic low in Flanders. It lost votes in thirteen *arrondissements* and gained in only three. Its best result at *arrondissement* level was 39.6% in Ypres and its worst 19.2% in Antwerp (also its worst loss, of 8.1%). Its best result at canton level was 52% in Kruishoutem.[15]

The profile of the CVP voter is similar, but not by any means identical, to that of the PSC voter. The CVP electorate has a female majority (55% to 45%) but a slightly smaller one than the PSC. A larger proportion of the CVP electorate (34.7%) are under forty; a larger proportion (35.6 as against 29.6% in the PSC) are workers, and a smaller proportion farmers (15.3%). Identification with the working class is felt by 57% and with the middle class by 37%, against 43.5 and 42.6% respectively for the PSC. Identifying themselves as practising Catholics are 92.7%, but then Flanders is in general more Catholic. CVP voting is therefore determined by religious practice coupled with working-class identification, and less with age and sex than for PSC voters.

In Brussels, both CVP and PSC voters are more likely to be *indépendants*.

Women (52.2%), over-sixties (54.2%), farmers (75%), middle-class identifiers and those who identify with no class (51.4 and 60% respectively)
and practising Catholics (61.8%) are the groups which predominantly vote
CVP. Indeed, only 12.5% of non-practising Catholics/non-Catholics
voted CVP.

More workers vote CVP than SP in Flanders. Figures for 1979 show
that 53.4% of the CVP vote is female and that 49% of Flemish women
vote CVP (only 40% men). The Party's voters are mostly between
thirty-five and forty-five (23.3%), but it has more young voters (7.6%)
than any party except the VU; indeed of all voters under twenty-five, more
vote CVP than for any other party (35.7%). Of CVP voters 41.6% are
workers, 21.7% *employés*, 16.7% *indépendants*, 10.6% managers and
9.4% farmers. Of all workers, 41.4% vote CVP and it remains the largest
party in every social category. Of all practising Catholics 62% vote CVP,
and surprisingly 17.3% declared non-believers voted CVP, a recent evolution. Of its electorate 73.3% are practising, 22.5% non-practising and 4.75
non-believers. The CVP retains its broad appeal as a non-class party and
has become less clearly confessional as religion has become a less important, but still a by no means negligible factor in political choice.

The CVP appeals to three basic groups: Catholic workers, the 'middle
classes' (small traders and businessmen) and the farmers. The Christian
trade unions, the Middenstand organisations and the Boerenbond are
closely associated with the party and co-exist more easily than the warring
factions of the PSC. This has made for an even more pragmatic and
'classless' party than the PSC, with a strong element of hard-nosed
defence of Flemish interests and a degree of cultural nationalism, coupled
paradoxically with an attachment to Belgium, as conceived by the CVP,
hence the expression the 'CVP-state'.

At the beginning of the 1980s, under pressure from figures such as its
party president Leo Tindemans (1978-81), the CVP moved into a tougher
and less centrist position on economic issues. Its chief slogans in the 1981
election were 'Take it or leave it: a strong new policy' and 'The truth is
harsh, but only the CVP dares to say so'. This involved a harsh line on
responsibility for the crisis both in class and community' terms (no more
concessions to the unions or to Wallonia). The five main elements of the
seventy-page manifesto[16] were 'economic reconstruction, support for
private initiative and the market, support for the family, an end to politicisa-
tion of economic policy, and the defence of Flemish interests'. The main
themes were the need for a strong government capable of implementing
policy, energetic action to reduce costs of production (taxes, social security
contributions, energy costs and, especially, wages), a resultant decrease
in public expenditure, and a decrease in state interventionism. At the same
time, measures are proposed for selective stimulation of certain
sectors (agriculture, viable restructured sectors and new industrial

sectors). Taxation and social security policies should support the family and be more selective. There is strong support for 'free' (Catholic) education.

The CVP shows its colours as a Flemish party, defending Flemish economic, social and cultural specificity. It accepts the Reform of the State, but insists on regional fiscal responsibility; in fact, it does not support greater devolution and above all is opposed to full regional status for Brussels, which it believes should simply have a special status. The CVP supported the regionalisation of five key industrial sectors, including steel for which Wallonia would then have to take financial responsibility.[17] In the international field, it strongly supports a federal Europe, seeking to 'give a new impulsion to the European Community' with greater political, monetary and industrial integration as urgent necessities. Europe needs to play a greater role in world affairs, especially in the North-South dialogue. NATO too needs strengthening, and the CVP supports its 1979 decision on Theatre Nuclear Forces (TNFs: Pershing and Cruise missiles), although from time to time CVP MPs joined protests against deployment.[18] After the 'Wende' (shift) to a centre-right coalition in 1982, the party under Wilfried Martens sought to remain loyal to the centre-right coalition. This was an easy choice in 1985, but it had to demarcate itself both from the aggressive liberalism of the PVV and from the Volksunie, especially in a government that gave low priority to the Reform of the State. Mr Martens went into the 1987 elections with the slogan 'no turning back' and at first was personally opposed to a reversal of alliances, but electoral losses, the PS gains and the attitude of the PSC made such a reversal inevitable. He agreed to continue in order to strengthen the new government, but also to moderate its federalism. There were moves in the CVP both in 1987 and 1991 to go into opposition but that was almost impossible, as no government could be formed without them.[19]

The organisation of the CVP is very logical, with parallel organs at every level:[20] the *kongres* (congress); the *partij bestuur* (party council), the *bureau* (executive) and the president. The basic level of organisation is the local *section* based on the *commune*, but it may be sub-divided into branches. Each section must be recognised by the *bestuur* in the *arrondissement* and a condition of recognition is a minimum membership equivalent to 7% of CVP voters in the *commune* or 3% of the total electorate. The *section* congress, consisting of all members, meets at least once a year and elects the *bestuur*, congress delegations for the *arrondissement* and the national level, and the president. It approves the statutes, subject to national 'model' rules, by a two-thirds majority, and adopts the manifesto for local elections. The *bestuur* consists of a number of members elected by the congress for three years, equal to the number of councillors in the *commune*, of whom one-third must be under thirty-five and at least one-fifth women and one-fifth men, plus some *ex-officio* members. The *bestuur* is responsible for medium-term policy decisions, and decides on alliances with other parties. It elects the *bureau* (president and members, each with a portfolio), which must include two women, for three years. The *bureau* is responsible for the day-to-day administration of the party. The CVP had 109, 554 members in 1966, 114,843 in 1960, *c*. 126,000 in 1976 and *c*. 130,000 in 1982, and has *c*. 140,000 today.

There is a similar structure at the *arrondissement* level, where the congress is made up of section delegates and some *ex-officio* office-holders. It elects the president and *bestuur* (president, fifteen members plus one per 500 party members, plus national *bestuur* members domiciled in that *arrondissement* and up to one-third co-opted members), and it elects the *bureau*. The *arrondissement* bodies are mainly concerned with parliamentary elections, campaigns and candidate selection.

The provincial organisation is more sketchy, consisting of a *bestuur* which has a number of members equal to twice the number of CVP deputies and provincial councillors in the province. The *bestuur* elects a *bureau*, fixes alliances and chooses candidates for provincial senators. Alliance decisions (for the *députation permanente*, for example) must be approved by the national *bestuur*.

At the national level, there is a congress consisting of delegates of the sections, members of the *bestuuren* of the *arrondissements*, and members of the national *bureau*. It meets at least once a year and may be called into session by at least five *arrondissements*. It normally meets to approve any new government in which the CVP is to participate. It adopts the programme, controls the work of the *bestuur*, and may amend the statutes by a two-thirds majority. It elects the president, whose term is a maximum of eight years. It elects a number of *bestuur* members (fifteen plus one per 5,000 members, of whom one-fifth must be women). The *bestuur* also includes CVP ministers, the *bureaux* of the Senate and House CVP groups, and up to one-third co-opted members. Every *arrondissement* and province must have at least one member. It may sack office-holders and exclude members by a two-thirds majority. It considers bills, decrees and policy statements from the CVP. Deputes must inform both their group and the *bestuur*, which considers current policy issues, of all their initiatives. The *bestuur* elects a *bureau*, which meets weekly and is composed of the president, nine non-deputies and some *ex-officio* members (the chairmen of the House and Senate CVP groups, four deputies and four senators, CVP ministers and the chairman of the CVP-*Jongeren* [youth organisation]).

At the *commune* level, polls are supposed to be held for candidate selection, but the *bestuur* may, by a two-thirds majority, decide that this need not be done.[21] Except where Parliament is dissolved suddenly, there should be polls at the *arrondissement* level for candidates to the House and Senate, but again these are rare. Most often, the *bestuur* of the *arrondissement* draws up a 'model list' for approval by an *arrondissement* congress. In any case, the national *bestuur* can modify the list by a three-quarters majority, adding names or changing the order. Polls are now very rare, and the reason for this is the perceived necessity of maintaining the delicate equilibrium between unions, 'middle class' and Boerenbond representatives. There is a theoretical age-limit for both deputies and senators of sixty-five and an anti-cumulation rule, but these may be set aside by the national *bestuur* by a two-thirds majority.[22]

There is also a *'comité de concertation'* with the PSC, composed of both *bureaux*, to discuss common problems. It is supposed to elect a joint national PSC/CVP president, but this post has remained vacant and the two parties have tended to drift apart.[23]

The Socialists

As we saw in Chapter 1, the first Socialist party, the Parti Ouvrier Belge,[24] was founded in 1885, avoiding the term 'Socialist', which even then was considered a threat to the party's essentially pragmatic outlook. Its basic doctrinal charter, the *Charte de Quaregnon* (1894), remained in force long after its quasi-revolutionary rhetoric had been superseded in the pre-1914 period by more specific pragmatic demands, to the point where the reformist current in the party forced through an anti-clerical alliance with the Liberals in 1912. The party first entered the House in 1864 with twenty-eight seats and first entered the government in 1916. Apart from a short Catholic Socialist government in 1925-6, it only participated in *'Union Sacrée'* governments in the early post-1918 period, and in the crisis years in the 1930s. However, it soon overtook the Liberals and became the second party, and even became the largest party in 1925-9 and 1936-9. After the end of the *Union Sacrée* period in 1921, it moved to the left, but in the 1930s it espoused the non-Marxist and nationalist theses of Hendrik De Man in his quasi-Keynesian *Plan de Travail*. De Man became president in 1939, succeeding the 'grand old man' of Belgian Socialism, Emile Vandervelde, on his death. He dissolved the party in 1940, and entered into open collaboration with the German occupation forces. A new party without collective union affiliations, the PSB was born clandestinely from the activity of P.-H. Spaak in exile in London; it was less clearly a 'workers' party' than its predecessors. Since 1946, it has always been the second largest 'family', reaching a high of 36.7% in 1961 and a low of 25.1% in 1981. Before the ravages of the 'community parties', its low was 29.7% in 1949. It has often been in government since 1945: in the period 1944-7 in 'national' or 'left' coalitions, in 1954-8 with the Liberals, in 1961-5, 1968-73, and 1981 in coalitions with the CVP/PSC, and in 1973-4 and 1977-81 in broader 'tripartite' or 'community coalitions'. Only twice since the late 1940s has it provided the prime minister: Mr Van Acker in 1954-8 and Mr Leburton in 1973-4.

In the matter of regionalisation the PSB/BSP long resisted the inevitable. The holding of separate and simultaneous congresses of the Walloon and Flemish organisations in 1967 did not wreck national party unity, and a number of expedients, such as linguistic parity in all governing bodies and a system of co-presidents (since 1971), were tried until the collapse of the Egmont pact and the resulting radicalisation of positions made separation inevitable. The party split in 1978 into the SP in Flanders, more pragmatic and open to Christians (made clear in its 1979 manifesto entitled *Doorbraak* [breakthrough]), and the Walloon PS with a diametrically opposed view on 'community questions'. Initially the PS and SP were close to each other in doctrine, but over time the two have moved apart in cultural, economic and, above all, defence policy issues.[25] With the end of the Cold War those differences have lost their prominence but the SP and PS remain as far apart as ever on community issues. Each of them is embedded in a regional consensus.

The Parti Socialiste (PS). The basic unit of organisation[26] is a local section in each *commune* which holds periodic general meetings and elects a committee to run its affairs. Organisations may affiliate to the PS; such bodies have no voting rights but they may set up joint committees with the party at various levels for common action. The local section has a model statute laid down by the *bureau*.

In each *arrondissement* there is a FA (*fédération d'arrondissement*) with a model statute. There are in all fifteen *fédérations* plus the one in Germany where Belgian troops serve and the overseas *fédérations*. The most important *fédérations* are those of Charleroi, Liège and Brussels. The *fédération* holds periodic congresses, which elect a committee and delegates to the national congress. The secretaries of all the FAs form a *collège*, which the national *bureau* may consult on administrative matters. In each canton (provincial electoral unit), there is a cantonal committee for campaign work. In the four Walloon provinces, there is a provincial committee – composed of not less than two delegates per FA – which holds a provincial congress at least once a year; this nominates the Socialist candidates for the *députation permanente* and as provincial senators. The *fédérations* of Brussels and Brabant also co-ordinate their activities. If the *bureau* of one FA so requests, the provincial committee must call a meeting of the FA (congresses or committees).

The *fédérations* of Brussels and the four Walloon provinces have a regional committee and congress, which is responsible for taking decisions on regionalised (107 *quater*) matters. The Walloon congress meets at least once a year or more often if it is called by the regional committee or by at least three Walloon FAs. Representation (in addition to the *bureau* and the regional committees which attend as of right) is on the basis of delegates from the appropriate FA.

At the national level there is the party congress, which has to meet at least once a year and always before the opening of the parliamentary session. Congresses may be called by the *bureau* or by a minimum of three FAs representing at least one-fifth of all members; one will also be held to endorse PS participation in governments. The congress defines party policy, elects the president, receives a report from the *bureau* which it may censure, and elects the *bureau* for two years. If a FA so demands, voting takes place by the block vote of each *fédération*, which has one delegate per 250 members. *Bureau* members, deputies and *députés permanents* may attend and speak, but they may not vote. The congress is run by a *bureau* and a *commission des résolutions* (compositing committee).

Between congresses the supreme body is the *conseil général* (CG), which appoints party officials, editors of party publications and candidates as co-opted senators, and discusses urgent policy issues which the *bureau* may submit to it. Three FAs can demand a meeting of the *conseil général*. The voting members are delegates of the FA (one per 750 members) elected by their congress for three years, deputies and the *bureau*. Representatives of various Socialist organisations may attend. In the *bureau* there are twenty-five voting members: the president, the two vice presidents (the presidents of the Walloon regional committee and of the Brussels *fédération*), the general secretary, and twenty-one members elected by the congress. Ministers, the parliamentary group chairman, and representatives of various Socialist organisations and of Action Commune – which includes the Fédération Général de Travail de Belgique (FGTB) – are non-voting members.[27] The *bureau* appoints the deputy general secretary, and takes day-to-day political decisions, consulting the *conseil général* if necessary. The executive, consisting of the president, the vice presidents, the general secretary and the deputy general secretary are responsible for day-to-day administration and finance.

A wide range of bodies surrounds the party: its youth, women's, educational and cultural organisations, as well as the unions (represented by the FGTB), co-operatives and *mutualités*, which form the Action Commune. These make up the '*monde socialiste*'. The party shares the Institut Emile Vandervelde with the SP as its research institute.

The party's statutes provide for the statutes of the parliamentary groups to be submitted to the *conseil général* for approval, and lay down that all parliamentary initiatives must be concerted within the group; matters not in the party programme must obtain a favourable opinion from the party *bureau*. The PS is one party which still holds polls to designate parliamentary candidates, especially in Wallonia (not in Brussels). This practice is declining since the congresses of the *arrondissements* usually decide against a poll; however, in 1978 polls were organised in the *arrondisse-*

ments of Charleroi (9,800 voters), Mons (8,170) and the Walloon part of Brabant (2,500). No other *arrondissements* held any polls.[28]

In 1972, the PS had 112,140 members in Wallonia and 28,433 in Brussels. In 1975, the numbers had risen to 118,502 in Wallonia and fallen to 24,636 in Brussels, a slight fall. It had 135,000 in 1979 in total. Now, the party has about 140,000 members.[29] In a typical Brussels section there will be about 150 active members. Looking at the profile of the PS voter,[30] 51.9% are women, 26.3% are under forty and 35.2% are over sixty. Workers account for 64.4%, 16.8% are *employés* (white-collar workers) and only 1.8% are farmers; 43.5% identify with the working class and only 17.9% are practising Catholics. Hence, the major characteristics of the PS electorate are that they are older than average, almost equally male and female, working-class and non-practising though nominal Catholics. Of Walloon workers, 60.6% voted PS and of those over sixty the proportion was 44% (only 17.7% in Brussels). Of practising Catholics only 16.5% voted PS (this figure is actually increasing) and of non- practising 56.1%. Of workers over sixty, over 65% voted PS, whereas only 49.6% of workers under forty did so. The PS has an above national average share of voters who left school at the basic leaving age, more workers, and fewer pensioners or housewives. Of the PS electorate 10.83% situate themselves on the left, 40.13% on the centre-left and 21.02% in the centre.[31]

The PS obtained 12.7% of the national vote in 1981 (13.0% in 1978) and 37.1% of the vote in Wallonia (37.5% in 1978); in Brussels it won 12.8%, evidence of its long-term decline there. Its best results were in Hainaut (41.4%) and Liège (37.4%) and its lowest vote was 24.7% in Luxembourg. At the *arrondissement* level, its best result was 47.9% in Huy-Waremme, and its lowest 23.3% in Neufchâteau-Virton, Luxembourg province. In some Luxembourg cantons it even received less than 10%. In 1985, the PS won 39.4% in Wallonia (an increase of 3.1%) and 14.8% in Brussels, sweeping up much of the former RW vote. The result was above 1981 and 1978 but not above 1977, and corresponded to early 1970s results. It won over 50% of the vote in fourteen *cantons*. The progress continued in 1987 with 43.9% in Wallonia and 20.6% in Brussels (15.6% of the national vote, as against 19.5% for the CVP). In 1991, it fell back to 39.2% in Wallonia and 15.4% in Brussels (13.5% of the national vote, 16.8% for the CVP and 12.0% for the PVV and SP). It was average compared to other PS results since 1965. Its best *arrondissement* was Huy-Waremme with 53.8% and its best canton was Huy with 61.6% and its worst Bastogne with 11.9%. Its best Brussels vote was 33.5% in St Gilles.[32]

The quite close-run election of Guy Spitaels as president (Spitaels gained 53% as against 47% for the left-winger Ernest Glinne) led to a number of changes in the PS. He turned it into a more modern party with a clearer doctrine. This was the aim of the 1981 congress, which had been planned since 1979, but only the energy of Spitaels enabled doctrinal and administrative congresses, entitled '*Rénover et Agir*', to be held in March and October 1982. There has also been the opening to federalists and Catholics such as Yves de Wasseige, Jean Mottard and Marie Caprasse, who have been elected on PS lists. This was strongly contested in Charleroi and by more traditional party members, but on the whole the more autonomist direction of the PS has been easily accepted. There has also been a clear 'presidentialisation' of the party, with the considerable use of the personality of Guy Spitaels in the election campaign after 1981, which was a new and effective phenomenon.[33]

The PS programme for the 1981 elections was, like the other party programmes, a closely argued and detailed text.[34] Its mainspring was the need to find a coherent response to the economic crisis, without accepting the logic of the market economy as inevitable. The basis of the PS response was to give absolute priority to employment and measures to create and conserve employment, especially for the most disadvantaged groups, using an interventionist approach to industrial and taxation policy. The party accepts the need to control production costs, but refuses to see salaries as the sole element involved. It also accepts the need to limit public spending, but only in a moderate way, and covering all areas (including defence) and safeguarding acquired social rights, with a greater effort towards national solidarity being required of those with higher incomes, through a more equitable tax system. Above all, the state – in the form both of intervention and of public enterprise – is seen as having a positive role in reviving the Walloon industrial infrastructure in a socially acceptable manner.[35] The PS has moved to a rigorously autonomist position, espousing a federalist viewpoint for the first time. Not only does it fully assume the reforms of 1980 and urge their completion, but it proposes to regionalise five key industrial sectors: steel, textiles, energy production, glass and shipbuilding, with powers of the regions being extended to other areas such as applied research, agricultural policy, major public works and nuclear materials policy under public (regional) control.

The PS is not influenced by the economic crisis to abandon its ambitious objectives in the social field, for youth, for equal opportunities for women, in environmental protection (which should be increased by better planning and land-use legislation), in health care, housing (a major effort needed) and consumer protection. Measures are favoured to improve the situation of immigrants, including the right of EC nationals to vote in local elections. The PS remains fully committed to the NATO alliance, but wishes to see reductions in military expenditure and measures to reduce tension. In the days of the Cold War it was opposed to the neutron bomb and favoured the so-called 'zero option' on TNFs: the dismantling of Soviet SS-20s in exchange for non-deployment of Pershing and Cruise missiles. The party remains strongly in favour of the EC, but seeks a more dynamic community with genuine social and regional policies. It seeks to maintain public development aid at the present 0.55% of GDP at least, and to extend the north-south dialogue with developing countries.

The programme was pragmatic rather than ideological, although it proposed some important structural reforms. The '*Rénover et Agir*' congress sought to give the party a clearer ideological basis, anchored in a coherent analysis of the crisis, resolute federalism, and support for the new phenomenon of an active '*vie associative*' (literally 'associational life'), with involvement in environmental, consumer and labour battles at the grassroots, which have hitherto by-passed traditional party structures.[36]

As party president Guy Spitaels exercised tight control over all aspects of policy, activities and appointments in party and government. Soon after being elected to that post he set the party on its present course of support for federalism, which led to taking up the cause of José Happart who headed the PS European elections list in 1984. This strategy involved presenting the PS as the quintessential Walloon and Brussels party defending the Francophone cause, rolling up all other federalist partners and movements and denying them any political space. With this strategy went a degree of political moderation and pragmatism: the party did not commit itself to the cause of labour union militancy during the industrial conflicts in 1982-6. The party's position, both on federalism and on economic and social policy, should place the party at the head of the main stream and never isolate it – only on that basis could it return to power. The strategy failed in 1985, despite excellent election results, but succeeded in 1987.

Yet for many in the party both that strategy and Spitaels' tight control that had led to their marginalisation demanded too high a price for returning to power. On the other hand, as Philippe Moureaux put it much later, the party could not afford to remain in opposition much longer, or to go into opposition in 1991. For it do to so would have enabled the liberal revolution, as in Britain, to create too many irreversible situations in such key areas as social security, indexation of wages and the public sector. By 1987 it was urgent for the party to return to power, even if it had to accept the basic thrust of the economic policy of the previous coalition and could only slightly moderate it.[37] Nevertheless, these negotiations were very difficult for the PS and lasted a long time. It took the dramatic disappearance of Guy Spitaels to pressure his party into a final acceptance of the terms. Even then, many party opponents thought that the party's socio-political and federalist commitments had both been sold short. So 40% of congress delegates opposed the deal, including the powerful Liège and Charleroi *fédérations*, including their leaders such as Roger van Cauwenberg (Charleroi) and Jean-Maurice Dehousse and José Happart (Liège).

Yet, until its last phase the 1988 government worked well, its leading figures being Martens and Dehaene from the CVP and the PS vice-premier

Moureaux. Behind the scenes, Spitaels retained his influence over the party and the PS ministers at all levels, through direct contacts and through his weekly meetings with them as party president. He also selected ministers. After the 1991 election, Spitaels rather surprisingly opted, not as some had expected, for a national ministry such as foreign affairs (which went to the SP) but for the presidency of the Walloon executive. As a result, he was replaced as party president unopposed by Philippe Busquin, one of his loyalists, who had been in the minority in Charleroi in 1988, been minister for social affairs in 1988-91, and had a good election in 1991. He continues the Spitaels strategy, but can be expected to operate a more collegial regime. He has already readmitted some members of the 1988 opposition to the party *bureau* from which they had been excluded, but there have been severe conflicts within the Liège *fédération* despite the government's overall moderation.

The Socialistische Partij (SP). As a permanent minority in Catholic and nationalist Flanders, the SP has lived in a completely different environment from the PS. It was forced much earlier than the PS to become a strongly Flemish party, and its style, rhetoric and policy have had to be more pragmatic and more nationalist in order to survive in an essentially hostile or indifferent environment which it could do little to control or shape. Since it has almost as large a share of the national vote as the PS, the SP's weakness should not be overstated, but given the greater size of Flanders this has left it in a minority position as the only left-of-centre party (except the very small Flemish wing of PCB/KPB), with only two seats in the nine-member Flemish executive. In both 1978 and 1981 the SP obtained 12.4% of the national vote, which represented 20.9% of the Flemish vote in 1978 and 21.1% in 1981. This is its lowest result, its highest having been in 1961 (29.7% of the Flemish vote – CVP 56.6%). It has traditionally been the second largest party, but with only about half the vote of the CVP. In 1981, it fell into third place behind the PVV.

After 1977, the long-term decline stabilised and even halted. Despite a small overall gain in 1981, results were variable, with gains and losses. The worst loss was in the Antwerp *arrondissement* (2.3%) and its best gains were in Hasselt (2.6%) and St Niklaas (2.3%). For the four Flemish provinces, its 1981 results were Antwerp 20.5% (–1.1%), Limburg 23.9% (+1.5%), West Flanders 21.4% (–0.7%), and East Flanders 19.8% (+0.2%). The best *arrondissement* was Hasselt with 28.3% (+2.0%) and Ostende 26% (+1.5%). These results show the very even spread of the SP vote and the tendency towards greater evenness. In Brussels, the SP (competing with the PS) obtained 3.0% (–2.4%) and yet for the Senate 6.3% (+0.7) and in the *arrondissement* of Leuven 21.3% (–1.6%).[38] The SP had an excellent European election in 1984, with 17.1% (+4.7%) and held part of their gain at the 1985 election with 14.5%. In Brussels, it won

5.0% (+1.5%), its best result since 1968. It won 32% in Hasselt and over 35% in the cantons of Zonnebeke, Landen, Renaix and Boom. In 1987, the SP won 24.2% of the Flemish vote (+ 0.5%) and 5.1 (+0.1%) in Brussels. In 1991, it fell back badly to 19.6% of the Flemish vote and 3% in Brussels. Its smallest loss (–1.7%) was achieved in Leuven with the new president Frank van den Broucke. Its best result was 27% in Hasselt and its poorest was 16.6% in Ghent-Eekloo.[39]

The profile of the SP voter[40] is somewhat different from that of the PS voter though not totally dissimilar. In 1968, 55.6% were male (against 48.1% in Wallonia and 45% in Brussels for the PS). This had become accentuated by 1979 with 60% of SP voters being male. The party had marginally more voters under forty (29.8% against 26.3% for the PS); in 1979, 5.3% were under twenty-five, 37.8% were 25-35 and 20.5% were 35-45, which means that 52% were under forty-five, representing a considerably change in the age structure of its voters. The occupational structure was 58% workers (64.4% for the PS) in 1968 and 60.3% in 1979. It had 27% of *employés* (16.8% for the PS) in 1968 and 22.5% in 1979, and more (9.4%) *indépendants* than the PS, (5.6%) in 1968 and 11.3% more in 1979. It had 5.3% middle- and upper-grade management in 1979 and 0.7% farmers, fewer than in 1968 (1.5%). Its Catholic electorate is much larger (34.5%) than that of the PS, but well below all other Flemish parties except the PCB/KPB and the extreme left. If nominal Catholics are included (1979), it had an electorate which is 78.2% Catholic, not far behind the PVV (79.3%). In 1979, 28.7% of its voters were declared non-believers, and 1.6% were of 'other religions', probably Jews. In 1968, 24.6% of all men in Flanders voted SP; only 19.4% of the women did so. By 1979, 21% of men and 16% of women voted SP. Talking of age, in 1968 it was in the 40-60 age group where the largest proportion voted SP (24.1%); in 1979 it was in the 25-35 age group (18.7%). Among workers 32.2% voted SP in 1968 and 22.3% in 1979 (41.4% for the CVP). Even among the lowest income groups (under 28,000 BF income per month), only 20% voted SP and 45% CVP. Whereas among managers and trades-men its support had risen to 18%, it had fallen to 2% of farmers (3.3% in 1968). Only 31.5% of those (1968) with a clear working-class identifica-tion voted SP, but 84% of its voters were such identifiers. The party has become younger and more middle-class, more open to Catholics, but more male.

The organisation of the SP is very similar to that of the PS *sections* at the *commune* level, with a general assembly and committee. The general meeting must meet to prepare for *arrondissement* and national congresses and to appoint delegates. The committee must include at least 25% women and 25% members under thirty-five.[41]

Arrondissement organisations (AF). The AF holds a congress which elects its executive. This must include 25% women and 25% of members under thirty-five; up to half its membership may be elected officials (deputies and others). *Sections* within an electoral canton co-operate in an *ad hoc* structure, as do the AFs within the same province, particularly for the nomination of candidates for the *bestendige deputatie/députation permanente* and as provincial senators.[42]

National organisations. The congress is the highest body, meeting at least once a year and giving its approval to the political report of the *bureau*. It elects, every two years, the party president (since 1989 Frank van den Broucke), the *bureau* and the administrative commission. The congress delegates are appointed by their *fédérations* on the proposal of the *sections*, on the basis of one delegate per 300 members. Members of the *algemene raad* (general council), the *bureau* and the administrative commission, deputies and provincial councillors may also participate, but not vote. The *algemene raad* meets to appoint the general secretary and co-opted senators, and to discuss major political issues. Voting members are deputies, MEPs, members of the *bestendige deputaties* and delegates of the AFs (one per 500 members, elected for two years). More day-to-day work is split between an administrative commission (responsible for administration, finance and audit, and information) and the *bureau* which deals with political questions. However, since the administrative commission (twenty members) includes the president and four representatives of the *bureau*, a close overlap and co-ordination exist between the two bodies. The *bureau* deals with political matters, but must present a report and a political resolution on future policy to the congress. It has nineteen members (sixteen of them elected by the congress on proposals from the AFs, besides the president, the secretary general and the latter's deputy).[43] The party has a retirement age of sixty-five for elected office-holders and rules against '*cumul*', which became stricter from 1983 onwards. It now rarely organises polls to select parliamentary candidates; in 1978 there were none, and in the *arrondissement* of Antwerp the federal congress specifically voted down a proposal for one.[44] The party had 107,553 members in 1972, 107,155 in 1975 (representing about 13% of its electorate, the highest of any party)[45] and 130,000 in 1979. There is a committee for *concertation* with the PS, composed of the two *bureaux*, but it rarely meets; indeed the two parties have moved further apart since the split in 1978.

SP has always been more pragmatic and less ideological in its policy than the PS. Its statutes speak of the 'establishment of a classless society, permitting the full self-realisation of every individual', and state that 'the action of the party is in the humanist tradition'. Under Karel van Miert, the party was modernised and became more open to new ideas, to Catholics, and to the new environmental and other grassroots groups of activists. At the same time, it has lost the national Belgian viewpoint which characterised it as a junior partner of the PSB in the old unitary PSB/BSP, and has fully adopted Flemish positions on the Reform of the State and cultural matters. It has begun to review its policy with a series of conferences devoted to the development of specifically Flemish Socialist policies in various fields (housing in June 1978, education in March 1981). It has also distanced itself from the PS on foreign policy matters, strongly opposing – even when in government – the use of Belgian territory for Pershing and Cruise TNFs, considering these weapons unnecessary and provocative,and emphasising instead the need for negotiations. However, the SP is *not* anti-NATO, nor is it unilateralist or neutralist. The SP took the lead in the anti-Pershing/Cruise movement in the early 1980s, and achieved considerable success both in mobilising opinion and in the European election of 1984 and in the national one in 1985. However, its foreign policy positions made it an unlikely coalition partner at that period, quite apart from other considerations.

After the departure of Karel van Miert to the European Commission in 1989, the presidency was taken over by Frank van den Broucke, a young and relatively inexperienced leader. The party leadership is more collective in style than in the PS. The key leadership figures had become Claes, the foreign minister, and Tobback, the interior minister.

The SP has many of the same strategic problems as the PSC. It is the clear junior partner in the socialist family and is a minority in right-leaning Flanders. It is obliged to adopt strong Flemish positions in line with other Flemish parties, which sometimes makes co-operation with the PS difficult. It is only the assumed requirement of 'symmetry' at all levels that has ensured that the SP could be in the Flemish regional executive in 1987 and 1991.

The Liberals

The Liberals were the first group to organise a political party in Belgium, and ever since the history of the Liberal family has been one of splits and reunifications. Brussels has always been a strong Liberal centre, which has made the 'community tensions' more difficult to handle. It was the Alliance Libérale in Brussels, founded in 1841, which took the initiative in organising the first Liberal congress (1846), which led to the formation of the Parti Libéral. The party was later to be split between a conservative wing on one side, differing from the Catholic right wing only in its anti-clericalism, and the 'Radicals' led by Paul Janson on the other, who favoured universal suffrage and social reform imposed by the state. The two sides splintered in 1881 and only reunited in 1990. The party played an important part in political life down to 1884, forming many governments between 1848 and that year, when the Catholic party obtained an absolute majority which it was to retain till 1919. By that time the Liberals had bee supplanted by the Parti Ouvrier Belge (POB) as the country's second largest political force. During the period of Catholic rule between 1884 and 1919, the party often acted in close concert with POB; both were 'out' parties excluded from power, both were anti-clerical, and both supported universal suffrage, which would break the Catholic monopoly. After the First World War, and indeed until the *Pacte Scolaire* of 1958 finally ended the battle over education, the party had been torn. In economic doctrine, it was more attracted to alliances with the CVP/PSC, but anti-clericalism remained enough of a live issue to make an anti-Catholic Liberal-Socialist alliance a real possibility. As a result the Liberals served (apart from tripartite coalitions) in the aftermath of both world wars and in periods of severe economic crisis in both kinds of coalitions – Liberal/CVP/PSC in 1921-5, 1931-2 and 1932-5, and in Socialist-Liberal governments in 1946-7 and 1954-8. The last Liberal prime minister was Frère-Orban – in 1878-84.[46]

In the 1960s the Liberals evolved rapidly in several directions. The party gradually and with success dropped its anti-Catholic bias and in Flanders began to attract Catholic voters (by 1979, 10% of all practising Catholics and 22% of non-practising Catholics voted PVV). With the creation of the more left-leaning PSC/CVP-PSB/BSP coalition after the strikes of 1960-1 and the 1961 election, the old Parti Libéral was reformed as a more overtly neo-Liberal party, which obtained the support of some ex-PSC figures and personalities from smaller right and centre parties, under the name Parti de la Liberté et du Progrés (PLP/PVV) under Omer van Audenhove. The new party accepted the Pacte Scolaire, and sought to become a *rassemblement* for believers and non-believers, in defence of the free market and Belgian national unity. The dominance of the French-speaking Brussels group in the party was also reduced.

The party was unable to remain untouched by the community problem which swept through the country in the 1965 and 1968 elections. This was in spite of its record performance in doubling its vote between 1961 and 1965, reaching a high-point of 21.6% in the latter year which was almost held in 1968 (20.9%), thereafter to decline between 1971 and 1978. There was a shift in Brussels in 1970, which shattered Liberalism in the capital and created considerable confusion. The first group to break away from the 'official' Brussels PLP/PVV was the Flemish group, calling itself the Blauwe Leeuwen (Blue Lions), which left in December 1969 in protest against the refusal of the 'unitarist' and 'Francophone' PLP/PVV to grant parity in the party organs in Brussels. Then the French wing split into a rump 'official' group and a group which sought co-operation with the FDF in the coming elections for the Brussels *agglomération*. First of all, the PLP as a whole and other Francophone parties in Brussels joined in the *Comité du Salut Public* (echoing the French Revolutionary institution) which led an aggressive anti-Flemish campaign in the 1970 *commune* elections. After these elections, a group under Georges Mundeleer split off in protest against co-operation with the bilingual list of Mr Vanden Boeynants in the Brussels *commune*. Out of this was born the PLP de la Région Bruxelloise, which formed an electoral cartel with the FDF, but in which Mr Mundeleer did not participate, tabling his own list along with the rump PLP.

The cartel, under the name Rassemblement Bruxellois, won an absolute majority in the council and 49.8% of the vote, leaving the PLP (official) and the Mundeleer Liberals with 4.1 and 1.9% respectively. In some of the Brussels suburbs, the PLP and the Blauwe Leeuwen were also in competition. As the two wings of the party were separating in 1972, the two Brussels groups also held separate congresses. In the 1974 election the pro-FDF group, renamed the Parti Libéral Démocratique et Progressiste (PLDP), formed a cartel with the FDF–RW which, when the results were compared with the 1971 election (FDF and the PLP and Mundeleer lists together), showed a serious loss for the Liberals. The PLDP became the Parti Libéral and this in 1975 re-absorbed most of the old unitary PLP. What remained of it was shown in the 1976 *commune* elections to be marginal.[47]

Meanwhile, the PVV and PLP became autonomous at the national level, each holding a separate congress while at the same time maintaining some national structure (national congress and president). When the RW split in 1976, its centrist wing under Périn, Gol and Knoops joined the PLP in the formation of a new party, the Parti des Réformes et de la Liberté Wallonne (PRLW) under André Damseaux (November 1976). It held its first congress in January 1977, and declared itself 'pluralist, reformist and federalist'. While liberalism in Brussels continued to decline (only one deputy in 1978), the PRLW prospered. The fusion of the PL and PRLW was thus proposed and carried out at congresses in May and June 1979, creating the Parti Réformateur Libéral (PRL), which declared itself to be 'pluralist, popular and favourable to a federalism of union'. It elected the ex-RW Jean Gol as president. The Liberals retained a national chairman, Pierre Deschamps (PRL), ensuring co-operation between the PRL and the PVV.[48]

The Parti Réformateur Libéral (PRL). The structure of the PRL is relatively classic,[49] with local *sections* and an *assemblée générale* of all members electing a committee; *arrondissement fédérations*, with a congress, a *bureau* and an executive; provincial organisations, and a national organisation with a congress, a *bureau*, an executive and a president. There was also, till 1983, a '*régionale*' for Brussels, presided over by Mr van Halteren, mayor of the city, also first vice-president of the PRL. Jean Gol took control of the new party (he had only entered the Liberal fold in 1976 when the PRLW was formed) with the help of a mere 300 ex-RW militants. André Damseaux retired from the leadership, and Gol obtained

80% of the congress vote against Michel Toussaint. He has created a presidential style, surrounded by a strong team of ex-RWs and 'new men' such as Robert Henrion. The pieces have been put back together again in Brussels, and the old liberalism and the new tendencies have been integrated by a judicious association of the 'old barons' of the party with decision-making. Candidates are chosen by congresses or polls – there were several polls in the province of Hainaut in 1978.[50]

Traditionally, the Liberals have been the third party in Wallonia. However, it was second in 1965, 1968 and 1981, third to the Communists in 1946 and fourth in 1971 behind the RW and the PSC. It saw its peak of 26.5% in 1968 and low points of 9.3% in 1946 and 10.5% in 1958. Indeed, before 1965 the party never attained more than 12% of the Walloon vote. The Brussels comparisons became difficult after 1971. Its low points were 13.4% in 1946 and 13.5% in 1971, and peak was 33.4% in 1965. With the FDF-PLDP cartel in 1974 obtaining 39.6% and the PLP/PVV only 5.9%, it would appear that the decline continued. In 1977 the PL obtained 9.4% and in 1978 a mere 6.4%. The 1981 elections saw a considerable recovery to 16.1%. The main bastions of the Liberal party in Wallonia are Nivelles (with 27.7% in 1981, against 1978, 17.7%), Luxembourg (27.1/20.7%) and its poorest results are in Hainaut (18.8/14.7%), Liège (21.6/16.5%) and Namur (22.7/20.4%), where it registered its smallest gains (+ 2.3%). Its best *arrondissement* was Arlon-Marche-Bastogne with 29.3% and its worst was Charleroi (15.7/11.6%).[51] In 1985 the PRL increased its share of the Walloon vote to 24.2%. Its share in Brussels rose dramatically to 26.0% as it mopped up UDRT and FDF votes. Its best results, with over 40%, came in the cantons of Bastogne (48.3%), Flobecq (43.1%), Fauvillers (42.7%) and Bouillon (41.3%) in the Ardennes. In Brussels its best results were in Uccle (30.8%) and Ixelles (28.8%). At the 1987 elections, the party fell back to 22.2%, behind the PSC. In Brussels, its vote fell again marginally to 25.3%; in 1991 it fell again to 19.8% of the Walloon votes and 21.7% in Brussels. It gained no benefit from being the main opposition party at a time of anti-government swing. However, its strength in Brussels stabilised above the catastrophic levels it had reached in the 1970s.[52]

The profile of the Liberal voter in Wallonia and Brussels is as follows.[53] The (1968) electorate of the Liberals was 51% female in Wallonia and 51.9% female in Brussels. The age profile shows the Walloon Liberals with 42.4% of their electorate under forty and 22.7% over sixty (in Brussels only 28.6% are under forty, and 24.9% are over sixty). As for the socio-economic structure, 15.8% of workers (the lowest share for any Walloon party), 23% *employés*, 20.9% *indépendants*, 23% managers and 11.2% farmers. This gives them the highest proportion of *indépendants* and *'cadres'* (middle/upper management); 59% identified with the middle class and 11.7% with the more elevated 'bourgeoisie'. The proportion of middle-class and 'bourgeois' identifiers was even higher in Brussels (59.3 and 17.8%). Practising Catholics accounted for 43.9% (only 28.4% in Brussels). Of all voters under forty, 32.1% (twice the PSC figure) voted Liberal. Of all Walloon workers, only 8.6% did so, as against 38.7% of *indépendants* (26.4% for the PSC). Of practising Catholics 24% and of nominal Catholics/non-believers 22.4% voted Liberal; but in Brussels 30.6% of the latter did so. It is therefore in Brussels, at least till 1968, that the traditional anti-clerical bourgeois liberalism had most clearly survived. The PRL had 28,000 members in 1972, 34,700 in 1975 and 40,000 in 1980.

Gradually, as the 'school war' lost relevance, the Liberals have moved to the right of the PSC, becoming a pluralist conservative party but retaining, in Wallonia especially, both among traditional supporters and among the ex-RW contingent, some of the radical liberalism of the past, updated as federalism and radical individualism. The economic crisis and the related pressure from new parties like the UDRT have led the Liberals to espouse a more radical neo-liberalism, inspired by the Chicago School and even by Margaret Thatcher. Jean Gol has repeatedly taken up the themes of the need to attack bureaucratic statism, to reward effort and to re-establish order in government, in the firm and in the family. At the same time the PRL opposes greater Walloon federalism as likely to add to these dangers, despite the earlier federalism of the PRLW. The strategy of the Liberals after the formation of the PRL was to maintain their position in Wallonia and to advance in Brussels (they did better than this) by taking votes from the PSC and FDF. This was so that they would constitute *the* strong conservative force in Wallonia and Brussels as a counterweight to the PS, and force the PSC to change alliances – as it reluctantly did in 1981. In line with this image, the PRL attracted well-known military figures previously outside politics, such as General Close, who took up the issue of the Soviet danger and linked the need for a strong defence with the need for a strong conservative policy internally.[54] This was part of a more right-wing profiling of the party.

During the centre-right coalition, the PRL seemed often to see the PSC as its main opponent. Thus, for example, the PRL refused to support PSC interior minister Nothomb over the Heysel affair when British football fans rioted and Italian supporters were killed. It was also the PRL that (with the PVV) was most strongly opposed to taking up the community issue during the 1981-5 coalition government. The PRL is in that sense only as federalist as it needs to be in its Walloon environment.

The party was torn between populist positions on economic issues and on immigration in Brussels and moderation necessary to remain in the Walloon mainstream. The party strongman Jean Gol was identified as minister of justice with tough measures on immigration, which drew the ex-FDF mayor of Schaerbeek, Roger Nols, into the PRL. Yet Nols himself, a Jew, rejected the positions on immigration of Brussels candidates in 1991. The Brussels PRL had to absorb and retain the populist vote of the former UDRT and keep voters from moving to the Front National.[55]

There were problems with the party leadership. During the centre-right period when Gol was a minister, the presidency was assumed by Louis Michel, but Gol remained in *de facto* control. After 1988 there were experiments with various formulae, including a twin presidency, but this did not work. In 1992 Jean Gol reassumed the presidency, but in reality, he had never relinquished control of the PRL. The party was unable to make gains or to profit from the government's discomfiture in 1991. At the time of writing it still faces problems over its future strategy, and has formed an alliance with the FDF.

Partij voor Vrijheid en Vooruitgang (PVV). The PVV began to obtain autonomy in the late 1960s and was organised as an autonomous party at a congress held in Blankenberge in May 1972 with Willy De Clercq as president and Mr Grootjans and Mr Vanderpoorten as vice-presidents. It declared itself open to all who supported Liberal ideals irrespective of religion or philosophical beliefs. The congress also dealt with more delicate issues such as abortion, which the PVV wants to see liberalised. Indeed, a PVV senator co-sponsored the abortion bill that finally passed into law in 1990.

Throughout the postwar period the PVV had been only the third party in Flanders, until 1981 when it took second place – which it lost again in 1985, 1987 and 1991. In some years (1968, 1971, 1977) it had fallen to fourth place behind the Volksunie as well. Its low point was 7.7% of the Flemish vote in 1946 and its high point 20.6% in 1981. Since then it has been declining with 17.3% in 1985, 18.5% in 1987 and 19.0% in 1991. Thus it ended the coalition period (1981-7) with a loss. Its vote in Brussels has remained stable and modest: 5.7% in 1981, 4.6% in 1985, 5.8% in 1987 and 5.4% in 1991. Its best result at the cantonal level in 1991 was 44.5% in Hovebeke and its worst was 9.6% in Westerloo. Its best *arrondissement* was Oudenaerde with 29.9%. The two liberal parties (PRL and PVV) seem generally to have achieved divergent results during the 1980s, never gaining ground at the same time.[56]

In 1968 51.7% of the PVV electorate was female, but by 1979 there had been a radical change in that 56.3% of its electorate was male. In 1968 30.5% of PVV voters were under forty; in 1979 5.5% were under twenty-five; 23.9% were 25-35; 22.9% 35-45; 21.2% 45-55; 21.2% 55-65 and 11.0% over sixty-five (the lowest figure apart from the VU). Thus, 52.3% of its voters were under forty-five (50.2% for the CVP and 53.5% for the SP). In 1968, 25.7% of its electorate were workers (31.8% in 1979), the lowest percentage of workers for any party; 24.3% were *employés* in 1968 (22.5% in 1979); 19.3% were *indépendants* (22.7% in 1979); 19.3% were managers (21.8% in 1979), and 9.3% were farmers in 1968 (5.5% in 1979). Only 38% identified with the working class while 49.8% identified with the middle class or 'bourgeoisie'. In 1968, 65.3% were Catholics. In 1979, 33.5% were practising Catholics, 46.0% nominal Catholics, 3.2% of other religions (Jewish) and 17.5% non-believers. Of all workers only 8.5% voted PVV (1979) and of all *indépendants* 15% did so (less than for the CVP).[57]

The PVV structure is fairly classic. Its membership numbered 43,794 in 1975 which has since grown to about 55,000, organised in local *sections* based in *communes*. Each *arrondissement* has a *fédération*, with its own congress and *bureau*. At the national level there is a president, a *politiek komittee* which takes major decisions between congresses, and the *uitvoerende bureau* (executive) which runs the party's day-to-day affairs. Periodically there are ordinary and extraordinary congresses. The PVV shares with the PRL the Centre Paul Hymans, (1956), a Liberal research institute, and it had set up an institute to train party cadres, the Instituut voor Volksopleiding en Kaders (training institute) Omer van Audenhove.[58]

The PVV is, as we have seen, pluralistic, i.e. open to Catholics, but it also favours freer abortion. On economic and social policy, defence and international relations it has become markedly more right-wing. Its basic programme *Handvest* (manifesto) *van het Moderne Liberalisme* – the Kortrijk manifesto (1979) – is, according to Mr Grootjans, 'influenced by theses of Milton Friedman, who has provided the intellectual basis for modern Liberalism'.[59] The manifesto makes it clear that the PVV is calling for a new start, a new liberalism attuned to 'economic realities' and to the 'doubts and alienation' created by 'ambiguous and meaningless political compromise'. It states that the whole programme 'is based around one central theme: the restoration of a belief in the freedom of the individual in a free society as the first pillar of our society, made sick by bureaucratisation and state intervention'. The manifesto advocates a new 'radical' liberalism, to provide a more coherent liberal ideological perspective in government. It identifies the individual's free choice in a market economy as its central value, and supports measures to 'free the market', reduce costs by controlling bureaucracy, the welfare state and trade union pressure. It supports the small independent enterprise, the rehabilitation of profit, and the acceptance of structural change. In social policy it seeks more self-help and selectivity. It takes a strong stand on defence issues as a necessary guarantee of freedom, and supports greater integration in the European Community.[60]

The PVV was the driving force behind the economic programme of the centre-right coalition. The party chairman Guy Verhofstadt was seen as a Belgian Thatcher, but tough as he was, he eventually found himself restrained and frustrated by the Christian Democrat parties and especially by their trade union wings. For the CVP and even more the PSC an austerity programme might be a powerful but pragmatic necessity, but their ideological commitment to deregulation, privatisation and tax cuts was never equal to that of the PVV. The PVV's radicalisation was clearly a reason for the breakdown of the centre-right alliance. As the PS moderated and the PVV radicalised, a reversal of alliances in Wallonia became desirable and possibly inevitable. With experiments such as the creation of a shadow cabinet along British lines, the PVV has remained rather isolated in its ideological purity. Guy Verhofstadt remains true to that line and is seeking to continue it. The threatened candidacy of a former PVV minister, Herman De Croo, for the party presidency in November 1992 was evidence of internal unrest at this line and a clear signal that some in the party wanted to steer a more consensual course in order to make the PVV an attractive coalition partner to the CVP, or an acceptable partner in a so-called '*coalition laïc*' (a non-confessional coalition of Liberals and Socialists) which Verhofstadt as *informateur* in 1991 had failed to achieve even in the classic tripartite form, and which the CVP had at one point wanted.

This internal dissidence fizzled out. Neither the tough opposition of the PVV in the 1987-91 legislature, which only brought a very modest gain, nor Verhofstadt's attempt to form a red-blue Socialist-Liberal coalition broke the mould. Verhofstadt came to see the PVV itself as too narrow, as an obstacle to the realisation of the ideas in his citizens' manifesto (spring 1991). He has argued that the main problem in Belgian politics is the distance and alienation between political leaders and citizens created by the strength of the intermediate organisations such as unions, *mutualités* and state enterprises, through which politicians control the lives of citizens and are themselves controlled. He sees left-right divergences, class struggle, clerical/anti-clerical divergences as being now irrelevant, the real division being between those who support the individualism of each citizen and the parties with links to organisations (*verzuilings*) – the CVP/PSC and PS/SP.

Thus a new political instrument was needed, since the PVV itself was to some degree part of the system and was also unattractive to those outside, in other parties or none, who agree with Verhofstadt's analysis. The PVV was wound up at a congress held in Antwerp on 12-15 November 1992, and replaced by the Vlaams Liberale Democraten (VLD). New members, some 700 in all, came mostly from the Volksunie and, in smaller numbers, from the CVP. The most prominent was Jaak Gabriels, the former president of Volksunie, who believed that once the Reform of the State was completed, many more of its members would come over to the new party. At the time of writing the VLD is still led by Guy Verhofstadt and its founding manifesto closely follows its 'citizens' manifesto'. Its key themes are deregulation, privatisation, less state intervention, reform (limitation) of the social security system, and maintenance of a minimum critical mass of central Belgian competences.[61]

The community parties

The denomination 'community parties' only came into current use in the 1960s, applying to the Volksunie (VU), in Flanders; the Front Démocratique des Francophones (FDF) in Brussels and the Rassemblement Wallon (RW) in Wallonia. As we have seen, the Flemish movement was much older, having been represented in Parliament by the Front Partij (1920s) and the Vlaams National Verbond (VNV) in the 1930s. The Volksunie was only formed in 1954, and at first grew slowly. But increasing Flemish consciousness and the strikes of 1960-1 provoked a response in both Brussels and Wallonia. This led to Walloon lists and then the RW and the FDF, both from 1965. The three parties are pluralist, but the VU leans to the right, the FDF is of the centre, sometimes with serious disputes between its ex-Socialist and ex-Liberal tendencies, and the RW, especially after 1976, leaned to the left. After 1981, the RW split again and when its leading figure, Paul-Henri Gendebien, left to join the PSC, it virtually ceased to exist. The PS then virtually swept up the Walloon movement.

The Rassemblement Wallon (RW). Before the dramatic strikes of 1960-1, which saw the creation of the left-wing Mouvement Populaire Wallon, Walloon federalism had developed here and there – in the Liberal and Socialist parties, in the Walloon *Résistance* (and the Congrès National Wallon of 1945) – without finding any clear organisation and focus. It remained a defensive reaction to the rise of the Flemish movement. After 1961 various other Catholic Liberal Walloon movements also came into being: the Wallonie Catholique, Rénovation Wallonne and Wallonie Libérale.

In 1964, the Front Wallon pour l'Unité et la Liberté de la Wallonie was created out of the MPW and another small party, and 1965 saw the creation of the more left-wing Parti Wallon du Travail (PWT) under Mr Périn. In that year the PWT and the Front Wallon each obtained one seat and, together with the FDF, 2.3% of the national vote. In Wallonia the two lists obtained 2.4%. After the election the PWT, the Front Wallon and some independents formed the Parti Wallon, later (1968) the Rassemblement Wallon. The RW made significant electoral progress, in alliance with the FDF in 1968 (10.8% in Wallonia); in 1971, with 21.2% and fourteen seats, it became the second Walloon party, but the 1974 election saw it decline to 18.8%. The 1977 elections, after the RW had been in power, were disastrous for the party, which had also meanwhile split; it obtained only 9.1%. In 1978, its results stabilised at 0.4%, but in 1981 once again it was beset by a split which reduced it to two seats and 5.5% of the Walloon vote, with many votes going to the dissident lists led by the former party chairman P.-H. Gendebien, and others going to the Socialists who put some ex-RW members on their lists. In 1978, a more representative year, the best RW vote was in the province of Namur (10.9%) and its worst in the province of Luxembourg (5.5%). In 1981 again its best result was in Namur with 8.5% and its worst in Luxembourg (2.5%). Its best *arrondissement* in 1978 was Thuin with 20.5% (5.0% in 1981 due to the dissident candidacy of Gendebien) and its worst 2.5% in Arlon-Bastogne. The best 1981 result was in Namur with 12.6% (+ 0.2%) and Nivelles 9.8%.[62]

The typical RW voter is male (50.4% in 1988), under forty (47.8%), working-class (42.0%) or middle-class (44.9%), 31.5% are *employés*, 17.1% *indépendants*, 20% *cadres* and only 1.4% farmers. It is more working-class than the PSC, and 43.9% are practising Catholics. Of all workers 5.8% and of all non-believers 8.2% vote RW. The party is based on local *sections*, and *sections d'enterprises* in some large factories. Its main organs are the congress, its *bureau fédéral* (seventy members) and the *bureau* (president, vice-president and general secretary). In 1979 it had 9,500 members.[63]

The RW went into the 1974 elections as a candidate for office. The inter-community dialogue seemed at last to be producing results, and a government involving the community parties was a possibility. The Steenokkerzeel conclave had not made enough progress for an 'opening' to the FDF-RW and the VU to be possible. However, the Lambermont talks of May 1974 made possible a 'small opening' to include the RW only in the PSC/CVP-PRL/PVV Tindemans I government in June. The RW's *bureau fédéral* had authorised, not without some doubts even at this stage, a small opening without the FDF. The party congress at Tournai in October 1974 saw Gendebien elected president in place of Mr Périn who had become a minister. Gendebien defined the party as 'federalist, progressive and pluralist' and its role as 'the left wing and motor of the majority, especially on regionalisation and social issues'. On a number of issues – the slowness of the preparatory regionalisation (necessary because the new government, despite later attempts, was never enlarged to have the necessary special majority for a full regionalisation); budgets; the rules for the state holding company; trade union elections – the RW's *bureau* and deputies chafed at the bit and requested the government to act.[64]

Almost from the start, two strategies were being pursued: that of the ministers, led by Périn, of maintaining the government in office in spite of and even against party interests (indeed Périn cared little for the fate of the RW as such), in order to advance the inter-community dialogue and provoke later, as the Socialist initiatives in June 1976 were to do, the conditions for a definitive regionalisation, as in the Egmont pact. The other strategy, pursued by Gendebien and the party as such, was favourable to the party staying in the government in order to ensure a continuation of the 'dialogue', but was also concerned about a distinct future for the RW and the ideas it represented.[65] These tensions built up continually from mid-1975, and were exacerbated by the 'F-16 versus Mirage' affair in which the RW *bureau* and deputies initially opposed support for the 'non-European' F-16 and finally agreed only with bad grace after receiving concessions, in order to keep the government in being. At the same time, it redoubled its pressure on the government to implement the Law on Provisional Regionalisation (August 1974).

From October 1975 there arose a serious division between the ministerial group and the party itself, which reached a rapprochement with the FDF. The 'Périn report' on institutional reform was badly received by the *bureau fédéral*, and the strange affair of the Flemish counters in the Schaerbeek town hall[*] led to tensions between the 'base' of the RW and the ministerial group. As it later transpired, the Périn-Gol-Knoops group was already looking for an alternative option, in negotiating its collective membership of either the PSC or PLP, and to that end Périn created a political base in the Club Réformes Europe-Régions, a factional organisation inside the RW, in July 1976. On the other side, Gendebien presented (26 October 1976) on behalf of the *bureau restreint*, without consulting the *bureau fédéral*, a doctrinal manifesto, and proposed a congress on 4 December. The atmosphere had not been improved by the poor RW results in the *commune* elections. In most party *sections*, there was no debate between the factions, but a split pure and simple. The Périn group took the offensive and left the RW to join the PLP – later to become the PRWL. This eventually required a government reshuffle to give posts to 'loyal' RW men. In the interests of the community dialogue, the RW remained loyal to the government until it became clear that the dialogue was making no progress; it then voted against the budget in March 1977, precipitating an election which proved disastrous for it.

The doctrinal congress of 4 December 1976 tilted the RW to the left, but the party was still open to Christian Democrats, for whom, together with Progressives, it was able to act as a centre-left pole, forming a component of a progressive majority in Wallonia with the PS after regionalisation. It was to be a progressive, libertarian, new-left party with an important ecological and '*auto-gestionnaire*' strand. After Gendebien left the presidency in 1978 to run for the European Parliament, the new leadership under Henri Mordant moved closer to the FDF; this, in 1981, caused the second split in which the former MPW elements and Gendebien left the RW because of their opposition to the RW and Wallonia

---

[*]   This was a linguistic quarrel in a Brussels borough, where the FDF mayor established separate counters in the town hall to serve Flemish-speakers. This action was ruled illegal, and when he still refused to accept bilingual counters, they were symbolically destroyed in a farcical night commando raid by the Gendarmerie.

being tied to Brussels. Some ran on Walloon lists (Gendebien obtained 15% in Thuin) and others were given places on the Socialist lists. The RW subsequently found itself in deep trouble, and reduced to two deputies.

The 1981 split saw one group gravitate towards the Rassemblement Populaire Wallon (RPW) close to the PS, others went to join the Parti de l'Indépendance Wallon, yet others joined Ecolo, and Gendebien, its leading figure, formed the Alliance Démocratique Wallonne (ADW) which formed a compact with the PSC in 1987. In 1985 Walloon activists voted for several parties: the trade union-related Société et Participation (SEP), which registered 2.6%, the Parti Wallon (0.4%) and some other smaller Walloon lists. In 1991, an alliance of the FDF and the Parti Populaire Wallon won 1% of the Walloon vote. The PS has now positioned itself as the federalist party *par excellence*, so denying the Walloon movement any electoral space.[66]

The Front Démocratique des Francophones (FDF). The FDF was formed in 1965 by federalists and non- federalists in Brussels to defend the French language, and immediately obtained 10% of the Brussels vote and three seats in the House. Its rise thereafter was spectacular, with 18.6% in 1968 and 34.5% in 1971 when, with allies, it also captured an absolute majority in the Brussels *agglomération*. Its share of the Brussels vote was 39.6% in 1974, 34.9% in 1977 and 35.1% in 1978, but it collapsed dramatically to 20.3% in 1981.

As a result of the theory of the 'significant majority in each region', the FDF entered the 'Egmont pact government' which, if it had survived, would have created a separate Brussels region. It remained in power in the Vanden Boeynants interim government and in the Martens I government till early 1980, when CVP pressure made its position untenable; it was in power but obtaining no results. It left the government – or was forced out of it, especially as the Francophone Front (PS-PSC-FDF) collapsed at the same time. After this experience, the FDF sought to strengthen its links with the RW in a Brussels-Wallonia alliance of solidarity. This produced the split in the RW and the electoral disaster in 1981: the electorate, faced by the economic crisis, was proving to be less and less concerned with community issues as such.

The FDF is a 'pluralist' party with Liberal, Christian and Socialist components. In more recent years the Liberal wing has often felt itself to be marginalised, hence the resignation of the FDF deputy Havelange in 1981. The party has also overcome clerical-anticlerical divisions, supporting abortion in 1973. However, it is more centrist than the RW, whose federalist theses it espoused in 1970.[67]

The FDF had also proclaimed some left-of-centre positions on workers' co-management and energy policy, but it remains largely the defender of the Brussels *indépendants*. Its statutes declare it to be 'a pluralist and federalist party committed to political action for the defence of the rights of the French community in Belgium and of the Brussels region'.[68] They also refer to the party's support for the Walloon cause (a recent amendment). In its 1981 election manifesto the party argued that the key crisis in Belgium was an institutional one, and demanded full regionalisation to give Brussels equal status with the other regions and (a new demand in line with its alliance with the RW) improvement of arrangements for Wallonia. It also still demands that boundaries of the Brussels region be extended beyond the nineteen *communes*.[69] On economic and social issues it regards the maximum autonomy for Brussels as the best guarantee that its absolute priority – the fight against unemployment – will be met. It proposes 'another kind of economic growth in public and social services', maximum support for SMUs, and an end to pro-Flemish employment policies in Brussels. In its view, Flemish interests take 15% of taxation from Brussels and return 6% of public spending, which they thus control; the unitary state is powerless and paralysed. The party places a new emphasis on an energy policy based on energy-saving and new energy sources (it is reticent on nuclear energy), with state intervention, and proclaims itself to be an 'ecological party', especially in seeking an improvement in the quality of urban life – public transport, green belts, parks – in Brussels, better planning, and conservation of buildings and districts.[70] On welfare policy, equal pensions for all (especially *indépendants*) is an absolute priority. With a woman leader, Mme Spaak, up till 1983 the FDF was always committed to women's rights and to measures against racism and political violence. On education, it argues for co-operation between the public and Catholic school systems. It is pro-EC and federalist, supporting the idea of a 'Social Europe of the Regions', open to the Third World. On defence, its stance in the Cold War was to oppose unilateral disarmament, but to favour mutual reductions by negotiation and a more autonomous European defence.

The FDF considers that the other Francophone parties made too many concessions to the Flemish in Brussels when the Brussels region was created in 1989, and opposes the minority safeguards and all other special characteristics of the Brussels region which, in its view, reduce its competences and its Francophone character. Yet the party belongs to the regional majority and in its election manifesto in 1991 made much of the work on housing, regional employment and the environment accomplished by Didier Gosuin, its regional state secretary.[71]

In the early 1980s the FDF faced the same basic strategic dilemma as all regional parties as the community issue took second place to the economic crisis and its vote fell. Thus in 1978 it had obtained 35.4% of the Brussels vote, making it easily the largest Brussels party, but after its brief spell in government and the decline in salience of the community issue, its share fell to 22.6% in 1991; it declined further to 10.9% (3 seats) in 1984, when it lost its MEP, and to 10.8% in 1987 (3 seats). The party was faced with hard choices: it sought to break out of its isolation in Brussels by discussions with other Brussels parties, but no common front of Francophone Brussels parties proved possible. Talks were held with the PSC (1983-5), but again no alliance was concluded. Both earlier and at the same time, alliance with the RW and other Walloon groups seemed to take the party to the left.[72]

These manoeuvres led to a series of splits in the late 1970s. Some FDF members returned to their original liberal home. The *'enfant terrible'* of Brussels politics, the mayor of Schaerbeek, Roger Nols, embarrassed the party by his preference for rightist populism and flirting with the PRL and UDRT, which led him to support the special powers bill of the centre-right government after 1981 while the official FDF line was to oppose it. After the municipal elections of 1982, Nols left the FDF over the issue of immigration. The overtures to the PSC and the appeals by PS leader in Brussels, Philippe Moureaux, to form a progressive alliance in Brussels led a group of FDF leaders around Serge Moureaux (brother of Philippe Moureaux) and Léon Defosset to leave the party and set up the Rassemblement Démocratique Bruxellois (RDB) in 1984, which allied with the PS at the 1985 elections. The FDF was more isolated than ever. Yet the establishment of the Brussels region in 1989 enabled the party to rediscover a modest regional vocation and to evolve the Walloon alliance strategy in 1991. The decline was reversed and the party registered 11.9%, with 3 seats.[73]

FDF membership has declined from 10,990 in 1975 to about 7,500. The party's voter profile is 64.1% female; 20.8% under forty and 25.0% over sixty; 15.3% workers, 39.0% *employés* and 12.7% *indépendants*; 59.3% identify with the middle class and 17.8% with the upper middle class; and 25% are practising Catholics, the lowest figures except for the PS.[74]

Given its limited territorial coverage, the FDF has a somewhat simpler organisation than the other parties: the basic unit is the *section* which has a general assembly, a committee and a president. *Sections* are grouped into *commissions de district*, which cover electoral districts and draw up their lists for provincial elections in Brabant and propose candidates for ratification by the *comité directeur* as provincial senators. The presidents of *sections* meet in a committee to coordinate activities. At the centre the supreme authority is the bi-annual congress (the *conseil général* may call other congresses), in which *all* members may participate and vote. It elects the party president and general secretary for two years, and votes on party policy.

Between congresses, the *conseil général* is the supreme body, and may even amend the statutes by a two-thirds majority. It is composed of delegates of the *sections* (one from each, plus up to seven extra for up to

1,000 members and then one per 300 additional members); delegates (10% of the total) of FDF communal councillors; all provincial councillors, *agglomérations* councillors, mayors, *échevins*, administrators of the RTBF and other state bodies, representatives of the women's and youth organisations of which there are ten and twenty respectively, all deputies, senators and MEPs. It meets at least four times a year, and in any case whenever there is a government crisis. The smaller *comité directeur* (meeting monthly at least) is an executive arm of the *conseil général*, chosen from within it on the same principles of representation. The *bureau permanent* is the day-do-day decision-making body, smaller but including the president and general secretary, all deputies and a number of members elected by the *comité directeur* from among its own members and representatives of the women's and youth organisations. The *bureau permanent* can therefore have up to forty or fifty members, but it may delegate certain decisions to a smaller group (e.g. president, vice-president and general secretary). The party also has a *commission electoral* which makes up the lists for national elections on the basis of proposals from the sections, but these lists must be approved by the *comité directeur*. The party has its own research institute.[75]

The Volksunie (VU). The Flemish movement has been more solidly anchored in a distinct culture and has tended to lean to the right. The predecessors of the Volksunie were certainly on the radical right, but the Volksunie itself is a broad church with several tendencies under the nationalistic umbrella. It has always had a pragmatic wing open to participation in both national and regional government coalitions provided only that some progress towards the goal of federalism was achieved.

As we have seen, the Flemish movement first entered Parliament in 1919, under the banner of the Front Partij, with five seats. This party was defeated in 1932, and gave way to the more radical and right-wing Vlaams Nationaal Verbond of Staf De Clercq, which won sixteen seats in 1936 and seventeen in 1939. The collaboration of some Flemish nationalists with the Nazis caused the movement to be discredited after 1945, and only in 1949 did a dissident group from the CVP contest the elections under the name Vlaamse Concentratie. In 1954 this group was enlarged and became the Volksunie (VU),[76] entering Parliament with 3.9% of the Flemish vote and one seat in the House. Its low point was reached in 1958 with 3.4% (one seat), and its high point with 18.8% of the Flemish vote and twenty-one seats in 1971. Despite a fall in its vote in 1974, it then reached its highest-ever number of seats, with twenty-two. Its participation in government and hence its approval of the Egmont pact cost it dear. Its vote fell back to 11.5% in 1978, and the dissident (anti-Egmont) Vlaams Blok was formed, receiving 2.1% of the vote and one seat (1981, one seat). Its high point in Brussels was 6.2% in 1976 – in 1981 it obtained 5.94%.

The party's best vote (1981) was in Limburg (17.3%) and its worst in Antwerp (14.9%). Its best *arrondissement* was Tongeren-Maaseik (Limburg) with 20.7%. The VU vote is very evenly spread.[77] In 1985 it obtained 12.7% of the Flemish vote and in 1987 12.9%, but in 1991, after being in government again, this fell to 9.3%, less than the Vlaams Blok. It is now in serious danger, having lost support to the VLD. This was the party's lowest result since 1965. The VU won over 10% in few *arrondissements* in 1991: Tongeren-Maaseik (17.8%), Hasselt, Roulers-Tielt, Furnes-Diksmuide-Oostende). In Brussels it won 1.8% (-0.9%).[78]

The VU (1968) vote was 51.5% female and 49.5% under forty, with only 14.3% over sixty. Workers accounted for 28%, white-collar workers also for 28%, *indépendants* for 19%, managers for 18%, and farmers for 6.4%; 42% identified subjectively with the working class and 50.6% with the (lower) middle class; 74.2% (second only to the CVP) were practising Catholics. In 1979, 50.5% of the VU's electorate were women, 11.3% were under twenty-five, 23.9% were in the 25-35 bracket, and 22.9% were 35-45; thus 46.8% were under forty-five and only 13.2% were over sixty. 37.1% of VU voters were workers, 35.1% *employés*, 20.6% *indépendants*, 6.2% managers and 1.0% farmers. 54% were practising Catholics and 36.4% were non-practising Catholics and only 9.1% non-believers. The main determinants of VU voting were (young) age and middle-class identification among workers.[79]

The organisation of the VU is fairly typical of all Belgian parties, but is relatively complicated. In each *commune*, there may be several *sections*, each electing its executive (for two years), which itself elects (with the approval of the *arrondissement* executive) its chairman and secretary and its representatives in the *arrondissement raad*. Elected officials may attend such meetings, but they must not be in a majority. Where there are several *sections* in a *commune*, their representatives (five votes plus one extra vote per fifty members above twenty-five members), two representatives of the *arrondissement* executive and elected members (deputies and councilors) make up the *politieke raad* (political council), which elects its own executive (a quarter of its members are required to be women and aged under thirty-five). It runs *communal* election campaigns and chooses *communal* candidates. All decisions on cartels and alliances must be approved by the *arrondissement* executive. Each *arrondissement* has a council made up of representatives of the *sections*, co-opted members (up to 15%), chairmen of political councils, VU leaders on councils and provincial chairmen. The *arrondissement* council elects its executive of seven members plus a chairman and secretary, who must be elected by a two-thirds majority. At the national level the party is led by a *partij raad* which is composed of *arrondissement* chairmen, ministers, deputies, senators, MEPs, representatives of *arrondissements* (one per 1,000 members) and some other *ex-officio* members. It can co-opt up to ten extra members by a two-thirds majority; it elects a *partij bestuur* and five committees for organisational matters. The party chairman is elected by a two-thirds majority of the *partij raad*. The *partij bestuur* elects a smaller political committee (chairman, vice-chairman, general secretary and parliamentary group chairmen) and an administrative committee; it chooses candidates based on proposals by the *arrondissements*, approved by the *partij raad*.[80] The party now has 60,000 members, of which about 9,000 are in Brussels.[81]

The VU claims to be a social and federal party. It espouses radical Flemish nationalism, which it identifies with the concept of a Flemish state rather than with the *Groot Nederland* (Greater Netherlands) idea. It bases its analysis on the failure of the present political system and of the national parties. It sees the link with Wallonia as a permanent financial liability, and argues instead for 'political autonomy for a Flemish state in a federal system'. The federal concept is needed in order to safeguard links with Brussels, which it regards as a Flemish city. It favours an 'integral federalism' with all tasks being performed at objectively the most appropriate level. It has therefore proposed a 'confederal model' for Belgium in which the Flemish state would enjoy the greatest possible autonomy, and with Brussels (limited to the nineteen *communes*) as a confederal capital where both communities would enjoy equal rights.[82] In more recent times, the message has become radicalised. The party argued in its 1981 manifesto 'No half measures: Flemish money in Flemish hands and a Flemish state', thus condemning the 1980 regionalisation as totally inadequate. Its nationalism is based on progressive slightly left-of-centre social and national radicalism; it favours greater equality but rejects both doctrinaire Marxism and Liberal egoism. It favours a 'social Flanders' with special policies for the family and weaker social groups, more local democracy and more democratic decision-making in the trade unions. On education and culture it is nationalist and pluralist. In the economic sphere, it gives priority to a Flemish employment policy, and has proposed a five-year plan to create 50,000 jobs by a new industrial policy based on a 'new co-operation between classes'. Profits must be rehabilitated as the mainspring of investment, public expenditure controlled, and tax and social contribution charges on businesses and wage costs stabilised. For some vital 'national sectors' such as energy the party has favoured a more radical approach with partial nationalisation and greater state control. Peace and disarmament are an important component of party policy: the VU seeks the nationalisation of the arms industry, resolutely opposes the installation of NATO Cruise missiles on Belgian territory, and seeks an increase in development aid.[83] Its policies make it difficult to classify it on a right-left spectrum, but its 'gut-level' centre of gravity is probably to the right of centre, although on some issues it is closer to the SP than to either the CVP or the PVV.

The extreme left

No party has ever been able to carve out any significant space to the left of the Socialists, but for a lengthy period the extreme left retained a marginal representation in Parliament. Now, with the collapse of the Communist party and of Communism in Eastern Europe, there is no parliamentary extreme left and even outside Parliament it remains small and marginal.

The Communists. The Belgian Communist party (PCB/KPB) was born in 1921 with only about 500 members of a forced marriage imposed by the Communist International on two antagonistic groups: the *'Ancien Parti'* — the Parti Communiste de Belgique led by Van Overstraeten, which was anti-parliamentary and favoured workers' councils – and the Parti Communiste of Jacquemot which grew out of the group called L'Ami des Exploités, whose ideology was more moderate. They wanted to return the old POB to a more left-wing class line. In 1925 the Comintern imposed the cell structure for the then 700 members and in 1928 ordered the expulsion of the 'leftist' Trotskyite faction. In the 1930s the party moved into the trade unions and obtained some success, especially in the Borinage coal mines, and membership grew above 8,500 at its high point. It espoused the notion of a *'front uni à la base'* (united front at the grassroots), until its VII Congress in 1935 when it adopted the *Front populaire* line. In 1937 a specifically Flemish wing, the KPB, was formed. There is some evidence that, even before the German invasion of the Soviet Union in June 1941, the PCB or rather groups within it were organising strikes and working-class resistance to the Germans in the Walloon industrial areas, but the party as such followed the Comintern line that the war was 'imperialist'. After June 1941 the PCB entered active resistance and played a major role in the underground in the *Front de l'Indépendance*, a pluralist co-ordination body.[84]

The party's parliamentary representation began in 1925, when it won 1.64% of the vote and two seats. Before 1936 it had never held more than three seats, but it did obtain votes as high as 6% in some areas. With the radicalisation of the late 1930s, its support increased to 6.06% with nine seats in 1936, and 5.36% with nine seats in 1939, but it played no part in parliamentary politics. In the early post-war period it saw considerable success, obtaining 12.7% and twenty-three seats in 1946. As in many European countries, it participated in several coalition cabinets between 1944 and 1947 — when the Cold War began in earnest. Throughout the 1950s and 1960s its support fell and then remained stable, but it was isolated in a political ghetto. The manner of the post-war reorganisation of the Socialist unions (FGTB) had also ensured that Communist influence would be small.

In the early 1970s, with its own evolution in response to the Euro-Communist movement and the greater openness of the PS to some form of *union des progressistes*, the PCB saw a brief opportunity to escape from its isolation, at least in Wallonia where this limited strength was greatest, but this remained unconsummated. In 1985, the PCB/KPB lost its last surviving deputy. It polled a mere 1.2% in Brussels and 0.5% in Flanders, less than the Trotskyite Partij van de Arbijd. In Wallonia it exceeded 6% in three *cantons*. By 1987 it had fallen to 0.8% overall, that is 1.5% in Wallonia, 1% in Brussels and 0.5% in Flanders. In 1982, the PCB/KPB had one Flemish communal councillor in Antwerp, none in Brussels, and 33 in Wallonia, but these had gone by 1988; it had no provincial councillors in 1985, 1987 or 1991. It put up no lists in Brussels or Flanders in 1991 and only stood in Mons (1.4%), Charleroi (1.3%) and Thuin (1.1%) and obtained in all 8,997 votes (0.5%) of the Walloon vote. The party's paper, the *Drapeau Rouge*, ceased publication in 1991 and the party itself has now wound itself up.[85]

Its greatest strength lay in Wallonia with a peak of 21.7% in 1946. Even as late as 1968 it had 9.8%, and it retained significant pockets of support of over 10% right down to 1981. However, its support in Flanders never exceeded 5.5%, even in 1946. Its voters were mostly male, working-class and non-Catholic, with above-average support among both younger and retired voters. It remained a unitary party, but it became federalist and Euro-Communist after 1979, arguing for a *rassemblement des progressistes* against monopolies and for measures against the economic crisis. But neither the crisis nor the peace movement enabled it to increase its support.

Partij van de Arbijd/Parti du Travail Belge. This party, previously AMADA (*Alle Macht aan de Arbijders*), is the strongest far-left party. In Flanders, especially, it overtook the Communists in the 1980s, and elected a provincial councillor in Antwerp in 1987. Its greatest strength is in the Antwerp docks. It obtained 1.2% in 1981, 1.0% in 1985 (3.5% in Antwerp) and 0.5% in 1991. In Wallonia its support has fallen to around 0.4%.[86]

The extreme right

Until the recent emergence of the Vlaams Blok, the van Rossem list in Flanders and the Front National in Brussels, the extreme right was both marginal and fragmented. At every election there were new and extremely temporary extreme-right lists, often in violent competition with each other for a limited electoral potential. The pre-war far-right parties such as the Rexists of Léon Degrelle and the Vlaams Nationaal Verbond (VNV) disappeared at the liberation in 1945. In its early years the Vlaams Blok could more accurately have been classified as a small Flemish nationalist splinter group than as the genuine extreme-right party it has now become, although it has retained its Flemish nationalistic ideology. The only other party to emerge from marginality was the Poujadist Union du Respect du Travail (UDRT/RAD). We shall examine the UDRT and then the Vlaams Blok and the Front National. It may well be that the extreme right is on the way to establishing itself as a permanent feature of the Belgian political landscape, but it is too early to be certain.

The UDRT/RAD. The UDRT originated in an initiative of a small group of leaders of *Défense Sociale*, the organ of the Fédération Générale des Travailleurs Indépendants (FGTI) and in particular of Robert Hendrick. In late 1977 they formed the Centre d'Action Démocratique which, with the energetic support of Mr Pauwels of the FGTI and *Défense Sociale*, became the UDRT in April 1978, adopting a seventeen-point charter. Between then and the 1978 elections, the UDRT concentrated on Brussels and on forging links with potential competitors, the basically Flemish Parti Radical of Paul Delahaye, the Union Radicale Belge, the Verenigde Onafhankelijke Partij (VOP) and, most important, the Centre Démocratie et Solidarité (CDS), led by Mr Delforge, that were the last remnants of the old PLP in Brussels. These groups formed a cartel for the 1978 elections, and in 1979 the UDRT/RAD enlarged itself to include the Parti Radical and some VOP and CDS members, and became a party with about 5,000 members mostly in Brussels. It established local *sections* for each *arrondissement*, provincial *bureaux*, a national congress open to all members, and between congresses a more restricted *assemblée générale*; an eighteen-member *conseil national* of which fifteen members are elected by the *assemblée générale* and three co-opted, and a *bureau exécutif* consisting of the co-presidents – Hendrick (Francophone) and Delahaye (Flemish) – and two other members and a treasurer. The party has also set up campaign and information cells. The structure is unitary.[87]

Its voters were mostly young, in the 26-35 age group; 30% are *cadres*, 28% *indépendants* and 11% *employés*.[88] At the 1978 election it took 0.88% of the national vote, with 0.7% in Flanders, 0.8% in Wallonia and 2.3% in Brussels, with 5.84% in Arlon as its best score. It had one deputy in Brussels. In 1981, it obtained 2.71% of the national vote and 0.9% in Flanders, 2.72% in Wallonia and 6.97% in Brussels, with 10.84% in Uccle as its best result. This time it had three deputies (two Francophone and one Dutch-speaker), *all* in Brussels, enabling it to form a group in the House of Representatives. The party was disappointed with these limited gains.[89]

The UDRT rejects labels such as 'Poujadist', and declines to be considered right- or left-wing. It is a 'different' party or an anti-system party. Its main targets are the established political parties, which it regards as parasites on the business community and incapable of reform, being too meshed in a system from which they profit. It attacks this 'political class' and its relationship to the *partenaires sociaux*. It rejects the 'dictatorship of the unions and employers', but is much more hostile to the unions than to the employers' body, the FEB. It does, however, dislike large multinational capital, favouring the small businessman. But this has been a problem in the party, since its leadership wants to broaden its base from being merely a defence body for *indépendants*. Thus, with difficulty, the candidates' list for 1981 was purged of obvious representatives of the *indépendants*. It opposes state interventionism and seeks radical reform of the tax system (maximum rate 35%), and reduction of bureaucratic regulations, unproductive public expenditure or bureaucracy, and 'excessive' social welfare. It proclaims attachment to the rights of entrepreneurs and to the free market. It seeks equal pensions for all and 'privatisation' of much of the welfare system. It argues for a stop on immigration from non-EC countries and controls on welfare abuses by immigrants. On many issues such as defence and foreign policy it has no position, and on the Reform of the State it developed no policy until the debates of 1980. It favoured decentralisation to the provinces rather than the present type of regionalisation, which it regards as a rather costly bureaucratic exercise. It may best be compared, as already mentioned, to the Danish Progress Party, which is likewise suspected of extreme right-wing tendencies, while in reality it is probably better classified with the paradoxical label 'right-wing anarchist'.[90]

The party gave its tactical support to the Martens-Gol government in 1985, but it was in effect squeezed by the '*recentrage*' of a centre-right government,[91] which took up in a less radical way many of the UDRT's themes. At the same time more radical extreme right-wing groups emerged. In 1985 it polled only 0.3% in Flanders, 1.6% in Wallonia (-2.5%) and 5% in Brussels (-3.7%), that is 1.2% on a national basis and one seat (-2). In 1987, its leader Mr Hendrick entered into a pact with the PSC in Brussels and was elected on the joint list. Elsewhere, the UDRT obtained 0.3% in Wallonia. In 1991 it only presented a list in Brussels, where it obtained a mere 0.3%, and it is now defunct.

The Vlaams Blok (VLB). The Vlaams Blok,[92] initially perhaps a radical Flemish Nationalist party but already with some far-right propensities, was formed in 1978, from a split in the more mainstream Volksunie. It won its first parliamentary seat in 1978, holding it at subsequent elections in 1981 and 1985, and gained a second one in 1987. Its share of the vote remained in the range of 1.4% (1978) to 6.6% (1991). It first attracted more serious notice at the 1988 municipal elections, with 17.7% in Antwerp and then in the Euro-elections of 1989, when it won 4.1% and its leader Karel Dillen was elected to the European Parliament. At the 1991 elections, the Vlaams Blok increased its vote to 6.6% and returned twelve deputies. Some of the party's results were indeed dramatic. With 25.1% it became the first party in Antwerp, Belgium's largest city (473,000 inhabitants). In Brussels (only 20% Flemish) it won 3.9% of the total vote. In other large Flemish towns it also achieved significant results.[93]

For the extreme right to be able to take off significantly, emerging from its traditional electoral and organisational ghetto, a suitable political environment, organisation and leadership must clearly come together in a critical mass. The end of the 1980s and beginning of the '90s saw the emergence for the first time since the Second World War of credible far-right movements, able to act as the mobilisers and standard-bearers for the right. In view of the divide between the communities in Belgium (which extended to the extreme right even in 1936), there could not be one single Belgian extreme right-wing party. In Flanders there is the Vlaams Blok and in Wallonia and Brussels the Front National. We should look more closely at these two movements – their origins, policies and international links.

The origins of the Vlaams Blok are initially rooted in the history of the Flemish movement; the party did not take up the stark positions of the modern extreme right on issues such as immigration till later. It was formed effectively as a splinter group from the Volksunie after that party's participation in government in 1977-8 and its acceptance of a plan for the Reform of the State (the Egmont pact) that the more extreme elements of the Flemish movement inside and outside the Volksunie considered to be a betrayal of the Flemish cause. The Vlaams Blok was then formed in 1977 out of two dissident parties: the Vlaams Nationale Volkspartij of Karel Dillen and the Vlaams Volkspartij of Senator Lode Claes. The party won a single seat at the 1978 election (1.4%), which it retained in 1981 and 1985, without making any significant impact. At this stage the party seemed part of a murky pond of extreme-right Flemish nationalist move-ments, with roots back into the Frontist (the first nationalist party in the inter-war period) and VNV movements of the 1920s and 1930s, and hence it had little wider appeal. For example, there were close relations between Karel Dillen of the Vlaams Blok and the violent and militant Vlaams Militanten Orde (VMO). In the later 1980s the Vlaams Blok picked up some of the Flemish wing of the Poujadist UDRT/RAD. In 1987 the Vlaams Blok vote rose to 1.9% and it won two seats. However, its real breakthrough came at the municipal elections in 1988, with 20% in Antwerp, and then at the Euro-elections in June 1989 when it obtained 4.1% and returned one MEP, the party chairman Karel Dillen, compared with 1.3% in the 1984 Euro-elections.

In the European Parliament Dillen joined the Technical Group of the European Right with the French Front National and the German

Republikaner, chaired by Jean-Marie Le Pen. Membership of this group gives the Vlaams Blok a European platform, significant resources from the European Parliament budget, and wider contacts and credibility on the European stage. These advantages were no doubt assets in achieving its national breakthrough at the November 1991 national elections. The Vlaams Blok began in the later 1980s to espouse the common themes of the European far right: on immigration, defence of European culture and values, the need for strong government, and opposition to Marxism and liberal values, along with its original emphasis on a Flemish nationalism, which is now seen as part of a broader European nationalism. It therefore opposes European integration and federalism, which it regards as destructive of national identities, while supporting co-operation; thus the ideology and policies of the Vlaams Blok have to be seen as the radical continuation of the Flemish movement with its deep historical roots.

The Front National.[94] The extreme right was much weaker and slower to develop in the French-speaking part of the country, despite the Rexist tradition and the high concentration of immigrants in Brussels. With the sole and short exception of the dramatic success of the Rexist party of Léon Degrelle in the 1936-9 period (twenty-one seats and 271,000 votes in 1936, but only four seats and 104,000 votes by 1939), it was never able to create a solid organisation or mass movement. In more recent years, the extreme right in French-speaking Belgium has seemed '*groupusculaire*', fractious, divided, introverted, insubstantial, amateurish and unable to produce effective leaders. Furthermore, it has seemed unable to chose a clear strategy. It wavered between forms of 'entryism' on the fringes of the traditional parties of the right (PRC and PSC), romantic violence and 'destabilisation' through links with paramilitary groups and limited infiltration of the security services, ideological debate such as the so-called 'revisionist', or neo-occidentalist philosophies as against seeking electoral support.

Numerous groups have proliferated, merged, split and reformed in a complex process of interlocking memberships. The most important of these were the Front de la Jeunesse (FJ), active between 1974 and 1981, which mixed political activity and an overt use of violence; the Parti des Forces Nouvelles (PFN), which contained a very strong National Socialist and revisionist strand; and the Front National-Nationaal Front (FN-NF) established in 1985. There were also groups and individuals straddling the divide between overtly extreme-right groups and the 'respectable' right in the traditional right-wing parties. Here one can point to the CEPIC, a rightist '*courant*' inside the Parti Social Chrétien until that party's new president, Gérard Deprez, closed it down in 1982 after publicity surrounding its activities and rumoured relations with the violent far right had brought the whole party into disrepute. In a grey area between the 'traditional' parties and the unambiguous extreme right, there proliferated innumerable small ephemeral groups, circles, associations and even parties (such as the Parti Libéral Chrétien, PLC), which acted as a bridge or a siphon between the two wings.

With the example of the French Front National showing that a mass far-right political movement was once again possible in a Western democracy, and the alienation of a significant portion of public opinion from Belgian democratic politics and increased opposition to immigration and multiculturalism, the option of giving priority to electoral politics in order to build a mass far-right party had been a reality. A standard bearer had to emerge to organise and mobilise the inchoate electoral potential. After an initial period in which the PFN seemed likely to emerge, it was the Front National under Daniel Féret which won the Darwinian battle. In this scenario it may well have been the patronage of the French party under Le Pen that tipped the balance.

The French Front National had won its own battles against rival movements by seeking to develop a broader populist mass appeal and to distance itself from the backward-looking National Socialist ideologies that persisted in both France and Belgium. Hence Le Pen visited Belgium on 28 September 1984 at the invitation of the renegade PRL mayor of Schaerbeek, Roger Nols, who was initially to be the creator of a broad populist Belgian movement, mobilising both the far right and a section of the electorates of the collapsing UDRT, PSC, PPL and even some of the populist working-class electorate. Indeed on that occasion, Le Pen said: 'The main reason for coming to Belgium is to found a new party...a similar movement (to the FN) will arise in Belgium.'

The Nols movement never took off, although 'Clubs Nols' and the mayor's own municipal list were established, and Nols himself was never prepared to break totally with the PRL, on whose list he was elected a deputy even in 1991 although in 1995 he stood for the Front National. In a sense it was *faute de mieux* that the Front National with the same brand-name became the new vehicle and benefited from the patronage of Le Pen until the FN and PFN amalgamated in May 1991, although relations had been cooling since the alliance between the FN and the Vlaams Blok in 1989. Indeed the Front National leaders from France concluded that the FN-NF was amateurish, chaotic and without solid basis. However, the arrival of the PFN after the merger in 1991, in spite of eliminating the only serious rival to the FN-NF, brought in the 'contagion' of the PFN ideology and hence made the new FN-NP an object of suspicion to the French FN. Currently, in application of Le Pen's amendment to the old *Communist Manifesto* slogan that he renders as '*Patriotes de tous les pays, unissez-vous!*', but also in search of an effective Belgian partner, the Vlaams Blok now has the FN's preference.

The situation in French-speaking Belgium is open and will probably be resolved by the success or failure of the FN-NF.

Thus the FN-NF emerged as the main standard-bearer of the far right. In 1985 the strongest far-right list was the PFN list called '*Forces*', which obtained 0.9% in Brussels compared to 0.6% for the then new FN-NF, but by 1987 the latter had taken the lead with 1.2% to 0.6% for the PFN. By 1991, the only other far-right party with any serious strength was AGIR which won 4.7% in Liège, double the FN-NF score. Had all far-right lists coalesced earlier, they would have elected one deputy in 1987 and perhaps two in 1991.[95]

What were the issues and policies of FN-NF? They were the usual ones of the far right: immigration, repatriation of immigrants, rejection of rights for immigrants; law and order; the alleged corruption of democratic politics; a degree of economic populism, criticism of the immobilism of the traditional democratic parties and reference to the need for strong leadership; a certain anti-Americanism which emerged during the Gulf war; opposition to European integration; and moral issues such as abortion and pornography, which it strongly opposed.

Despite some more than intermittent international contacts, some links between the 'tough' democratic right and extreme-right *milieux* to develop common action against 'subversion', and possibly some murky connections between extreme-right ideologies and paymasters and violent groups, all of which admire the 1970s Italian '*teoria della distensione*', conspiracy theories of the extreme right in Belgium mostly distract from the more banal realities. There is some mutual assistance, sharing of slogans and speakers, and especially same basking in the reflected glory of the French FN, but the right's gains in support have been due more to similar problems and contradictions in western societies. Its variable success relates to distinct national circumstances, organisation and leadership.

The Greens

The Greens – Ecolo in Wallonia and Brussels and Agalev ('*Anders Gaan Leven*', 'Live Differently') in Flanders – are now an established part of the political landscape, and since the 1987 elections, but especially since those of 1991, have been on the point of emerging from marginality and becoming a serious potential partner in the political process. They can be considered more than a 'single issue' party or a mere vehicle for protest voters. They are now almost a distinct political family.

There were several 'ecologist' lists in both Flanders and Wallonia in 1978, with various political characteristics – socialist, pluralist and purely environmental protection. None of the ecologist lists made much impact in Flanders, but Agalev was the most significant. In Wallonia, Ecolo was the most successful list, obtaining 1.26% in Wallonia (Charleroi, Neufchâteau, Virton, Nivelles, Namur). Its best result was in the *arrondissements* of Namur (2.78%), Nivelles (2.78%) and Liège (2.04%). Its best cantonal result was in Namur (5.21%). The ecologists found it easier to penetrate rural than urban areas in Wallonia and the reverse in Flanders. The 1981 elections saw an important advance for Ecolo, despite the divergences between the various tendencies which had threatened the movement, especially in Brussels: it obtained 4.8% of the national vote, as against 0.8% in 1978, returning four deputies and four senators. Ecolo (Walloon) and Agalev (Flanders) each obtained two seats, with 6.3% and only 3.5% of the vote respectively. In Brussels and in Hainaut Ecolo obtained 7.5% of the vote, which was above the national average. The ecologists were more united in Flanders, but their division in Brussels was not detrimental to their advance. The movement has suffered from internal disputes and discussions about its structure and ideological orientation, especially in Brussels, where in the 1981 election two other lists, Ecologie Bruxelles and Ecolo-J, were tabled as well as Ecolo, although these other lists, largely pertaining to Brussels in particular, obtained little success. Ecolo was dominant in Wallonia, as was Agalev in Flanders. Such divergences are of course only to be expected in a movement brought together from such diverse origins and sensibilities (rural, urban, ideological and so on).[96]

At the 1984 European elections, the steady advance of the Greens continued, with Agalev winning 4.3% of the vote and one seat and Ecolo 3.9% and one seat also. European elections offered an easier target for small 'protest' parties, but even so the Greens' results in the 1985 legislative elections were respectable and represented an advance on their 1981 national results: Ecolo 2.5% (+ three seats) and Agalev 3.7% (+ two seats), although neither party reached its 1984 European score. Ecolo made gains in six Walloon *arrondissements* but lost in seven for a net gain of 0.3% in Wallonia, but in Brussels it made dramatic gains from 3.1% in 1981 to 5.5% in 1985. Agalev advanced from 0.6% to 1% in Brussels and reached 6.1% (+ 2.2%) in Flanders, its greatest gains being in Leuven (+ 3.1%) and Turnhout (+ 3.1%). It exceeded 10% of the vote in Kontich (10.2%) and came near in Kapellen (9.6%). The 1987 legislative election saw continued moderate advance: Agalev won 4.3% of the vote (+ 0.8%), exceeding its 1984 Euro peak. Ecolo won 2.6% (+ 0.1%), below its 1984 peak. The 1988 municipal elections saw consolidation of the Ecolo/Agalev positions in local government, with gains in all Walloon towns of over 30,000 inhabitants, except Liège and Verviers, and a total vote of 9.6% in those towns. The 1989 European elections were once again a new peak for both parties. Ecolo took 6.3%, a dramatic jump from its 3.9% in 1984 and even more so from 2.6% in 1987. Agalev gained 7.2%. At the 1991 elections, those peaks could not be held, although Ecolo virtually doubled its 1987 score with 5.1% and overtook Agalev, whose gains were more modest with 4.9% (+ 0.4%).

In 1991 Agalev won 7.8% of the Flemish vote, with a peak in Leuven with 12% and its low of 3.7% in Zoutleeuw. It obtained over 10% in six cantons (Ghent, Leuven, Turnhout, Kontich, Zonhoven and Kapellen). Ecolo obtained 13.5% of the vote in Wallonia and 9.4% in Brussels. Its best Walloon vote was 16% in Soignies and 15.3% in Namur, and in Brussels its best result was 14.1% in St Gilles.[97] The advance of the Greens stopped in the 1994 European elections.

The Ecolo and Agalev electorate is young, being over-represented in the 17-24 and 24-35 age groups and under-represented among pensioners and housewives. It is over-represented among students, first-time voters and the middle and professional classes (C1 + C2). It is the least 'confessional' of all the parties: 84% of Ecolo voters believe that the church should not intervene in political issues. Ecolo (27.7%) and, even more so, Agalev (36.3%) voters classify themselves as on the left and centre-left, second only to the PS and SP. Despite some tendency for Green leaders to reject the left-right cleavage, their voters seem to accept it.[98]

Ecolo and Agalev emerged in the 1970s, a period of deconfessionalisation among the Belgian parties. A significant activist and electoral potential developed in the new pro-materialist tendencies, stronger initially in Flanders, that gave rise to left libertarian social movements. These new protest movements centred on four main topics: protest against the environmental impact of industrial and transportation projects (canals, roads, chemical factories in Flanders; rivers and excessive building in the Ardennes in Wallonia); neighbourhood movements in the cities, especially in Brussels; the Third World movement, stronger in Flanders; and pacifist and anti-NATO movements. The feminist and anti-nuclear power movements were less important in Belgium than elsewhere. There was a profound sense among these severe activists that none of the existing parties were responding to these new issues.

Both parties emerged from the new social movements and dissatisfaction with the existing parties. They went through a series of phases: incubation till about 1979, development of structure and strategy till 1981, and thirdly institutionalisation. Agalev began as a mere '*werkgroep*' of activists founded by the Jesuit teacher Luc Versteylen. As the name implies, it was concerned with lifestyle issues and from 1973 onwards organised a series of environmental protests, using 'happenings' in a style borrowed from Dutch movements. At first the group endorsed candidates on conventional lists (1974) and then from 1977 fielded its own lists, but without establishing any party structure. At first this was only semi-serious, but electoral success brought in new activists and new pressures. There was a split with Versteylen, and Agalev went its own way in 1981, entered Parliament and established a minimal structure in 1981/2.[99]

The initial core of Ecolo activists came from the radical elements in RW who soon took up Green issues and democratic participation as key elements in a radical programme. This group established a Belgian section of Amis de la Terre (Friends of the Earth) and the grassroots urban renewal movement Atelier de Recherche et Action Urbaine (ARAU). At this stage there was no monopolistic organisation. Several Green lists were established in 1978, especially in Brussels. In January 1978 a Green convention had founded Ecolo and adopted a programme. However, it was not dominant enough to unify the movement totally in 1978 and several lists remained incomplete. These crystallised into a more leftist (*fundi* in German terminology) group in Brussels and a more moderate group, favouring the formation of a more structured party and parliamentary activity, based in Namur. By 1981 the Namur group had come to the fore. After the modest results of the 1985 elections, a new factional battle flared up between the radical Brussels wing and the Namur-Liège Ecolos, who had even favoured some co-operation with the PSC/PRL regional government and with the PS in the Liège municipal government. The leftist faction split and formed Vert et Gauche Alternative (VEGA), but Ecolo retained the loyalty of Green voters in Wallonia.

Both parties proclaim a 'different', more democratic and participatary type of politics. Each party has about 1,200 members. Only about 0.52% of their voters are members – less than the proportion in the conventional mass parties such as the PS or CVP. Yet Ecolo and Agalev number about 700 activists equal to about 35% of members; thus the membership is smaller but far more activist than in other parties. They do not elect a party president but prefer forms of collective leadership, through a group of spokesmen or federal secretaries. The parties have local groups in each district, *arrondissement* groups that hold assemblies and elect an executive secretary. In Agalev, the national conference elects two members per *arrondissement* to the national steering committee while in Ecolo it is the regional conference that exercises this power. These conferences – the supreme decision-making bodies in the respective parties – are all member and not delegate conferences (as in the FDF); there are limits on terms of office and cumulation of offices. Ecolo seems a more parliamentary, more elastic party, and less plugged into the social movements than Agalev.[100] Increasingly it is adopting a profile as a Francophone party.

Though separate, Ecolo and Agalev have made joint proposals on the Reform of the State. Both parties espouse all the typical Green positions: investing in sustainable growth, conservation, social justice, participation and federalism. From being a mere protest party, Ecolo especially has adopted a more responsible profile. Its 1991 list included well-known lawyers and economists. It declared itself ready to enter into alliances and seek compromises. Its leading figure appeared on his first full-length TV broadcast in a suit and tie. The leadership has also proposed reducing the number of federal secretaries (in effect the party leadership) from five to three.

In 1987 Ecolo was briefly considered as a regional coalition partner; in 1991 Ecolo/Agalev were seriously involved in discussions for a 'non-confessional' national coalition (PS/SP, PRL/PVV, Ecolo/Agalev) and by the summer of 1992 were the only opposition parties remaining in the inter-community dialogue and genuinely sought comprise. Their economic proposals are presented with a new realism and based on a costing. They have also said that they oppose more immigration. One distinctive point is their scepticism about the Maastricht treaty and its impact on Belgian economic policy. They oppose the 3% PSBR limitation. They joined the majority (CVP/PSC and SP/PS) and the Volksunie in agreeing on the *Accord de la St Michel* in September 1992, which represented a major new stage in the Reform of the State and obtained approval of an eco-tax package as the *contre-partie*.

Like the community parties but unlike the far right, Ecolo and Agalev are in the process of being co-opted into the system.

NOTES

1. See, for example, CVP statutes (1989), Parti Socialiste, *Statuts*, adopted 1983; *Statuts du FDF*, 18 December 1989, *Statuten van de PVV*, 1982 and 1986.
2. On the role of the Mechelen Congresses, see Luykx, op. cit., 124-5.
3. For a brief history of the origins of the Catholic Party, see Luykx, op. cit., 123-7, and *Dossiers du CRISP*, no. 10, 'Les Partis Politiques en Belgique' (hereafter *CRD* 10), 3.
4. J. Fitzmaurice, 'Belgium', in F. Jacobs, (ed.) *Western Political Parties*, Longman, London, 1989.
5. *CRD* 10, 11-14, for the structure of the PSC.
6. On the MOC, see G. Spitaels, *Le Mouvement Syndical en Belgique*, Editions de l'Université de Bruxelles 1975, 59-61. On its recent moves, see *Le Soir*, 10 April 1982, 2.
7. On the CEPIC, see *CH du CRISP*, no. 787, 'Le Centre Politique des Cadres Chrétiens (CEPIC)'.
8. For all election results in this chapter, see *CH* 826, 'Les élections législatives du 17 décembre 1978', and for 1981 *La Libre Belgique*, 10-11 Nov. 1981, p. 3. Walloon area: *CH* 826; Flemish area: ibid., 4; Brussels area: ibid., 32 and 33.
9. Data from X. Mabille and E. Lentzen, 'Les Elections du 13 octobre 1985', CH 1095/6 (1985) and X. Mabille, E. Lentzen, P. Blaise, 'Les Elections du 24 novembre 1991', *CH* 1335/6 (1991).
10. The data on the electorate of the various parties is taken from N. Delruelle, R. Evalenko and W. Fraeys, *Le Comportement Politique des Electeurs Belges*, Editions de l'Institut de Sociologie de l'Université Libre de Bruxelles, 1970, tables V and VI, and analysis, 48-91, for 'statistically valid' determinants of voting preferences. For the Flemish parties later (September 1979), figures are taken from a poll cited in R. van Malderghem's 'Welke zijn de nieuwe publiek en volksgroepen die de Socialistische Beweging aanspreekt?', *Socialistische Standpunten*, 2/81, 87-95; for poll data, 94-5.

11. *Le Soir*, 10-11 November 1981, 2.
12. X. Mabille, 'La législature 1981-85', *CH* 1088 (1985), 14-20.
13. See note 10 for source.
14. *CH* 1095/6 and *CH* 1355/6.
15. See note 11 for source.
16. 'Verkiezingsprogramma van de CVP', published in *Tele-Zeg*, 3-4.
17. 'Verkiezingsprogramma 1981', 5-21.
18. Fitzmaurice, op. cit.
19. H. de Ridder, *Le Cas Martens*, Duculot, Paris/Louvain-la-Neuve, 1991, 201-5.
20. See CVP statutes (1974, 1977, 1979), published in *Tele-Zeg* (1980), especially articles 17, 18 and 19 for the *arrondissement* structure, and articles 28-35 for the national structure.
21. *CH* 820, 'Le renouvellement des candidatures en vue des élections législatives du 17 décembre 1978', 11-17.
22. Ibid., p. 16.
23. See Statutes of the PS adopted at Namur, 26 Nov. 1978, for the organisation of the PS.
24. For a brief history of the POB, see R. Abs, *Histoire du Parti Socialiste Belge*, Editions Fondation Louis de Brouckère, Brussels, 1979, 17-46.
25. *CRD* 10, annex, p. 1.
26. Statutes, adopted at Namur, in 1983, for the organisation of the PS.
27. PS Statutes, articles 17-28 on the congress.
28. *CH* 821, 2-7, on polls held in 1978.
29. Fitzmaurice, op. cit.
30. See note 11 for source.
31. L. Voyé, B. Bowing-Legros, J. Kerkhofs and K. Dobbelaere, *Belges, heureux et satisfaits. Les valeurs des belges dans les années 90*, De Boeck, Université Libre de Bruxelles, 1992, 243-5 and tables on 259 (hereafter L. Voyé *et al.*).
32. *CH* 1095/6 and *CH* 1335/6.
33. For an examination of the election of Mr Spitaels and the changes he has brought about, see an article published in three parts in *Le Soir* of 11, 12 and 13 January 1982 (page 2 each day), entitled 'Le PS dans un drôle de cure d'opposition'.
34. *Le Programme du Parti Socialiste élections législatives, 1981.*
35. Ibid., chapter I: 'Le riposte socio-économique du Parti Socialiste' for the economic programme.
36. See Programme Electoral du PS, adopted on 26 October 1991, especially pages 1-2, 3-5 and 9-18.
37. Ibid.
38. *CH* 1095/6 and *CH* 1335/6.
39. See note 11 for source.
40. 'Statuten van de SP' adopted 8 and 9 March 1980.
41. Ibid., paras 7 and 10.
42. Ibid., paras 2-38, on the various national bodies.
43. Article 50 for the age-limit and article 53 on the '*cumul*'.
44. *CH* 820 (I), 17-21.
45. *CRD* 10, 14 and 34 and Keesing's *Political Parties of the World*, op. cit.
46. Statutes, article 1.
47. See Van Malderghem, op. cit., (note 11).
48. For the early history of the Liberal Party, see Luykx, op. cit., 94-7 and 181-3.
49. R. Willemyns, 'Politieke ideologie en vrijzinnigheid', *Socialistische standpunten*, 5/81, 264-79.

50. For the problem of the Brussels Liberals, see Luykx, op. cit., 586-8, and *CRD* 10, 2-3 and annex, 3-4.

51. *CRD* 10, 27, and annex, 3-4 and *CH* 1095/6 and *CH* 1335/6.

52. *CRD* 10, 11-14.

53. On Jean Gol and the changes he introduced, see *Le Soir* 15 and 16 May 1981, 'Voyage au Parti Réformateur Libéral' (each day on p. 3).

54. X. Mabille, 'Les Parties Politiques à Bruxelles', *CH* 1086/1087 (1985), 33-50.

55. *CH* 1095/6 and *CH* 1335/6.

56. See note 11.

57. *CRD* 10, 11-14.

58. Quoted in *Le Patronat Belge*, op. cit., 291.

59. See 'Herstel het Beleid' Programme for the 1991 elections.

60. *Ibid.*

61. Jos Bouveroux, *De Partij van de Burger: de verruiming van de Vlaamse Liberalen*, Standaard Uitgeverij, Antwerp, 1992.

62. See *CRD* 10, 5-6, for the origins of the RW.

63. See note 10.

64. See note 11.

65. *CRD* 10, 11-14.

66. For an account of the RW in power, see *CH* 786: 'L'évolution du Rassemblement Wallon d'avril 1974 à mars 1977'.

67. *CH* 786, 32-3.

68. For the origins and character of the FDF, see *CRD* 10, 3-4, 10-11 and 24.

69. Statutes of the FDF (1977, amended 1981), article 1.

70. FDF 1981: 'Maître chez soi', 5-15.

71. *Programme 1991: Rassemblement FDF-RDW: Francophones au coeur de l'Europe (1991)*

72. X. Mabille, 'Les Partis Politiques à Bruxelles', op. cit., 33-44.

73. *CH* 1095/6 and *CH* 1335/6.

74. *CRD* 10, 34.

75. See note 11.

76. See Statutes, esp. articles 5-6 (congress), 7-10 (*conseil général*), and 23 (*commission électorale*).

77. *Volksunie: Identity, history and programme*, published in English by the Volksunie, 1979 4-5, and *CRD* 10, 4.

78. *CH* 1095/6 and *CH* 1335/6.

79. See note 11.

80. *Statuten van de Volksunie*, esp. articles 48-73, for the party's national organisation.

81. *Volksunie: Identity, history and programme*, op. cit., 4.

82. M. van Haegendoren, 'De Volksunie ziet het zo', *Vlaams Nationaal Standpunten*, 6/7 1980, 8-10.

83. 'Vlaams Staatshervorming: Blauwdruk voor en Konfederaal Model' (June 1981).

84. The origins and early history of the PCB are set out in R. Lewin (ed.), *Le Parti Communiste de Belgique (1921-44)*, CHEMA 1980, 17-27, and in the inter-war period, 41-53.

85. See Statutes of the PCB (XX Congress, Charleroi 1971) and the resolution adopted by the central committee on 27 October 1980: 'Fonctionnement démocratique du Parti', which seeks to create both more open political debate and some regionalised structures.

86. Ibid.

87. *CH* 924, UDRT-RAD (I), 3-5 for origins and 13-16 for structure of the UDRT/RAD.

88. *Le Soir*, 15 June 1981, 'Descente au coeur de l'UDRT', 3.

89. *CH* 924, 11-13, for election results.

90. On UDRT/RAD policy see *CH* 941 and 942, 'L'UDRT- RAD' (2 parts), esp. 2-11 for its 'anti-system' analysis and 17- 40 for its programme.

91. X. Mabille, 'Les Partis Politiques à Bruxelles', op. cit.

92. *CH* 1095/6 and *CH* 1335/6.

93. C.T. Husbands, 'The Extreme Right in Belgium since 1945', in Ed. P. Hainsworth.

94. CH 1095/6 and *CH* 1335/6.

95. J. Fitzmaurice, 'The Extreme Right in Belgium: Recent Developments', in *Parliamentary Affairs*, Summer 1992.

96. G. Braes, *L'Affront National: le nouveau visage de l'extrême droite en Belgique*, EPO, Brussels, 1991, 111-25.

97. See note 10.

98. See *CG* 1095/6 and *CH* 1335/6, also J.F. Istasse, 'Les Elections Communales du 9 octobre 1988 en Wallonie', *Socialisme*, no. 210, 1988, 409-20.

99. *Belges heureux et satisfaits*, op. cit., 248-55 and 259-62.

100. H. Kitschelt and S. Hellemans, *Beyond the European Left: Ideology and Political Action in the Belgian Ecology Parties*, Duke University Press, Durham NC, 1990, for the origins of Ecolo and Agalev, 31-47.

7

OTHER POLITICAL ACTORS

In complex modern societies, and Belgium is no exception, political parties are by no means the only political actors. There exists a wide range of economic and social pressure groups that are, with the political parties, intervenors in the political process and mediators of public opinion. It is not unusual for such groups to have close links with a political party, such as those between the British Labour party and the trade unions. This is a civil society.

What, however, has characterised Belgium is the density, segmentation and influence of such networks, which make the country the example *par excellence* of a co-sociational democracy. The key characteristic of this system has been called by political scientists *'verzuiling'*, literally 'pillarisation' or 'segmented pluralism'.[1] Of the various definitions of this concept that have been attempted, Val Lorwin's is perhaps the most comprehensive.[2] For him it is a system of relations between organisational pillars based on ideological families; that system is fundamental to the Belgian political system. Other observers have emphasised the notion of distinct, segmented 'worlds' based on self-sufficient pillars.[3] Common to all analyses is the notion of networking between organisations and a political party and the close links between the *zuilen* (pillars) and the state.

Thus Belgian consensualism is seen not merely as a coalition between political parties alone, but between *zuilen*, a system of consensus between social forces, between the different 'worlds'. Thus, political decision-making involves dialogue and concertation with what are called the *'partenaires sociaux'* (lit. social partners), the two sides of industry or, more widely, between the government and various *'interlocuteurs'* (partners) in institutional fora and the direct involvement of these bodies in the public bodies that administer and provide services.

For some, indeed initially most, this system was regarded positively as a means of guaranteeing and protecting the rights of minorities (e.g. non-Catholics in Flanders) and maintaining forms of pacification in a highly segmented society. Others, in the 1970s particularly, while perhaps attacking specific aspects of the system, such as a perceived lack of internal democracy in organisations such as trade unions, regarded the active involvement of what is called the '*vie associative*' (civil society) in public debate and political decision-making as a positive extension of democracy. In reality, as we shall see, this tendency was less a support for *verzuiling à la belge* than an attack on it from a different angle: support for forms of consensual dialogue, but without the dead weight of the *zuilen*.[4]

By the 1970s, two quite different radical critiques of the phenomenon of consensual *verzuiling* emerged. Some on the left, especially what might be called the small left (remnants of the PSC, AMAMA/TPO) and the new left movements, and Greens, argued that not only the top-down nature of the system, but the very concept of consensualism and 'class collaboration' implied in the search for consensus and splitting the difference in the traditional manner tended to stifle the emergence of radical socio-economic reform and shored up the present system. Others – on the radical right (to be found in the PVV under Guy Verhofstadt), in the UDRT, and in small business organisations[5] – criticised the neo-corporatist nature of the system. This criticism was in one way similar to that of the left. They argued that the constitutional bodies – the cabinet and Parliament – had abdicated responsibility, which had become increasingly closed as decision-making disappeared into a Bermuda Triangle of 'concertation' between government and the *interlocuteurs sociaux*. As a result, for them as for the left, radical change had become impossible.

At another level, reinforcing the first critique, the various organisations themselves – not only trade unions, but also employers' organisations – had become unrepresentative, too politicised, too clientelist, too protective of their own power as organisations. This theme emerged strongly in the 1980s and was a major driving force behind the new centre-right coalition in 1981. The PVV in particular, under Guy Verhofstadt, sought, as in Thatcherite Britain, to roll back corporatism as a necessary prelude to rolling back the state through deregulation and privatisation. The success of the PVV campaign was only moderate. It could never accumulate the centralised power that the British system gave to Margaret Thatcher. The existence of the regions and the communities, the need to compromise with their PSC/CVP coalition partners, with their strong *zuil* links, with the trade unions and even pressures from the Liberals' own *zuil* organisations[6] prevented the campaign from achieving more than modest success before 1988 and the return of the PS/SP to government. One might indeed conclude, especially comparing the PVV's experience with Thatcher's, that this amply proved the point that the *zuilen* were an obstacle to radical change. Whether that is good or bad depends on one's ideological viewpoint. To the radical left critics one might reply that there never was even a remote chance of a radical shift to the left, *zuilen* or no *zuilen*, whereas in the climate of Thatcherism and Reaganomics of the early 1980s there was a very real possibility of a radical shift to the right, which the *zuilen* actually prevented.

The special characteristics of Belgian *verzuiling* and, with it, consensualism *are* undergoing change and *are* being weakened, less as a result of any conscious assault on them than through the agency of social change. It is from this angle that a renewed debate about *verzuiling* has been launched with, for example, the establishment of an official committee in the Vlaams Raad in 1990 to study the phenomenon.[7] The issue is whether the *verzuiling* system still corresponds to social reality. If it does not, then its 'privileges' will increasingly come under critical scrutiny. What are the broad social and political changes that have affected the *verzuiling* system?

Belgium, like all Western societies, has seen a process of ideological de-alignment and atomisation. The ongoing secularisation and de-confessionalisation and the parallel process of the disappearance of 'scientific socialism', education, travel, the impact of the media – all have contributed to this process of atomisation. Belgians in the 1990s are less ideological, more open, more pragmatic, more issue-driven (ecology, aid to Africa, immigration, etc.) more individualistic, more sceptical about all traditional political parties, churches and *zuil* organisations. They seek politics *à la carte*.

The share of the vote of the three traditional families has consistently fallen since the middle 1960s. New political movements, outside the old *zuil* structure, have come up as responses to new political issues. Now, the Belgian political landscape is more complex. Alongside the three political '*mondes*' there is a group of community parties (FDF and Volksunie and, earlier, the now-defunct RW). There is the Green current (Ecolo/Agalev). There is also now a clear far-right tendency (Vlaams Blok and FN). Electoral opinion is more volatile and shifting, and the undisputed dominance of the old parties can no longer be assumed. In 1961, the three traditional families together still had 90.3% of the votes cast. The two main *zuil* parties (CVP/PSC and PS/SP), then still unitarist, had 78% of the vote and an easy two-thirds majority in both chambers. At the 1991 elections the three old families (now six parties) obtained only 70.1% and the two main families secured just a bare majority in votes (50%) and 120 seats out of 212 in the House.[8]

Above all, the rise of a new division in the 1960s, which was not taken into account by the *verzuiling* system – namely the community cleavage that at times could assume by far the greatest saliency in Belgian politics – has also created a new situation. It has been necessary to organise forms of dialogue between communities as well as between the *zuilen*. The new development has overlaid and challenged the traditional system. New Flemish and Walloon *zuilen* aggregating the Flemish and Walloon parts of the traditional *zuilen* in order to undertake a dialogue with the other community *zuil*, have come into existence alongside the traditional *verzuiling* within each community.

The new ideological de-alignment, especially strong among younger voters, has made organisations based on the *verzuiling* principle less and less attractive. People want more pluralistic, *à la carte*, service-oriented organisations. Today's younger Belgians can easily contemplate the heresy of voting Green, going to a Catholic school, belonging to the Socialist trade union and the Christian *mutualité*, and attending Flemish national cultural organisations, or any other possible combination.[9] This has forced the organisations to de-emphasise their *zuil* characteristics and seek to compete on the basis of services. The Catholic *zuil* organisations – schools, hospitals and the like – have a consistently higher level of support than the CVP.[10] This may be a tribute to their efficiency, but undermines their political legitimacy in a *verzuiling* system.

If these trends continue, there will be consequences to be drawn in terms of the role of *zuil* organisations in the political process and for the functioning of the organisations themselves. As Agalev argued before the Vlaams Raad committee,[11] there will be tendencies to build more bridges between *zuilen*, and to create more neutral or pluralist associations and organisations. In the cultural and social fields (*matières personalisables*) the public authorities will have to consider new systems of distribution of subsidies based more on individuals than on organisations. At the same time, the problem arises of the representativity of organisations and their capacity to speak legitimately for their sectors and cut the kind of broad deals that have been so central to the Belgian method of decision-making. This is part of a wider debate about the governability of Belgium. In all probability, the breaking down of *verzuiling*, or *ontzuiling* ('depillarisation') will be gradual and undramatic, but it will make the cutting of political deals more complex and difficult than in the past.

We now turn to look at the various organisations: trade unions, *patronat*, middle-class organisations, farmers' unions, professional bodies and national cultural organisations.

THE TRADE UNIONS

Despite the country's early industrialisation, trade unionism developed late in Belgium. The Socialist leader, Hendrik De Man, ascribed this to the widespread co-operative movement which hindered union activity. Now, however, the level of unionisation is high. In the whole country, it is 67%, being over 80% in the northern Flemish provinces, 59% in Hainaut and 52% in Liège.[12] Although there were some isolated craft bodies as early as 1806, it is generally accepted that Belgian trade unionism was born in Ghent with the formation of, first, the weavers' association of Ghent in 1857 and then the Werkersbond in 1860, which grouped several organisations. At first there was only limited progress because of the inertia of the developing working-class and bourgeois opposition. The first clearly Catholic union (of cotton workers also in Ghent) was formed in 1886.[13]

Trade unionism until the Second World War

Trade unionism in Belgium soon developed along pluralist, ideological lines.

Socialist trade unions. From 1880, a large number of national *fédérations* was formed (Fédération Nationale des Travailleurs du Bois; 1883), to be followed in the early twentieth century by *centrales industrielles* (industrial unions) which by 1914 represented 58% of affiliated members, a proportion which had risen rapidly from 11.5% in 1911.[14] The Parti Ouvrier Belge (POB) brought the movement under direct party control: Article 9 of its statutes (1892) provided for only national *fédérations* and later national *centrales industrielles* joining the party. In 1898 it established the first centralised union organisation under a committee appointed by the party's *conseil général*, called the *commission syndicale*, which had no independent policy line. In 1907, the commission obtained its own statutes and organised congresses.[15] At the same time 'independent' (non-party) unions were admitted, provided they accepted the basic tenets of POB ideology. The *commission syndicale* was renamed Commission Syndicale du POB et des Syndicats Indépendants. Party and unions developed a degree of mutual independence, and the unions even publicly regretted the refusal of the POB to join the 1939 Pierlot government. The *commission syndicale* also reinforced its authority over the *fédérations* and *centrales*, jealous of their right to call strikes and call them off. The year 1922 saw the first proposals to give these powers to the central body; at the time the proposals were rejected. In 1937 the *commission* was transformed into the quite independent (at last formally) Confédération Générale du Travail de Belgique (CGTB), which was accorded these vital powers; it also had control over the Caisse Nationale de Résistance (strike funds) first set up in 1909.[16] At the same time, the structures of the *fédérations* and *centrales* had been greatly simplified by numerous amalgamations.

Christian unions. The first Christian union, as already mentioned, was the cotton workers', founded in Ghent in 1886. It was 'anti-Socialist', but nevertheless met opposition in Catholic circles. The 1893 papal encyclical *Rerum Novarum* gave the movement new impetus. The same process of initial diversification followed by amalgamation and consolidation occurred as in the Socialist unions. By 1906, there were thirteen *fédérations*, mostly in Flanders, and only in 1908 was the first Walloon union set up: the Fédération Nationale des Francs Mineurs.

Moves began in 1904 for the creation of centralised organs. Thus the

Secrétariat Général des Unions Professionnelles Chrétiennes was set up, but it had no power over the *fédérations*. This weakness led to the creation in 1909 of two separate Flemish and Walloon confederations, based respectively in Ghent and La Louvière. These were fused in 1912 to form the Confédération Générale des Syndicats Chrétiens et Libres de Belgique (CSC).[17] The next period saw the CSC considerably reinforce its powers. In 1922 it gained control over the strike fund, and in 1930 it obtained further powers over decisions on industrial action; the *fédérations* could still launch strikes, but only if the CSC did not object. In the CSC the *fédérations* were weak and the organisation as a whole was largely Flemish-dominated.

Liberal unions. The Confédération Générale des Syndicats Libéraux de Belgique was founded in 1930. It is the smallest of the three *confédérations*, but the most centralised. It has no *fédérations* but is based on geographical sections. Its influence is slight at the grassroots level but greater at the national level.[18]

Independent unions. These are found in the public service and in some specialised sectors (taxis, trams, train drivers, docks). Before the Second World War, the most important was the Confédération Nationale Indépendante des Travailleurs (1938).[19] The independent unions formed the Cartel des Syndicats Libres de Belgique in 1959 with private and public sector affiliates of respectively 62,000 and 52,000 members.

The trade unions and the war

The Nazi occupation put an end for five years to traditional trade unionism, and left scars which were later to provoke changes in structure for the Socialists and at least in policies if not structures for the other confederations. The occupation led to a radicalisation. Unions were faced with the choice of underground resistance or joining (as proposed by the then leader of the POB, Hendrik De Man) the Union des Travailleurs Manuels et Intellectuels (UTMI), set up in 1940 by Dr Voos to federate the three organisations and the Nazi *Arbeitsorde* in an overtly collaborationist body. Neither workers nor employers ever supported UTMI. The traditional unions ceased to exist, and factory committees, often left-inclined (anarcho-syndicalist), led impressive resistance and strike activities, especially in the Liège steel industry, exacting wage rises from the occupying power in a massive strike in 1941. From the coordination body of these committees (Mouvement Métallurgiste – MMU) and the Communist organisation Comité de Lutte Syndicale (CLS) came the Mouvement Syndical Unifié (MSU), formed in early 1944. Its manifesto, *Pour une révolution constructive*, was a left-wing radical statement which in the new climate would inevitably represent a challenge to the old CGTB after the liberation. The Communist CLS also created the Confédération Belge des Syndicats Unifiés (CBSU), and in the public service the Syndicat Général des Services Publics (SGSP) was formed in 1942.[20]

Post-war developments

The Christian and Liberal unions faced no major difficulties in reestablishing themselves after 1945. The same cannot be said for the CGTB, which was threatened by three new and dynamic organisations on its left. On 8 September 1944 it called for an '*assemblée de réunification*', to include the CSC, but the latter withdrew after an inaugural meeting. After many difficulties, a unification congress was held in Brussels on 28 and 29 April 1945, which led to the formation of a new organisation uniting the four previous ones (CGTB, MSU, SGSP and SBSU) into the Fédération Générale de Travail de Belgique (FGTB). The balance of power was established in the way shown in the Table below. This gave the Communists (CBSU) a far from negligible influence in the new body. A new declaration of principles was adopted which was to the left of previous positions, and which made the FGTB independent of all political parties. For some time, internal problems continued. Communist *centrales* continued to act semi-independently, and the '*tendances*' continued to show up in congress votes. After the Communist take-over in Prague in February 1948, the *bureau* excluded the Communist secretaries, and in April all Communists on the national committee resigned but many Communist members stayed on as individuals. After 1950 the movement maintained its unity, aided by the *Question Royale*, over which the FGTB launched a general strike against Leopold III.[21]

	Membership	Seats in the secretariat
CGTB	248,259	3
CBSIJ	165,968	2
MSU	59,535	1
SGSP	51,789	1

The structure of Belgian trade unions

The Socialists. The régime set up in 1945 lasted till the strikes of 1960-1 and was then replaced by a 'transitional régime' (1963-78). In 1978, the statutes were modified to ensure a regionalised structure for the FGTB in line with the moves towards political federalism. In 1965, a structure was adopted which gave two-thirds of the representation at the congress to the *centrales professionnelles* and one-third to the *régionales interprofessionnelles*. The *régionales* are weaker than the *centrales* and do nothing but reflect the make-up of the *centrales* in that region, being composed as they are of delegates of the *centrales*. The *centrale* is made up of *centrales professionnelles régionales* and the *sections d'entreprises* (workplace sections).[22]

The FGTB faced a major crisis which split it on community lines at the time of the 1960-1 strikes. The *comité national* met on 16 December 1960 to consider two motions: the Smets motion (for a national day of action and a campaign against the *loi unique*) and the Renard motion (for a general strike). Smets and Renard were the two key leaders of the FGTB. Smets was a moderate, whereas Renard was a radical and a federalist, who contributed greatly to the FGTB's (and later the PS's) policy of major structural reforms in the economy. The Renard motion was lost by 475,823 votes to 496,487 (mostly Flemish) and 53,112 abstentions (mostly from Brussels).[23] The movement was strongest in Wallonia, and its *de facto* leadership came from the unofficial Walloon coordination committee. Out of this came pressure, led by André Renard, for a degree of federalism inside the FGTB. This pressure was most evident in Liège and on the political level in the new Mouvement Populaire Wallon (MPW). The internal debate led to an agreement on a 'transitional régime' in June 1963. The agreement did not institute federalism, but provided for linguistic parity in the FGTB *bureau* and secretariat, but not in the congress. It provided for a sort of '*sonnette d'alarme*' (alarm-bell) procedure on any matter where there was a '*rupture*', either between the *centrales* and *régionales* or between Walloons and Flemish.[24] In such a case, a compromise was to be sought which would be approved by a majority of Walloon and Flemish regions and *centrales*. There were rules on the right to establish '*tendances*' and for regionalised publicity activities.[25] These procedures were never invoked, but they certainly incited mutual searches for compromise. In 1966 the first purely Walloon position emerged and led to the creation of an *assemblée générale des régions wallonnes*. Also in that year, a '*comité des sages*' thus proposed an addition to the 1963 agreement, which permitted the creation of inter-regional organisations on community lines and created a *conseil national de politique economique* of twenty-three members to work out general economic policy, coordinate the programmes of the regions and *inter-régionales* (IR) and make proposals for action. It met on twenty-nine occasions between 1968 and 1975.[26] This body was the first to incorporate the principle – strongly supported by the Liégeois and the public sector workers – that the *centrales* and *régionales* should have equal representation in all organs.

Each IR then set up its own machinery and statutes, each reflecting its traditions and preoccupations both as to its structures and issues treated. In the Flemish IR, both the *centrales* and *régionales* are represented, but in the Walloon IR[27] only the *régionales* are represented. Both have a secretariat (four members in each), a *bureau* composed of representatives of the *régionales* (and *centrales* for the Flemish IR), and an *assemblée générale* composed (in the Walloon IR) of the executive committee of the *régionales* and, on the Flemish side, of the *bureau* plus representatives of the *régionales*.[28]

The Walloon IR has concerned itself with the 1971-5 and 1976-80 plan options, the public sector and the implementation of Article 107 *quater* (regionalisation) of the Constitution. It has worked actively in the Conseil Economique Wallon (CEW), an advisory body set up under two 1970 laws.[29] The Flemish IR has concentrated on seaports policy, energy policy and the policy of the BRT (Flemish TV network), on which it has created joint working parties with the SP.[30]

The 1978 reform simply legalised these arrangements, harmonised the structures of the IRs to include both *centrales* and *régionales,* and established a third Brussels *inter-régionale*.[31]

The Christian trade unions. The national organisation, as laid down in 1947, of the CSC is not dissimilar to that of the FGTB. Its congress is its supreme body, which meets at least every two years. Otherwise the most powerful body is the committee which, meeting every two months, defines policy between congresses. The committee is the true decision-making body of the CSC. It is made up of the *bureau journalier*, one representative of each *régionale* and *centrale* and a representative of the Catholic church. The *bureau* (twenty-four members: twelve representatives of *centrales*, seven provincial representatives and five members of the *bureau journalier*) and the *bureau journalier* (president, general secretary and members appointed by the committee) run the day-to-day administration of the CSC.[32]

The CSC, despite its 'Christian' appellation, is relatively open. In it, the *centrales* have less power than in the FGTB. The president, elected by the committee, has a considerable position. Walloon members are, at all levels, officially in the minority according to the statutes.

Later, and less directly, the CSC faced the same federalising pressures as the FGTB.[33] Also, as in the FGTB, pressure came from Wallonia. The response was slower and more pragmatic. The first signs came at the 1966 congress, and in 1967 a committee was set up to look at the problem. One response was to 'regionalise' the existing Commission pour les Problémes Régionaux et Sectoriels into two regional committees. On the Walloon side, pressures were accelerating, and manifested themselves above all in the Liège area. They showed strongly at the 1971 'congress on the democratisation of the firm'. A *'groupe des 40'*, including all CSC Walloon leaders, was set up in 1975. Motions were passed in various *régionales* in favour of a more advanced policy, co-operation with the FGTB workers, and a separate Walloon economic strategy against the economic crisis. In 1978 the *'groupe des 40'* reported in the form of a 'Walloon action programme'.[34]

In the face of the these developments, the CSC *bureau* decided on 10 October 1978 to set up three regional committees each with 50-100 members, drawn equally from the *centrales* and *régionales* and the CSC *bureau*. There was a clear determination of 'national matters', for which the regional committees were not to be competent. It was now, however, fully accepted that there should be regionally differentiated approaches. The Flemish committee was much less active than the Walloon committee; meeting first in March 1979, it then only discussed formal organisational matters. The Walloon committee continued its work on the 'Walloon action programme'.[35]

Liberal Trade Unions. The Liberal *confédération* includes a public-sector and private-sector section. Otherwise the structure is very unitary. The sections and sub-sections are directly linked to the *centrale générale* for the region irrespective of profession or trade. The Liberal trade union's main distinguishing feature is its belief in solidarity between employers and workers in respect of liberal principles as the basis of 'justice and social peace' (Article 3 of the 1962 statutes). If favours German-type participation in management, and conciliation at the national level in appropriate bodies.[36]

Relative membership

Before 1939 the FGTB was the largest union, but it was overtaken by the CSC in 1959, though the gap narrowed again in the 1970s and then widened.[37]

	FGTB	CSC
1910	63,370	49,478
1945	447,992	342,099
1959	731,281	737,286
1962	685,862	772,208
1965	750,318	844,410
1979	1,112,757	1,273,000
1985	1,097,594	1,367,589

The Liberal trade unions had 30,000 members in 1930, 100,000 in 1940, 122,000 in 1972 and 210,396 in 1985.[38] In trade union elections, the CGSLB has averaged about 6%. Its share has climbed steadily from a mere 3.75% in 1958 to 8.41% in 1983. Its greatest strength has been in Brussels (12.08% in 1983). Its strongest categories have been among the non-ferrous metals sector, among bus drivers and white collar workers, reaching over 10% in the categories. The independent unions had 114,000 members in 1972.[39]

The largest FGTB *centrales* are the public service one (CGSP) with 253,125 members, the *centrale générale* with 246,589, the metallurgists with 204,762 and white-collar *centrale* with 286,747 members. In the CSC, the largest *centrales* are metallurgists, with 232,557; carpenters, joiners and builders with 190.526, rural employees with 187,271, food and drink and services with 132,413. The textile *centrale*, with 120,486, has lost ground. Membership is more spread than in the FGTB. In the CSC, the big three *centrales* only represent 40% as against 70% in the FGTB. The public sector is much weaker in the CSC, with only 230,000 members, including teachers.[40]

The regional distribution is also different. For the FGTB, 42.66% of its members (in 1985) were in Wallonia, 42.97% in Flanders and 14.47% in Brussels, compared to 19.88% of CSC members in Wallonia, 68.32% in Flanders and 11.8% in Brussels. The CSC has slightly increased its membership, more coming from Brussels and Wallonia over the last decade, but not significantly to alter the long-standing pattern.[41]

The FGTB is a mainly Socialist, Walloon and French-speaking union, oriented mainly to the public sector and heavy industry. The CSC is more private-sector-oriented, less ideological and predominantly Flemish, with close links to the CVP. Membership, political orientation and, since the late 1970s, union structures, are fully regionalised.

Policy and doctrine

The FGTB has clear origins in the Socialist movement, and its first doctrinal statement was that of the POB. It cherishes the ideal of a Socialist transformation of society, and in practice too it has emphasised its residual attachment to notions of class struggle by its reluctance to be 'co-opted into the system'. It seeks to maintain a different economic logic from the capitalist system, in that its social demands are not subordinated to the economic performance of the enterprise. The practical policies of the union have been to favour expansion by neo-Keynesian methods and above all in more recent years by structural reforms which would make greater use of the public sector. These would represent 'breaks in the capitalist wall'. This policy, though first developed in 1954-5, has remained unchanged, subject only to increasing radicalisation and autonomist pressures in Wallonia.[42]

The CSC has a much less clear doctrine. It favours dialogue rather than the notion of class struggle. Its main aim is the wellbeing of the workers, but achieved in a much more *ad hoc* manner. It has favoured participation, and above all it holds the view, different in essence from the FGTB, that union power involves responsibility. Its Walloon wing is, as we shall see, much more radical and has found common ground with the FGTB in Wallonia.[43] The Liberals, as we have seen, seek – even more than the CSC

– non-conflictual class-cooperative solutions to disputes and naturally oppose collectivist or interventionist strategies.

Links with political parties

According to their statutes, all three unions are independent.[44] As we have seen, the FGTB abandoned direct affilication to the Parti Ouvrier Belge in the reforms of 1945. The CSC opened its doors to non-Catholics. Yet the two main unions – FGTB and CSC – retain important links with the PS/SP and CVP/PSC respectively. In that sense, the Mouvement Ouvrier Chrétien (MOC) in Wallonia and the Algemeen Christelijke Werknemersverbond (ACW) in Flanders serve as a sort of arms-length intermediary. The MOC is an umbrella that coordinates the CSC, Mutualités Chrétiennes (ANMC), the Christian co-operatives (FNCC), La Vie Féminine and the Jeunesse Ouvrière Chrétienne (JOC). The MC decided in 1972 to adopt a more pluralist position and give support to the short-lived party Solidarité et Participation (SeP) in the 1980s, but it still retains close links with the Démocratie Chrétienne element in the PSC. In Flanders the ACW plays the same role, but plugs directly into the CVP, which reserves seats on CVP lists out of its governing bodies for the ACW. The Socialists have also created a link organisation between the parties, the FGTB, the *mutualités* and co-operatives (FEBECOOP). The Flemish inter-regional secretary sits in the SP *bureau* and the Brussels and Walloon inter-regional secretary in the *bureau* of the PS. After some estrangement between the FGTB and the PS in the early 1980s, when the union felt that the party provided it with inadequate political backing, a new political agreement was reached in 1986. Before 1961 the Liberal CGSLB had more structured links with the old Liberal party, but since then the Liberal parties have tended to support the independent unions as well, causing tensions and a more independent stance by the CGSLB.[45]

Co-operation between the unions

The split of the unions into two large blocs with different political links and regional bases has greatly weakened the movement, especially during periods when the PS/SP are in opposition, as between 1981 and 1988 when both the CSC and the FGTB were in danger of being manipulated pawns in the political strategies of the parties. In the 1982 and 1986 labour conflicts, the CSC was seen as more moderate. The FGTB in Wallonia was at times in danger of appearing to be the instrument of the PS opposition. This could show up in two ways: it could increase militancy, or it could impose moderation in order to prevent union militancy tarnishing the image of the PS, as it sought to return to power. The more natural centre-left CVP/PSC and PS/SP coalition is in a sense not only a coalition of political parties, but a concentration of social forces including the two union federations.

At the industrial level the Front Commun (joint front) has been developed as an instrument to overcome the political division in the union movement that could reduce its industrial muscle, especially since the FGTB is weak in Flanders and the CSC even weaker in Wallonia. The Front Commun has often been temporary, relating to localised or sectoral co-operation in a particular dispute, such as in the public sector or the railways since 1961, where both unions have co-operated on opposition to SNCB restructuring plans, or in localised areas, especially in Wallonia. The technique has been less frequently used in Flanders and has proved almost impossible at the national level, although the two unions do present joint approaches to government on various issues.[46]

In Wallonia, a more general rapprochement took place between 1978 and 1982. The so-called Sabic (CSC)-Yerna (FGTB) group drew up a joint proclamation in March 1979, organised several joint campaigns and agreed on a joint programme adopted at Cornemeuse in October 1981, followed by contacts with the PS, PSC, RW, RDW, MOC and SeP, with a view to constituting a progressive majority behind the platform. These efforts petered out in 1982.[47]

EMPLOYERS' ORGANISATIONS

The development of employers' organisations cannot be dissociated from the growth of the industrial proletariat and their trade unions. Early *'intérêts des producteurs'* were largely directed against producers' clients,[48] and only in the 1880s was the need felt for a defensive organisation. Initial attempts were not successful; thus only in 1895 was the Comité Central du Travail Industriel (CCTI) formed, and this was as much involved in lobbying for industrial interests with government as with confronting union power. It was transformed in 1913 into the Comité Central Industriel (CCI) and in the war it began, with severe misgivings, to participate with the unions in bi-partite or corporate (with government) bodies such as the *conférences nationales du travail*. By 1935 the CCI grouped together firms employing 100,000 workers. In 1946 the Fédération des Industries de Belgique (FIB) was formed.[49] It was made up of *fédérations*, on the basis of one per industrial sector, which greatly homogenised the structure of the various organisations. Its most important component *fédérations* were Fabrimétal, Fédération des Industries Chimiques de Belgique, Confédération Nationale de la Construction and Groupement des Hauts Fourneaux, all of which had their own organisation and considerable influence in their own right. In parallel, the tertiary sector was organising itself. In 1953 the Fédération du Commerce des Banques et des Assurances was set up and was transformed into the Fédération du Commerce, des Banques et des Assurances was set up and was transformed into the Fédération des Entreprises non-industrielles (FENIB). In 1973 FENIB and FIB merged to form the Fédération des Entreprises Belges (FEB).[50]

The main aims of such bodies are to provide and centralise services and information for its members on business and tax law, marketing information and suchlike; to deal with the trade union *confédérations*; to negotiate with government on issues of concern to industry, and to present the concerns of industry to public opinion and improve its image. At the same time, business organisation has been regionalised. The earliest regional organisation was the Vlaams Economisch Verbond (VEV), founded in 1926 as part of the drive to increase the Flemish role in national economic life. Its present Walloon counterpart, the Union Wallonne des Entreprises (1967), took over from the earlier Union Industrielle Wallonne (1954), and the Union des Entreprises de Bruxelles was set up in 1971. On a more local level, the traditional *chambres de commerce* remain active, and they too have their own national organisation.[51]

There has been a tendency for employers' organisations to develop an autonomy, becoming actors on the political scene distinct from the firms of which they are made up, but at the same time there is close identity between the leadership of the employers' organisations (FEB and individual sectoral *fédérations*) and the managers or owners of large companies.[52] Nor should it be forgotten that the small group of holdings which exercise a dominant position in the Belgian economy, together with several large multinationals, represents a political force in its own right quite independent of the official organisations. It can and does exercise a major, but often hidden, influence on decision-making.

Employers' organisations, especially since the onset of the economic crisis in the 1970s, have been developing a more offensive ideological line[53] in the face of what they see as 'the constant denigration of profit and the free market' not only by what they characterise as 'active minorities' – which include the consumer movement, ecologists and the left-wing press – but also by official media such as the RTBF (the French-speaking television network). In this new 'crisis of values and authority', the *patronat* (employers or employers' organisations) sees a threat to established procedures of *concertation* between the two sides of industry, since the authority of trade union leaderships is also under threat, and must therefore react more radically. That is not to say that the *patronat* has ever liked *concertation* as such, but it has come to accept it as a stabilising element, as the devil it knows, which has made possible a certain consensus, an accommodation with union power.[54] The new situation has created uncertainties and faces the *patronat* with new and 'unrealistic' demands – 'unrealistic' in the sense that they deliberately ignore the 'laws of the market' and the need, as seen by the employers, to control costs, which to them largely means labour costs. These phenomena are noted especially in Wallonia, where 'the spirit of class struggle and a doctrinal and unrealistic attitude' is said to characterise the Walloon trade unions. Trade union power is now being abused, according to the employers. There has also been an attempt to present the unions, with their mass membership, finances and political influence as inevitably more powerful than the employers' bodies, which are often divided among themselves.

The reaction to this perceived situation has been to seek to influence public opinion, to show the superiority of free enterprise against state interventionism and abuse of power by the unions. The FEB has sought to improve its structure and its coherence, co-operating with other groups (*fédérations*, 'middle-class' organisations and the regional *patronat* such as the VEV). A counter-offensive has thus been launched.

In relation to the trade unions, this has involved since 1976 the notion of a reinvigorated system of *concertation* based on a consensus around defined and agreed objectives, expressed solemnly in a '*pacte social*' (social contract). As one of its main promoters, Fabrimétal, argued, such an approach would have made possible class co-operation within the firm, permitting wage moderation and restructuring in response to the economic crisis, and accepting the logic of market forces in a concerted fashion, enabling the shocks to be attenuated. As to the state, it would be limited to giving general orientations in economic policy, creating favourable conditions for firms by reducing taxation and welfare insurance costs, and indeed reducing the 'work disincentive aspects' of the welfare state. It should only enter the *concertation* arena as an arbiter of last resort. It should also severely reduce public expenditure, and limit public aid to industry in difficulty (on this some sectoral *fédérations* such as Febeltex, concerned with the textile industry, dissent). These doctrines became more radical after the beginning of the 1980s. Many employers' leaders and managers have forsaken their more traditional allegiance to the CVP/PSC and turned increasingly since 1979 to the less divided and more dynamic PVV under Willy De Clercq, and the revitalised PRL under Jean Gol. Among the smaller businessmen, the self-employed, café-owners *et al.*, the more radical defence of the free enterprise system offered by the Liberals and even the UDRT, especially in Brussels, has caught on and largely explains the poor results of the PSC/CVP at the 1981 elections.

With the arrival in power of the centre-right coalition in 1981, which the *patronat* has wanted for several years, the employers' organisations became less defensive and more aggressively anti-trade union, and more openly promoted deregulation, increased competition and less *concertation*, which was indeed abandoned by the Martens-Gol government in 1982.[55] The *patronat* supported the use of special powers to break the link between wages and the price index, even though all previous governments, even those with Liberal ministers, had sought *concertation*. In more recent years, the FEB has returned to a more moderate expression of its basic values. It concentrated on competitiveness and preparation for a Single Market in 1993, but has not espoused the more radical privatisation and deregulation theses of the PVV.[56] Not only has it been faced with the return of the PS/SP after 1988, but has also faced difficult internal balancing acts between the larger firms predominant in the councils and SMEs and between export orientation and domestic oriented firms.

MIDDLE-CLASS AND PROFESSIONAL ORGANISATIONS

Middle-class organisations, in Belgian terminology, means independent traders and owners of very small businesses. These constitute a large bloc which, although it has declined, remains a considerable influence. Their organisations include the Fédération Nationale des Chambres de Commerce de Belgique, the Nationaal Christelijk Middenstandsverbond in Flanders, close to the CVP and the more neutral Fédération des Unions Syndicales de Classes Moyennes in Wallonia. There is also the Entente Wallonne des Associations de Classes Moyennes and the Inter-Syndicale des Indépendants de la Région Bruxelloise, which 'regionalise' these organisations. The main concerns of these bodies have been restrictions on opening hours for supermarkets, taxation rates, rigidities in labour law and their unfair pension situation. On all these points they have had some success, notably via a special ministry for middle-class affairs.[57]

Organisations representing the liberal professions, in particular doctors, are very powerful.[58] There have been several strikes by doctors since the early 1970s both to obtain increases in the fees they may charge and to combat any creeping socialisation of medicine. The Ordre des Médecins (medical association) has also attempted to play a part in influencing opinion in such sensitive ethical issues as abortion.

FARMERS' ORGANISATIONS

The most powerful farmers' organisation has always been the Boerenbond in Flanders and, from 1931, the Alliance Agricole in Wallonia.[59] These bodies formed one of the '*standen*' in the old Catholic party before 1945. They remain close to the CVP/PSC, and many deputies from these parties – Dupont (PSC), Héger (PSC), Martens (CVP) and De Keersmaeker (CVP) – have been close to these farmers' organisations. There is also the much less important, politically neutral Fédération Nationale des Unions Professionelles Agricoles Belges. These organisations are active at the national level, but since vital price and other decisions on agriculture are now taken by the EC, they have had to increase their sphere of activity to the European level. They have in any event been fairly successful in keeping the Belgian government to a high-price position in EC negotiations.

THE WALLOON AND FLEMISH MOVEMENTS

In addition to the socio-economic organisations and *zuilen*, which as we have seen have become completely regionalised, there is what is called the Flemish movement, composed of a series of nationalist, cultural and social organisations, and later the much less structured Walloon movement.

These movements hardly constitute a nationalist *zuil*, but do include a dense network of organisations dedicated to promoting a distinct regional identity. Those organisations, especially in Flanders, have successfully influenced both the political parties and built a more active Flemish consciousness in public opinion.[60] To a less extent, perhaps as a defensive reaction, the same has happened in Wallonia since the late 1960s. There have been both *zuil*-type organisations within each community, and there have been pluralist cultural organisations. On the one hand, there are the three political cultural foundations – the Davidsfonds (CVP), the Willemsfonds (Liberal) and the Vermeylenfonds (Socialist). There has been a decision of the Vlaams Raad in 1976 to set up five umbrella organisations to subsidise the *zuil* organisations (Catholic, progressive Catholic Socialist, Liberal and neutral).[61] It is this approach that is being reevaluated in the renewed debate on *verzuiling*. On the other hand there are patriotic associations such as the Ijzerbedevaartkomitee (Ijzer Pilgrimage Committee), which organises an annual pilgrimage to the Ijzer tower to commemorate those who died in 1914-18 on the Ijzer front; this in fact is an occasion for Flemish nationalist demonstrations and speeches, and for numerous Flemish practical groups, such as the Belgie in de Wereld organisation for Flemish people abroad (1963), or the Vlaamse Touristenbond (1922) that caters for Flemish travel and tourism. More politicised are the Vlaamsvolksbeweging, the extreme Taal Aktie Komite (TAK), and the semi-Fascist Vlaamse Militanten Orde VMO) which are rejected by the mainstream Flemish movement. Mainstream associations are coordinated by the Overlegcentrum der Vlaamse Vereningen umbrella organisation.

The Walloon movement is much newer and much less dense. Organisations such as Wallonie Libre, Rénovation Wallonne and the Mouvement Populaire Wallon (MPW) grew out of the 1960-1 strikes. The organisations of the Walloon movement are more political than purely cultural or practical and, unlike most organisations of the Flemish, are left-leaning.

THE ROLE OF PRESSURE GROUPS

The *zuil* organisations draw in and hold together all members of the *zuil* and emanate a sense of unity, strength and sufficiency. The various *zuil* organisations can exercise pressure within the *zuil*, especially on the *zuil* party to promote certain objectives in the political arena. From time to time, as for example in the *fronts communs*, there can be co-operation between components of different *zuilen* to put pressure on government. The government and pressure groups co-operate and exchange information extensively and government often makes strenuous efforts to co-opt major organisations into disarming them by involving them in compromises.

Apart from a dense network of consultation between government departments and relevant organisations, there is a more formal involvement of organisations in both national and regional advisory and administrative bodies.[62] Since 1968 collective bargaining has taken place within the tripartite system of '*concertation*' at national, industry and firm level. The most important advisory bodies are the Conseil Central de l'Economie (government, unions, employers) with the tripartite councils for each sector: the Comité National de l'Exportation Economique (1960), the Conseil Supérieur des Classes Moyennes (1949) and the Conseil National de la Consommation (1964) for consumer issues. Occasional tripartite *conférences nationales de travail* are held on issues such as the cost of living index and general wages targets. Consultative activity has also been regionalised. There are now *conseils economiques régionaux* for all three regions. These bodies must be consulted on all draft decrees that are put forward. These councils have ten members from the unions, ten from employers, farmers and middle-class organisations and seven from the appropriate council (parliamentary assembly).[63]

In addition, socio-economic organisations sit in a network of administrative and supervisory bodies that exercise decision-making powers in various economic sectors. This is particularly the case in sectors such as energy, steel, banking and credit, social welfare administration, and price control. For example, interest groups have seats on bodies such as the Comité de Contrôle de l'Electricité et du Gaz (pricing policy), the Comité de Concertation et Contrôle de Politique Sidéurgique, and the boards of *parastataux* ('quangos' in British parlance) that operate many social services and economic activities.

THE PRESS AND MEDIA

Despite the growth of television, the press remains an important actor on the political scene. It still has a wide readership;[64] 4,595,900 people take one or more daily papers (56.4% of all Belgians over 16–60% in Flanders and 52% in Wallonia). The press has an important agenda-setting function and is seen as a major influence on the formation of opinion, though now secondary to television. The sale of newspapers was static in 1990 (–0.5% in Flanders and +0.5% in Wallonia). The industry employs 5,855 people (1990), an increase of 1.72% on 1989. The number of journalists rose even more sharply (+ 6.7%).

This relatively healthy overall situation hides several less encouraging elements. In more recent years, it has become increasingly difficult to maintain adequate political pluralism. Ownership concentration of titles among a limited number of press groups has increased as a number of specifically socialist newspapers, such as *Le Peuple* (1973 circulation 60,000), the Flemish Socialist papers *De Volksgazet* (78,000) and *Vooruit* (32,000) have either been forced to close or have been transformed since the late 1970s. For a time the new SP/left paper *De Morgen* was able to survive as a specifically Socialist-leaning paper, but more recently it has lost this specific cachet. As a result, as long ago as the 1960s, only 36.4% of PS voters and 28% of SP voters read Socialist papers and only 24.4% of PRL voters read Liberal papers. For PSC (60.8%) and CVP (52.8%) voters, the position was better. Since then, these percentages have without doubt fallen drastically. There has been a tendency for ownership to be concentrated in a small number of powerful groups: Vlaams Uitgevers Maatschappij (VUM), which publishes *De Standaard*; Rossel – which publishes *Le Soir* and *La Meuse*; and the largest, De Persgroep Hoste NV (*Het Laatste Nieuws, De Nieuwe Gazet*). For publicity purposes, there are two large groups, l'Union des Journaux Belges and the Régie Générale de Publicité. The number of papers has also contracted as the Table below indicates.[65]

Type of daily newspaper	1971	1978	1990
Political	47	39	36
Economic, financial	2	1	
Agricultural, commerce	2	2	12
Arts, literary, scientific	–	–	
Total	75	64	48

These figures have been stable since 1987. Of the political dailies one is German, twenty are published in French and fifteen in Dutch. The press has been totally regionalised. There has been no French paper in Flanders since 1971 when the last one (in Ghent) closed down. There is little cross-community readership outside the wider Brussels area. A Walloon paper such as *Le Journal de l'Indépendance/Le Peuple*, published in Charleroi, has only 2.3% of its sales in Flanders. *La Libre Belgique* sells 14.5% of all its copies in Flanders, including Brabant (4.8%). *De Morgen* sells 16.3% of its copies in Brabant (including Brussels). Even the two major newspapers, *Le Soir* (2.9% in Flanders) and *De Standaard* (nil in Wallonia), have no cross-community sales.

The main papers in each region with readership figures are as shown in the following Table:[66]

Flanders	*Wallonia*	*Brussels/Brabant*	*German region*
De Standaard 1,102,400	Indépendance/Le Peuple 315,300	Le Soir 517,000	Grenz Echo 45,800
Het Laatste Nieuws 684,400	La Meuse 335,400	La Dernière Heure 230,600	
Het Volk 567,700		La Libre Belgique 192,300	
Gazet van Antwerpen 537,200			

Concentration both of papers and advertising agencies – cross-ownership is considerable, with capital from Société Généale, RTL and Kredietbank in VUM, Rossel or Multimedia – presents a threat to the independence of the press on sensitive issues such as pollution, the arms trade and the role of the banks in the Third World, to name only a few.[67]

Radio and television are a public service in Belgium, now financed by both a licence fee and by advertising. It has now been fully reorganised, with competence for broadcasting being fully communitarised, including the content of advertising. There are three distinct public radio and television corporations: the Radio-Télévision de la Belgique Française (RTBF), Belgische Radio-Televisie (BRT) and the Belgisches Rundfunk (BRF) for the German community. The corporations have normal public service obligations of neutrality, balance, impartiality, right of reply and educational broadcasting, and their statutes, the appointment of their boards, and political and administrative supervision are the responsibility of the community council. Only the level of the licence fee remains national. There has been and remains a constant tendency to politicise the BRT and RTBF. Members of the boards are elected by the community councils using the D'Hondt system of proportional representation. Candidates are nominated by the political groups. In some parties, e.g. the FDF, 'their' RTBF or BRT board members are *ex-officio* members of the party's national executive. Beyond that, staff appointments have been politicised and a certain *proportz* applied in appointments. The BRT is politically more centrist and the RTBF leans to the left, which led to a major quarrel between government and opposition between 1981 and 1988. The BRT has remained more structurally centralised in order to retain a strong Flemish presence in Brussels, it has taken more readily to advertising, and it has adopted a Dutch model of allowing air time to outside bodies on a pluralist basis. The strong and early presence of cable television in Belgium undermined the RTBF and BRT monopolies, as alternative external sources of programmes both in Dutch (from the Netherlands) and in French (from France and RTL), and of course in German and English (BBC 1 and 2) as well, are available. Indeed, the RTBF share of the Francophone audience is only about 48% and the BRT share not much higher at 59%.[68]

NOTES

1. For an analysis of the origins and use of the term in Belgium, see J. Billiet, 'Verzuiling en Politiek: Theoretische beschouwing over België via 1945', *Belgisch Tijdschrift voor Nieuwste Geschiedenis*, 13-1 (1982), 83-113. The term originated in the Netherlands with Lijphart.

2. See, for example, Val Lorwin, 'Conflicts et Compromis dans la Politique Belge', in *Courier Hébdomadaire (CH) du CRISP*, 323 (1966), 3.

3. For example, L. Huyse, *Passiviteit, Pacificatie en Verzuiling in de Belgische Politiek*, Standaard Uitgeverij, Antwerp, 1970.

4. See characteristic views of the Belgian *patronat* in the late 1970s and early 1980s in J. Moden and J. Sloover, *Le patronat belge*, CRISP, Brussels 1991, especially 71-149.

5. See 'Handvest van de Moderne Liberalisme', adapted in Kortrijk in 1979, which according to Mr Grootjans, was 'influenced by the thesis of Milton Friedman, who has provided the intellectual basis for modern Liberalism' – quoted in Moden and Sloover, *op. cit.*, 58. For a more recent PVV view, see evidence to the Vlaams Raad committee on *verzuiling*, reported in *De Financieel Ekonomische Tijd*, 22 June 1990.

6. For example, Louis Bril, a PVV deputy, former minister and founder of the small-business organisation Liberaal Verbond der Zelfstandigen (LVZ), opposed the official view; see *De Standaard*, 19 September 1990.

7. Vlaams Raad, *Handelingen* 29 (26 March 1990), 1-159.

8. X. Mabille, E. Lentzen, P. Blaise, 'Les Elections du 24 novembre 1991', *CH* 1335/6 (1991), 37.

9. For an analysis of these developments, see S. Hellemans, 'Stijd om de Moderniteit', *Kadoc Studies*, Leuven, 1990.

10. M. Van Hagendoorn and L. Vandenhove, 'Le Monde Catholique Flamand', *CH* 1070, 1080/1, 1084/5 (1985).

11. See Serge Govaert, 'Le débat sur la Verzuiling en Flandre', *CH*. 1329 (1991), 21.

12. G. Spitaels, *Le Mouvement syndical en Belgique*, Editions de l' Université de Bruxelles, 1974, 74.

13. Ibid., 9-13, for the early history of Belgian trade unionism.

14. Ibid., 13.

15. Ibid., 15.

16. Ibid.,15-16.

17. Ibid., 19.

18. Ibid., 20-1.

19. Ibid., 21.

20. On the unions in the war see *ibid.*, 21-3.

21. Ibid., 24.

22. Ibid., 29-31.

23. CH866, 'Evolution aux Structures Internes de la FGTB et de la CSC, 1980, 3.

24. Ibid., 4.

25. For details, ibid., 4-8.

26. Ibid., 8.

27. Ibid., 11-12.

28. Ibid., 9-10.

29. Ibid., 12.

30. Ibid., 13-15.

31. Spitaels, op. cit., 45-7.

32. *CH* 866, 16.

33. Ibid., 17-19.
34. Ibid., 20.
35. Spitaels, op. cit., 64-7.
36. P. Jones, *International Directory of the Trade Union Movement*, Macmillan, London and Basingstoke 1979.
37. E. Arcq and P. Blaise, *Les organisations syndicales en Belgique, Dossiers du CRISP* 23 (1987), annexes 2 and 3.
38. Figures from Spitaels, op. cit., 48-52; Coldrick and Jones, op. cit.
39. Spitaels, op. cit., 65.
40. *Dossier*, annexes 2+3 for regional membership distribution for CSC and FGTB.
41. Ibid.
42. On the FGTB doctrine, see ibid., 36-40.
43. On the CSC doctrine, see ibid., 53-8.
44. *Dossier*, 14.
45. On political links of the FGTB, CSC and CGSLB and particularly links between the PS and the FGTB, see *Dossier* no. 23, 14.
46. See *Dossier*, 23, and E. Arcq, P. Blaise and X. Mabille, 'Coalition Gouvernementale et Fronts Communs', *CH* 1123 (1986).
47. *Dossier*, 23.
48. J. Moden and J. Sloover, *Le Patronat Belge* (CRISP – 1981), 10.
49. Ibid., 11.
50. Ibid.
51. Ibid., 11-12.
52. Ibid., 13-14.
53. The discussion of the ideology of the *patronat* is taken from ibid., esp. 21-41 (analysis of the offensive against business); 42-61 (on industrial relations) and 71-149 (for the riposte).
54. However, in an interview with *Libre Belgique* (27 April 1979), Mr J. de Staercke of the FEB considered 'concertation to be now impossible, at least in the short term'. This was already a sign of later attitudes.
55. E. Arcq, 'Les Organisations Patronales en Belgique', *Dossier* no. 33 (1990), 10.
56. *Dossier* no. 33, 40.
57. *Dossier* no. 11, 'La Décision Politique en Belgique', 17.
58. Ibid., 17.
59. Ibid., 17, and E. Arcq, op. cit., 16-17.
60. For details, see ibid., 17-19.
61. S. Govaert, op. cit., 24.
62. For details, see ibid., 12-13.
63. *Mémento Politique*, Antwerp, Kluwer 1989, 150-4.
64. Data on newspaper sales and readership taken from *La Presse* (trimestriel de l'Association Belge des Editeurs de Journaux), no. 145 (Sept. 1991).
65. La Presse, op. cit., 17.
66. Ibid.
67. H. Verstraeten, *Pers en Macht*, Kritak, Leuven 1980. Table 1 (p. 14).
68. See K. McRae, *Conflict and Compromise in a Multilingual Society: Belgium*, Wilfried Laurier University Press, Waterloo, Ont., 1985, 237-348.

8

FOREIGN AND SECURITY POLICY

Foreign and security policy has rarely been a matter of serious domestic political conflict in Belgium, except at one or two key 'turning points', when efforts were made to reorient the country's foreign policy. These key points were the Flemish national and Socialist opposition to the French Alliance in the early 1920s and the choice of the Western Alliance in the early 1940s that was bitterly opposed on the left and not merely by the hard core of the PCB. Otherwise the brutal reality has been that options are few, and in any case largely dictated by outside events and by the great powers, as with Belgium's initial and long-lasting neutrality. This has been accepted pragmatically by successive generations of Belgian leaders.

A decisive turning point came in 1945. The bitter failure of neutrality was so obvious that, unlike in 1918, the lesson was readily accepted by an overwhelming majority both of the political class and of public opinion. As the division of Europe and the formation of two blocs became inevitable in 1945-8, Belgium made a clear choice for the Western camp, joining the Western European Union and NATO as a founder member. Then in the 1950s, as the second division of Europe took place – this time a voluntary one between the countries of the nascent European Community and the rest, which were for the most part loosely organised in EFTA – Belgium again, somewhat understandably, chose to belong to the most binding inner core of the EC.

As a loyal but never passive member of these two central organisations, the EC and NATO, Belgium has become a 'professional small state', and discovered with great virtuosity that a pragmatic mediating small state can exercise an influence out of all proportion to its size and power. It has sought in a sense to extend the 'Belgian method of compromise' to the international organisations to which it belongs, and has done so with both men and methods. Men such as P.-H. Spaak, Leo Tindemans and Pierre Harmel were able to leave a lasting mark. Belgium played a key behind-the-scenes role in numerous crises in both NATO and the EC: the empty chair crisis in the Community in 1965; the issue of British membership of the EC; the Maastricht negotiations; the elaboration of the détente doctrine in NATO in 1967, leading to the CSCE agreement in Helsinki in 1973; and the NATO twin-track decision crisis between 1979 and 1984. In every

244

case, Belgian diplomacy played a moderating role seeking to avoid irreconcilable conflict and encourage compromise solutions.

The foreign policy-making process

Several articles of the Constitution refer to foreign and defence policy. Article 68 lays down that the King commands the armed forces. In fact he did so personally in both world wars, but that is now inconceivable. However, Articles 118 and 119 provide that the organisation of the armed forces must be fixed by law and their size voted annually. The King (the government) declares war and makes peace (Article 68), but no cession, addition or exchange of territory may be made other than by law. The King concludes all treaties, but trade treaties and those imposing a charge on the state, imposing obligations on Belgian citizens, or dealing with matters already regulated by law, must be approved by Parliament. Other treaties must be communicated to Parliament. These provisions taken together place the conduct of foreign and defence policy in the hands of the Crown, but with certain limitations imposed by the need for parliamentary approval and the enactment of implementing provisions.[1]

Modern diplomacy has created far simpler forms of agreements than in the past, often called 'executive agreements'. These are accepted in Belgium and are concluded by officials or ministers, without the formality of a treaty. Nevertheless, if they involve measures which would, under Article 68, require parliamentary approval, such agreements do not by their form alone escape this requirement, as the *Cour de Cassation* and the *conseil d'état* have made clear in several decisions.[2]

Article 59 *bis* of the Constitution created a novel situation. Under it, the councils of the communities are competent to conduct international co-operation in relation to cultural matters and 'personalisable' matters (health, social etc.). This means that treaties in these fields must, according to Article 16 (1) of the Special Law of 8 August 1980, be approval not by the national Parliament but by the community council.[3] Such treaties are presented by the community executive. The doctrine seems to suppose that because the King concludes treaties, even those under Article 59 *bis* must therefore be negotiated by the central government. This seems a limitation on the rights of the executives, which is not self-evident from Article 59 *bis* of the Constitution, although the executives would, at the least, have the right to be consulted on the negotiations. However, in an important keynote speech on Walloon external relations delivered on 2 April 1982 in Liège, Mr Moureaux (PS), president of the Francophone community executive, set out a much more radical view to the effect that the conduct of external relations in the 'devolved areas' fell entirely to the community executives and not to the national government, and that included the conclusion of agreements. He went on to outline the measures which the executive had taken or intended to take in order to give effect to this viewpoint, which included the creation of a *commissariat* for external relations, a proposal for community observers in a wide range of international organisations, and the conclusion of agreements in the newly devolved field of '*personalisable*' matters. We see here an almost unique arrangement, however cautiously undertaken: a lower level of government in a semi-federal system involved in international relations. The Francophone community has already made some use of these provisions, even before the 1980 reform, to conclude agreements with foreign states or sub-states such as Québec on cultural and educational matters.

The ambiguity between Article 68 (of course, a much older 'unitarist' constitutional provision) and the newer Article 59 *bis* has led to a flourishing legal debate.[4] Some such as Mr Moureaux obviously hold the view that Article 68 has been implicitly amended by Article 59 *bis*. Others have disagreed. Behind this is a concern for the unity and coherence of Belgian foreign policy, and over possible difficulties with foreign powers – since few are willing to conclude treaties with entities that are not sovereign states, although Francophone states such as Benin have done so. The only example of a state in which the subordinate federal entities had such a wide and theoretically autonomous external competence, without any requirement or possibility of intervention by the central state as claimed by the maximalists, was the Soviet Union. This was not an encouraging example in the 1980s and now no longer exists. At the same time, there was an anomaly in that the regions had been given no external competences by the 1980 Special Law. An additional problem was the issue of representation in bodies such as the European Community when matters for which the central state was no longer competent were under discussion. There was also the question of compliance with treaties – both these concluded by communities, but which they failed to respect, and those such as the EC treaties and legislation that imposed obligations on the Belgian state, as the ECJ has clearly ruled,[5] in areas where the central state has no internal power to intervene, given the strict and hermetic distribution of competences between state, regions and communities. As we saw in Chapters 4 and 5, these issues were considered as part of the Martens VIII Reforms of the State in 1988-9 and some partial solutions were introduced, and others were prefigured in the government agreement of 1988 as part of the Third Phase, but were not implemented till 1993.

The basic premise of the 1988 coalition agreement was maximalist. The communities and the regions were to be given a clear competence to negotiate and conclude agreements, resolving in their favour the earlier ambiguity about their competence to do so. Their only obligation towards the federal government would be prior information about an intended agreement and nothing more. They are now fully sovereign within their own fields of competence, internally and externally. The regions were intended to receive an equal status with the communities.[6] These problems were resolved in 1993 by a revision of Article 68, making clear the right of the communities and regions to negotiate and conclude treaties in their own fields of competence. This new position was then enshrined in a revision of Article 16 of the Special Law of 1980.

It was also laid down that the regions and communities should be associated and consulted in the fixing of Belgian positions in international bodies, especially the EC where community and regional competences are affected. In devolved areas, even more radically, Belgian legislation and the Maastricht treaty now allow the communities and regions to speak and vote for Belgium in the EC Council of Ministers, which requires prior coordination to determine the common view.

During the debate in the joint House/Senate committee in 1991, there were some second thoughts[7] about so radical and unlimited a grant of external competences to the communities and regions, since this could create conflicts between competing foreign policies, threatening credibility and leading to non-implementation by the communities and regions of international obligations, especially EC directives.

In the provision finally accepted, the federal government not only has the right to be informed in cases of agreements with countries with which Belgium has no diplomatic relations and in some other defined cases, but it can impose a suspensive *concertation* with the community or region. The federal government was also given reserve powers to ensure implementation of EC legislation and compliance by the communities and regions with their own treaties.[8]

Parliament (or the councils) usually gives approval in the form of law (or decree) with a single article stating approval of the treaty, which *does not* form part of the law and therefore may not be amended. Article 68 implies that for all treaties other than territorial ones Parliament may give its agreement by a method simpler than that of a law. However, a provision in a finance act to spend money on the execution of an international delegation does not suffice.[9]

Once approved, treaties are normally ratified, but the Constitution does not require this. A more difficult question is that of promulgation. To be binding, laws must be promulgated (Article 129 of the Constitution) and, the *Cour de Cassation* has ruled, so also must individual treaties. The law of 31 May 1961 (Article 8) covering treaties is not clear on the manner of promulgation.[10]

Problems have arisen in relation to treaties and internal laws and norms. EC regulations (or directives under the ECSC treaty) are directly applicable and binding, and some EC treaty provisions have also been held to be directly applicable. In 1970 the Constitution partly caught up with the development of European and international law, with the addition of Article 25 *bis* which regularises the transfer of sovereignty to international bodies (such as the EC). The ECSC treaty had involved a very broad interpretation of the Constitution; but it was accepted by the government that the European Defence Community (EDC) would have required an amendment, as was probably the case for the EC treaty.[11] Article 25 *bis* has some limitations; it does not permit the permanent transfer of powers without the possibility of reversal, nor does it permit the transfer of unlimited powers. The 1968-71 *constituant* Parliament was unable to deal with the issue of the relationship between treaties and derived international-al norms (such as the EC legislation) and domestic law, which has caused some problems in the doctrine – though few in practice. The courts have accepted the primacy of EC law, although this interpretation went the other way from a 1926 decision of the *Cour de Cassation*, which was generally accepted till only a few years ago. The 1968 *Déclaration de Révision* included Article 68, but no final action was taken. The Senate proposed to modernise the article and solve the problem of 'primacy', and impose a stricter condition for the approval of treaties under Article 25 *bis*. The 1978 and 1981 *Révisions* also include Article 68 for this issue. This has now been remedied.

The practical conduct of foreign policy

From the earliest days of the Belgian state, foreign policy-making has been a central concern of governments. The foreign ministry, once called the department of foreign affairs, was among the original five departments of state together with the war department and in 1908 a department for the colonies.[12] It was always an important department sometimes taken by the prime minister or in earlier times by the *formateur* – 1831, 1832, 1836-40, 1847-52, 1852-5, 1870-1, 1878-84, 1917-18, 1935-6, 1938-9 (Spaak), 1939 (Pierlot), 1946 (Spaak) and 1947-9 (Spaak). In more recent times, the post has usually not gone to a vice-prime minister, but it is a senior cabinet position, and often (though not always) goes to a representative of a different party from the prime minister. Spaak (PS), Simonet (PS) and Claes (SP) have been foreign ministers in cabinets headed by PSC or CVP premiers whereas Harmel (PSC) and Tindemans (CVP) were foreign ministers in cabinets headed by party colleagues.[13]

Although the ministry has remained a single administrative unit, its name has successively altered. In 1958 it added foreign trade and in 1961 technical assistance (to developing countries), renamed 'development' in 1968.[14] At times the various components – foreign affairs and foreign trade and development – had separate full ministers, as in 1968-71 and 1977-8, whereas on other occasions one component would be covered only by a state secretary. In the 1960s there were experiments (not very successful) with deputy foreign ministers or state secretaries for European affairs (e.g. H. Fayat, 1965-6) and a full minister for European affairs in the 1966-8 government (R. Van Eslande [CVP]). Until 1981, there was again no secretary of state. Then, from 1981 until 1990, Mr De Keersmaeker (CVP) served as secretary of state for European affairs and agriculture, and there was no full minister of agriculture. In the Martens VIII cabinet in 1992, there was a secretary of state for Europe in 1992 as well, placed under the minister of trade, which gave the PS an involvement in European policy.

Prime ministers have come increasingly to play a major rôle in foreign affairs, not least in EC matters due to the regular European Council meetings. This is particularly true of figures like Leo Tindemans and Wilfried Martens, two of Belgium's few internationally known politicians. The King, too, has a role to play in foreign policy; he is kept well informed of events by the ministry and may from time to time directly advance Belgian interests.[15] Major decisions in foreign policy will require discussion in cabinet, and may create serious divisions in the government coalition, such as SP opposition to the NATO council's decision in 1979 on theatre nuclear forces (TNF). Other more routine or urgent matters will be examined in the cabinet's external policy committee. Where coordination is important, as between various departmental viewpoints (this is especially marked in connection with EC affairs, which touch areas well beyond those normally affected by foreign affairs, such as agriculture and social policy), the Comité Ministériel de Coordination Economique et Sociale (CMCES) is the responsible central body, it in turn being backed by the civil servants' committee, the Commission Economique Internationale. This was not without difficulties because the CMCES was overloaded with domestic policy issues and the external policy committee was not ideal for many of the economically oriented foreign policy issues which had been in the forefront of attention in the 1950s and 1960s. The issue was solved at least for European issues by the creation – under Vicomte Davignon, the long-term *chef de cabinet* of successive ministers – of *ad hoc* groups of officials. Ministers concerned with EC affairs also met. Under the first government of Leo Tindemans, the CMCES made a comeback and became a powerful coordinating and centralising body with more sub-committees, at least nine of the CEI being set up to support the CMCES. The foreign affairs committee was virtually abolished, but it has now been revived.[16]

The ministry itself, like all other ministries, is headed by a director general, but the political department under figures such as Davignon and later Alfred Cahen has always played an important role. It employs 3,576 staff of whom 1,838 are abroad and in international bodies. In 1970, the figure was 1,298 and 1,675 in 1982. It remains a small ministry.[17]

Under the general secretary is a legal service, a department for European policy coordination, and a 'think tank'. There are directorates-general for administration; for external economic relations (area directorates), supported by a Comité Consultatif du Commerce Extérieur for chancery matters; for political affairs with seventeen area and regional services; and for information and cultural matters. Finally, there is an administration for development co-operation, assisted by a consultative Conseil de Coopération au Développement.[18]

The communities have also established administrations responsible for external relations. There is a member in each executive responsible for external relations, sometimes but not always a president. That is also true for the regions – which, however, have only just acquired external competences but were always required to be associated with decisions, as we have seen. The Francophone community established in 1982 its Commissariat Général aux Relations Internationales.[19] This body, with a staff of ninety,[20] administers fifty agreements, fifteen of which have been concluded by the community itself, services membership in Francophone community bodies and maintains delegations in Québec, Paris, Geneva and Kinshasa. The Walloon region has co-operated with the CGRI since 1986. The Flemish community, which of course combines community and regional competences, has also created a *commissariat general*[21] under the ministry of the Flemish community where the matter is under the direct responsibility of the secretary-general and the responsible member of the executive, whose external relations it coordinates and executes. It has a staff of thirty-six.[22] In the German community, the president of the executive retains overall coordination of external relations, but each minister can act in his own sphere. Agreements have been concluded with the other communities, where agencies provide technical assistance. Annual bilateral meetings are held with German-speaking states – the Federal Republic of Germany (before 1990 also with the GDR), Austria, Luxembourg.[23]

The national foreign ministry has established a liaison desk with the communities and regions, and the preparation of Belgian positions in the EC councils involves contacts with the regions and communities whose ministers can be associated with CEI meetings if discussion at a political level is needed. The coordination committee between the federal and community/regional executives established in 1984 was supposed to meet monthly but has only functioned sporadically,[24] although it has begun to work better.

The role of Parliament and the councils

We consider here both the role of the national Parliament and the councils of the communities and regions in relations to foreign policy issues. The House and Senate established one or more committees to deal with foreign affairs from an early stage. Initially there was in both chambers one committee per government department, but in the 1960s the number of committees dealing with an aspect of foreign policy, trade, development, co-operation, defence and security, and EC affairs multiplied dramatically. Both the House and the Senate (which in general is less interested in foreign affairs than the House) established separate committees for foreign affairs, foreign trade, development and defence, and the House also had a European affairs committee (1962-79).[25] In addition, the finance committee deals with opinions from other committees, with the foreign affairs budget, and with the committee for revision of the Constitution, and from time to time also with foreign affairs competence issues. Important foreign affairs matters such as the statute of the Council of Europe, Marshall Aid, the bill on direct elections and the ECSC and EEC treaty ratifications went to special committees, but there has since been a certain consolidation. In the House there are foreign affairs and defence committees, each with twenty-three members, and each chaired by an opposition figure.[26] In addition, as we shall see, there is the European advisory committee which operates jointly with MEPs. Of course, other committees such as those dealing with agriculture and the environment often deal with external relations, especially EC matters.

The work of those committees is mostly devoted to information meetings on foreign affairs and EC matters, interpellations, the departmental budget and treaties. Otherwise, the foreign and defence committees deal with few bills. From time to time, they give opinions to other committees such as those on direct elections.

These committees work in the same way as other committees of their respective chambers, and therefore all deputies and senators can attend – a facility of which greater use is made in foreign affairs than in other areas.[27] The FACs tend to hold more hearings than other committees and to hear more outside and even non-Belgian personalities such as EC commissioners (Chesson in 1975, Delors on Maastricht). They also make use of some of the less frequent and even unusual procedures such as joint meetings (i.e. defence and foreign affairs) or joint House-Senate committee meetings; they did so, for example, to hear the then UN secretary-general, Waldheim, in 1975. A joint defence-foreign affairs session was held on 24 September 1991 on the decision to send troops to Zaïre, and in January 1991 the House foreign affairs committee held a televised debate on the Gulf war situation and again on 21 August 1991 on the Soviet coup.[28]

In the 1990/1 session the House foreign affairs committee held thirty-six public sittings (totalling 62 hours); nineteen closed sittings (14 ½ hours) and three joint meetings (one with defence), considered seventy-seven interpellations and examined thirty-five budgets and bills, but only considered one important treaty. The House defence committee held nineteen public sittings (26 hours), eleven closed sittings, considered eleven interpellations, and completed 215 bills and budgets.[29] Membership of the committees tends to be long-standing and expertise builds up. The committees have numbered among their members many past and future ministers and party leaders, currently Jean Gol (PRL). Their staffs are small: ten in all for each chamber.[30]

Treaties are mostly (*c.* 90%) examined in the foreign affairs committees of the two chambers.[31] Some go to the finance committee (taxation). More specialised transport and social agreements go to the responsible specialist committees. Treaties can be and often are dealt with without the need for a report where they raise no difficulties; this happened with 296 out of 491 treaties tabled between 1961 and 1981.[32]

There are few plenary debates on foreign affairs in either chamber and they are rarely controversial. However, exceptions have been the Scheldt treaties, the purchase of the F-16 in 1975-6 the NATO twin-track decision, and intervention in Zaïre. Ministerial statements and plenary interpellations (even on issues such as Zaïre or the Gulf war) have been rare, yet in the 1990/1 session there were several: Zaïre (11 October and 8 November 1990), agricultural imports from Eastern Europe (25 October 1990), Brussels as the seat of the European institutions (8 November 1990).[33]

European Community matters are a special case. As early as the debate on ratification of the Rome treaties in 1957, the idea was raised of a special parliamentary body to exercise an augmented form of control, especially since under Article 2 of the ratified bill the government must present an annual report on EC matters. Thus in 1962, a European affairs committee was set up in the House (Article 83 of the rules) to examine 'the consequences and application of the treaties'. It was not supposed, like the Danish market relations committee, to exercise a prior control over ministers. Indeed the rules stated: 'It shall not exercise a power of control, but promote contact and information.' Before 1970 it was relatively effective, though never dynamic. Throughout its existence it has held ninety-five meetings but only twenty-three since 1970, mostly on direct elections. Of course, in the old non-elected Parliament it could have MEPs as members, since they were also members of the Belgian Parliament. It debated reports from the government (when these were tabled) and from delegations to the European Parliament (seven reports), the Council of Europe, and the Benelux and WEU assemblies.[34]

MEPs may attend any committee meeting and speak but of course not vote. They are now no longer members of the Belgian Parliament (rule 25). A Comité d'Avis chargé des Questions Européennes has been established under rule 100 in the House. Chaired by the president of the House, it is composed of ten deputies and ten MEPs (out of twenty-four); in the 1990/1 session, it held fifteen meetings (38 hours). It can draft resolutions for tabling in the House and the Senate. The Comité d'Avis drew up a report in preparation for the *assises* (held in Rome in November 1990), on EMU and on the IGCs. It heard Mr Williamson (EC secretary-general) and Mr Ravasio, personal representative of President Delors in the EMU-IGC, and it sent a delegation to the *assises* and to the COSAC (national parliamentary committees) conference held in Luxembourg. A report was drawn up on procedures. Under it Belgian MEPs can ask written questions of the government, and standing committees examine matters on the agendas of EC Council meetings. The Comité d'Avis has also met to evaluate European Council meetings.[35] It is thus much more active than its predecessor. The president of the House at the time of writing, Charles Ferdinand Nothomb (PSC), has sought to promote much more active 'parliamentary diplomacy' both on EC matters and on Central Europe.

The councils of the communities and, to a much lesser extent, of the regions exercise competence in external relations. The CCF, Vlaams Raad and even the Deutscher Rat have committees with external competencies.[36]

Belgian foreign policy

From independence to the Second World War. Belgium's lack of options has in no way diminished the importance of international relations, which have been and remain vital for the survival and prosperity of a small, virtually indefensible trading nation with an open economy. Indeed, the very existence of Belgium is due to the support of certain great powers at the crucial moment after the September 1830 revolution in France had obtained an initial success. Britain and France combined to ensure the survival of the fledgling state. Other powers, such as Russia and Prussia (later the German empire), supported the Dutch cause but were unable to impose this 'legitimist' viewpoint in the face of the Franco-British front.[37] Belgium therefore lived from 1830 till 1914 under an international statute, which imposed neutrality on the state in perpetuity. This was the price – a small one – which had to be paid to ensure its survival and the withdrawal of the Dutch armies from its territory. Belgian independence and territorial integrity were guaranteed by the major powers such as Britain, France and Prussia.

The fundamental options of Belgium's foreign policy were thus defined by its international statute.[38] The country had in effect to refrain from participation in alliances or other combinations of powers which made up the fabric of nineteenth- and early twentieth-century international relations. Its concerns were therefore essentially localised or economic: to foster good relations with its immediate neighbours: France, Germany and the Netherlands (to repair the damage caused by the revolution), to maintain good relations with its main guarantor, Britain, and to develop freer trade by a number of commercial treaties. As a liberal and neutral state, it became the haven for opponents of repressive regimes such as the French Second Empire and Bismarck's Germany, which caused pressure to be brought to bear on it – which it could not always resist – to curb their activities. These, however, were mere incidents of little fundamental longer-term importance, despite the controversy they generated inside and outside Belgium. Likewise, the severing of diplomatic relations with the Vatican in 1880, controversial as it was, had few genuine international consequences, representing in reality more a symbolic gesture in the internal struggle between the temporarily ascendent anti-clerical Liberals and the Catholic church.

The only matters of substantive importance in foreign policy in the period up to 1914 were colonial policy, at first the personal venture of Leopold II and after 1908 of the state, and the difficult question of military policy. There was initially a great reluctance on the part of the Belgian state to become a colonial power. The expense and military obligations involved and above all the dangers of conflict in Africa with other major colonial powers, some of which could vitally affect Belgian security in Europe, were factors in this negative attitude. However, the King pursued colonisation in the Congo as a private policy. Gradually, first by giving him the necessary constitutional waiver to become head of a second state and then from 1900 by providing loans and guarantees, the Belgian state became progressively involved, until in 1908 a take-over became both necessary and unavoidable. Thus Belgium joined the ranks of the major colonial powers.[39]

Military policy became an issue in the later nineteenth century – in connection with the fortification of Antwerp, the level of military expenditure, and the injustice of the conscription system which allowed young men of wealth to escape their obligations by purchasing a replacement. There was always a strong body of opinion, led by Leopold II and his successor Albert I, seeking a stronger defence policy: Belgium should be able to defend its neutrality effectively. But others were sceptical, believing such a rôle to be impossible in a modern war. The debate concentrated in the 1870s on the new defence concept of a withdrawal from the old 'barrier' fortresses, dating from 1715, to a redoubt at Antwerp to serve as the base from which foreign allies could launch a counter-attack. This provoked tension between the communities and the strong opposition of the progressive local, particularist and anti-militarist Antwerp Meeting Partij. The real value of such a defence policy was in any case doubtful, but this internal opposition showed the limits to which any government could go.[40]

However, the dangers facing the new state were real enough: the threat from the Netherlands – until the Five Articles Treaty of London of 1839 whereby reasonable relations were restored; Prussian opposition to Belgian military measures; and the ambitions of Napoleon III, who sought to reverse the order established at the Congress of Vienna. After his fall in the Franco-Prussian war, the rise of Germany as the leading continental power was the chief menace to Belgium. As early as 1866, Bismarck had discussed with Napoleon III a partition of Belgium, his aim then being to buy off France without offending Britain, but after easily defeating France in 1870, Germany had no need of any such compromise in order to complete its unification. Britain firmly opposed any action by France to involve Belgium in that war. Nevertheless, Belgium mobilised 83,000 men in great haste, but the rapid defeat of France at Sedan avoided any use of Belgian territory by either side.[41]

The period 1871-1914 was one of alliance-building, from which Belgium was excluded by its statute. The *Entente Cordiale* (1904) became the Triple *Entente* with the inclusion of Russia in 1907, while the central powers of Germany, Austria Hungary, Turkey and Italy constituted the opposing bloc. The 1899 disarmament congress at The Hague failed, and the period to 1914 was marked by an arms race, and competitive colonial expansion (the division of Africa took place at the Berlin congress of 1884/5), punctuated by periodic crises which might as easily have led to a generalised European war as did the fatal shots at Sarajevo in July 1914. It became ominously clear in the period before 1914 that German military plans probably involved the use of Belgian territory in their enveloping attack against France – the famous Schlieffen plan; the question of Belgium's attitude to such a passage was raised during the visit of King Leopold II to Potsdam in January 1904 and again during a visit by King Albert in November 1913.[42]

Belgium was committed to defending its neutrality against attack from *any* quarter. That was the dilemma: all knew where the attack would come from, but no alliances could be prepared to counter the threat in order to preserve a fictive 'neutrality'. In 1887 new fortified positions were built on the Meuse at Liège and Namur. At the same time, partisans of a field army capable of a more active defence joined those who were supporters of personal military service in the interests of equity (under this, buying out would no longer be allowed). However, an early attempt at such a reform failed in the House by 69-62 in July 1887. Leopold II personally entered the battle for a stronger and fairer army, as did his successor, Albert. The law of 1902, increasing the army's strength from 130,000 to 187,000, likewise failed to come to grips with this problem, which only happened in 1909 together with other measures reinforcing the defensive triangle Antwerp-Liège-Namur. Finally, with international tension rising, Parliament approved an increase in the length of military service from fifteen months to two years.

All these efforts were inadequate. Germany issued an ultimatum to Belgium on 2 August 1914, and entered Belgian territory two days later. By 20 August, Brussels had fallen and by October, despite the efforts of her allies in the Mons area, Belgian forces only held a small strip of territory on the River Ijzer in the north-west, a salient with Ypres,

Dixmude and Nieuwpoort on the coast as its outer extremities. So it was to remain until the end of the war, with the government sitting in Sainte-Adresse near Le Havre in France.

The key diplomatic issue had been the belligerent status of Belgium. It had fought to defend its independence and neutrality, but it was not *ipso facto* a member of the *Entente*, despite having fought alongside the *Entente* powers. It declined to sign the treaty of London of September 1914, by which those powers pledged themselves not to conclude a separate peace. It did, however, obtain in 1916 the 'declaration of Sainte-Adresse' by which the *Entente* powers undertook to conclude no peace which did not restore Belgium to full independence.[43]

Some sought to push Belgium fully into the Allied camp and increase its peace demands, for instance over the matter of the River Scheldt. King Albert rejected such an approach and even refused an integrated military command. He continued to conduct his independent diplomacy, following up President Wilson's 1916 peace appeal; he later supported an active Belgian role in the first, abortive Franco-German contacts in July 1917. These failures led eventually to Paul Hymans becoming foreign minister and de Brocqueville resigning as prime minister in July 1918. Indeed, continued German demands on Belgium made compromise impossible.

At the Versailles peace conference in 1919 Belgium appeared as a power 'with limited interests'. However, it had formulated wide-ranging demands in a series of notes, the first of which was sent to the Allied powers on 18 September 1918, before the end of the war. These demands involved the ending of its compulsory neutrality, the return of areas ceded to the Netherlands in 1831 and 1839, resolution of the Scheldt question, the return by Germany of the *cantons de l'est* (Eupen-Malmédy); the acquisition of further colonial territory in Africa; and reparations for war damage. But Belgian was not an Allied power – by its own choice – and so had no seat in the inner circles of the conference such as the Council of Ten (the leaders of the five major Allied powers: the United States, Britain, France, Japan and Italy) or the 'Big Three' meetings (the United States, Britain and France). Also, Belgian demands either affected the neutral Netherlands, which President Wilson rejected, or in the case of Luxembourg, which she sought to annexe, clashed with the goals of a larger power, France. Belgium had therefore to be content with reparations spread over thirty years and with 2 billion gold francs as an immediate payment; a commission on the Scheldt, which achieved little; League of Nations mandates over Rwanda and Burundi in Africa; the acquisition of Eupen-Malmédy; and the ending of its imposed neutrality. Later, in 1921, an economic union with Luxembourg was achieved.[44]

Between the world wars,[45] Belgium followed three basic lines of foreign policy and sometimes two of them in parallel, joining the League of Nations and working actively within it for effective collective security policies and disarmament. Thus it signed the Kellogg-Briand pact of 1926, condemning recourse to war and offering disarmament negotiations. It also sought closer economic relations with the small Nordic democracies and the Netherlands, a policy which led to the Oslo convention (1930) and the aborted Ouchy convention (1931). These attempts, which could also have had political effects, were blocked by Britain for economic reasons. It is no accident that these were also the countries which sought most keenly to give the League some value in terms of collective security. Belgium also signed the Locarno pact of 1925 whereby several powers, including Germany, France and Britain, exchanged mutual guarantees obligations to assist other contracting parties against aggression.

In the period before 1930, Belgian was a hardliner over Germany and sought, without much success, to maintain a vigorous *Entente* relationship with Britain and France. Thus it signed a military pact with France in 1920, but failed to achieve a similar agreement with Britain. When Germany defaulted on reparations in 1923, Belgium joined France in occupying the Ruhr. The Dawes (1924) and Young (1929) plans limited reparations but did ensure some payment, until the powers accepted an end to them at the 1932 Lausanne conference. Belgium was tough while other powers vacillated, but without effect; it did not understand, any more than France, the need to allow the Weimar democracy in Germany to breathe and live. The Third Reich of Adolf Hitler was at least in part the consequence of this attitude.

After 1933 – when reparations had been ended, the League became ineffectual and France and Britain showed in successive crises that they lacked the will to oppose the Nazi dictator – Belgium returned to voluntary neutrality, backed by greater military effort. Like France, she sought to preserve the *'acquis'* of Locarno, but a different spirit was abroad, exemplified by the total failure of the 1932-3 disarmament conference and Mussolini's proposal for a four-power 'directorate' in Europe, which would have involved the tearing up of both the Versailles and Locarno treaties. Belgium sought to moderate what she still saw as French 'extremism' in relation to Germany, and sought international agreement to limit German rearmament. Such appeasement and weakness (but not total weakness!) were the muddled elements of its policy in the face of increasing international tension, which remained in both the military and diplomatic fields – contradictory and without any clear line.

Attempts at greater military strength alternated with periods of reduction. The room for manoeuvre was limited by the combined opposition of Socialists and the Flemish movement (which was suspicious of a foreign policy too closely linked to France) to greater military efforts. Thus, in line with the tough policy in the Ruhr question, national service was increased to fourteen months in 1923, but it was later cut to ten months again and the size of the army was reduced in 1926 in the optimism of the

spirit of Locarno. Pressure for six months' service led to a new compromise in 1928: a 43,000-man army, with 23,000 on eight months'
service and 21,000 on 12-14 months. In 1936, when Hitler remilitarised
the Rhineland, service was increased to seventeen months, but the 1920
pact with France was rescinded.

In the face of the worsening situation, the only apparent policy was that
of avoiding conflict with Germany. Some Flemish opinion also saw in
such a policy the opportunity to break with the *Entente* policy, which was
based inevitably on a close relationship with France. Therefore in 1936
the government defined a new policy. Paul-Henri Spaak spoke variously
of a policy 'exclusively and wholly Belgian' or of one 'which does not
imply a return to neutrality, but which is merely independent'. Leopold
III said that the country's military policy 'should serve only to preserve
us from war, wherever it comes from'. Despite the words, this *was*
neutrality, and Britain, France and even Germany gave guarantees to
respect it in 1937. Each crisis thereafter was met with declarations of
neutrality and mobilisation of the army – as occurred in the 1938 Sudeten-
land crisis, 'solved' by the Munich agreement, and when war did break
out in September 1939.

Post-war foreign policy.[46] In the war against Hitler, Belgium became a
fully-fledged Ally. Its government-in-exile spent the war in London, and
the country became a founder-member of the United Nations in San
Francisco in 1945. Like most other countries, it hoped that the wartime
alliance would continue into the post-war world, enabling the United
Nations to function effectively to keep the peace as the League had so
singularly failed to do. Despite not inconsiderable Communist influence
in the Resistance, which caused some local problems, Belgium was
liberated by the Western Allies, and by its own choice belonged to the
Western alliance which formed with the onset of the Cold War. Opinion
had matured in the face of the bitter realities of being a small country
confronted by major aggressive powers. It was clear that Germany no
longer represented a threat, but that with the onset of the Cold War, which
paralysed the collective security mechanisms of the UN, a new threat had
appeared in Europe: Soviet power, which now stood on the river Elbe.
Despite assurances, one by one all the states of eastern Europe had Soviet
Communist-style regimes imposed upon them. The greatest impact was
made by the last to fall: Czechoslovakia, which till 1948 had maintained
enough external independence initially to accept Marshall Aid and a
degree of internal democracy. The 'Prague coup' in which the Communist
Party seized power was a clear sign that Stalin had abandoned his cautious
efforts to avoid conflict with the Western powers while making stealthy
advances. The threat was now perceived everywhere in western Europe.
It would work either through military pressure or by an internal collapse

provoked by the severe economic problems arising from post-war recovery. Reaction was rapid and healthy: Belgium no longer sought refuge in the escapism of 'neutrality'.[47]

The reaction to the needs of post-war recovery and the later perceived threats from the Soviet Union as the Cold War deepened led to a series of initiatives in international co-operation, which profoundly modified Belgium's foreign policy. From being a traditional 'loner', reluctantly accepting aid in each crisis, she became an active and enthusiastic member of a series of interlocking European and Atlantic alliances. She was indeed one of the few to see the need for co-operation between European states and to act on that viewpoint with the formation of the Benelux union in 1944. The three small 'Benelux' countries (Belgium, the Netherlands and Luxembourg), all heavily dependent on trade, had suffered from the inter-war protectionism and 'beggar-my-neighbour' policies, and foresaw bleak prospects in a post-war Europe in ruins and with trade flows interrupted. To provide an enlarged market, they formed a customs union under a treaty signed in London on 5 September 1944. Despite some difficulties – safeguard clauses were agreed in 1953 and there was failure to move towards monetary union and supranational institutions as prefigured in 1949 – the Benelux was a success in itself and a model for later European integration.

Belgium was an active founder-member of the various European organisations formed in the late 1940s and early 1950s. Some of its statesmen, most notably P.-H. Spaak, became powerful advocates of European integration, which grew out of the congresses of the European movement (The Hague, 1948; Brussels and London, 1949). Belgium joined the Council of Europe (1950), but largely though not exclusively because of British opposition, it failed to meet the federalist aspirations of its founders and was thus a disappointment.

There has always been a certain ambiguity – perhaps a deliberate one – over the relationship between European integration and Atlantic co-operation. For some they were complementary approaches – this, at first anyway, was undoubtedly the view of the United States. But for others they were at least potentially contradictory, with European integration seeking to create Europe as a 'third force', independent but standing in an equal (or more than equal) alliance with the United States. No doubt this was one reason why Britain has always been so reserved about 'Europe', but Belgium never saw contradiction in it but rather complementarity. It joined the European Coal and Steel Community set up following the Schumann declaration in 1950 which formed the basis of the 'Europe of the Six'. When the European Defence Community (EDC) – to which we return later – failed to win approval in the French National Assembly, the Benelux states were among the most concerned at the loss of momentum, and worked tirelessly for the '*relance*' of European integration, spurred on by Jean Monnet when president of the ECSC's high authority. It was the Benelux memorandum, in fact drafted by Spaak and the Netherlands foreign minister Mr Beyen, which formed the basis of the '*relance*' at Messina in June 1955. Spaak presided over the ministerial committee which drafted the two Rome treaties, signed in 1957, setting up Euratom and the EEC, both of which obtained ratification in the Belgian Parliament without any difficulty.

At the same time, there had been important developments in Atlantic co-operation. With the hardening of the Cold War, the US secretary of state unveiled the Marshall Plan in July 1947 from which Belgium obtained US$ 113 million over the following ten years. A European organisation of sixteen nations, the OEEC, was set up to coordinate recovery and the use of Marshall Aid, and the European Payments Union was set up as well to facilitate trade where currencies were often not convertible. Belgium joined both these bodies, a timely initial reaction to the dangers of collapse of the European economies which could have posed as great a threat as direct Soviet military intervention or pressure.

On the military level Belgium, with Britain and France and its Benelux partners, joined the Western European Union (1948) and NATO (1949), which initially involved twelve countries. To meet its obligations under the new integrated NATO command structure, Belgium was required to increase its armed forces from 69,000 men in 1950 to 169,000 in 1953, and to introduce a period of twenty-four months for national service. These measures, taken by a homogeneous PSC/CVP government, met severe opposition in Parliament from the Communists, Socialists (despite Spaak) and even Liberals, and in street demonstrations, which forced the government *de facto* to reduce service to twenty-one months.

Whether popular or not, the key issue had now become, especially under American pressure, the rearming of Germany. Efforts were made as early as 1951 to include it in NATO but these failed. This was the genesis of the Pleven plan, which surfaced in 1952, for a European Defence Community (EDC), in which a German force would be part of a supranationally controlled European army linked to NATO. An early problem was the refusal of Britain to join the scheme. No doubt many 'European' activists saw this initiative as part of the general drive towards European integration. Geopolitical hindsight, as well as the fact that, despite the failure of the EDC, Europe was able to move ahead with the Messina '*relance*', reveals that the EDC was much more closely linked to the German rearmament problem than to European integration. The plan was therefore much more strongly opposed in Belgium than either the ECSC or the later EEC and Euratom treaties. The EDC was ratified by 148-49 in the House of Representatives (there were only seven Communists) and by 125-40 in the Senate (three Communists), showing considerable Socialist and even Liberal opposition. When the plan fell in the French National Assembly, time had moved on sufficiently to allow the direct integration of Germany and Italy into both the WEU and NATO, under the Paris agreement of October 1954, with only nine votes against in the Belgian Parliament.

For Belgium the following period was marked (apart from the colonial problems, which are considered separately) by EC issues, NATO and related military questions, and by the pursuit of an active policy for détente. It supported all efforts to speed up European integration, and indeed it was the Belgian commissioner (later EC president), Jean Rey, who gave the EC its first real appearance on the world stage as negotiator in the 1962 Kennedy Round trade talks. Belgium strongly supported British entry to the Community and opposed the attempts by Charles de Gaulle to weaken the Community's supranational nature. However, Belgian policy was always prudent and conciliatory. In the 1965-6 empty chair crisis, Spaak as foreign minister worked to act as a bridge between the 'Five' and Gaullist France, an approach which was effective in bringing France back into the Community councils.

Also, Belgium actually worked for a new impulse towards a stronger and more integrated European Community. Prime Minister Tindemans was the author of a report, requested by the European Council and delivered on 29 December 1975, on European union, which supported the notion of a common 'decision centre' on foreign policy and a common foreign policy, following up in a sense the initiative of the Davignon report (1970) which formed the basis of political co-operation in the EC. The second central theme of the Tindemans report was support for more powers fro Parliament and the Commission. It also enthusiastically pressed for direct elections, although public opinion was not particularly favourable to this initiative, showing stronger opposition (16%) than all the other member-states except Denmark and Britain.[48]

This last point is not without significance. Belgian public opinion, which is not unfamiliar with Europe since the major EC institutions are in Brussels, has been merely passively supportive despite the strong support given by political leaders. The EC has only rarely been an internal political issue, and then almost always in a negative sense: protests by farmers over inadequate price increases; protests by small traders in 1970-1 against the introduction of VAT; the Walloon reaction in 1980 and 1981 to Commission reservations about state aid to the Walloon steel industry; and reaction to a Commission recommendation to Belgium in 1981 on the level of public spending. However, Belgian opinion does remain conscious of the need for an effective community.

In 1967 following its expulsion from Paris by de Gaulle, NATO was transferred from Paris to Brussels (the civil organisation) and Casteau near Mons (the military HQ). In the 1970s, support for NATO policies and the military obligations arising from them became less automatic. In 1973 attempts to deprive students of the right to postpone their military service resulted in serious demonstrations which at times took on an anti-NATO colouring. The government was forced to temporise and make concessions, looking more towards a differentiated army with a core of full-time professionals and a six-month national service period. The 'sale of the century' to replace the outdated Lockheed F-104 fighter, involving costs of BF 30 billion over ten years, caused serious political repercussions. There was a prolonged campaign of demonstrations against the purchase, and objections were raised by Walloon federalists in the FDF-RW against the choice of the American F-16 in preference to the French (hence European) 'Mirage'. The RW ministers were instructed by their party executive to veto the deal in the cabinet, but did not do so. The government was lucky (the attitude of the RW deputies being in doubt) to have its policy approved by the House of Representatives on 12 June 1975 by 113-92 with three abstentions.[49] The issue of the regional distribution of employment arising from this deal, and the conflict over the three Belgian-Dutch treaties on Scheldt navigation and the water-flow rate on the Meuse/Scheldt which were opposed in Wallonia (1975), highlighted the increasing tendency for all issues, even those of foreign policy, to become involved in regional controversy.

At the same time, these military debates were the precursor of a new trend, which became evident in the controversy surrounding the decision of NATO in December 1979 to install theatre nuclear weapons in Europe – in principle in Belgium, Germany and Italy – to meet the alleged superiority of the Soviet tactical nuclear forces equipped with the SS-20. Despite some reactions to specific military decisions from the Socialists, foreign policy in Belgium had hitherto been a matter of broad consensus, barely worthy of debate. However, this consensus had broken down and both sides took up more trenchant positions. The SP (Flemish Socialists), under the impulsion of its chairman K. van Miert and defence spokesman Tobback, became increasingly hostile to the NATO decision and insisted on the need to open serious discussions with the Soviet Union *before* any installation took place. However, the SP was likely to oppose any such installation in Belgium, especially while in opposition. This attitude found support from some sections of the PS, the Volksunie, the Greens and church groups, influential on the left wing of the PSC. This was evident in the massive demonstration in Brussels (200,000 people) on 25 October 1981 as part of the Europe-wide campaign against the NATO decision. The defenders of a strong defence posture, such as General Close, retired for making public statements attacking the weakness of government defence policy, also became more active and less defensive. General Close became an active protagonist of the NATO case on many platforms, publishing a book on the issue and entering politics as a PRL deputy.

Belgium had begun at an early stage to explore the possibilities of détente; in 1966-7 the foreign minister, Pierre Harmel, began a series of contacts with East European (Romanian, Polish, Yugoslav) leaders, which were broken off by the Soviet invasion of Czechoslovakia in August 1968 but then resumed from 1970 when he became the EC's unofficial spokesman in the discussions preparatory to the opening of the CSCE conference in Helsinki.

Belgium remained loyal to the NATO twin-track decisions and indeed agree to deployment of the forty-eight Cruise missiles at Florennes, though it had attempted to promote renewed détente in order to make the deployment unnecessary. Not long after deployment, the changes in the Soviet Union made the 1987 IWF treaty possible and the missiles could be withdrawn. In its traditional manner, Belgium sought to mitigate internal conflict.

The European Community has increasingly become the central focus of Belgian foreign policy. There has always been at the very least a passive consensus in Belgian public opinion favouring European integration.[50] Belgium has appeared to fuse its national interests with the Community. It has been taken as axiomatic that in a small open economy at the crossroads between France and Germany what was good for the EC was also good for Belgium. It has favoured both the pursuit of deeper integration and prudent enlargement, but always with due regard to stability. In the 1960s it was never the Belgian view that France under General de Gaulle should be isolated or forced into a corner; or equally that Thatcher's Britain should be too directly confronted. There again, it is the Belgian political method applied to the EC. When Communism collapsed in central and eastern Europe in 1989/90 and the Berlin wall came down, Belgian instincts were for stability and security, through the Community. The Community integration had to be accelerated to bind Germany into the West and to provide a sheet anchor for the whole of Central Europe.

Always, Belgium's specific national interests in the Community are secondary to its broader strategic concerns and have been subordinated to them in the last analysis; indeed they have been, if not marginal, then at least capable of resolution by compromise. This has applied over issues such as state aid to the coal industry in the 1960s and later to the steel industry, agriculture, regional fund aid, location of the European Parliament in Brussels, and even the recent debate about the Belgian contribution to Community financing under the so-called Delors-2 package.

Yet, with Economic and Monetary Union under Maastricht, a more substantial and problematic issue has surfaced for the first time. The so-called objective conditions for admission to Stage 3 of EMU in 1997 include a requirement that the public sector deficit should not exceed 3% of GDP. At present the Belgian public sector deficit stubbornly remains at 6% despite a long austerity programme which has brought it down from

15% in 1981. This issue was difficult when the Dehaene government was formed in 1992. It made any agreement with Ecolo/Agalev impossible and there were difficulties for the Socialist parties. For the first time, there would have to be a debate about Europe. Supporting Europe would clearly cost something, and the case would have to be made. That is not to say that a strong Danish-style anti-EC reaction was to be expected in Belgium but merely that it had become an issue.

Colonial issues

As we saw in Chapter 1, there was a sharp increase from the mid-1950s in internal pressure towards decolonisation, both in Belgium and in the Congo, and external pressure at the United Nations and from the 'neutralist' block (later the Group of 77). Matters came rapidly to a head after bloody riots in Leopoldville in January 1959. In January 1960, a 'round table' meeting of Congolese and Belgian leaders was held which led to independence on 30 June 1960, after elections which were won by the partisans of Patrice Lumumba.[51]

The new state had a disastrous beginning, with tribal warfare and an army mutiny breaking out on 6 July. The threat to the large remaining Belgian community and to Belgian interests led the government to intervene militarily in the former colony. This action was condemned by the UN Security Council, and Belgian troops were replaced by UN forces. Belgium also showed considerable sympathy, stopping short of recognition, for the breakaway Katanga régime led by Moïse Tshombe. These events, coupled with the murder of Lumumba, who had been dismissed as premier because of his move to the left and to a more 'neutralist' foreign policy, caused a violent anti-Belgian reaction both in the Congo, renamed Zaïre, and in the Eastern bloc and Third World states.

Diplomatic relations with Zaïre were only restored in 1963 after the Katangese separatist state had been defeated by UN troops. Further unrest led to a new armed intervention by Belgium in 1964, but difficulties with the United Nations were less acute this time since the Belgian aim was clearly to rescue white residents in danger. Financial and other problems between Belgium and Zaïre were provisionally resolved by an agreement in 1965, but the *coup d'état* by General Mobutu in November 1965 created new problems. Tension continued from time to time over financial and economic issues, and the internal situation remained unstable, leading to revolts in Katanga which forced the Belgian government to withdraw technicians. The virtual nationalisation of the Union Minière company of Katanga in 1966 also provoked difficulties. From 1969 relations improved, with the visit of a Belgian economic mission to Zaïre, a state visit to Belgium by Mobutu in 1969 and a visit to Zaïre by King Baudouin in 1970 for the tenth anniversary of the country's independence.

Problems continued sporadically, not least because of the activities of Mobutu's political opponents in Belgium and the Franco-Belgian intervention in Shaba province in 1978 to rescue white residents. It is difficult to avoid the conclusion that Belgium did not adequately prepare its colony for independence, and, as a consequence of the important interests in mineral extraction (uranium, copper) of such companies as the Union Minière, attempted to maintain at best a paternalistic and at worst a neo-colonialist interest in the internal affairs of Zaïre well into the 1960s.

NOTES

1. For discussion of these constitutional requirements, see Mast, op. cit., 320-6.
2. Ibid., 322 and footnote 57.
3. Ibid., 324.
4. See Yves Lejeune 'Les Grands Thèmes' in F. Delpérée and Y. Lejeune (eds), *La Collaboration de l'Etat des Communautés et des Régions dans le domaine de la Politique Extérieure*, Academia, Louvain-La-Neuve, 1988, 11-31.
5. See cases 68/81 to 73/81, *Commission* v. *Belgium* judgement of February 1982, Court Record 1982 at p. 153.
6. On the Coalition Agreement and its implementation, see E. Arcq, P. Blaise, E. Lentzen, *Enjeux et Compromis de la Législature 1988-91*, CH due CRISP Nos. 1332-3, 10-17.
7. See *Documents Parlementaires*, Chambre 1167-3 (1989/90) and Chambre 1167-6 (1989/90).
8. New Articles 59 *bis* and 68 of the Constitution.
9. See ruling of the *Cour de Cassation*, 25 Nov. 1955, published in PASSIS (Law Reports), 1956, 285.
10. Mast, op. cit., 329-30.
11. See W.J. Ganshoff van der Meersch, *Organisations Européennes*, vol. I, Bruylant, Brussels: 1963, and P. Hayoit de Termincourt, 'Conflict Tussen het Verdrag en de interne Wet' (speech of the Procureur-Général, 20 Sept. 1963), *Rechtskundig Weekblad*, 1963/4, cols 73-94.
12. Luykx, op. cit., 407-8.
13. Ibid., 409 – 18 *passim* and 710-20 *passim*.
14. J.J.A. Salmon, 'Les Commissions des affaires étrangères du Parlement Belge', unpublished paper for the Colloquium on Parliamentary Foreign Affairs Committees held in Florence, April 1981, 8-9.
15. A. Molitor, *La Fonction Royale en Belgique*, CRISP (1978), 51-9.
16. C. Sasse, *Regierungen, Parlamente, Ministerrat*, Bonn, Europa Union Verlag, 1975, 52-6.
17. *Mémento Politique*, Kluwer, Antwerp, 1989, 163.
18. *Annuaire Administratif et Judiciaire*, 1981/2.
19. On the CGRT, see Charles Etienne Lagarse, 'La Communauté Française et les Relations Extérieures', Delpérée and Lejeune, op. cit., 51-6.
22. *Mémento Politique*, op. cit., p. 165.
23. Guido Genren, 'La Communauté Germanophone et le Partage des Compétences Internationales', in Delpérée and Lejeune, *op. cit., 61-4*.

24. Baron de Vleeschouwer, 'Le Rôle du Ministère des Affaires Européennes', in Delpérée and Lejeune, *op.cit.*, 35-9.
25. Salmon, op. cit., 9-10.
26. *Mémento Politique, op. cit.*, 39-43 (House) and 65-9 (Senate).
27. Salmon, op. cit., 28.
28. Chambre des Représentants, *Rapport Annuel*, session 1990/91, 71-2.
29. *Rapport Annuel*, 71, and for subjects of interpellations 1328-32.
30. Ibid., 42.
31. Figures in ibid., 24-5.
32. Ibid., 54.
33. *Rapport Annuel*, 133-4.
34. For details on EAC, ibid., 10-18.
35. On the work of the *Comité d'Avis*, see *Rapport Annuel*, 160-4.
36. *Mémento Politique*, op. cit., 112, 117, 122.
37. Frans van Kalken *Histoire de la Belgique*, Office de Publicité, Brussels, 1959, 565-9 and 574-5.
38. Ibid., 579-81.
39. Ibid., 641-52, and Luykx, op. cit., 239-42.
40. Van Kalken, op. cit., 594-6 and Luykx, op. cit., 186, 187 and 320-1.
41. Van Kalken, op. cit., 591-3.
42. Luykx, op. cit., 260.
43. Ibid., 266-9, for diplomatic developments during the war.
44. Van Kalken, op. cit., 703-6.
45. For a summary of policy between the wars, ibid., 718-20; and Luykx, op. cit., 300-1 (Franco-Belgian military agreement), 344-5, 353-4, 365-7 (neutrality in 1936) and 379-81. For a more detailed account, see H. Jaspar, 'Locarno et la Belgique', *Revue Belge*, 1925, and Ministry of Foreign Affairs, 'La position Internationale de la Belgique 1934-39'.
46. For post-war foreign policy (on which this section is based), see Luykx, op. cit., 460-4, 471, 478 (EDC), 483-4, 545-7, 668-9 and 671.
47. Ibid., 460-4.
48. See D. Hearl, 'Belgium: Two into three will go' in Herman and Hagger (eds), *The Legislation of Direct Elections to the European Parliament*, Gower Press 1980.
49. Luykx, op. cit., 568-70.
50. J. Fitzmaurice, 'Belgium and Luxembourg' in J. Lodge (ed.), *The 1989 Election of the European Parliament*, Macmillan, Basingstoke and London, 1990, 37-47.
51. Luykx, 498-501, and W.J. Ganshoff van der Meersch, *Fin de la souveraineté belge au Congo*, Brussels, 1963.

9

CONCLUSIONS: THE FUTURE

Whither Belgium? The modern Belgian state was born in 1830 as one of the first manifestations of the new collective forces of modern nationalism and liberal democracy. Yet it was this very force that was to prove its undoing, as the Flemish movement demanded from the new French-speaking state consideration commensurate to its size and economic power. It was undermined because it did not correspond to the modern triptych of one people, one nation, one state. Now one may ask whether, as earlier, the new federal constitutional settlement is once again the precursor of a new political model of a 'Europe of the regions'.

This is an open question, not least because the solidity of the new federal settlement is itself an open question. Certainly the debate on the *Accord de la St Michel* and the outpouring of national sentiment caused by the death of King Baudouin in August 1993 showed that there was almost no support for separatism and not much more for confederalism. On the contrary, there seemed to be a groundswell of support for the maintenance of the unity of the Belgian state – which, it should be emphasised, is not identical to a desire to return to the old centralised unitary state. How strong and genuine is this sentiment? Can it survive a strong centrifugal tendency created by prolonged economic recession? Is the explanation for its appearance that people will cling to any available raft in a storm?

Whatever the answer, there can come a point where a critical mass of public opinion comes to consider that change can only be for the better. At that point the delicate balance of the present federal settlement would be upset. Were such a situation to develop in one or both of the communities, then the present settlement would not be viable in the longer term. Far from being a source of stability, it would herald a radical confederalist or separatist solution.

However, Belgium will not develop in isolation from developments in the rest of Europe. On the contrary, as we have seen, it is one of the most open of European economies and societies. Outcomes will be determined by a complex dialectic between the internal dynamics of Belgian society and the balance between the two main communities and the external political, social and economic forces that play upon it. In this age of mass communications, the progressive internationalisation of the economy, Belgium's commitment to European integration and the open and receptive traditions of Belgian political culture, it would not be possible – even if it were considered desirable – to close Belgium off from these outside influences. Yet the exact way in which they impact on Belgium will depend on their interaction with forces inherent in Belgium itself. The outside forces of internationalisation and Europeanisation will not in themselves predetermine whether the current federal model succeeds or fails. However, they may reinforce trends already developing within Belgium or provide the initial impetus for a new trend. Thus the collapse of Communism and with it the post-Yalta order have made it possible – but of course by no means inevitable – to envisage separatism as an outcome. On the other hand, European integration, while initially at least during the pre-1989 period militating against separatism, is now more neutral in its impact. It may however support a middle way based on federalism within a Europe of the regions.

APPENDIXES

A

BELGIAN MONARCHS

Leopold I	1831-65
Leopold II	1865-1909
Albert I	1909-34
Leopold III	1934-51*
Baudouin	1951-93
Albert II	1993-

* Abdicated.

B

BELGIAN GOVERNMENTS SINCE THE LIBERATION (1944)

	Prime Minister	Period of office	Party composition
1.	Pierlot V (PSC)	1944-5	CVP/PSC-PLP/PVV-PSB/BSP-PCB
2.	Van Acker I (PSB)	1945 (Feb.-Aug.)	CVP/PSC-PLP/PVV-PSB/BSP-PCB
3.	Van Acker II (PSB)	1945-6	BSP/PSB-PVV/PLP-PCB-UDB
4.	Spaak II (PSB)	1946 (Mar.)	BSP/PSB
5.	Van Acker III (PSB)	1946 (Mar.-July)	BSP/PSB-PCB-PLP/PVV
6.	Huysmans I (PSB)	1946-7	BSP/PSB-PCB-PLP/PVV
7.	Spaak III (PSB)	1947-9	PSC/CVP-PSB/BSP
8.	Eyskens I (CVP)	1949-50	CVP/PSC-PLP/PVV
9.	Duvieusart (CVP)	1950 (June-Aug.)	CVP/PCC
10.	Pholien (PSC)	1950-2	CVP/PSC
11.	Van Houtte (CVP)	1952-4	CVP/PSC
12.	Van Acker IV (BSP)	1954-8	BSP/PSB-PLP/PVV
13.	Eyskens II (CVP)	1958 (June-Nov.)	CVP
14.	Eyskens III (CVP)	1958-61	PSC/CVP-PLP/PVV
15.	Lefèvre (CVP)	1961-5	PSC/CVP-BSP/PSB
16.	Harmel (PSC)	1965-6	PSC/CVP-BSP/PSB
17.	Vanden Boeynants I (PSC)	1966-8	PSC/CVP-PSB/BSP
18.	Eyskens IV	1968-71	PSC/CVP-PSB/BSP
19.	Eyskens V	1972 (Jan.-Nov.)	PSC/CVP-PSB/BSP
20.	Leburton (PSB)	1972-3	PSC/CVP-BSP/PSB-PLP/PVV
21.	Tindemans I (CVP)	1974 (Apr.-June)	CVP/PSC-PLP/PVV
22.	Tindemans II	1974-7	CVP/PSC-PLP/PVV-RW
23.	Tindemans III	1977-8	CVP/PSC-PSB/BSP-FDF-VU
24.	Vanden Boeynants II	1978-9	PSC/CVP-PSB/BSP-FDF-VU
25.	Martens I (CVP)	1979-80	CVP/PSC-PS/SP-FDF
26.	Martens II	1980 (Jan.-Apr.)	CVP/PSC-PS/SP
27.	Martens III	1980 (May-Oct.)	CVP/PSC-PS/SP-PRL/PVV
28.	Martens IV	1980-1	CVP/PSC-PS/SP
29.	Eyskens VI (CVP)	1981 (Apr.-Nov.)	CVP/PSC-PS/SP
30.	Martens V	1981 (Dec.-1985)	CVP/PSC-PRL/PVV
31.	Martens VI	1985	CVP/PSC-PRL/PVV
32.	Martens VII	1985-8	CVP/PSC-PRL/PVV
33.	Martens VIII	1988-91	CVP/PSC-PS/SP-VU
34.	Martens IX	1991-2	CVP/PSC-PS/SP
35.	Dehaene I	1992-5	CVP/PSC-PS/SP
36.	Dehaene II	1995	CVP/PSC-PS/SP

C

COMPOSITION OF THE HOUSE OF REPRESENTATIVES

(% of national vote and no. of seats held)

	1946 %	seats	1949 %	seats	1950 %	seats	1954 %	seats	1958 %	seats	1961 %	seats	1965 %	seats	1968 %	seats
PSC/CVP	42.5	92	43.6	105	47.7	108	41.1	95	46.5	104	41.5	96	34.4	77	31.8	(PSC 2) 69
PS/SP	31.6	69	29.8	66	34.5	77	37.3	86	35.8	84	36.7	84	28.8	64	28.0	59
PRL/PVV	8.92	17	15.25	29	11.25	20	12.1	25	11.1	21	12.3	20	21.6	48	20.9	47
FDF/RW	–		–		–		–		–		–		2.3	5	5.9	12
VU	–		2.1	0	–		2.2	1	1.9	1	3.5	5	6.7	12	9.8	20
PCB/KPB	12.7	23	7.5	12	4.7	7	3.6	4	1.9	2	3.1	5	4.6	6	3.3	5
UDB	2.2	1	–		–		–		–		–		–		–	
Ecolo	–		–		–		–		–		–		–		–	
Agalev	–		–		–		–		–		–		–		–	
UDRT	–		–		–		–		–		–		–		–	
Vlaams Blok	–		–		–		–		–		–		–		–	
Front National	–		–		–		–		–		–		–		–	
Van Rossem (libertarian list)	–		–		–		–		–		–		–		–	
Others	–		–		–		–		–		2.9	2	2.1	0	–	

	1971 %	1971 seats	1974 %	1974 seats	1977 %	1977 seats	1978 %	1978 seats	1981* %	1981* seats	1985 %	1985 seats	1987 %	1987 seats	1991 %	1991 seats	1995 %	1995 seats
PSC/CVP	30.1	67	32.3	72	36.0	80	36.3	82	PSC (7.1) 26.4 (19.3) CVP	61	(7.9) 29.2 (21.3)	(20) 69 (49)	(8.0) 27.5 (19.5)	(19) 62 (43)	(7.7) 24.5 (16.8)	(18) 57 (39)	(7.7) 24.9 (17.2)	(12) 41 (29)
PS/SP	26.4	61	26.7	59	27.1	62	25.4	58	PS (12.7) 25.1 (12.4) SP	61	13.7 28.2 14.5	35 32	15.6 30.5 14.9	40 72 32	13.5 25.5 12.0	35 63 28	11.9 24.5 12.6	18 39 21
PRL/PVV	15.9	34	15.2	30	15.5	33	16.4	37	PRL (8.6) 21.5 52 PVV (12.9)	52	10.2 20.9 10.7	24 22	9.4 20.9 11.5	23 48 25	8.1 20.1 12.0	20 46 26	(10.3) 23.4 (13.1)	(18) 39 (21)
FDF/RW	11.2	24	10.9	25	7.1	15	7.1	15	4.2	8	1.2	3	1.2	3	1.5	3	–	
VU	11.1	21	10.2	22	10.0	20	7.0	14	9.7	20	7.9	16	8.1	16	5.9	10	4.7	5
PCB/KPB	3.1	5	3.2	4	2.1	2	3.2	4	2.3	2	1.2	0	0.8	0	0.1	0	–	
Ecolo	–		–		–		0.8	0	4.8	4	2.5	5	2.6	3	5.1	10	4.0	6
Agalev	–		–		–		0.9	1	2.7	3	3.7	4	4.5	6	4.9	7	4.4	5
UDRT/RAD	–		–		–		1.4	1	1.1	1	1.2	1	–		0.2	0	–	
Vlaams Blok	–		–		–		–		–		1.4	1	1.9	2	6.6	12	7.8	11
Front National	–		–		–		–		–		–		0.1	0	1.1	1	2.5	2
Van Rossem (libertarian list)	–		–		–		–		–		–		–		3.2	3	–	
Others	–		–		–		–		–		2.3	0	2.0	0	1.5	0	2.9	0

Note: The total size of the House in 1946 was 202 seats. It was increased to 212 seats at the 1949 election. In 1995 it was changed to 150.

* Figures in brackets give separately the PSC and CVP, the PS and SP, and the PRL and PVV percentages of the vote and of seats.

INDEX